The French Revolution:

Conflicting Interpretations

The French

Revolution:

Conflicting

Interpretations

SELECTED AND EDITED BY

FRANK A. KAFKER

AND

JAMES M. LAUX

University of Cincinnati

 RANDOM HOUSE *New York*

Preface

*T*his anthology stresses variety rather than consensus. One of its primary aims is to acquaint readers with the work of many of the leading historians of the French Revolution—the great names of the past as well as present-day scholars. We have not sought to give special prominence to any one view or school of revolutionary studies; instead we have tried to include selections by historians of different countries, different political persuasions, different religious beliefs, and different historical methodologies. All we have asked is that they present their points of view with knowledge and clarity. And in our search for such selections, we have not limited ourselves to those easily accessible or already in English. Ten of the selections, for example, are translated from the French.

We have also tried to organize the readings around some of the most important historical problems of the Revolution and the conflicting interpretations of them. In so doing, we have chosen selections that are long enough to show not only the author's viewpoint, but also the arguments he uses to support it; and we have not confined ourselves to two contrasting interpretations when others might be considered equally cogent. We hope that the student will see that some of the explanations and analyses offered here have more validity than others and that he can arrive at preliminary conclusions on at least some of the historical problems presented.

Of course, some noted historians are not represented and some major problems not discussed. But, we believe, these gaps can be filled. The interpretive works on the Revolution by such historians as Alexis de Tocqueville and Alfred Cobban are short and easily available. Issues such as the long-range causes of the Revolution or the relation between the French Revolution and other revolutions of the eighteenth century have been treated elsewhere in single paperback editions. In any event, given the vast historical literature on the French Revolution—an embarrassment of riches—gaps are inevitable. Some indication of this literature can be found in the bibliography.

The spelling, capitalization, and punctuation of the individual authors have been retained. When we as editors have added explanatory material to any piece, such additions have been enclosed in brackets. To distinguish these brackets from the author's brackets in the original text, we have italicized the contents of author's brackets.

We are very happy to acknowledge the help of Paul Burrell and Kornel Huvos, our colleagues at the University of Cincinnati, who have been generous with their time and learning.

F. A. K.

J. M. L.

Contents

The French Revolution:

Conflicting Interpretations

I

THE OUTBREAK
OF THE REVOLUTION
(1787–1789)

*W*ho led the overthrow of the Old Regime in France?
*Although on July 14 Frenchmen celebrate the victory
of "the conquerors of the Bastille," historians long ago decided
that the story was much more complicated. Many of them have
accepted an interpretation popularized by Georges Lefebvre in
his* Coming of the French Revolution: *"The first act of the Revolution, in 1788, consisted in a triumph of the aristocracy. . . .
But, after having paralyzed the royal power which upheld its
own social preeminence, the aristocracy opened the way to the
bourgeois revolution, then to the popular revolution in the cities,
and finally to the revolution of the peasants—and found itself
buried under the ruins of the Old Regime." [1] Thus, the outbreak
of the Revolution occurred in four stages; it was carried out by
four different social classes; and it was dominated by class conflict. We include here a short version of Lefebvre's interpretation,
that contained in his survey* The French Revolution. *The three
selections that follow it may be read as tests of Lefebvre's thesis.*

*Jean Égret's article deals with what Lefebvre calls the "aris-
tocratic revolt," and especially with the part played by the parlements, the chief law courts of France. Égret studies the extremely
varied social backgrounds of the judges. As a result, the word
"aristocratic" takes on many shades of meaning. Does his article*

[1] Georges Lefebvre, *The Coming of the French Revolution,* trans. Robert R.
Palmer (Princeton, N.J.: Princeton University Press, 1947), p. 3.

simply add nuance to Lefebvre's account, or does it undermine it?

Elizabeth Eisenstein's article concerning the "bourgeois revolt" directly challenges Lefebvre. She finds that the leaders of revolutionary reform in 1788–1789 were a loose-knit coalition of such aristocrats as the Marquis de Lafayette, such clergymen as the Abbé Sieyès, and such commoners as Target, liberals drawn from all three estates. Consequently, she thinks Lefebvre's term "bourgeois revolt" is inaccurate.

Finally, George Rudé analyzes the class composition of the "popular revolt" in Paris during the three days from July 11 to 14, 1789. From the evidence he has collected, can one say that these rioters were men from any one particular class and that the disturbance was class inspired?

In judging the Lefebvre interpretation as a whole, one may also ask the following: if it be true that the leaders of these four stages in the coming of the Revolution were formed primarily by their class backgrounds, how is one's class determined? Marxists stress a person's relation to the means of production—whether, for example, he works the land or owns it, whether he is a laborer in the city or a capitalist. Others believe that such factors as family ancestry, occupation, and education must also be taken into account. What criteria does Lefebvre use when he divides eighteenth-century society into aristocrats, bourgeois, city masses, and peasants? Are these classifications too imprecise, too simple?

Moreover, does he exaggerate the importance of class to the neglect of the individual? In all times, men from similar social backgrounds have chosen different political routes. For example, some aristocrats supported the king in 1788 and many Parisian workers did not riot on July 14. Were such cases exceptional or common, inconsequential or momentous? The answers to these questions have an importance far beyond the study of the French Revolution, for they would illuminate to what extent man is a creature of his class and to what extent he is a free agent, a power in his own right.

A SERIES OF CLASS REVOLTS *

Georges Lefebvre

Georges Lefebvre (1874–1959) is generally considered the foremost twentieth-century historian of the French Revolution. Born in the north of France, the child of poor parents, he attended local public schools and the University of Lille. For the next twenty-five years he taught at provincial and Parisian secondary schools. At first he did research on medieval history, but after several years he turned to the study of the Revolution. In 1924, at the age of fifty, he presented his four-volume doctoral thesis on the peasants of the Department of the Nord during the French Revolution. This pioneering study of the life of the common people during the Revolution made his reputation. He then taught at various universities and published volume after volume on such topics as the outbreak of the Revolution and the revolutionary mentality, as well as highly regarded surveys of the revolutionary and Napoleonic epochs. In 1932 he succeeded Albert Mathiez as editor of the Annales historiques de la Révolution française, *and in 1937 he was appointed to the Chair in the History of the French Revolution at the University of Paris. Though he retired in 1945, his formidable energy, intelligence, and devotion to the French Revolution continued to the end.*

THE ARISTOCRATIC REVOLUTION, 1787–1788

The French Revolution was started and led to victory in its first phase by the aristocracy. This fact is of primary importance, but for differing reasons both the Third Estate and the aristocracy

* From Georges Lefebvre, *The French Revolution from Its Origins to 1793*, trans. Elizabeth Moss Evanson (New York: Columbia University Press, 1962), pp. 97–130. Copyright © 1962 Columbia University Press. Reprinted with some minor changes in translation by permission of Columbia University Press, Inc. and Routledge & Kegan Paul, Ltd.

took pains to thrust it into the background. The immediate cause of the Revolution was a financial crisis originating with the war in America. Necker had financed the war by borrowing, and his successor, Calonne, had used the same method to pay off arrears. The deficit grew to such proportions that on August 20, 1786, Calonne sent Louis XVI a note declaring state reform imperative.

Calonne and the Notables

The fiscal administration was so confused that the situation can be described only roughly. A statement of financial expectations drawn up in March, 1788, the first—and last—budget of the Old Regime, estimated expenditures at 629 million livres and receipts at 503 million, leaving a deficit of 126 million, or 20 per cent. Contemporaries attributed the deficit to court wastefulness and financiers' profits. Some economies could be and were made, but servicing the debt alone required 318 million, more than half of expenditures. The government could have reduced expenses only by repudiating the debt; raising taxes seemed out of the question, as taxes were already considered too high. At any rate there was one resource left. Certain provinces paid very little in taxes; the bourgeoisie less than the peasantry, the nobility and clergy least of all. From a technical point of view, the crisis could be easily resolved: equality of taxation would provide enough funds.

Calonne did not prove bold enough for fiscal equality, but he at least proposed to extend the [government's] salt and tobacco monopolies through the whole kingdom and to replace the *capitation* and twentieths [1] by a direct land tax, a "territorial subvention," to be levied without exception upon all landowners. At the same time he planned to stimulate economic activity and consequently swell treasury receipts by freeing the grain trade from all controls, by abolishing internal customs barriers, and by suppressing certain indirect taxes. Going even further, he intended to give responsibility for apportioning taxes to provincial assemblies elected by landowners without distinc-

[1] [The *capitation* and the twentieth (*vingtième*), as well as the *taille*, were direct taxes levied by the Crown. During the course of the eighteenth century they came to fall most heavily on the peasants, while the privileged groups were able to avoid paying most of their share.]

tion as to order, and to relieve the clergy of its own debt by selling the Church's manorial rights. Financial stability would
strengthen royal power, reducing opposition from the parlements
to insignificance. Unity of the kingdom would be advanced. The
bourgeoisie would be permitted to take part in government
administration.

Although the sacrifices required of privileged groups were
modest—they would still be exempt from the *taille* and from the
tax which Calonne proposed to substitute for road-service obligations (the *corvée des routes*)—he entertained no illusions as to
how the parlements would receive his plans. He might have
attacked them openly had he been able to count upon the king's
support, but the fate of Turgot and Necker[2] gave him no en-
couragement. Moreover, although royalty still carried prestige,
Louis personally had none. He was devoted to the hunt and
liked to work with his hands; he drank and ate to excess; he
liked neither high society, gambling, nor dancing; he was the
laughing-stock of his courtiers; and rumours of the queen's conduct made him appear ridiculous. Marie Antoinette had gained
the reputation of a Messalina and had lost face in the Diamond
Necklace Affair of 1785. Calonne was therefore resigned to prac-
tise indirect methods. He thought out a plan to convoke an
assembly of notables consisting primarily of various noble elements. By selecting them himself, and banking on administrative
influence plus respect due the king, he expected that they would
prove amenable and that their acquiescence would in turn impress the parlements. But the calling of an assembly was an initial
surrender: the king was consulting his aristocracy rather than
notifying it of his will.

When they convened on February 22, 1787, the notables were
angered by the proposal to elect provincial assemblies without
distinction as to order, by the restriction of their powers, and
by the attack on the clergy's manorial rights. As could be expected, they censured the direct land tax and asked that they
first be given a treasury report. They declared themselves desirous
of contributing to the welfare of the state—but they intended to
dictate their own terms. Louis saw that Calonne would get nowhere with the assembly, and dismissed him on April 8.

---

[2] [Both of these ministers had proposed reform programs which aroused
opposition. Louis XVI had given neither of them wholehearted support. Turgot was dismissed in 1776; Necker resigned in 1781.]

Brienne and the Parlements

At the head of those who opposed Calonne stood Loménie de Brienne, archbishop of Toulouse, who wanted to become minister and did so without delay. To soothe the notables he submitted the treasury accounts to them, promised to retain the three orders in the provincial assemblies and to leave the clergy's manorial rights alone. But he took over the plan for a territorial subvention and to it added an increase of the stamp duty. The notables replied that it was not within their power to consent to taxes, an allusion to the Estates-General. On May 25 their assembly was dissolved. Calonne's device had failed; it was obvious that Brienne had next to proceed to the parlements.[3]

The Parlement of Paris made no protest over registering freedom of the grain trade, commutation of the *corvée des routes,* and institution of provincial assemblies. But it drafted remonstrances against the stamp tax and rejected the territorial subvention, openly referring this to an Estates-General. A *lit de justice* was held on August 6; the parlement declared it null and void, then started proceedings against Calonne, who fled to England. On August 14 the magistrates were exiled to Troyes. Other sovereign courts supported them. Brienne quickly retreated, and on September 19 the reinstated parlement recorded restoration of the old taxes.

Brienne fell back on loans, but the same problem faced him: he had to have consent of the parlements to borrow. A few members agreed to negotiate and did not hesitate to set their decisive condition—that the government should promise to convoke the Estates-General. Brienne asked for 120 million livres to be raised over a five-year period, at the end of which—in 1792 —the Estates-General would be convened. But, uncertain of a majority, he suddenly had an edict presented by the king himself on November 18 in a "royal session," that is, a *lit de justice* in which traditional ceremonies of convocation had not been

---

[3] [During the reign of Louis XVI, an edict often became a law in the following manner: the Crown prepared the edict, which was then sent to the leading law court of France, the Parlement of Paris. If the Parlement accepted the edict, it was registered. If it objected to parts of the edict, it drafted remonstrances. The king could override these objections by a *lit de justice,* that is, he could appear before Parlement in person or by proxy, sit on a pile of cushions (a *lit*), and order the registration. Then, according to the king, the edict had the force of law, but the Parlement frequently did not accept this interpretation.]

observed. The duc d'Orléans protested and the registering of the edict was declared void. Louis retaliated by exiling the duke and two councillors. The parlement came to their defence, condemning *lettres de cachet* and demanding that royal subjects be given personal freedom. To ward off an attack by force, on May 3, 1788, it published a declaration of fundamental laws of the kingdom, stating that the monarchy was hereditary, that the right to vote subsidies belonged to the Estates-General, that Frenchmen could not be arbitrarily arrested and detained, that their judges were irremovable, the customs and privileges of provinces inviolable.

The government had evidently resolved to imitate Maupeou.[4] On May 5 armed soldiers took up posts around the Palais de Justice until two members of the parlement who had been placed under arrest gave themselves up. On May 8 Louis succeeded in registering six edicts drawn up by Lamoignon, keeper of the seals [Minister of Justice]. According to them the power of registration was transferred to a "plenary court" composed of princes and crown officers, and at the same time the judiciary was reformed at the expense of the parlements—without, however, abolishing venality [the sale of government offices]. The *question préalable*—torture preceding the execution of criminals—was abolished (the *question préparatoire,* used to extract evidence during a judicial inquiry, had ended in 1780). Last of all, a fresh blow was dealt the aristocracy: a litigant could now refuse to accept the ruling of a manorial court by referring his case to royal tribunals.

This time resistance was more widespread and more violent. The provincial parlements and most of the lower tribunals protested. The assembly of the clergy, already annoyed by a recent edict granting Protestants a civil status, criticized the reforms and offered only a small contribution as its "free gift" [the Church's periodic grant of money to the government]. Riots broke out in Paris and several other cities. On June 7 the citizens of Grenoble rose and rained missiles upon the garrison from the rooftops in what was known as the "Day of Tiles." The provincial assemblies set up at the end of 1787 satisfied no one; several provinces clamoured for their old estates vested with the right to vote taxes. In the Dauphiné nobility and bourgeoisie

---

[4] [A minister of Louis XV from 1768 to 1774, who had attempted to tame the parlements.]

met together at the château of Vizille on July 21, 1788, to convoke the Estates on their own authority. Brienne gave way.

The treasury was now empty. Pensions had had to be cut.
Stockholders received nothing and notes from the Bank of Discount were made legal tender. Having no money, Louis had to
leave it to the Prussians to invade Holland and support the
Stadholder against his burghers. The Stadholder broke his alliance with France and joined with the English. Brienne yielded
again, this occasion being the last: the Estates were to convene on
May 1, 1789. He resigned on August 24, 1788. The king recalled
Necker, whose first act was to dismiss Lamoignon and reinstate
the Parlement of Paris. On September 23 the parlement hastened
to stipulate that the Estates-General would consist of three orders,
as in 1614. Each order would have the same number of representatives, would make i's decisions separately, and would have
a veto over the others. The nobility and clergy were made
masters of the assembly. This was the aristocracy's victory.

During these events privileged groups—especially those in
Brittany—had acted together in forming propaganda and resistance organizations to protest royal authority; they had intimidated and sometimes won over the intendants and army
leaders; occasionally they had roused sharecroppers and domestics.
These revolutionary precedents were not to be forgotten. The
parlements above all had taught a lesson: the Third Estate would
duplicate their tactics when the Estates-General met. They had
even presumed to indict a minister, making Calonne the first
émigré.

THE BOURGEOIS REVOLUTION

To annoy the ministers a number of commoners, notably lawyers,
had favoured the revolt of the nobility. Many others, such as the
Rolands, expecting nothing, remained neutral. The summer of
1788 brought no evidence that bourgeois would take part in
events. But news that an Estates-General was to be convened
sent a tremor of excitement through the bourgeoisie: the king
was authorizing them to plead their case. In this early stage
accord with the aristocracy was not out of the question: the
example set by the Dauphiné, where nobles granted commoners
vote by head and equality of taxation, was welcomed enthusiastically. The atmosphere changed abruptly when the Parle-

ment of Paris showed its true colours on September 23. Suddenly the popularity of the magistrates vanished. A clamour arose throughout the kingdom. "Public debate has assumed a different character," [the journalist] Mallet du Pan stated in January of 1789. "King, despotism, and constitution have become only secondary questions. Now it is war between the Third Estate and the other two orders."

Formation of the Patriot Party

The rupture was still not complete. Some of the liberal great lords joined the upper bourgeoisie to form the "National," or "Patriot," party. The "Committee of Thirty," which seems to have exerted considerable influence within the party, counted among its members the duc de La Rochefoucauld-Liancourt, the marquis de Lafayette, and the marquis de Condorcet, along with Talleyrand, bishop of Autun, and the abbé Sieyes. Mirabeau also appeared at its meetings. Sieyes and Mirabeau were in contact with the duc d'Orléans, who had at his disposal a large sum of money and who wielded unquestionable influence within his extensive appanage. Personal connections as well as bonds created by the many associations that had sprung up in the eighteenth century—academies, agricultural societies, philanthropic groups, reading circles, Masonic lodges—were utilized in the provinces as in Paris. Some have attributed to the Masonic Grand Orient, whose grand master was the duc d'Orléans, a decisive role. But the duc de Luxembourg, its administrator-general, remained devoted to the aristocratic cause, and the lodges were full of nobles. It is difficult to imagine that Masonry could have sided with the Third Estate without being split by conflicts, of which we have no evidence.

Although propaganda of the Patriots provoked counterarguments, the government raised no objection to controversy: the king had invited his subjects to air their thoughts and viewpoints concerning the Estates-General. Under pretext of replying to his appeal, a flood of pamphlets appeared, and their authors slipped into them whatever they wanted to say. The Patriots none the less used brochures with cautious skill—they limited themselves to requesting as many representatives for the Third Estate as for the nobility and clergy combined, invoking the example of the provincial assemblies and the Estates of the Dauphiné. The order of the day was to overwhelm the government with petitions, for which the municipalities assumed, willingly or not, full responsibility. Actually, all were counting on Necker.

Necker and the Doubling of the Third Estate

The minister of finance took care of the most urgent fiscal needs by drawing upon the Bank of Discount and by granting financiers, as security for their advances, "anticipations" on future tax receipts. He did this only to gain time until the Estates assembled, since he expected them to abolish fiscal privileges. If the nobility dominated the Estates the government would be at its mercy. Necker was therefore inclined to favour the Third Estate without being under its power. By doubling that order, and by limiting the vote by head to financial questions, all could be reconciled: equality of taxation would be adopted, while constitutional reform would bring conflict and require arbitration by the king. There can be no doubt about Necker's own view concerning the type of government to be instituted. He admired the British system—a House of Lords would soothe the aristocracy; admission to public office regardless of distinction by birth would satisfy the bourgeoisie.

He had no intention of revealing these plans. As an upstart financier, a foreigner, a Protestant, he had always been suspect in the eyes of the aristocracy, the court, and the king. Several of his colleagues—especially Barentin, the new keeper of the seals —opposed him. Determined above all else to preserve his power, he advanced with measured step. Like Calonne he hoped to persuade the notables to approve doubling of the Third. To this end he again convened them on November 6, 1788, but they disappointed him. On December 12 the royal princes sent Louis an entreaty which, by virtue of its clarity and moving tone, can be considered the manifesto of the aristocracy.

> The State is in danger . . . a revolution of governmental principles is brewing . . . soon the rights of property will be attacked, inequality of wealth will be presented as an object of reform: already the suppression of feudal rights has been proposed. . . . Could Your Majesty resolve to sacrifice, to humiliate, his brave, his ancient, his respectable nobility? . . . Let the Third Estate cease attacking the rights of the first two orders . . . let it confine itself to asking a reduction of the taxes with which it is perhaps overburdened; then the first two orders, recognizing in the third citizens dear to them,

may renounce, in the generosity of their feelings, the prerogatives relating to pecuniary matters, and consent to bear public obligations in the most perfect equality.

But Necker went further and with the support of a few colleagues won the day—probably because Brienne's fall had displeased the queen and the nobility's rebellion had antagonized the king. An "Order of the Council" of December 27 granted doubling of the Third Estate. Louis XVI has since been criticized for not specifying the voting method at that time. This reproach is groundless, for in his report Necker mentioned that voting by order was to be the rule. But the decree failed to record this, and the minister had already hinted that the Estates-General might consider it appropriate to vote by head on tax questions.

The Third Estate cried victory and affected to consider the vote by head won. The nobility denied this interpretation and in Poitou, Franche-Comté, and Provence violently protested the doubling which had given rise to that conclusion. In Brittany class struggle degenerated into civil war; at Rennes fights broke out at the end of January, 1789. The Third Estate, annoyed, moved towards radical solutions. In a famous pamphlet issued in February, "What Is the Third Estate?" Sieyes described with cool rancour the hatred and scorn inspired in him by the nobility: "This class is assuredly foreign to the nation because of its do-nothing idleness." At the same time Mirabeau, in a speech which he had planned to deliver to the Estates of Provence, praised Marius "for having exterminated the aristocracy and the nobility in Rome." Fearful words, heralding civil war.

The Elections and the Cahiers

The electoral rules could have handicapped the bourgeoisie either by giving existing provincial estates the right to appoint deputies or by reserving a proportion of seats in the Third Estate to provincial delegates. Some of the nobles recommended these devices; Necker brushed them aside.

The method of election varied considerably, but the ruling of January 24, 1789, generally prevailed. It designated bailiwicks (bailliages) and seneschalsies (sénéchaussées) as electoral districts, even though these judicial areas were unevenly populated and differed widely in size. Contrary to precedent, whether or not he possessed a fief every noble was summoned to appear in the assembly of his order, but those ennobled by personal title only were relegated to the Third Estate—an error, for it wounded their pride. To elect clerical deputies, all parish priests met with the bishops, whereas monks and canons were merely allowed to send representatives. Most parish priests were of the Third Estate and, commanding a majority, often neglected to elect their aristocratic bishops as delegates. The electors who chose the Third Estate's deputies assembled in bailiwick meetings after themselves being named by tax-paying heads of families within villages and parishes. They were elected directly in the villages, by two stages in the large towns. In each of the small bailiwicks designated "secondary" electoral districts, the meeting was allowed only to draw up a *cahier de doléances,* or list of grievances, and send one-quarter of its members to the assembly in the "principal" bailiwick to which it was attached. Peasants outnumbered all others at these meetings, but, lacking education, were incapable of expressing their opinions and were all the more intimidated because the meetings began with discussion of what should be included in the *cahiers.* They almost invariably elected bourgeois deputies.

Among the representatives elected by clergy and nobility were able men who opposed reform, such as Cazalès and the abbé Maury, but owing to circumstances only the liberals—Duport, Alexandre de Lameth, and notably Lafayette—took a leading role. Deputies of the Third Estate were for the most part mature, often rich or well-to-do, educated, industrious, and honest men. Sometimes they had received special distinction—Bailly and Target were members of the Académie Française—but more often they had earned a reputation in their particular province. Mounier and Barnave were well known in the Dauphiné, Lanjuinais and Le Chapelier in Brittany, Thouret and Buzot in Normandy, Merlin de Douai in Flanders, Robespierre in Artois. A telling characteristic of the bourgeoisie was that it had long idolized the marquis de Lafayette, noble deputy from Riom, and that the most celebrated of its own deputies, Sieyes and Mirabeau, came from the privileged classes. This foretells what position the nobility could have assumed in a reformed society by siding with the bourgeoisie.

Sieyes and Mirabeau were both from Provence. Sieyes, the son of a notary in Fréjus, had become canon of Chartres and was elected deputy from Paris. He guided the Third Estate during the early weeks. His pamphlets earned him a reputation as an oracle.

It was he who developed the theory of "constituent power," declaring that sovereignty resided in the nation alone and that representatives of the nation were to be invested with dictatorial power until a constitution could be written and put into effect. He was the loyal interpreter of the bourgeoisie and later made the significant distinction between "active" and "passive" citizens. But, lacking application or special talent as an orator, he quickly shut himself off in isolation. Mirabeau, on the other hand, possessed the realistic foresight of a statesman, knew how to handle men, and was unexcelled in eloquent oratory. Unfortunately his scandalous youth and cynical venality made it impossible to respect him; no one doubted that the court could buy him at will. Neither he nor Sieyes could direct the Third Estate. Its work remained a collective achievement.

Necker could have exerted considerable influence over the drafting of the *cahiers de doléances*. Malouet, an official in the naval ministry and a deputy of the Third Estate from Riom, pointed out to him that he must draw up a royal programme to guide public opinion, impress the nobility, and—most important —restrain the enthusiasm of the Third Estate. Necker very likely sensed the wisdom of this suggestion, but he had already been soundly criticized for permitting the doubling and was now inclined to consider his moves carefully. He rejected this additional risk, content with having persuaded the king to remain neutral.

The bourgeois were therefore free to participate in drafting lists of grievances from the parishes. Some model *cahiers* were sent out from Paris or were drawn up regionally; lawyers and parish priests sometimes set pen to paper for the cause. A number of *cahiers* were nevertheless original: indifferent to constitutional reform, they were content to criticize the overwhelming burdens laid upon the populace. But these should not necessarily be taken as an accurate reflection of what the lower classes felt most deeply, for in the presence of a manorial judge peasants were not always likely to say what they thought. Moreover, the proletarians rarely participated in deliberations. Grievances sent out from the bailiwicks are even less representative, since bourgeois members simply eliminated from the original lists those demands which displeased or did not interest them. The popular classes of town and countryside were concerned not only with attaining fiscal equality and tax reduction, but with suppressing the tithe, manorial rights, and seigneurial authority, with gaining observance of collective usage, regulating the grain market, and instituting controls to curb capitalist expansion. The people threatened aristocratic property along with aristocratic privileges, and bourgeois aspirations as well. But since the populace did not have access to the Estates-General, king, aristocrats and bourgeois were left alone to settle their triangular conflict.

In their *cahiers* the nobles and bourgeois were of one accord in expressing devotion to the monarchy, but they also agreed upon the need to replace absolutism with rule of law accepted by representatives of the nation; with reasonable freedom of the press and guarantees of personal liberty against arbitrary administrative and judicial ruling; with reform of various branches of the administration, including ecclesiastic reorganization. To the desire for national unity was joined a keen desire for regional and communal autonomy which would end ministerial despotism by loosening the grip of a centralized administration. Both classes agreed to religious toleration, but secularization of the state stopped at this point: they wished to leave the privilege of public worship to the Catholic Church and did not consider abolishing religious instruction or Church poor relief, nor did they deny clerics the right to register births, marriages, and deaths. The clergy was not satisfied with this much: it would not allow criticism of its doctrines through the press or the same treatment for heretics as for true believers. Even a recent edict granting legal status to Protestants had provoked protest. Except for these qualifications, not inconsiderable in themselves, the clergy agreed with the other two orders. More or less generally conceived, liberty was a national desire.

Class conflict was none the less evident. The privileged classes resigned themselves to financial sacrifices—with strong reservations as to the extent and method of contributions demanded of them—but they were generally opposed to the vote by head and expressly stipulated that the orders be preserved and honorific prerogatives and manorial rights be retained, whereas for the Third Estate equality of rights was inseparable from liberty.

But this did not mean that royal arbitration was destined to fail. No one challenged the king's right to approve legislation or the need to leave executive power intact. By renouncing the exercise of arbitrary will and by governing in accord with the Estates-General, the Capetian dynasty would only emphasize its national character; royal authority would not be lessened if reformed. There were many men among the aristocracy and bourgeoisie who, whether they actively desired it or not, might have leaned towards compromise. Among the nobles obedience to the princely will might have quelled opposition. Such bourgeois as Malouet and Mounier wanted above all to end despotism and judged that wrangling among the orders would perpetuate it. With little concern for the peasants, they were willing to respect the manorial authority and honorific primacy of the noble. Among each of the orders fear of civil war, already perceptible, secretly pleaded for conciliation.

A great king or a great minister might have taken the initiative towards a settlement. But Louis XVI was not Henry IV; Necker was clearsighted, but his background paralysed him. The nation was left to itself.

The Victory of the Bourgeoisie

Far from thinking of compromise, the court tried to get rid of Necker. The Parlement of Paris, repentant, gladly offered its assistance. In April rumour had it that a new cabinet would be formed and would promptly adjourn the Estates-General *sine die*. The issue of verifying powers aroused contention among the ministers: Barentin held that precedent accorded power of verification to the Council of State [the king's Cabinet]; Necker objected. Louis ended by supporting Necker, thereby averting a palace revolution but leaving the question of who was qualified to verify powers undecided. This conflict probably accounts for the postponement of the opening of the Estates from April 27 to May 5.

Prudence advised that the deputies should assemble far from Paris, but Versailles was the preferred choice—by the king so he could hunt; by the queen and her entourage for their own pleasures. The court also acted unwisely in clinging to a protocol that humiliated the Third Estate. Each order was assigned a particular dress, and they were segregated for presentation to the king on May 2. In the procession of the Holy Ghost, on May 4, they paraded in separate groups from Notre Dame to Saint Louis. Representatives of the Third, dressed in black, were indistinguishable except for the commanding ugliness of Mirabeau, but were applauded confidently by an immense crowd. The nobles were decked and plumed. The dark mass of parish priests came next, then the king's musicians, then bishops dressed in dazzling robes. This war of ceremony lasted until July 14: in royal sessions the Third affected to dress like the privileged orders; Bailly gave notice that deputations he led to the king would not kneel before the royal presence.

The Hôtel des Menus-Plaisirs on the Avenue de Paris, actually an ordinary storehouse, had been prepared for the meetings of clergy and nobility. Behind it, on the Rue des Chantiers, a room built for the notables was enlarged and redecorated for plenary sessions, which were presided over by the king. But because nothing else was large enough to hold the Third Estate, this "national hall" was turned over to it on ordinary occasions. Spectators sat on the speakers' platforms, thronged in and out, and were allowed to join in discussions, a habit which persisted until the end of the Convention. This careless arrangement increased the importance of the Third Estate and subjected the more timid to pressures of intransigent and rash opinions.

Louis opened the meeting on May 5. His brief address was applauded. Barentin, who could not be heard, followed. Then Necker, with the aid of an acting official who relieved him from time to time, harangued the anxious deputies. His listeners were soon disappointed and seriously annoyed. For three hours the minister of finance explained the detailed situation of the Treasury and the proposed improvements, made no allusion to constitutional reform, expressed confidence in the generosity of the privileged classes, then repeated the method of voting which had been announced in December. ·On the following day the nobility and clergy began to verify their powers separately. The Third Estate refused to follow suit. The Estates-General was paralysed.

Deputies from Brittany and the Dauphiné favoured outright refusal to vote by order, but that would have been an infringement of legality, and the politicians did not want to take chances so early in the game. The representatives were not yet familiar with one another, and no one knew how far each would agree to advance. Some found the ardour of the Bretons alarming. A delaying tactic was necessary, and Necker's refusal to grant the Council of State power of verification provided an escape. The Third Estate alleged that each order had to establish whether the two other orders were legally constituted, and that powers should therefore be inspected in common session. During this stalemate the Third refused to constitute itself as a separate order: no minutes were taken, no rules established; not even a steering committee was set up. They consented only to choose a "dean," who after June 3 was Bailly. At the beginning the Third had taken the name Commons (*communes*) for itself. Although no one other than a few of the more erudite knew exactly what the medieval communes were, the word evoked a vague memory of popular resistance to feudal lords, an idea strengthened by what knowledge they had of English history. To the Third Estate the name meant refusal to recognize a social hierarchy that had relegated it to third rank.

This attitude had its drawbacks. The people were told that the Third Estate was responsible for delaying the abolition of fiscal privileges. When Malouet tried to negotiate by offering to guarantee the rights and property of the aristocracy he was roundly criticized. Everyone, however, sensed the need for some new tactical issue, and it was the clergy which furnished them with just that. The nobility, in no way perturbed, on May 11 announced itself constituted as a separate order. Because a large proportion of the parish priests supported the Commons, the clergy instead proposed that designated members of the three orders meet in conference. To humour the other order, the Third Estate agreed. But the discussions of May 23 and 25 came to nothing: the nobles retreated behind precedents which the Third Estate either challenged or fought with arguments of reason and natural right. They next tried to get the clergy to agree that the three orders should be fused. The bishops sensed imminent defection from the parish priests and asked the king to intervene. On May 28 Louis asked that the conferences be resumed in the presence of his ministers, and on June 4 Necker drafted a conciliatory proposal: each order should first verify the powers of its own members, then announce the results to the others and consider any objections that were raised. If no agreement could be reached, the king was to deliver a final decision. Once more the Third found itself in a difficult position. This time it was the nobility that came to its rescue by rejecting royal arbitration except for the "complete" delegations—those which, as in the Dauphiné and in several bailiwicks, had been chosen in common by the three orders. This was the signal for revolutionary action.

On June 10 the Third Estate followed a proposal from Sieyes and invited the privileged members to join it. Those who did not appear to answer a roll call would be considered to have defaulted. The roll was begun on June 12 and finished on the 14th: several parish priests had responded, but not one noble. After two days' debate the Third Estate on June 17 conferred the title "National Assembly" upon the combined and enrolled orders. It immediately arrogated to itself the power to consent to taxation, confirming existing taxes provisionally. Had sovereignty passed to the nation? Not exactly. On June 20 Bailly acknowledged that these revolutionary resolutions required the king's approval.

Louis had no intention of approving them. The Dauphin had died on June 4, and the king had withdrawn to Marly, where the queen and royal princes instructed him. The nobility finally abdicated in favour of the throne and begged the king to make the Third Estate return to the path of duty. On June 19 the majority of the clergy declared itself in favour of fusing the three orders. The bishops hastily called for assistance. Royal ministers and even Necker agreed that intervention was necessary. The Council of State announced that a royal session would be held on June 22. But what would the king declare then? With the support of [the ministers] Montmorin and Saint-Priest, Necker hoped to manage the Commons by simply ignoring their decrees rather than by overriding them. At last he came out into the open, proposing to establish equality of taxation, to admit all Frenchmen to public office, and to authorize the vote by head in constituting future Estates-General, stipulating that the king would agree to this only if the Estates met as two houses and if he were granted full executive power with a legislative veto. Necker protected aristocratic prerogatives and property with the vote by order, but Barentin objected: did this mean they were to adopt the British system of government? Louis hesitated, postponing the decision. The royal session was put off until June 23.

On June 20 the Third Estate discovered its hall closed without notice or warning. It finally found asylum in a neighbouring tennis court, where, because there was talk of retiring to Paris and seeking the protection of the people, Mounier stepped in and proposed the famous oath, that they remain united until a constitution was established. A threatened *lit de justice* had provoked enough indignation to incite the deputies, with few exceptions, to sign the oath. The Third Estate, like the Parlement of Paris, rebelled in advance against the royal will.

On June 21 Louis admitted his brothers to the Council and, finally, withdrew his support from Necker, whose programme was defeated the next day. On the 23rd an impressive show of armed force surrounded the Hôtel des Menus-Plaisirs, from which the public was excluded. Received in silence, Louis had Barentin read two declarations of capital interest in that they revealed quite clearly what was at stake in the struggle. They granted the Estates-General power to consent to taxes and loans and to various budget allocations, including the funds set aside for upkeep of the court. Personal liberty and freedom of the press would be guaranteed; decentralization would be carried out through the provincial estates; an extensive programme of reforms would be studied by the Estates-General. In sum, the proposals meant that a constitutional system, civil liberty, and achievement of national unity were to be the common inheritance of monarch and nation. Louis made an exception only for the clergy: its special consent was required for everything touching upon ecclesiastic organization and religious matters. Furthermore, he appeared as arbiter among the orders—if the Third Estate's decrees were overridden, so were the binding mandates that the privileged orders had invoked to compel voting by order and to postpone equality of taxation. Verification of powers would follow the system proposed on June 4. The orders were authorized to meet together to deliberate matters of general interest. The king strongly hoped that the clergy and nobility would agree to assume their share of public burdens.

But Louis failed to impose equal taxation and remained silent upon the question of admittance to public office; he expressly retained the orders and excluded vote by head from such matters as organization of future Estates-General, the manorial system, and honorific privileges. The throne thereby committed itself to preservation of the traditional social hierarchy and aristocratic pre-eminence. As a result of this decision, the Revolution was to mean conquest of equality of rights.

The king concluded by ordering the Estates to separate into orders and by giving them to understand that he would dissolve the assembly if its members did not obey. He then departed, followed by the nobility and most of the clergy. The Third Estate did not stir. Brezé, grand master of ceremonies, repeated his sovereign's command, to which Bailly replied: "The assembled nation cannot receive orders." Sieyès declared: "You are today what you were yesterday." Ignoring, as the Parlement of Paris had done previously, the existence of a royal session, the Third Estate confirmed its own decrees and declared its members inviolable. The expressive and significant statements made by Bailly and by Sieyes deserve to be those remembered by posterity, but Mirabeau's epigraph has proved more popular: "We will not stir from our seats unless forced by bayonets." The Commons could not have carried out this challenge, but the court thought itself in no position to find out, as agitation had already reached menacing proportions. After this point, resistance to the Third Estate disintegrated: a majority of the clergy and forty-seven nobles joined the Commons; on June 27 the king asked the others to follow suit.

The legal, peaceful revolution of the bourgeoisie, achieved by lawyers who borrowed their methods from the Parlement of Paris, was to all appearances victorious. On July 7 the Assembly appointed a committee on the constitution and two days later Mounier delivered its first report. From that day, and for history, the Assembly was the Constituent Assembly. On July 11 Lafayette submitted his draft for a declaration of human rights.

Appeal to Armed Force

The Third Estate did not lose its composure. Dictatorship of the constituent power, advocated by Sieyes, was not instituted. Royal approval was still considered necessary. The modern idea that a constitution creates its own powers before it regulates them had not yet been formulated; instead, Louis XVI, invested with his own power rooted in history, would contract with the nation. On the other hand, although the Third Estate fused the three orders, it did not proclaim their disappearance within the nation, nor did it call for election of a new assembly: the bourgeoisie therefore did not aspire to class dictatorship. On the contrary, it seemed possible that a moderate majority would be formed: the clergy, the liberal nobility, and a segment of the Commons favoured a party of the middle. Most of the nobles, however, made it known that they by no means considered the matter settled, and when troops were seen thronging around Paris and Versailles the king was suspected of preparing a show of force. He had excuses: agitation was growing; hunger multiplied disturbances; at the end of June disorderly conduct of the French Guards [a regiment of royal troops] caused a riot in Paris.

The court had not yet fixed a plan of action. To draw one up, it had to get rid of Necker and his friends. The maréchal de Broglie and the baron de Breteuil had been called in. Wisdom commanded that a cabinet be formed secretly, ready to appear when sufficient forces were on hand. This was a game with fearful consequences. We can understand that the king regarded deputies of the Third Estate as rebels and that the nobility considered surrender a humiliation. But if a show of arms failed, the blood spilled would stain both king and aristocracy. Nevertheless, on July 11 Necker was hastily dismissed and banished from the kingdom; his friends were replaced by Breteuil and his cohorts. No further steps were taken. But the Assembly expected the worst, and the bourgeois revolution seemed lost. They were saved by popular force.

THE POPULAR REVOLUTION

Resort to arms transformed the struggle of social orders into civil war which, abruptly changing the character of the Revolution, gave it a scope that far surpassed what the bourgeoisie had intended or expected. Popular intervention, which provoked the sudden collapse of the social system of the Old Regime, issued from progressive mobilization of the masses by the simultaneous influences of the economic crisis and the convocation of the Estates-General. These two causes fused to create a mentality of insurrection.

The Economic Crisis

Starting in 1778, the surge in production which had followed the Seven Years War and which is known as the splendour of Louis XV, was checked by difficulties rooted in agricultural fluctuations, a continual problem of the old economy. These setbacks became established in cyclical depressions and caused what their historian[5] called the decline of Louis XVI. First, unusually heavy grape harvests provoked a dreadful slump in the wine market. Prices fell by as much as 50 per cent. They rose somewhat after 1781 because of scarcity, but short supply then meant that the wine sector could not recoup its losses. Wine-growing was still practised in almost every part of the kingdom and for many peasants was the most profitable market product. They suffered cruelly; those who were sharecroppers found their income reduced to nothing. Grain prices were the next to fall, remaining relatively low until 1787. Finally, a drought in 1785 killed off much of the livestock.

Rural inhabitants constituted the majority of consumers, and because their purchasing power was reduced industrial production was in turn threatened after 1786. Traditional interpretation has laid primary blame for industry's troubles upon the

[5] [C.-E. Labrousse, *Esquisse du mouvement des prix et des revenus en France au XVIIIe siècle* (Paris: Dalloz, 1933) and *La Crise de l'économie française à la fin de l'ancien régime et au début de la Révolution* (Paris: Presses Universitaires de France, 1943).]

commercial treaty with Britain [the Eden Treaty of 1786]. Although this was not the most important cause, it certainly did obstruct industry temporarily, since production had to modernize if it was to withstand foreign competition. Unemployment spread. The countryside, where domestic industry had developed, suffered as much as the cities.

The lower classes therefore had no reserves left when they faced the brutal prospect of famine after grain crops failed in 1788. The price of bread rose steadily. At the beginning of July, 1789, a pound of bread sold for four sous in Paris—where the government nevertheless sold its imported grains at a loss—and twice as much in some provinces. At that time wage earners considered two sous per pound the highest price they could possibly pay and still subsist, for bread was their staple food and average daily consumption ranged from one and a half pounds per person to two or three for an adult manual labourer. Necker ordered large purchases from abroad, and, as usual, labour centres [*ateliers de charité* or public workshops] opened up, while measures were taken for distributing soup and rice. The previous winter had been severe, and the cruel effects of high prices did not lessen as the harvest season drew near. For over a half-century we have known, chiefly from the works of Jaurès, that the prosperity of the kingdom of France was responsible for the growing power of the bourgeoisie, and in this sense it is with reason that [the historian] Michelet's interpretation has been attacked, for the Revolution broke out in a society in the midst of development, not one crippled and seemingly threatened with collapse by nature's Providential shortages. But the social importance of this enrichment should not deceive us. Since colonial profits were realized mainly through re-exportation, the nation's labour force did not benefit as much as we might think, and, while a long-term rise in prices swelled the income of large landowners and bourgeoisie, wages failed to keep pace. We now know that production was dislocated and curtailed in the last decade before the Revolution, and we can justifiably state that the living standard of the masses was steadily declining. Famine, when it came, overwhelmed the populace.

"The people" (artisans, shopkeepers, hired help) as well as proletarians ("the populace"), peasants—small proprietors and sharecroppers who did not raise enough to support themselves or wine-growers who did not raise any grain—as well as townsmen unanimously agreed that the government and upper classes were responsible for these afflictions. Income declined but taxes did not. Tolls and duties on consumption became more hateful in times of high prices. If the wine market was restricted it was because excises limited consumption. There was no bread because Brienne removed controls on grain exports and shipments in 1787. True, Necker had stopped exports, subsidized imports, and reinstituted market sales. But he was too late. "Hoarders" had gone to work. Anyone in authority, all government agents were suspected of participating in hoarding. The "famine plot" was thought to be more than a myth. Tithe collectors and lords were just as odious—they were hoarders because their levies cut into a poor harvest and consumed the peasants' supplies. The final blow was that collectors and lords profited even more from the high prices that increased poverty. And, finally, the solidarity of the Third Estate was shaken: the grain merchant, the baker, and the miller were all threatened; the bourgeois, partisan of economic freedom, clashed with popular hostility towards capitalism, since the people by nature favoured requisitions and controls. In April Necker authorized requisitions to replenish the markets, but the intendants and municipal officials rarely used this power.

As the months of 1789 passed, riots kept the tired and frightened officials in a constant state of alert. On April 28 Parisian workers from the faubourg Saint-Antoine sacked the manufactories of Réveillon and Henriot. Throughout the kingdom markets were the scenes of disturbances. Grain shipments, forced by milling and transportation conditions to use roads and rivers in plain view of famished hordes, were sometimes halted. The army and constabulary exhausted themselves rushing from one place to another, but were not inclined to deal harshly towards rebels whose privations they shared and unconsciously began to feel a common sympathy with them. The armour of the Old Regime was rapidly disintegrating.

Agitation was especially pronounced in the countryside. There the tax burden was crushing; tithes and manorial dues drove the peasants to desperation. Sentiment in the peasant community was divided among journeymen, sharecroppers, small proprietors, and large-scale tenant farmers, but on all matters of taxation it was solidly opposed to royal authority and the aristocracy. Tremors of agrarian revolt could be felt well before July 14—in Provence at the end of March, around Gap in April, in Cambrésis and Picardy in May. Near Versailles and Paris game had been exterminated, forests cleaned out. Moreover, the people were afraid of each other because begging, a regional trouble, spread before their eyes. Many journeymen and small landowners became mendicants. The poor left their villages to crowd into towns or else became vagabonds, forming groups which coursed through the country. They invaded farms even at night, forced themselves in by the fear of burning and of attacks on livestock, trees, the crops that were just beginning to grow, or by threatening to pillage everything. Officials had their own reasons for worrying about the crops and let the villagers arm themselves for protection. As fear of brigandage spread, panics broke out. The slightest incident was enough to put a timid person to flight, convinced that brigands had arrived, sowing fear wherever he fled.

The "Good News" and the Great Hope

But we cannot be sure that economic crisis would have driven the people to aid the bourgeoisie if the calling of the Estates-General had not deeply moved the populace. The goals appropriated by the bourgeois they elected scarcely concerned the lower classes, but an event so foreign was welcomed as "a good piece of news" presaging a miraculous change in men's fates. It awoke hopes both dazzling and vague of a future when all would enjoy a better life—hopes shared by the bourgeoisie. This vision of the future united the heterogeneous elements of the Third Estate and became a dynamic source of revolutionary idealism. Among the common people it gave to the Revolution a character that can be called mythical, if myth is taken to mean a complex of ideas concerning the future which generate energy and initiative. In this sense the Revolution in its early stages can be compared to certain religious movements in nascent form, when the poor gladly discern a return to paradise on earth.

Arthur Young [the British traveller and agricultural reformer] has recorded that on July 12, while walking up a hill near Les Islettes, in the Argonne Forest, he met a poor woman who described her misery to him. " 'Something was to be done by some great folk for such poor ones,' but she did not know who nor how, 'but God send us better, *car les tailles et les droits nous écrasent* ' " (for the *taille* and [*manorial*] rights are crushing us).

Since the king consulted his people, he pitied their plight. What could he do if not remove their burdens—taxes, tithes, fees? He would therefore be content if they went ahead and helped him: after the elections aristocratic cries of alarm arose on all sides, for the peasants openly declared that they would pay no more.

At the same time this great hope inflamed fearful passions, from which the bourgeoisie was not exempt. The revolutionary mentality was imbued with them; the history of the period bears their deep imprint.

The Aristocratic Conspiracy and the Revolutionary Mentality

The Third Estate was at once convinced that the nobles would stubbornly defend their privileges. This expectation, soon confirmed by aristocratic opposition to the doubling and then to the vote by head, aroused suspicions that with little difficulty hardened into convictions. The nobles would use any means to "crush" the villagers; they would outwit their well-intentioned king to obtain dissolution of the Estates-General. They would take up arms, bar themselves in their châteaux, and enlist brigands to wage civil war just as the king's agents enlisted the poverty-stricken. Prisoners would be released and recruited. Nobles who had already hoarded grain to starve the Third Estate would willingly see the harvest ruined. Fear of the aristocracy was everywhere rapidly linked with fear of brigands, a connection that fused the results of the calling of the Estates with those of the economic crisis. Moreover, foreign powers would be called on to help. The comte d'Artois was going to emigrate and win over his father-in-law (the king of Sardinia), the Spanish and Neapolitan Bourbons, and the emperor, brother of the queen. France, like Holland, would be invaded by the Prussians. Collusion with foreign powers, which weighed heavily in the history of the Revolution, was assumed from the beginning, and in July an invasion was feared imminently. The whole Third Estate believed in an "aristocratic conspiracy."

The burden of royal centralization and the conflict of orders dominated the Third Estate's view of the crisis. Neglecting to accuse natural forces and incapable of analysing the total economic situation, the Third laid responsibility upon royal power and the aristocracy. An incomplete picture perhaps, but not inexact. The freeing of the grain trade, which Brienne had decreed, did favour speculators; to the argument that this would increase production the people replied that it would profit the aristocracy and bourgeoisie first, while they had to bear the costs. Similarly, if the Third Estate falsely imputed Machiavellian qualities to the aristocracy, it was true that the court, in agreement with the nobles, thought to punish the deputies for their insubordination; and it was true that the aristocratic conspiracy, although denounced prematurely, was soon to become a reality. In any case the mind of the Third Estate is of capital interest in showing the historian that events have their immediate roots not in their antecedents but in the men who intervene by interpreting those events.

If aristocratic conspiracy and "brigands" instilled many with enough fear to cause occasional panics, there were others who, although frightened, remained rational and faced danger resolutely. Consequently the labels "fears" and "Great Fear" unjustly imply that the whole Third Estate was struck dumb with terror. Actually the revolutionary mentality was capable of countering unrest with vigorous defensive reaction. The Third was kept informed by letters from its deputies and in turn encouraged its representatives with innumerable appeals. The bourgeoisie would gladly have pushed further: it wanted to take municipal control from the petty oligarchy made up of those who owned offices, many of whom had acquired noble titles. At Paris the electors who had chosen deputies organized a secret municipal council in the Hôtel de Ville at the end of June. Notables hoped to set up a "national militia" [soon to be called the National Guard]. This was proposed by Parisian electors to the Constituent Assembly, but deputies did not dare authorize it. A double purpose lay behind the desire to organize a militia: to resist royal troops should the occasion rise, and to hold the people in check. Meanwhile efforts were made to win over the army, not without success, since lower-ranking officers had no hope of advancement and the soldiers, who had to pay for part of their subsistence, were affected by high prices. The French Guards fraternized with crowds at the Palais Royal; at the end of June the people freed prisoners at the Abbaye. Several men are known to have distributed money among the soldiers or to have paid the July insurgents. Beyond doubt the agents of the duc d'Orléans did as much.

Finally, along with the defensive reaction there existed a punitive will either to cripple the aristocratic conspiracy, hoarders, and all enemies of the people, or to punish those enemies. From July on this took the form of imprisonments, acts of brutality, and popular massacres.

These three aspects of the revolutionary mentality—fear, defensive reaction, and punitive will—together constitute one of the keys to the unfolding narrative of the French Revolution. The conspiracy was to all appearances halted by the end of 1789, and repression slackened. The plot later reappeared, cloaked with many of the characteristics given it in advance, and foreign powers came to its aid. The resulting defensive reaction first stimulated the volunteers who poured in and then was responsible for the mass levy. Punitive will provoked the massacres of 1792 and, when danger again loomed in 1793, the Convention warded off further perils only by setting up the Terror. Fear and its accompaniments died out only, and gradually, after the uncontested triumph of the Revolution.

The Parisian Revolution

Against this background, Necker's dismissal was a torch set to a powder keg: it was taken as evidence that the aristocratic conspiracy had begun to act. News of the event circulated in Paris on Sunday, July 12. The weather was good and a crowd gathered at the Palais Royal, whose garden and arcades, recently opened by the duc d'Orléans, had become a centre of amusement. Groups clustered about extemporaneous orators; only one, Camille Desmoulins,[6] do we know by name. Soon processions of demonstrators reached the boulevards, then the Rue Saint-Honoré. The cavalry undertook to make them disperse and charged the crowd at the Place Louis XV. The French Guards in return attacked the cavalry. The baron de Besenval, military commander, mustered his whole following on the Champ de Mars that evening.

The Parisians did not think of rallying to the aid of the Assembly; they saved it, but only indirectly. They were concerned with their own fate, convinced that their city, surrounded by royal troops and brigands, would first be bombarded from Montmartre and the Bastille and then would be pillaged. Panics erupted continually during these "days," Act One of the Great Fear. The police were gone. Toll gates were burned. [The monastery of] Saint-Lazare was sacked. Person and property were seemingly endangered. Fright hovered over the capital, abandoned to its own resources.

A defensive reaction followed immediately. Barricades arose

---

[6] [At that time a penniless young lawyer and writer, he was soon to become a polemical revolutionary journalist. By 1794 he was a supporter of Danton and was executed with other Dantonists on April 5, 1794.]

in the streets, and gunsmiths' stores were wiped clean. The electors appointed a permanent committee and set up a militia. To
arm their forces, they took 32,000 guns from the Invalides on the
morning of July 14. In search of more, they went to the Bastille.
Its governor, de Launay, parleyed. Commanding only a small
garrison, he had ordered the outer courts evacuated. They were
quickly filled by the crowd. Behind walls ninety feet high, surrounded by a water-filled ditch seventy-five feet wide, he had no
cause to fear an attack. But he lost his nerve and opened fire.
Several men fell; others drew back in disorder, crying treason,
convinced that they had been permitted to advance only to offer
better aim. Shots rang out from those who were armed, and battle
was engaged, but on an entirely unequal basis: the assailants lost
a hundred men, whereas one sole member of the garrison was hit.
A census was later taken among the "conquerors of the Bastille,"
so we know a good number of the attackers. All classes of society
were represented among them, but most were artisans from the
faubourg Saint-Antoine.

The tide of battle was still uncertain when the French and
National Guards arrived from the Hôtel de Ville. Led by a former non-commissioned officer named Hulin and by Lieutenant
Élie, they entered the courtyard of the Bastille and under heavy
fire aimed their cannons at the gate. De Launay took fright and
offered to give himself up. Élie accepted, but the attackers protested—No surrender! Amid total confusion the governor had
the drawbridge lowered, and the crowd rushed across into the
fortress. Efforts to save most of the defenders were successful, but
three officers and three men were massacred. De Launay was with
difficulty led to the doors of the Hôtel de Ville, where he lost his
life. Shortly after, Flesselles, provost of the merchants [the title
of the chief municipal official of Paris], was also killed. Their
heads were paraded through the city on pikes.

Besenval ordered a retreat to Saint-Cloud. The electors took
over municipal control, appointed Bailly mayor, and offered
command of the National Guard to Lafayette, who soon afterwards gave the Guard a cockade of red and blue, the colours of
Paris, between which he placed a white band, the king's colour.
Through Lafayette the tricoloured flag, emblem of the Revolution, joined old France with the new.

No one considered the Bastille the stakes of the struggle, and
at first no one thought that its fall would determine the outcome.

Panics continued. But seizure of the Bastille, of mediocre importance in itself, broke the court's resistance. The forces Versailles had on hand were not enough to take Paris, especially since the loyalty of the troops was not certain. Louis hesitated. Would he try to flee? Against the urgings of the comte d'Artois he decided to give in. On July 15 he yielded to the Assembly and announced the dismissal of his troops. The next day he recalled Necker. On the 17th he went to Paris and accepted the cockade.

Few concluded from this that the aristocracy had laid down its arms, and wild rumours continued to circulate. The comte d'Artois and many others emigrated; according to one story an English squadron lay in wait off the coast of Brest. The permanent committee searched the edges of Paris for brigands. Finding only vagabonds, it sent them back where they had come from. The suburbs feared that they would be overrun with such wanderers, and panic spread. Bertier de Sauvigny, the intendant of Paris, his father-in-law, Foullon de Doué, and Besenval himself were arrested. Massacres began again: on July 22 Sauvigny and Doué were hanged at the Place de Grève; Necker returned just in time to save Besenval on July 30. These murders provoked strong protest, but now part of the bourgeoisie, roused by the obvious danger, joined the people in their fury—"Is this blood then so pure?" cried Barnave before the Constituent Assembly. Nevertheless, they could hardly deny that summary executions ought to cease. On July 23 a notary from the Rue de Richelieu proposed, in the name of his district, that a popular tribunal be set up; and on the 30th Bailly made a similar request. The Assembly paid no heed. Only in October did it institute prosecution for crimes of *lèse-nation* [treason against the people], to be handled by the Châtelet of Paris—an ordinary court. In July the Assembly did at least establish a "committee of investigation," prototype of the Committee of General Security; and the municipality of Paris organized another which was the first revolutionary committee. While debating the issue of privacy of correspondence during the summer, deputies of all representation, from the marquis de Gouy d'Arsy and Target, member of the Académie Française, to Barnave and Robespierre, firmly maintained that one could not govern in time of war and revolution as in time of peace—in other words, that the rights they were proposing to grant to all citizens depended upon circumstances. This was to become the doctrine of the revolutionary government.

The Municipal Revolution

In the provinces, too, Necker's dismissal provoked strong feeling and an immediate reaction. The populace was no longer content only to send addresses, now often menacing, to its representatives. In several towns the public coffers were broken open and arsenals or military storehouses looted. One committee undertook to set up a militia and issued an appeal to neighbouring communes, even to the peasants. The governor of Dijon was arrested; nobles and priests were confined to their dwellings—this was the first example of detention of suspects. At Rennes the townsmen persuaded the garrison to desert and then rose up. The military commander fled.

When news came of the fall of the Bastille and of the king's visit to Paris—an event celebrated in some places—the bourgeoisie took heart and laid hands on the instruments of control in almost every area. The "municipal revolution," as it is known, was in most cases a peaceable one: the municipal councils of the Old Regime took on notables or stepped down for the electors. Very often they had to create, or permit the formation of, a permanent committee. It was charged initially with organization of the National Guard, but gradually absorbed the whole administrative apparatus. Nevertheless, the people, having taken part in bourgeois demonstrations, demanded that bread prices be lowered. If this was not soon granted riots broke out, the houses of officials and those known as hoarders were sacked, and often the former municipal councils were ousted.

The municipal revolution thus differed from place to place and was often arrested half way. In every instance, however, the only orders obeyed were those of the National Assembly. The king no longer commanded authority. Centralization, too, was weakened: each municipality wielded absolute power within its own confines and over surrounding districts as well. From August on, towns started to conclude mutual-assistance pacts, spontaneously transforming France into a federation of communes. Local autonomy opened the field of action to a small group of resolute men who, without waiting for instructions from Paris, passed what measures they considered necessary to secure public safety. This was a basic stimulant to revolutionary defence.

Yet the other side of the coin was immediately visible. The Constituent Assembly enjoyed a prestige accorded none of its successors, but the populace observed only such decrees as suited it. What did the people want above all else? Tax reform, abolition of indirect levies, institution of controls over the grain trade. Tax collection was suspended; the salt tax, excises, and municipal tolls were suppressed; exchange of grains was either forbidden or continually thwarted. Proclamations and decrees against this had no effect. At Paris the populace went even further. Within the districts—divisions established for elections to the Estates-General—assembled citizens, like the electors before them, claimed to supervise the municipal authority they set up to replace the electors. In their eyes national sovereignty entailed direct democracy, an idea that would remain dear to the sans-culottes.

The Peasant Revolution and the Great Fear

The countryside had joined the towns, but revolution in Paris had even greater effect on rural areas. Agrarian revolt broke out in several regions. In the woodlands of Normandy, in the Hainaut and Upper Alsace, châteaux or abbeys were attacked by those seeking to burn archives and force surrender of manorial rights. In Franche-Comté and the Mâconnais peasants set fire to many châteaux, sometimes laying them waste. The bourgeoisie was not always spared: they, too, had to pay. In Alsace the Jews suffered. On the other hand, there was clear evidence of rural hostility towards a menacing capitalism whose instrument had become the manorial reaction: free pasturage was reclaimed, enclosures destroyed, forests invaded, commons taken back or demanded for the first time—the peasant revolution was a double-edged sword. Faced with this threat, the notables drew closer together. Urban militias were used to restore order. In the Mâconnais the bourgeoisie set up extraordinary tribunals beside the old provost courts, and thirty-three peasants were hanged. Revolt fired men's minds. Even more important, however, was a passive resistance which everywhere interfered with collection of the tithe or the *champart*[7] demanded from crops harvested. Only those who wished to pay did so. The Great Fear gave irresistible force to this movement.

Events in Paris strengthened fear of the aristocratic conspiracy, of foreign invasion which could carry it out, of recruitment of brigands for its service. Brigands were the source of even greater fear now that the wheat was ripe, and Paris, along with

[7] [A manorial rent payable in kind by the peasant to the lord.]

other large towns, was expelling beggars and vagabonds. Grain riots and agrarian revolts heightened tension. So did forays by National Guards who left towns to pillage châteaux or demand grain. The Great Fear grew out of six localized incidents no different from those which had unloosed so many panics, but this time they set off currents which were fed along the way by new outbreaks acting as relay reinforcements. Some of these can be traced for hundreds of miles, with branches that covered entire provinces. This extraordinary diffusion in a chain reaction gives the Great Fear its distinctive character and illuminates the mentality that made it possible.

A "disturbance" at Nantes alarmed Poitou. At Estrées-Saint-Denis, in the Beauvais, another spread fright in all directions. A third in southern Champagne sowed terror through the Gâtinais, Bourbonnais, and Burgundy. A fourth, originating near the Montmirail forest, close to La Ferté-Bernard, alerted Maine, Normandy, Anjou, and the Touraine. From the edge of the Chizé forest fear struck Angoulême, spread into Berry and the central mountains, alarmed Aquitaine as far as the Pyrenees. In the east, agrarian revolts in Franche-Comté and the Mâconnais drove fear to the shores of the Mediterranean.

Revolutionaries and aristocrats accused one another of having contrived the Great Fear. The enemies of the Revolution, charged the revolutionaries, sowed anarchy in an effort to paralyse the National Assembly. The bourgeoisie, replied the aristocrats, alarmed the people to make them take up arms and rebel just when the lower classes desired to remain at peace. This last version met with success because the Great Fear provoked a defensive reaction which turned upon the aristocracy. Near Le Mans and in Vivarais three nobles were put to death, and peasants in the Dauphiné provided a formidable relay station for panic by burning châteaux.

It was therefore repeated afterwards that fear had broken out everywhere and at once, spread by mysterious messengers and engendering agrarian revolt. It did not, in fact, cover the whole kingdom: Brittany, Lorraine, lower Languedoc, among other areas, were unaffected. The Great Fear lasted from July 20 to August 6. Documents show that some propagated it in good faith, and one significant fact is that it never touched the districts which had previously witnessed insurrection. Only in Dauphiné did it provoke a *jacquerie* [large-scale peasant revolt]. If it encouraged the revolution of the peasants it did not cause it. They were already on their feet.

The Night of August 4 and the Declaration
of the Rights of Man and the Citizen

While popular revolution spread, the Assembly's debates dragged on ineffectively. Was this the appropriate moment to publish a declaration of rights? Would it not be better to postpone any such action until the constitution was drawn up, so that the two could be reconciled? Arguments of a general nature were voiced with no mention of the reasons behind opposing views: the existence of orders and the privileges, both of which would be suppressed by the principles to be proclaimed. Aristocrats therefore favoured postponement, hoping to preserve a few of their prerogatives, while the Patriots, growing impatient, accused the nobles of undue obstruction, and the more clairvoyant suspected that privileges held by provinces and towns gave the nobility secret supporters within the Third Estate. On the morning of August 4 the Assembly ruled that it would begin by voting the declaration. But its members could expect discussion to provoke new resistance.

On the other hand, the popular revolution had to be resolved. The Assembly, which it had saved, had no choice but to endorse it, yet order had to be re-established, since the people were quietly waiting for the reforms their representatives would deem appropriate. The bourgeoisie in all probability could control townsmen, but the peasants were a different matter. They were destroying the manorial regime without concerning themselves about the Assembly. What course should be taken? If it resorted to the army and provost courts, the Assembly would break with the people and place itself at the mercy of king and aristocracy. The alternative was to grant satisfaction to the rebels—but then how would the parish priests and liberal nobles react? And it was their support which had assured the Third Estate's victory.

The terms of the decision and the tactics to carry it out were decreed during the night of August 3–4 by a hundred deputies meeting at the Café Amaury as a "Breton Club," which dated back to the end of April, when deputies from Brittany had, as soon as they arrived in town, adopted the custom of concerting their moves and had immediately opened their debates to colleagues from other provinces. They resolved to sway the Assembly by "a kind of magic." In matters involving the feudal system, the duc d'Aiguillon was to take the lead.

But on the evening of August 4 it was the vicomte de Noailles who made the first move, and there was no alternative but to support him. Without debate the Assembly enthusiastically adopted equality of taxation and redemption of all manorial rights except for those involving personal servitude—which were to be abolished without indemnification. Other proposals followed with the same success: equality of legal punishment, admission of all to public office, abolition of venality in office, conversion of the tithe into payments subject to redemption, freedom of worship, prohibition of plural holding of benefices, suppression of annates (the year's income owed the pope by a bishop upon investiture). Privileges of provinces and towns were offered as a last sacrifice. Nevertheless, the "magic" had worked its powers.

These resolutions had to be written up formally, so the debate opened again the next day and lasted until August 11. The final decree began: "The National Assembly destroys the feudal regime in its entirety." This was far from exact: they retained the law of primogeniture and honorific prerogatives, while requirement of an indemnity promised a long life to manorial fees. The tithe was suppressed without indemnity, but, just as fees could be collected until the method of redemption was determined, the tithe could be exacted until a law on public worship was passed.

Despite these qualifications, on the night of August 4 the Assembly achieved in principle the legal unity of the nation. It destroyed the feudal system and aristocratic domination over rural areas; it launched fiscal and ecclesiastical reform. The way was paved for discussion of a declaration of rights. This started on August 20 and continued without intermission until the 26th. Proclaiming liberty, equality, and national sovereignty, the text was in effect the "act of decease" of the Old Regime, which had been put to death by the popular revolution.

WAS THE "ARISTOCRATIC REVOLT" ARISTOCRATIC?*

Jean Égret

Jean Égret (1902–   ) is Professor of Modern History at the University of Poitiers. During the last twenty-five years he has written several books and articles on the early period of the Revolution, including La Pré-Révolution française, 1787–1788 (1962), a standard historical narrative for those years.

The importance of the role played by the parlements of France in the last crisis of the Old Regime has never been ignored, and the revolt of these sovereign courts[1] in 1787–1788 has often been described. We are less fully informed on the social class of these magistrates, whose uprising opened the way for the French Revo-

* From Jean Égret, "L'Aristocratie parlementaire française à la fin de l'ancien régime," *Revue historique,* CCVIII (July–September 1952), 1–14. The entire article is printed here except for the omission of some footnotes. Printed by permission of the author, the editor of *Revue historique,* and Presses Universitaires de France. Editors' translation.

[1] [The sovereign courts included the thirteen parlements, two sovereign councils very similar in functions to parlements, and some fifteen additional specialized high courts. These latter included several chambres des comptes and cours des aides, which dealt primarily with royal financial and fiscal matters.

In the parlements, the first president was at the top of the hierarchy, followed by the présidents à mortier. Other officials were the procureurs-généraux and avocats-généraux, who represented the royal interests, and the councilors—the large majority of the members of the parlements—who were the deliberative mass of the court. Specialized branches within the parlements included the chambres des requêtes and the chambres des enquêtes.]

lution. Detailed studies devoted to this matter are rare,[2] and general accounts not always reliable.[3]

A recently published collection of documents offers at least a partial answer to the historian's curiosity.[4] The information it presents, together with what we already know, sheds new light on the backgrounds of the members of the French parlements who held office at the end of the Old Regime.

Article VIII of the Edict of December 1770 had required those who obtained governmental posts conferring nobility to pay, in addition to the usual marc d'or [gold mark] that was due from all recipients of a royal pardon, favor, mission, or position, a supplementary fee equivalent to that paid for letters patent of nobility. If the candidate already was a nobleman, he was exempted from paying this marc d'or of nobility by furnishing proof of his rank to the king's Cabinet. A collection of the Orders of Exemption granted by the Cabinet has just been published.

Dealing exclusively with nobles who were candidates for positions conferring nobility, the Orders, as one would expect, concern primarily the highest positions in the robe [mainly the judicial hierarchy]. In practice these positions did not confer nobility, because the candidates for them already possessed it. Actually, this collection of Orders exempting payment of the marc d'or of nobility provides us with some first-class documentary evidence. From it we learn the family origins of most of the twelve first presidents (of fifteen in office in 1790), of the ten procureurs-généraux (of fifteen in office), of the fifty-nine présidents à mortier (of ninety-five in office), of the sixteen presidents of chambres des enquêtes and chambres des requêtes (of twenty-eight in office), of the twenty-six avocats-généraux (of thirty-three in office), and of the 426 lay [non-clergy] councilors (of 757 in of-

[2] Of particular value are A. Colombet, *Les Parlementaires bourguignons à la fin du XVIIIe siècle* (Dijon, 1937); E. Michel, *Biographie du Parlement de Metz* (Metz, 1853); F. Saulnier, *Le Parlement de Bretagne* (Rennes, 1908); A. de Mahuet, *Biographie de la Cour souveraine de Lorraine et Barrois et du Parlement de Nancy (1641-1790)* (Nancy, 1911); A. Duboul, *La Fin du Parlement de Toulouse* (Toulouse, 1890).

[3] H. Carré, *La Fin des Parlements (1788-1790)* (Paris, 1912), includes useful information, but the lists of members of the parlements given in the appendix are incomplete and contain errors. . . .

[4] A. de Roton, *Les Arrêts du Grand Conseil portant dispense du marc d'or de noblesse,* annotated and completed by J. de La Trollière and R. de Montmort (Paris, 1951). . . .

fice) admitted to the thirteen parlements and to the two Sovereign Councils of Colmar and Perpignan. All this information has to do with the period after the courts were reestablished [1774] and concerns those magistrates who obtained their offices from 1774 to 1789 and who still occupied them in 1790.

———•••———

Among the parlementary positions, it is best to deal separately with those which were neither purchasable nor hereditary, but which derived solely from the king, that is, the positions of first president and procureur-général, for they were filled by officials specifically representing the monarch within each court.

The first president was above all the agent of the king, who personally swore him into office. His primary function—a delicate and formidable one in a period of crisis—was to maintain relations between the king and the company [the particular court in which he served]. One would expect that the monarch would select him, without any restrictions, on the basis of his loyalty and his ability, and that he would preferably come from a province and a court different from those in which he was to carry out his duties. In fact, at the end of the Old Regime, only four first presidents were new to the companies over which they presided and to which they had been appointed by royal favor alone: Hocquart de Mony at Metz, Cœurderoy at Nancy, Malartic at Perpignan, and Baron de Spon at Colmar, all courts of secondary importance. Only Baron de Spon was, by his origins, a stranger to the sovereign courts; the other three belonged to the parlementary aristocracy. And this background, somewhat alarming for an agent of the king, even more strongly characterized all the other heads of the parlements in France.

In some courts, there were veritable dynasties of first presidents, so that the agents of the king, whatever their distant origin, became, as time went on, men of the local province. At Grenoble, Pierre-Albert de Bérulle was the fourth in his family line to be first president. During the eighteenth century, two ancestors had already preceded Camus de Pontcarré at Rouen and Pollinchove at Douai. The same development occurred at Aix-en-Provence where Gallois de la Tour, like his father before him, was both the intendant of the province and first president of the parlement; and again at Besançon and at Bordeaux, where Perreney de Grosbois and Le Berthon directly succeeded their fathers as first presidents. Is it surprising to see First President Le Berthon disregard his role as an intermediary, identify himself with a company that he should have dominated, and do this "with a perseverance that came close to obstinacy"? [5]

Still more amazing is the appointment of one of the présidents à mortier as first president of the very same parlement, thereby crowning an industrious career. As a matter of fact, the king's choice was narrowly limited in such a case, and the agent of the king really became the man of the company. In this way the second President Lefebvre d'Ormesson, who died in January 1789, and then the third President Bochard de Saron were successively chosen for the highest position in the Paris Parlement, after First President d'Aligre retired in October 1788. In the provinces the local parlementary aristocracy conquered the first presidency in the persons of présidents à mortier Le Gouz de Saint-Seine at Dijon (1777), Merdy de Catuélan at Rennes (1777), Cambon at Toulouse (1787), and Casamajor de Charitte at Pau (1789).

A procureur-général had less influence than a first president, since he did not take part in the assemblies of the chambers [special plenary sessions of the several chambers of a parlement]; nevertheless he was, in the words of one of them, "an agent acting in His Majesty's name, working with the men who administer the royal courts. He pleads cases and he is a party in cases —that is his career. . . . When he is not an interested party, he oversees and points out to the king and the representatives of royal justice everything that deserves attention. . . ." [6]

Obviously, dynasties arose from the inheritance of these positions, even though at the end of the eighteenth century they could no longer be purchased. At Besançon, Doroz was the third procureur-général in his family. At Paris, Guillaume-François-Louis Joly de Fleury filled—without any distinction—the position made famous by his father. At Rennes, the Marquis de Caradeuc succeeded his father, Louis-René de la Chalotais, although his talents were known to be very inferior. When the famous Le Blanc de Castillon retired in 1787, he left to his forty-six-year-old son the position of procureur-général at the Parlement of Aix. Before the age of thirty, the sons of Dudon of Bordeaux and of Godart de Belbœuf of Rouen were accepted as procureurs-géné-

[5] C.-B.-F. Boscheron des Portes, *Histoire du Parlement de Bordeaux* (Bordeaux, 1878), II, 331.

[6] Berger de Moydieu of Grenoble, in a letter to a minister (Archives des Affaires Étrangères, 1563, fol. 142).

raux *en survivance*[7] and were in line to succeed their fathers who were reaching their declining years.

Those who had not depended on their fathers to raise them to the highest ranks of the robe magistrature were former avocats-généraux, or more often former councilors, who had filled these positions for many years in the very same parlements where they became the *representatives* of the Crown, showing a loyalty that we may presume to be rather hesitant. Did not almost all of them belong to the local parlementary aristocracy? The list of procureurs-généraux at the end of the eighteenth century provides only two exceptions to this rule: Herman, who was procureur-général of Colmar and a former royal praetor [a municipal official] at Sélestat in Alsace; and Pierre de Bordenave, the son of an ennobled army officer, who began as a councilor and owed his unusual promotion to the post of procureur-général of the Parlement of Pau to the outstanding services that he had performed for this court.

———•—•—•———

Below the first president, every court had "several leaders [présidents à mortier] subordinate to the first president, but equal among themselves. They were ranked only by seniority. . . . On formal occasions they wore ermine on the standard red gown of the simple councilor. They also carried a round cap of black velvet trimmed with two stripes of gold braid; the first president had three stripes on his cap. . . ." [8]

Forty-three of the fifty-nine présidents à mortier admitted to office in the years 1774 to 1789 came from parlementary families. Those of Paris bore names already long illustrious in the Parlement and the Council of State. At Bordeaux, where earlier there had been a stubborn and ultimately successful opposition to the promotion of avocat-général Dupaty to the post of président à mortier (he did not possess all the requirements for noble rank), the three presidents admitted were all sons of presidents. At Pau, Grenoble, Besançon, and Toulouse, those newly promoted could all point to fathers and often to several ancestors who had served in the same court. The parlementary aristocracy still enjoyed an overwhelming preponderance in the recruitment of présidents à

[7] [One who has the right to succeed the present incumbent in office.]

[8] S.-N.-H. Linguet, *Annales politiques, civiles et littéraires du XVIIIe siècle* (London and Paris, 1777-1792), IV, 187.

mortier at Rennes, Douai, Aix, and Rouen. Only the parlements of Nancy, Dijon, and Metz appear less exclusive.

For the less exalted positions of presidents of the chambres des enquêtes and the chambres des requêtes, which existed in only some of the parlements, and for the positions of avocats-généraux, where the younger members of the high robe aristocracy often served their *novitiate*,[9] the members of the parlementary aristocracy numbered half of the magistrates admitted.

The 426 positions of lay councilor, held in 1790 by judges appointed in the last fifteen years of the Old Regime, were divided unequally—the parlementary aristocracy totaled 160 representatives; the *new men*, 266. This numerical superiority of new men among those who filled the lower ranking positions in the high magistracy is one of the most interesting things we learn from the collection published by M. de Roton. It goes counter, in fact, to a generally accepted view—that which asserts that during the last period of their history the parlements always recruited from the same families, who were destined in time-honored fashion to the same positions. The collection of Orders of Exemption also gives us rather precise information on the diverse origins of these new men.

In theory, one might expect wealthy commoners to have been tempted by parlementary positions, all of which sooner or later conferred hereditary nobility on their holders. In reality, most positions gave only *gradual nobility (patre et avo consulibus)*, that is, father and son in succession had to fill the position for twenty years each or die in office before hereditary nobility could be acquired by the third generation. In some privileged parlements, those of Paris, Besançon, Douai, Metz, and Grenoble, the positions gave *hereditary nobility in the first degree,* that is, after twenty years' service by a single magistrate.

Actually, and Jacques Necker pointed this out in his *Treatise on the Administration of Public Finance,* a "large number" of parlementary positions "do not serve as a source of new nobles. Since the kingdom is teeming with nobles, several sovereign courts do not readily admit into their membership bourgeois families who have not yet gained a footing in the nobility." [10]

---

[9] This expression is used by Linguet in the article just cited.

[10] J. Necker, *De l'administration des finances de la France* (Paris, 1784), III, 90–91.

Inspired by aristocratic pride and careful of their composition, several parlements demanded a fully acquired nobility for those candidates who were not the sons of judges. The Parlement of Rennes, by its regulation of January 2, 1732, appears to have led the way. The royal government recognized the uncompromising stand of the Parlement of Rennes in this matter, for by an Order of Council dated September 6, 1775, the Crown gave up the requirement of the marc d'or of nobility due from magistrates admitted by the sovereign court of Rennes, since they were sure to be noble already. In the second half of the century several other parlements—Nancy, Grenoble, Aix, and Toulouse—took similar resolutions, but the government did not, in their cases, give them official consecration. Although the principle was not established so categorically everywhere, the tendency appears to have been rather general. The Orders of Exemption prove that the majority of the new men admitted to all the parlements during the reign of Louis XVI were noblemen already. But even so, a closer study reveals some very important differences among the courts.

In the last quarter of the eighteenth century, all the parlements of France admitted nobles whose forebears did not owe their nobility to judicial service, but whose families could prove at least a century of noble rank. To gain exemption from the marc d'or of nobility, it was not unusual, after 1781, to see these noble gentlemen submit certificates from the genealogist Chérin proving that they possessed the nobility required for a position as second lieutenant in the royal army. This seems to suggest that these young men hesitated when choosing between two equally honorable careers. This recruitment of magistrates from the old nobility was flattering to the sovereign courts: it ratified the fusion of the two nobilities. This fusion was complete in the Parlement of Rennes, where all the new men, without exception, were *noblemen of long standing;* but everywhere else only a minority of the newcomers were.

Several families whose members entered the parlements during the reign of Louis XVI had achieved nobility in the course of the century by filling positions in the chambres des comptes and the cours des aides where they served for a time. The Chambre des Comptes of Dôle sent several men who had been ennobled there to the Parlements of Besançon and Dijon. At Aix,

Grenoble, and Dijon, there were both chambres des comptes and parlements; the first was often a stepping stone to the second. At Paris, two streams carried families from the chambre des comptes and the cour des aides to the Parlement. Somewhat lower positions conferring noble rank, such as those in the bureaus of finance, also led some families to their first positions in the robe magistrature; and the Parlement of Toulouse received two councilors whose grandfathers had earned noble rank as city aldermen.

There were other more expensive but easier ways to acquire nobility and to hasten the slow and regular ascent of a family. The position of secretary of the king, which was expensive but required only unimportant duties fully compatible with other activities, conferred nobility in the first degree. Necker denounced these hasty grants of nobility, which were not a reward for service.[11] A councilor in the Parlement of Normandy, Gressent, in his private journal, deplored this practice, "I am not a nobleman by birth, and it always injures my pride to see some loutish fellow whose father had been a secretary of the king enjoy all the advantages of nobility. . . ."[12] Indeed, during the reign of Louis XVI, it was a rare parlement which did not admit some sons or grandsons of secretaries of the king. The number of these wealthy parvenus was important at Paris, where they added up to more than a third of the new men. And in the persons of the Présidents à Mortier Bruny de La Tour d'Aigues, Micault, and Lassalle, they gained, at the outset, the highest judicial positions at Aix, Dijon, and Metz.

In this way the barriers that some courts tried to erect in order to bar candidates of lowly birth could be surmounted. The ease with which nobility might be achieved allowed the aristocratic parlements to keep commoners out without halting the recruitment of new members and without completely eroding the already declining value of these offices. The Orders of Exemption from the marc d'or of nobility, which were obtained by nearly all the new magistrates at Nancy, Grenoble, Aix, and Toulouse, show that in these courts the policy of excluding commoners was effective.

In the other parlements, however, many councilors do not

[11] *Ibid.*, III, 91–92.
[12] Comte d'Estaintot, *Notes manuscrites d'un conseiller au Parlement de Normandie, 1769–1789* (Rouen, 1889), p. 12.

seem to have obtained an Order of Exemption. This was true of all the new members admitted at Colmar; about two-thirds of those at Perpignan and Metz; more than half of those at Pau, Douai, and Bordeaux; a third of those at Dijon and Rouen; and a quarter of those at Besançon. It is possible that some of those presumed to be commoners already possessed at least a *noblesse commencée*.[13] Others, of course, were able to take advantage of useful connections that further research would reveal. In any event, it can no longer be said that all the parlements of France were closed to commoners at the end of the Old Regime and that it was impossible for sons of lawyers or lower ranking judges to take their seats on the *fleurs-de-lis* [a contemporary expression for the higher courts].

Thus there can be no doubt of the heterogeneous composition of parlementary circles in France at that time.

———◆◆◆———

Contemporaries noticed this extreme diversity, and it inspired comparisons and sarcastic comments. The Parlement of Rennes gloried in its unusual recruitment, and the Breton magistrates called themselves *The Robe's Knights of Malta*.[14] The Parlement of Paris was less highly esteemed. Bésenval said its members were "of a different nature from what are called men of high society."[15] And Vitrolles, the son of a councilor of the Parlement of Aix, commented that the first court of France was much more poorly constituted than that of Provence: "Almost all the members of the Parlement of Paris came from provincial families or from big business—from the Rue Saint-Denis, as one said then."[16]

Within each parlement, the councilors of high birth noted the distance separating them from the others. Chancellor Pasquier's remarks in his memoirs that recall his earliest days in the Parlement of Paris, in 1787, still breathe the disdain of the old robe families for the new men of common birth, who were so numerous in the court of the capital: "Of 150 magistrates,"

[13] [The status of a person who had started but had not yet completed all the formalities required to gain noble rank.]

[14] This was the expression of the Breton Councilor Desnos des Fossés, writing in the middle of the eighteenth century (cited by Saulnier, p. lxi).

[15] Pierre Bésenval, *Mémoires* (Paris, 1882 edition), p. 327. [Bésenval commanded the royal troops in Paris in 1789; his memoirs were first published in 1805–1807.]

[16] E. de Vitrolles, *Mémoires* (Paris, 1950 edition), p. 40.

wrote Pasquier, "half, at the most, belonged to families that had served in high judicial positions for generations; the other half had come rather recently from the families of lower ranking judges and from financial circles." [17] At Dijon, both of the double doors of the assembly hall of the chambers were opened when the councilors entered; but when it was the turn of the commissaires aux requêtes (almost all commoners) to enter, one of the doors was closed.

In each parlement, the group of présidents à mortier—recruited almost entirely from the parlementary aristocracy—personified the traditional outlook of the higher robe nobility. We have seen that it succeeded in exerting its authority over the king's representatives—the first presidents and procureurs-généraux. Pasquier tells us that at Paris, "the high bench, where the présidents à mortier sat, was still occupied by the illustrious names of the judiciary; they exemplified the most admirable virtues, but they included no men of outstanding ability and especially none with any talent for oratory." [18] Talent was not so scarce among the presidents of the provincial parlements: Mareschal de Vezet at Besançon, Joly de Bévy at Dijon, and La Croix de Sayve d'Ornacieux at Grenoble expressed with eloquence and authority the venerable claims to which Montesquieu's *Spirit of the Laws* had recently given a new form.

Could the old nobility count on the support of men recently ennobled, who were so numerous in some of the courts, who had hardly emerged from the Third Estate, who—as a liberal noble of Dauphiny put it—"still had relatives, friends, and all manner of ties and associations there," [19] men whom the old nobility would always distrust? Could they even count on the complete loyalty of the very young councilors (who dominated some courts at the end of Louis XVI's reign), even though they belonged to their own class?

———•◆•———

The Orders of Exemption from the marc d'or of nobility, which inform us about the family backgrounds of the judges admitted from 1775 to 1789, also indicate their ages. They prove

[17] *Mémoires du Chancelier Pasquier* (Paris, 1893–1895), I, 25.

[18] *Ibid.*, I, 24.

[19] The Chevalier du Bouchage, in a letter to the Marquis de Viennois, September 27, 1788 (Archives of the Marquis d'Albon).

that the clause of the Edict of November 1683, which required a minimum age of twenty-five years for new councilors, was rarely applied. The entry of very young councilors into a court did not have serious consequences when the turnover of the court's personnel was slow enough so that there was still a preponderance of old and experienced councilors. The Parlement of Toulouse, from a total membership of seventy-five, admitted only twenty-seven new lay councilors from 1775 to 1789; and so, in 1790, this parlement had only seventeen councilors under thirty-five years of age.

In other courts—Besançon, Douai, and Metz—where new councilors numbered more than half the total, but where the prejudices of the nobility, less intransigent than elsewhere, did not bar the admission of competent commoners, mature men still clearly comprised the majority.

This majority was weaker in the aristocratic Parlements of Aix and Grenoble, which had to admit the very young sons of families whose fathers were always in a hurry *to find them positions.*[20] It became a very slender majority in the Parlement of Rennes, where fifty-two of the sixty-five councilors in office in 1790 had been admitted during the reign of Louis XVI. Finally, in the courts of Dijon and Paris, where the turnover was especially rapid during this last phase of their existence, the lay councilors under thirty-five held an absolute majority in the assembly of the chambers on the eve of the Revolution.

All the contemporary memoirs outdo each other in insisting that this majority of young men exerted a decisive influence on the debates of the principal parlement of France [Paris] in 1787 and 1788. The First President of the Paris Cour des Aides, Barentin, deplored "their headlong and rash actions";[21] and a witness who was also a participant, the ex-councilor Sallier, reported that they "came to the assemblies of the chambers as if they were marching to battle. . . ." [22] Councilor Ferrand, an up-

[20] The expression of Reynaud, Procureur-Général of Grenoble, in a letter to the Minister of Justice Lamoignon, July 18, 1787 (Municipal Library of Grenoble, Q 6, fol. 86). . . .

[21] C.-L.-F. de Paule de Barentin, *Mémoire autographe sur les derniers Conseils du roi Louis XVI* (Paris, 1844), p. 86.

[22] G.-M. Sallier-Chaumont de La Roche, *Annales françaises, 1774 à 1789* (Paris, 1813), p. 79.

holder of the old tradition, pointed out to them how the very existence of the sovereign courts was endangered by their thoughtless enthusiasm for the convocation of the Estates-General, an enthusiasm described by Pasquier, who, with Sallier, lived through those feverish times: "From the moment when it became clear that our interests were at stake, we saw nothing more beautiful than to sacrifice them to what we believed to be the public good." [23]

Although one may question the recollections written many years later by Chancellor Pasquier, the conclusive value of the letters of the Parisian Councilor De Pont cannot be denied. He also was a member of the parlementary aristocracy. The son of the Intendant of Metz, he had discovered England and its institutions in 1786, when he was eighteen, and he wrote to Edmund Burke on November 6, 1789, that he would never forget that it was while listening to Burke speak "that his heart first beat in the name of liberty." [24]

————•◆•————

At the end of the Old Regime the parlementary aristocracy was not a caste closed to new men and new ideas. Only the Parlement of Rennes was restricted to noblemen of long standing. Along with the Provincial Estates of Brittany, it was a fortress of the Breton nobility. Bésenval's opinion on the provincial parlements, which were—unlike the Parlement of Paris— "composed almost entirely of nobles . . . and which formed, in a manner of speaking, a great family, to which all members were linked by sentiment and by interests," [25] was true for Brittany. But the Parlement of Rennes was an exception. Most of the others welcomed, not only the parlementary nobility and some nobles of long standing, but also, with varying warmth, noblemen of recent date and even commoners. At a time of crucial decisions, it was difficult to establish a close collaboration, a sincere *union of classes,* among courts of such varied composition.

[23] *Mémoires,* I, 28.
[24] Letter published with three others, all written by C.-J.-F. De Pont to Burke between 1776 and 1790, edited by H. V. F. Somerset, *Annales historiques de la Révolution française,* XXIII (1951), 365. [Burke's *Reflections on the Revolution in France* was written in the form of a letter addressed to De Pont.]
[25] Bésenval, p. 427.

Within each of them, who could stop the same jealousies from echoing the same scorn?

Differences in ages provoked other divisions. Several parlements had a majority of mature and cautious men; but in others youth triumphed. At Paris the chambres des enquêtes approved the boldness that the grand' chambre censured.[26]

Here, no doubt, we see the explanation of the hesitations, the contradictions, and the inconsistencies in the parlementary agitation of the years 1787–1788, an agitation which was the principal expression of what we usually call the *Aristocratic Revolution*.

[26] [The grand' chambre was composed of the leading members of the Parlement, those of the highest rank.]

WAS THE "BOURGEOIS REVOLT" BOURGEOIS?*

Elizabeth L. Eisenstein

Elizabeth L. Eisenstein (1923–   ), a native of New York City, received her Ph.D. from Radcliffe in 1953. Professorial Lecturer at American University, she has written a biography of The First Professional Revolutionist: Filippo Michele Buonarroti, 1761–1837 *(1959) and several articles dealing with the impact of printing on historical thought and Western European culture.*

This paper is concerned with discrepancies in Georges Lefebvre's presentation of the point at which, "strictly speaking, the Revolution of 1789 began"[1]—more precisely with how the author locates revolutionary initiative at this point. . . . The point at issue comes, according to the author's scheme, when the Paris Parlement on September 23, 1788, ruled that the Estates-General should be constituted according to the precedent set in 1614. Up to this point the "aristocratic revolution" was proceeding without intervention from other social sectors and appeared to be successful in accomplishing its purpose. The Bourbon monarchy had been forced to concede constitutional limitations upon royal power, and, crippled by bankruptcy, forced to act in accordance

---

* Excerpts from Elizabeth L. Eisenstein, "Who Intervened in 1788? A Commentary on *The Coming of the French Revolution*," *The American Historical Review*, LXXI (October 1965), 77–103. Reprinted by permission of the author, who has prepared this abridgment.

[1] Georges Lefebvre, *The Coming of the French Revolution*, trans. R. R. Palmer [from *Quatre-Vingt-Neuf*, 1st ed., Paris, 1939] (Princeton, N.J., 1947), 37. [*Hereafter page references to this book are given by numbers in parentheses following citations.*]

with this concession: by reinstating the Paris Parlement and agreeing to convoke an Estates-General to determine fiscal policy. In prior decades, since the era of the *Fronde* [the civil strife in France from 1648 to 1653], the political prerogatives of the intermediary orders had been weakened, those of the crown extended. A reversal of this trend after so long an interval of time may be appropriately classified as a "revolution." Major alterations in an unwritten constitution were being made. But one should note that this sort of revolution was not unprecedented. Prolonged experience, at home and abroad, could account for the behavior of the contestants in the struggle. As the author himself points out, these particular "beginnings of the Revolution" may be viewed as "the last offensive of the aristocracy." They represented, he says, "merely the crowning effort" of this class, the culmination of a struggle that had begun with the first Capetian kings (16). Similarly, earlier "times of troubles" had seen not only the coincidence of empty royal treasuries with noble sedition but also widespread outbreaks of urban *émeutes* [riots], peasant uprisings, and even municipal insurrections.

If we agree with Lefebvre that the Revolution of 1789 begins "strictly speaking" with an orchestrated wave of protest over the issue of representation at the Estates-General, it is because this is the first large-scale response to the prolonged political and financial crisis that differentiates it from all preceding "times of troubles." The organization of this protest movement could not have been anticipated since it had no precedents in the annals of French statecraft. [Its effectiveness in throwing the authorities off balance owed much to its coming from no familiar centers of sedition, no duly constituted groups in particular, but from many different amorphous groups who seemed to be at large.] As the author notes, as late as "the summer of 1788 there was no reason to anticipate that the bourgeoisie would intervene in the name of the whole Third Estate in the conflict between the royal power and the aristocracy" (51).

It is this unanticipated intervention in the fall of 1788, made in the name of the whole Third Estate, that seems to lie at the heart of the question: "Who started the French Revolution?" Who was responsible for this intervention? What scanty evidence the author supplies, relating to the social composition of the groups who intervened, does not bear out his implication that initiative passed from one class to another. This appears to be true however loosely or widely one cares to define the term "bourgeoisie" or even the much larger residual category "Third Estate." His evidence, to the contrary, suggests that a loose coalition of men drawn from all three estates provided the initial impetus for the protest movement and steered it through to obtain what is described as "The First Victory of the Bourgeoisie." On his own showing, intervention came from persistently undefined members of a shadowy "patriot party" led by a "Committee of Thirty," only nine of whose members are named. Not one of those named could be characterized as "bourgeois" or as members of the Third Estate.[2] When leaders other than those belonging to this committee are mentioned, moreover, a sizable proportion turn out also to belong to the first two estates. In every passage describing political action the names of the real men who initiated this action are presented to the reader. . . . But the blank-faced visage of the bourgeoisie is invariably substituted in analyzing the significance of this action, introducing it, summing it up, or generalizing about it.

Thus we are told about the first moves made to protest the Parlement's ruling: "In aligning themselves against the privileged classes, the bourgeoisie took the name hitherto claimed in common by all who opposed the royal power. *They* formed the 'national' or 'Patriot' party [*italics mine*]" (52). Who are *the real people* who took the initiative to form this more exclusive, class-oriented party?

> . . . Great noblemen, the duc de La Rochefoucauld-Liancourt, the marquis de La Fayette, the marquis de Condorcet, and certain members of the Parliament, Adrien du Port, Hérault de Séchelles, Le Pelletier de Saint-Fargeau. These men, to take the lead of the movement, joined with bankers like the Labordes,[3] academicians like the lawyer Target[4] and jurists and writers of note, such as Bergasse

[2] For the names see the following page.

[3] The earlier description of the aristocracy tells us (13) that a daughter of the banker Laborde became the Comtesse de Noailles, thus linking the Labordes with La Fayette's family circle. This sort of alliance of great nobles with the *haute bourgeoisie* points to the fallacy of dividing revolutionary leadership into aristocratic and bourgeois elements. It should be noted that financial connections linking both groups are not as significant as and do not necessarily correlate with social, familial, or personal affinities. Thus business associates may be excluded or snubbed—even down to the present—by aristocrats who prefer the company of members of their own class. D'Artois' investment in the Javel works (13) thus tells us nothing at all about his political or social orientation.

[4] On the important continuous role played by this academician, see numerous references to Target in the index of Lefebvre's book.

and Lacretelle, Servan and Volney. The party organized itself for
propaganda. Like the Parliaments and the Breton nobility before
them, each man made use of his personal connections. Correspondents in the depths of the provinces did the same. . . . The general
staff of the new party met in certain drawing rooms like that of
Mme de Tessé, soon to be Mounier's Egeria. Journalists harangued
in the cafés . . . (52–53).

The phrase "to take the lead of the movement" is misleading.
There was no "bourgeois" movement in the summer of 1788
organized by bankers, academicians, jurists, and writers for some
great noblemen to join or to lead. There was no party to organize
itself. None of those who "took the lead" could be depicted as
"fellow travelers," climbing on a bandwagon that was already
rolling. All of them were planning how to beat the drums and
wave the banners in order to attract a procession, as they did by
the winter's end. Although he sums the matter up—"the bourgeoisie from the first move showed shrewd political sense" (55)
—the author, instead, describes how nonbourgeois leaders made
the first moves, employed shrewd political tactics, utilized extensive personal connections, and expanded much printer's ink
in order to mobilize and organize resistance over the issue of
"doubling the Third."

> The question is whether a central intelligence directed this
> orchestra of protest. . . . A directing role can apparently be
> attributed only to the Committee of Thirty of which unfortunately
> we know very little. It met especially at the house of Adrien du
> Port and its membership is said to have included the duc de
> La Rochefoucauld-Liancourt, La Fayette, Condorcet, the duc
> d'Aiguillon[5] . . . Sieyès . . . and Talleyrand. . . . Mirabeau
> also came to the meetings. This committee inspired pamphlets,
> circulated models for the petitions of grievances, supported candi-
> dacies and dispatched agents to the provinces. . . . But the in-
> fluence of the Committee of Thirty . . . would be greatly exag-
> gerated were we to imagine that everything done in every town
> was merely in execution of its orders. The state of communica-
> tions allowed no such strict control. If the movement prospered it
> was because the local bourgeoisie proved its initiative . . . (53–
> 54).

[5] The Duc d'Aiguillon, a prime mover along with Target, La Fayette, and
the latter's son-in-law, the Vicomte de Noailles, in the night of August 4,
1789, is later described as "one of the greatest landowners in France" (161).

Possibly the local bourgeoisie did prove its initiative in the provinces although one wonders about the social composition of those correspondents in its depths. [Certainly it was not the Parisian bourgeoisie that took the initiative in their home town, but rather a socially heterogeneous, ideologically homogeneous collection of notables and nobodies drawn from the three estates.] All that the Parisian leaders seem to have shared in common was that their private social circles overlapped and that they "unreservedly adopted the new ideas" (52). The point is not that everything done everywhere was done on the basis of orders from the Committee of Thirty. It is rather that, as the author tells us, what central organization the state of communications permitted *was* provided by this group. On the basis of what happened in Paris and judging from the other evidence provided it seems plausible that where local initiative did come, it came from similarly heterogeneous provincial groups. . . .

We had earlier been informed, in the first act of the drama, that

> the aristocratic class developed an organization for political action, exchanging correspondence and passing instructions from town to town. The Committee of Thirty, which was soon to take over the leadership of the Third Estate, seems to have originated as a center of parliamentary resistance (33).[6]

If Parisian leadership of the Third Estate emerged from an organization developed by "the aristocratic class" (by heterogeneous groups of "notables" might be more accurate), why should not local initiative have emerged from a similar source? In fact, precedents established both by the royal ministers Calonne and Brienne, experimenting with newly formed provincial assemblies (24, 32), and by the "aristocratic revolution" in defense of old provincial estates, provided those who pressed the issue of "dou-

[6] The author does not account for the apparent contradiction involved in a center of parliamentary resistance that becomes a center of resistance to parliamentary authority. This is only one of many puzzles obscured by the very clarity of his scheme. Since one-half of the puzzle belongs to the first act, the other to the second, the reader, like the author, is apt to forget that the pieces belong together. Thus the Breton Third Estate is, on pages 18–19, represented by nobles and privileged persons. On pages 60–61 this same privileged body defies the nobles and clergy until fiscal equality long demanded by it is granted. The fact that municipal oligarchs did have different interests than the hereditary nobles would, in this case, solve the puzzle created by overdramatizing the solid front composed of privileged status groups in the first act. But no such simple solution of the first-mentioned puzzle occurs to me.

bling the Third" with their main arguments. The case of the
Vizille assembly—when "the aristocracy of Dauphiny got out of
hand" (32) and after successfully defying the royal minister conceded "double representation to the Third Estate, vote by head
and fiscal equality" (51)—is twice cited in this connection (51,
55).[7]

We are told also how the program to press double representation was executed:

> the scheme was to overwhelm the government with a flood of peti-
> tions for which the municipalities whether willing or not were
> obliged to take responsibility during the autumn of 1788. At Dijon,
> for example, the matter was put through as follows: Some twenty
> "notables"[8] met and decided to submit to their respective guilds
> and corporate bodies the questions of doubling the Third and of
> vote by head (56).

Favorable response from roughly twenty out of fifty guilds, resistance from the municipal authorities overcome by an invasion
of the town hall, and a petition sent to the King in the name of
the Dijon Third Estate followed. Similar action occurred in the
other towns of Burgundy. Who devised this "scheme," suggested
to the original twenty notables in Dijon, elsewhere in Burgundy,
and presumably throughout many other provinces in the vast
realm of France that they canvass the guilds and force, by direct
action, the signing of similar petitions by municipalities? "A
directing role can apparently be attributed only to the Committee

---

[7] Nowhere is the analysis more puzzling than in the account (32) of this action
by the Dauphiny aristocracy. "Still . . . dissatisfied, *because* Brienne . . .
had granted double representation [*italics mine*]" and vote by head to the
new provincial assemblies, this aristocracy demanded the return of their old
estates. They defied his refusal to grant this request, "obtained the support
of the bourgeoisie," and then at Vizille granted the very forms of representation that had, we were told, provoked their original defiance. By considering
the issue of Versailles versus the provinces rather than that of aristocrats
versus commoners this affair might seem less puzzling. Regional rivalries that
crisscrossed social cleavages tend to find no place in the book, but they were
of equal importance in determining the forms of conflict that set the stage
for the coming of the Revolution.

[8] As always, when specific examples come in the narrative, the blank-faced
bourgeoisie disappears. In dealing with the issue of revolutionary initiative,
social nomenclature which is vague appears to be more accurate than that
which is precise. The closer one gets to the real men involved the further
one is from clearly polarized class divisions. It should be noted that even
craftsmen in some cases "counted as notables" (44), along with urban oligarchs,
academicians, magistrates, and aristocrats.

of Thirty" (53). In the one example offered we see that the
burghers of Dijon were by no means unanimous in their response
to the issue pressed upon them. Thirty or so guilds did not
respond. Violence was required to force urban oligarchs to sign
and send the petitions.

Evidence drawn from countless such towns, located in all the
French provinces, would be required to determine precisely how
members of the Third Estate divided on this issue. One would
like to know, in the one example given, why some burghers and
guildsmen (in particular the local lawyers' guild) responded
favorably while others did not. But despite the evidence, bourgeois solidarity is blandly taken for granted. According to the
author's scheme, in fact, the bourgeoisie moved to the center of
the stage just as soon as the Paris Parlement pronounced its
verdict.

> . . . A wave of excitement passed over the bourgeoisie at the news
> that the Estates-General were to be convoked. For the first time since
> 1614 the king was authorizing the bourgeoisie to speak. At first no
> struggle was foreseen. . . . The assembly at Vizille had left a deep
> impression by conceding double representation to the Third Estate.
> . . . Agreement seemed by no means impossible.[9]

> But the outlook changed abruptly when the Parliament of Paris
> . . . ruled that the Estates-General should be constituted as in
> 1614. A clamor rose from one end of the kingdom to the other.
> Between night and morning the popularity of the Parliament van-
> ished (51).

The state of communications, which did not permit Parisian
organization to penetrate the provinces and left matters to local
initiative, apparently proved more efficient in transmitting news
of the Parlement's ruling. The question of who transmitted this
news and how it was transmitted is, however, by-passed. The
length of the interval between night and morning is not discussed. On how the news was received, we are offered some un-

[9] To suggest that agreement about representation seemed possible before the
Parlement's ruling conveys a prior preoccupation with this issue before it
was posed. The issues over which men might agree or disagree were still
invisible during the two and a half months from July 5 to September 23,
1788, when the wave of excitement rippled over literate sectors of the public.
It seems likely that no one, bourgeois or not, knew quite what to expect
after learning an Estates-General would meet, that all sorts of vague hopes
and plans were encouraged rather than specific expectations about how the
orders would be represented.

dated comments by Weber and Brissot, told that Mme. Roland and Rabaut-Saint-Étienne "now took passionately to public affairs," and informed of Mallet du Pan's remark: "The controversy has completely changed. King, despotism and constitution are now minor questions. The war is between the Third Estate and the other two orders" (52).[10] Mallet's remarks are dated. They came in January 1789, after three or more months of canvassing and campaigning on the issue of doubling the Third.

It seems to have been this canvassing and campaigning, accompanied by an outpouring of pamphlets that "astonished contemporaries" by their number (54), that accounted for the way hitherto quiescent subjects took passionately to public affairs in the winter of 1788–1789. But disappointment at the Parlement's ruling and immediate action designed to reverse it came first of all from groups who had already been active in the first act of the drama. Indignation, defiance, and effective action from such quarters are, however, muffled by the author and detached from the public storm of protest.

> As was to be expected, some of the privileged were inclined to grant the Third Estate a certain satisfaction of its pride. On December 5, 1788, the "nationals" in the Parliament of Paris prevailed on that body to declare, by formal order, that it had no intention of prejudging the number of deputies in the Estates-General, and that the number was not fixed by law (58–59).

"In private," we are also told, "some of the privileged expressed themselves definitely in favor of the Third Estate" (59). Presumably public expressions of such an attitude were not becoming to aristocrats. Yet something more than the tepid inclination to grant commoners "a certain satisfaction" is conveyed by a letter cited from one aristocrat to another.

> Some think the non-privileged, who are the base and pillar of the State, should be without sufficient representatives in an Assembly which is to regulate their destiny. This is really too insulting and will not work. In any case the thing has been seen through. It will be best to be careful of what is done. . . . But I perceive my dear count that I am repeating to you what you know and think (59).

[10] Eighteenth-century journalists, however intelligent, were less well informed than their modern counterparts and just as inaccurate. In fact, the war between the Third Estate and the other two orders saw the clergy split on the issue.

This was, to be sure, a private letter. But the convictions contained in it were implemented by public action coming from the same privileged social strata, resulting not only in the Parlement's reversal of its ruling but also in the official decree of December 27 granting double representation to the Third Estate.

These moves did not occur without considerable opposition from many aristocrats, whose resistance, we are told, led "many bourgeois to become more radical in their ideas" (61). Along with the later behavior of the Breton deputies and a shift in Rabaut-Saint-Étienne's views, two illustrations of this change in bourgeois attitudes are offered. One is a famous pamphlet by Abbé Sieyès: *What Is the Third Estate?* The other is a famous printed speech by Count Mirabeau, eulogizing Marius for exterminating the order of the nobility (61–62). It is typically difficult to describe the social position of both authors in terms of conventional social nomenclature. Mirabeau was a "deserter from the nobility" who "had lived by his pen in the service of Calonne and Calonne's enemies" (71). Sieyès was a frustrated member of the Second Estate barred from a bishopric as a commoner whose "pamphlets made him an oracle" (69). In their service to the Committee of Thirty both "were certainly in contact with the Duc d'Orléans" (54). As publicists drawn from the first two estates who were ultimately elected to represent the Third, they are ill-adapted to illustrate changes in attitudes on the part of a single social class. They seem better suited to illustrate the more amorphous social strata to which "men of letters" (a formidable pressure group in its own right) belonged, and from which the attack on both despotism and privilege, the thoroughgoing assault on all the traditional ruling elites first came.

On the evidence provided then, sensitivity to a ruling that was taken as an insult to the nonprivileged was not confined to the bourgeoisie. The canvassing, pamphleteering, and circulating of petitions to reverse this ruling were neither initiated nor directed by the bourgeoisie. What precedents existed for a contrary ruling and what action was taken to obtain a reversal from the Parlement did not come from the bourgeoisie. Yet all of these measures receive the same treatment as the scheme that was put through in the fall of 1788:

> By such means, the *bourgeoisie* set the "nation" into motion. *Its* maneuver was denounced then, and has been ever since. But the aristocracy, shortly before, had acted no differently. Every political

movement naturally has its instigators and leaders.[11] No one has ever dared to maintain that *the Third Estate,* invited to appear in the Estates-General, could have thought it natural to leave the aristocracy supreme in the assembly. Hence, what *the leaders of the patriot party* are blamed for is simply to have roused *the nation* to shake off *its* torpor and organize *itself* to defend *its* cause [*italics mine*] (56).[12]

One must bear in mind that what is meant by "torpor" is the political passivity of quiescent subjects accustomed for hundreds of years to leave decisions pertaining to affairs of state to others. Otherwise one is apt to overlook the necessity of explaining how that torpor was shaken off. There was as yet no "nation" to be set in motion or, a more problematic issue, to rouse or organize itself. Since no evidence is presented concerning "maneuvers" by the blank-faced bourgeoisie—since scattered unorganized commoners were not in a position to undertake such maneuvers—one is at a loss concerning the means by which they set "the nation" in motion. As already noted, the maneuvers of the leaders of the patriot party may be examined. It is not surprising that they appear similar to those employed by "the aristocracy, shortly before." For most of these leaders are the very same men whose tactics the author had described "shortly before"—in connection with aristocratic political organization—before he had them "range themselves" on the same side as the bourgeoisie. In fact, he shows them choosing sides before lines had been drawn, setting the terms of the debate, and canvassing opinion on it. How could they range themselves on the same side as men who had yet to be heard from? . . .

"No one has ever dared to suggest that the Third Estate could have thought it natural to leave the aristocracy supreme in the Assembly." The author himself shows that had the orders not been kept separate, it was feared that many members of the Third Estate would vote to be represented by aristocrats (55). What men thought "natural" before the French Revolution needs

[11] The presumption is that movements give rise to instigators and leaders. Some movements do, but, in my view, the reverse was the case with regard to the point at issue.

[12] The italics are employed to suggest ambiguity concerning the group whose behavior is involved, who set whom into motion, and who defended whose cause. At least four, possibly five or six collective terms are used: the bourgeoisie, the leaders of the patriot party, the Third Estate, the "nation," the instigators and leaders.

to be distinguished from what historians view as "natural" thereafter. Certainly few of the customs of the *ancien régime* appeared natural to men steeped in Enlightenment thought. But most of them probably appeared natural enough to men who were not. Both groups confronted what appeared by the late eighteenth century to be an "unnatural" vagueness about numerical representation in earlier meetings of the Estates-General. For, as antiquarians scouring the records discovered, the Third Estate, although officially summoned to send one delegate for each sent by the other two orders, had in fact sent many more than its share of delegates, outnumbering the clergy on one hand and the nobility on the other by different numbers which varied in each case[13] (and which made little difference since there was also an unnatural agreement about consistently voting by order [14]). To follow the precedent of 1614 precisely was in this regard impossible. When the Estates-General had to be resurrected, after its demise more than a century and a half before, such vagueness concerning quantitative representation no longer came naturally to any party concerned. The fact that some eighteenth-century provincial estates had already doubled the Third and were voting by head suggests what France suffered by letting the Estates-General atrophy during the seventeenth and eighteenth centuries. In place of a relatively flexible institution that could accommodate social change, Frenchmen confronted only a brittle precedent that had to be either artificially reconstructed or deliberately broken. No one could escape this either-or issue. Every notable had to rethink and make explicit his view of how the body politic should be constituted. The resulting division of opinion involved conflicting concepts of a well-ordered commonwealth, incompatible opinions about how it should be governed, and rival ambitions about who should govern it.

Was this division congruent with the division between the first

[13] This is not discussed by Lefebvre; I have taken it from J. M. Thompson, *The French Revolution* (New York, 1945), 4.

[14] Lefebvre points to the shrewdness of pressing the issue of doubling the Third while leaving open that of voting by head (55, 59–60). Indirectly he shows how the postponement of this latter issue was politically indispensable for the patriots. But he never makes clear that when propagandists *did* stipulate "voting by head" or when, as in the Dijon case, the municipal authorities balked on this issue (56), the separation of the orders was taken for granted by *everyone* as far as the elections to the Estates-General went. Voting by head referred *only* to the procedure to be followed at Versailles—after the doubled Third had arrived there.

two estates and the Third? Did it not first of all divide those who had just emerged victorious in their long struggle with the crown and expected to exploit this victory to the full? Should we not look to the "liberal" aristocracy, even before turning to the bourgeoisie, for a "full consciousness of historic mission" shaped by "the thought of eighteenth century writers" (50)? At least the men who thought it unnatural to leave the aristocracy supreme in the Assembly, who at any rate posed the issue in this way to their fellow countrymen happened—many of them— to be marquis, counts, bishops, *abbés,* in short, members of the first two estates. Why did *they* think it unnatural to follow, as best one could, the precedent of 1614? . . . The Parlement of Paris had decided the case otherwise. A recent analysis of the eighteenth-century robe nobility suggests why it was "natural" for this body to do so.[15] But the Committee of Thirty seems to have originated in robe circles. Members of the Paris Parlement: Adrien du Port, Hérault de Séchelles, Le Pelletier de Saint Fargeau, and the unnamed "nationals" who obtained a reversal on December 5, 1788, worked hard and successfully to create a clamor against the ruling of the very body to which they belonged. It is this sort of purposeful action by active minorities, working both inside and outside duly constituted bodies, that one may unambiguously call "revolutionary." Since it could not be anticipated by contemporaries, authorities could not take measures to forestall it. Since it did not fit familiar formulas derived from prolonged experience with assassination plots and seditions during earlier "times of troubles" and since it could be traced to no court or cabinet, no foreign agents, no one class or group or region, new kinds of conspiratorial hypotheses would be woven to explain it (including those which involved impersonal agents set in motion by an invisible hand).

Instead of being isolated and studied, in *The Coming of the French Revolution,* the behavior of these active minorities, composed of like-minded individuals drawn from all three estates, is treated as marginal or inconsequential. Evidence pertaining to this behavior is invariably subordinated to the clear scheme of each large class acting independently in its own interests. . . .

Should the Third Estate have contented itself, respectfully and submissively, with what the great majority of the aristocracy were

[15] Franklin Ford, *Robe and Sword: The Regrouping of the French Aristocracy after Louis XIV* (Cambridge, Mass., 1953).

willing to offer it? In any case it did not think so, and loudly demanded equality before the law. At this point, strictly speaking, the Revolution of 1789 began (36–37).

This kind of rhetorical question about what the Third Estate *should* have done does not help us much in our effort to understand how the Revolution came. Instead one might ask what the heterogeneous, scattered, and politically unconstituted members of the Third Estate *would* have done had they not been presented with a most appealing and very clear alternative to respectful submission. It seems likely that whatever they might have thought and done and however widespread was a latent resentment of aristocratic privilege, had they not been provided with many identical petitions to get signed and many similar pamphlets to read, local responses of a very limited short-wave resonance would have resulted. There are, even today, many different ways of demanding equality before the law. There were many more in the vast realm of France during the *ancien régime* where justice before the law was dispensed differently in different regions and for different social groups, where there was no uniform law before which any kind of equality could be demanded.

If in the winter of 1788 a single demand sounded "loudly," it was because a sufficient number of similar petitions, singling out for protest the Parlement's ruling and singling out from among all the issues relating to composition, election, convocation, and procedure this ruling might raise, that of double representation for the Third Estate, were forced through scattered municipalities throughout the realm. Since local initiative was required to force through the petitions and since this occurred in many scattered areas, one may agree, roughly speaking, that a considerable number of commoners throughout the country were not content to submit respectfully to what the constituted bodies offered. But when one remembers the long list of earlier insurrections and seditions, it seems evident that a failure to submit to established authorities was not what distinguished the protest movement of 1788 from earlier "times of troubles." Such insubordination had hitherto been spread out over much longer intervals resulting in "sporadic" episodes, or, when occurring in shorter intervals, had involved so many bewilderingly various localized issues and incidents that historians, even in retrospect, have difficulty patterning and polarizing them.[16] In the winter of 1788 protests came within a remarkably short interval and produced a remarkably uniform appearance. A considerable measure of central organization is suggested by the simultaneity of this action. The unprecedented use made of the duplicative powers of print largely accounts for the uniform character of the clamor.

This clamor, which rose from one end of the nation to the other, was made in the name of the Third Estate and appeared to come from that residual order of the realm. In some regions, we are told, "peasants and workingmen streamed into the halls and the whole Third Estate signed [or marked?] the petition" (56). Although they composed most of the nonprivileged, "the base and pillar of society," and although it was, as yet, by no means clear how the Third Estate was to be represented,[17] [the participation of peasants and workingmen in this action is generally not regarded as evidence of revolutionary initiative.] Whereas similar participation by a smaller residual category of literate commoners, who did not work with their hands and are diversely defined as "the bourgeoisie," is so regarded. Located in all the provinces of France, however, and presenting "an extreme diversity of condition" (46), this latter group were scarcely better situated than were their unlettered compatriots to ensure the uniformity and simultaneity that made the demands of the Third Estate sound loudly. They had yet to meet together, find some basis for a common accord, or discover how they differed.[18]

On the other hand, the leaders of the resistance to the crown had already gathered in Assemblies of Notables and had already discovered how they differed. The activities of the Committee of Thirty appear inexplicable if we assume, as the author seems to, that the "aristocratic revolution" was made by men who fought royal despotism only with old feudal war cries or the more up-to-

---

[16] On the debate over "vertical" alignments versus horizontal "fronts" resulting from the "thorny problem" of the involvement of social sectors in seventeenth-century seditions, see Leon Bernard, "French Society and Popular Uprisings under Louis XIV," *French Historical Studies,* III (Fall 1964), 454–74.

[17] It was proposed, as well as suggested in grievance lists, that the government should create a separate order of peasants or provide for the separate election of town deputies and rural ones (65).

[18] The delegates to the Third Estate who arrived in Versailles in May 1789 "were unknown to each other and it was impossible to tell how far they would go" (78).

date "thèse nobiliaire" in mind. His evidence shows that it had also been made by men who had more "liberal" views about how a modern state should be governed; who had, in addition to their public concern, private personal ambitions. From this evidence, we also infer that these liberal notables moved in social circles that included talented commoners, preferred the latter's company, respected their judgment and competence rather more than that of many of their peers. Such men, it turned out, comprised a minority of the aristocracy. But they were not, for that reason, paralyzed, silenced, or rendered inactive. They were a sizable and powerful minority who had already combined in a loose coalition with a sizable minority of talented commoners who were particularly skilled with their pens. They had already created an organization for political action and correspondence throughout the provinces, had already laid the basis for a shadowy "national" or "patriot" party. They did not lose their initiative when thwarted. To the contrary, they initiated action as leaders of an independent coalition party. . . .

In concluding his account of "the first victory" achieved by the "Bourgeois Revolution," the author conveys, always by indirection, that initiative remained in the same hands during the electoral campaign that followed the successful protest movement. The successful electioneering of the patriot party is contrasted with the failure of Necker and other royal ministers to draw up a list of candidates committed to a program of desired reforms. It is contrasted also with the clumsy, uncoordinated attempts at personal influence made, here and there, by the chairmen of bailiwick assemblies (66). "Since 1789 there have been political parties with much stronger organization than the patriots of that time but none has met with so little resistance on the part of the government" (67). Until 1789, however, the government had been engaged in mobilizing its forces against seditious elites: namely, the parlements, provincial assemblies, municipal corporations (not to mention a variety of religious orders, the long arm of Rome, and of foreign courts as well). It had no experience with an independent domestic opposition party led by a loose coalition of aristocrats, ecclesiastics, men of letters and of the liberal professions mobilizing opinion against these elites and utilizing for this purpose the full power of the printing press, earlier turned against the crown by the parlements, now, for the first time in France, released from the clandestine channels into which it had been forced.[19]

What is surprising is that even a rudimentary political party could be organized, lists of candidates drawn up, platforms of reforms proposed in less than a year before the Estates had convened—not that subsequent parties would be more strongly organized or that the government failed to forestall this one. With respect to this problem, the author tells us, "The Committee of Thirty . . . assumed a lead whose extent it is impossible to determine" (66–67). On the other hand, he has no doubts,

> It is hardly doubtful that enterprising bourgeois everywhere took concerted action[20] to steer the town and bailiwick assemblies, with as many parish assemblies as possible in addition, by suggesting candidates and circulating models for petitions of grievances. The models were either received from Paris, or, more often, drafted locally (67).

These "enterprising bourgeois" who suggested candidates and drafted local models, independently of those sent from Paris, are necessarily nameless. Two social groups are singled out as playing a predominant role: lawyers who "were very influential" and the village priests who "gave much aid." This is not the only instance, but it is the most transparent, where the vital distinction between being literate (as these village priests apparently were) and being "enterprising bourgeois" (as they surely were not)[21] is overlooked.

This distinction is so vital to all theories pertaining to the

[19] The King in his traditional invitation to his subjects to express their views when promising to call an Estates-General on July 5, 1788, "had not intended thereby to grant freedom of the press," but pamphleteers disregarded his intentions, releasing a flood that "astonished contemporaries" (54).

[20] However enterprising they may be, men who are located "everywhere" simply cannot take "concerted action" to steer an electorate toward a given slate of candidates. One group located in one place is required to see that all the others do not "steer" in all directions.

[21] Many bourgeois families sent one son into the priesthood as they sent another into law. But the former were more apt to be attached to cathedral chapters in towns than to village parishes. They were also apt to be the less enterprising among bourgeois offspring. Finally, to apply the term "bourgeois" to village priests as well as to "the upper level of the nobility . . . whose conditions of life drew them to the bourgeoisie" (14) is to stretch this much-abused term beyond its already frayed limits. There is something wildly askew about a structural model that includes the top layer of nobles and the bottom layer of the clergy within the middle ranks of "the middle class."

coming of the French Revolution, or to the "rise of bourgeoisie to political power," that it seems worth pausing over. Because the electoral assemblies were also deliberative, we are told,

> the most influential bourgeois, or those best informed on public affairs or most accustomed to speaking in public, namely the lawyers . . . [*dominated*] throughout the debates. In the bailiwick assemblies, the peasants lacking education and unable to express themselves, let themselves be docilely led. The result was that the representation of the Third Estate was made up uniquely of bourgeois (65).

In light of the vital distinction, we would argue that it was made up, almost uniquely (aside from three priests and a dozen noblemen [67]) of a nonprivileged literate laity. The acquisition of literacy, by whatever means and in whatever era since the sixteenth century, was the most important single determinant as far as the social composition of the Third Estate delegation went. As a group, literate commoners *had* no social structure or nomenclature—medieval institutions had not been designed to take them into account. But in countless villages and even in some small towns, they were nonetheless a very distinctive group. The village schoolmaster was yet to become as ubiquitous as the parish priest. The latter was out of the running as a delegate of the Third Estate. Lawyers "who lived in the villages or often visited them for manorial pleadings" (67) represented in some cases the only possible alternative.

One reason for so many varying definitions of "the bourgeoisie" is the impossibility of making this group, however regarded in terms of status, occupation, economic class, style of life, and so forth, congruent with the much more amorphous body of men who had, ever since the printing press, been rising from the ranks of a preliterate population by mastering the written word. To whom else could this population turn but to such men when all the traditional literate elites—teachers, preachers, officers, bureaucrats—were out of the running? One may only guess how many more priests, aristocrats, or high magistrates might have been elected instead of the lawyers and other literate commoners who were, had not the former been eliminated from the running. Evidence is offered that the leaders of the patriot party feared the number might have been significantly large:

> Seeming to fear the prestige of the privileged persons and to think

them capable of imposing on commoners to the point of being elected to represent them, the patriot party often demanded, even later on, that each order be required to choose its representatives from its own members (55).

This is presented to show, not how elections were partly rigged by rigorously enforcing the separation of orders, but rather as evidence of "the moderation of the Third" despite the atypical "trenchant tone" of Sieyès' pamphlet. "The patriot party, in fact, by no means asked that the Estates-General be elected without regard to the three orders" (55). Of course it did not ask this. To obtain an overwhelming majority composed of the doubled Third, parish priests, and liberal nobles, working under the leaders of the patriot party, the electorate had to be insulated until after the elections. The abrupt accession to political power of the Third Estate depended very precisely on how demands for "equality before the law" were formulated and phased. The sudden appearance of a commanding majority composed of hitherto politically quiescent, unknown literate commoners (often described as the political accession of the "revolutionary bourgeoisie") paradoxically depended just as much on preserving the medieval tradition of separate and qualitatively differentiated orders as it did on pressing the issue of doubling the Third, while holding in reserve—until after the scene of action had shifted from the provinces to the capital—insistence on merging the orders and voting by head. . . .

> Divide the human race into twenty parts and there will be nineteen composed of those who work with their hands and who will never know that there was a Locke in the world; in the twentieth part remaining, how few men are there who can read? and among those who can, there will be twenty who read romances to one who studies science. The number of those who think is excessively small and they do not think about troubling the world.[22]

If we substitute eighteenth-century Frenchmen for "the human race," Voltaire's observation, ironic or not, appears to be well founded. The excessively small number of eighteenth-century Frenchmen who could read, who had heard of Locke,

[22] Voltaire, "Lettres Philosophiques: XIII—sur M. Locke," cited by J. H. Randall, *The Making of the Modern Mind: A Survey of the Intellectual Background of the Present Age* (Cambridge, Mass., 1926), 363; see also a longer, differently translated version in *id.*, *The Career of Philosophy, From the Middle Ages to the Enlightenment* (New York, 1962), 870.

preferred science to romance, and could "think" were, most of them, surely not consciously thinking about troubling the world. They had never participated in noble seditions or popular *émeutes* before Voltaire's day; nor did they do so for a decade after his death. Their inner composure was possibly disturbed by silent dialogues with favorite authors whose messages tended to slip past inner censors much as they did, via clandestine channels, past outer ones. But whatever their fantasies—and no one can read the minds of book readers—they remained politically passive, probably the most orderly subjects of an occasionally disordered realm. Engaged, on the whole profitably, pursuing their diverse trades, occupations, and professions, they had, in fact, much to lose and little to gain from the disruption of domestic peace. Even after delegates drawn exclusively from this "excessively small number" of literate townsmen who "were for the most part mature men in comfortable circumstances . . . educated . . . proficient in some specialized calling . . ." (68) arrived at Versailles, six-hundred strong, the leaders of the patriot party had every reason to expect, if not peasantlike docility, at least solid support from these political unknowns. They had no reason to anticipate that future historians would regard their own role as subordinate to that of the deputies they dominated. At least another year would pass before their expectations would appear unwarranted. As the author notes, in discussing the National Assembly: "It is also characteristic that, at least at first, the most prominent leaders were men from the privileged classes" (69). . . .

On "the debated question of who 'started the Revolution,' " then, the author's evidence suggests that initiative came, beginning with the first Assembly of Notables called by Calonne in 1786 through the stormy year of 1789 and beyond, from a loose coalition of like-minded men drawn from all three estates. No conventional social nomenclature appears applicable to this group whose collective biography remains to be written. Judging by the frequency with which the same names turn up, in conjunction with the Committee of Thirty and the leaders of the patriot party, this group was not very large—roughly the same number as might appear in a composite portrait of our own "founding fathers" seems to be involved. Some sort of collective biography of these men appears to be indispensable to any understanding of how the Revolution of 1789 came. . . . Instead we are told that neither La Fayette, Mirabeau, nor Sieyès dominated "the scene to the point of personifying the Revolution of 1789, which remained the collective achievement of the Third Estate" (71). What has been described, however, was the collective achievement of more than one marquis, one *abbé,* and one count—the collective achievement of Sieyès, Mirabeau, La Fayette *and* Talleyrand, Condorcet, Adrien du Port, Hérault de Séchelles, Le Pelletier de Saint Fargeau, the Duc d'Aiguillon, La Rochefoucauld-Liancourt, Laborde, Target, Volney, Mounier, and so forth. In so far as a revolution such as that of 1789 may be personified or incarnated, this group of men did so. In so far as concerted collective action was involved, these men conducted it. As constant leaders of the patriot party who steered the protest movement of 1788 and the electoral campaign of 1789, who pushed through the transformation of the Estates-General into a National Assembly, who proposed and drafted the Declaration of the Rights of Man, who abolished all privilege on the night of August 4, they provided the basis for whatever unity or continuity may be perceived in the early phases of the French Revolution. . . .

To discuss how initiative passed into other hands thereafter would carry us far beyond the limits of this paper. Suffice it to say that unanticipated consequences more often than not result from a given course of action that is not grounded on precedent or prolonged experience. Here, at least, the revolutionary action initiated in 1788 proved unexceptional . . . and the leaders of the patriot party could scarcely have anticipated the subsequent roles they would enact in the drama. But they nonetheless did, by wielding all the considerable power and influence at their disposal, help determine the conditions under which the drama would be played out. Purposeful action directed toward desired goals is one thing; unanticipated consequences resulting from this action are another. This obvious distinction has to be stressed, in order to avoid entanglement in the empty and endless debate over whether the Revolution was "spontaneous" or "planned," the product of "circumstances" or "plot." The debate is empty because it is invariably held over a grand design, incorporating the full sequence of events which only began to unfold in 1789. This design is visible only in retrospect. It could not be foreseen by any contemporaries. Hence it could not have been planned or devised by any of them. The debate is endless because the sequence of events has no stopping point. It is still spinning itself out and will always be differently concluded for and by each successive generation. It is worth noting that those who weave conspiratorial legends or employ the "thèse de complots" [conspiracy thesis] are just as prone to ignore the real men who formed and led the patriot party as are those who insist on spontaneous mass or class action. In both cases, efforts to fathom a grand design result in perpetually unsatisfactory answers to the more limited range of questions which anyone curious about the coming of the French Revolution might be expected to ask: Who intervened in the conflict between crown and nobles in 1788–1789? How did they do so and why? To learn, for example, that many leaders of the patriot party were Masons or that their correspondents in the provinces belonged to "reading societies" does not get us very far. Or, rather, it leads us much too far with hints that we must look beyond a loose political coalition based on informal groupings of like-minded notables, in search of an invisible network controlled by a hidden hand (the Duc d'Orléans?) or manipulated by Protestants, aliens, libertine aristocrats, and would-be philosopher-kings. On the other hand, to be told that these leaders must have been, if not members of the bourgeoisie, then its agents, symbols, or incarnations and to examine the social structure of this ascending class in order to understand the behavior of these leaders does not get us very far either—or takes us much too far also in search of statistics pertaining to capitalist enterprise, industrial development, and landownership patterns. In both instances we are asked to look around, over, beyond, above, or below rather than at the assorted individuals whose group action we are curious about. What we have tried to suggest in the foregoing discussion is that evidence relating to this group action, undertaken by known individuals, using known means, to exert continuous pressure toward known ends is contained in *The Coming of the French Revolution*. But a static framework derived from a structural analysis is incapable of containing this sort of dynamic group action. Instead it keeps apart, as socially stratified, the very cluster of men who gravitated together, mutually attracted by political goals that appeared to be within their reach.

THE PARISIAN REVOLT:
WHO PARTICIPATED?*

George Rudé

*George Rudé (1910–   ) is one of several historians who,
since the mid-1950's, have investigated the life of the
common people during the French Revolution. Professor of History at the University of Stirling in Scotland, he has published
studies on the crowd in eighteenth- and nineteenth-century riots
and disturbances. His books include* The Crowd in the French
Revolution *(1959),* Wilkes and Liberty *(1962),* Revolutionary
Europe, 1783–1815 *(1964), and* The Crowd in History *(1964).
Disagreeing with such popular works as Hippolyte Taine's* The
French Revolution *and Charles Dickens'* A Tale of Two Cities,
*both of which describe most rioters as vicious and contemptible,
Rudé presents a much more precise and favorable picture of them
by analyzing their class backgrounds and their grievances. The
following selection is an example of his method.*

The captors of the Bastille [have been represented] as vagabonds,
criminals, or a mercenary rabble hired in the wine-shops of the
Saint-Antoine quarter. This is a legend that dies hard; yet not
only is there no evidence to support it, but all the available evidence directly refutes it. Nor should we, of course, be satisfied in
describing them with such general terms as "the workers of the
Faubourg Saint-Antoine," "the people," or "all Paris." There is,
in fact, small excuse for so doing: those directly involved in the

* From George Rudé, *The Crowd in the French Revolution* (Oxford: Clarendon Press, 1959), pp. 56–59, 180–181. Reprinted by permission of the Clarendon
Press, Oxford. Quotations originally in French has been translated by the
editors.

capture of the fortress were but a few hundred and, in their case at least, sufficient evidence has survived to enable us to get a reasonably clear picture.

The *vainqueurs de la Bastille,* as they came to be called, numbered between 800 and 900 persons. Those were they who managed, after careful sifting of evidence, to establish their claim to have taken a direct part in the capture of the fortress. Their names were carefully compiled and recorded and have come down to us in three separate lists, each one of which was, at various times during 1790, approved by the Constituent Assembly.[1] One of these lists—that drawn up and held by Stanislas Maillard, secretary of the *vainqueurs*—consists of the names of 662 survivors, of whom nearly 600 are those of civilians.[2] Although incomplete,[3] it is the only one that will serve our purpose, as here alone we find recorded the addresses and occupations, and even the militia units, of the persons concerned. It is, of course, only on the basis of such evidence that it is possible to build up a picture of the social or occupational status of the captors of the Bastille without resort to speculation or vague generalization.

There were few men of wealth among them. As Jaurès wrote: "In the list of the combatants there is no mention of men of property, the capitalists for whom the Revolution was in part carried out." [4] Three manufacturers are listed, 4 merchants, the brewer Santerre, 3 naval officers, 4 termed "bourgeois," and perhaps a handful of wealthy shopkeepers. The rest, apart from 61 soldiers and 15 cavalrymen of the National Guard—whose civil occupations are not given—are almost all small tradesmen, artisans, and wage-earners. Of these, about two-thirds are small workshop masters, craftsmen, and journeymen drawn from about thirty petty trades;[5] the remainder are engaged in manufacture,

---

[1] *Tableau des citoyens vainqueurs de la Bastille* (871 names), Musée des Arch. Nat. [Archives Nationales], no. 1166; *Tableau des vainqueurs de la Bastille* (954 names, many appearing twice) in F. Bournon, *La Bastille* (Paris, 1893), pp. 219–223; *Noms des vainqueurs de la Bastille* (662 names), Arch. Nat., T 514[(1)].

[2] Arch. Nat., T 514[(1)].

[3] Among notable omissions are Dénot, who chopped off de Launay's head; the abbé Fauchet; Fournier l'Américain; the architect Palloy; and Maillard himself.

[4] Jaurès, *Histoire socialiste,* I, 303.

[5] These include 49 joiners, 48 cabinet-makers, 41 locksmiths, 28 cobblers, 20 sculptors and modellers, 11 metal-chasers, 10 turners, 10 hairdressers and wig-makers, 7 potters, 9 monumental masons, 9 nailsmiths, 9 dealers in fancy

distribution, building, the professions, and general trades.[6] The wage-earners cannot always be clearly identified, but they appear to be (as we should expect in this case) in a decided minority: perhaps 60 in the small crafts and 85 or 90 in other occupations.[7] There was one woman among them—Marie Charpentier, *femme Hauserne*, a laundress of the parish of Saint-Hippolyte in the Faubourg Saint-Marcel.

These were the survivors; we know less about the ninety-eight said to have been killed during the siege. Jaurès, quoting the journalist Loustalot, wrote: "More than thirty left their wives and children in a state of such poverty that they needed immediate assistance." [8] There is further evidence to suggest that those killed included wage-earners and city poor. [The contemporary diarist] Hardy reports a burial service for Charles Dusson, aged 31, a journeyman edge-toolmaker of the rue de la Huchette, in the church of Saint-Séverin on 18 July.[9] Again, Jean-Marie Silvain Gomy, aged 17, one of Santerre's brewers, was last seen alive when he set out for the Bastille under arms on the afternoon of 14 July.[10] Five further corpses of civilians were brought to the Châtelet for identification: they included a journeyman shoemaker of the Faubourg Saint-Antoine, and a street-lighter of the rue des Noyers, off the Place Maubert; the rest remained unclaimed and unidentified.[11]

Of the survivors, at least, the great majority were citizens of the Faubourg Saint-Antoine. Four hundred, it is true, of the 635

---

ware, 8 printers, 7 braziers, 9 tailors, 9 founders, 5 jewellers, 5 goldsmiths, 5 stove-makers, and 3 upholsterers. For a similar classification see G. Bord, "La Conspiration maçonnique de 1789," *Le Correspondant,* May 1905, pp. 521–544. M. Bord must have used Maillard's list to arrive at his results, but he gives no reference.

[6] These include 11 wine-merchants, 3 café-proprietors, 2 innkeepers, 21 shopkeepers, 9 hatters, 3 manufacturers, 4 businessmen, 6 gardeners, 3 carpenters, and 7 stonemasons.

[7] The largest categories are: cabinet-makers (8–10), joiners (8), locksmiths (7–9), cobblers (5), print and paper workers (4), stocking-weavers (4), gauze-workers (22), porters (17), riverside workers and bargemen (8), shipyard workers (5), coachmen (4), stonemasons (5), stonecutters (4), ribbon weavers (3).

[8] Jaurès, *op. cit.,* I, 303.

[9] S. Hardy, *Mes loisirs, ou journal d'événements tels qu'ils parviennent à ma connaissance* (MS in 8 vols.; Paris, 1764–89. Bibliothèque Nationale, fonds français, nos. 6680–7), VIII, 388.

[10] Arch. Nat., Y 14119.

[11] Arch. Nat., Y 10634, fol. 150; 12698; 10598.

whose origins have been traced, were of provincial birth,[12] yet most of them had become settled inhabitants of the *faubourg*: no less than 425, out of 602 whose addresses are given, lived in one or another of its parishes.[13] Of the remainder, 60 came from Saint-Gervais, Saint-Paul, and other districts adjoining the Bastille from the west, 30 from the central markets,[14] perhaps a dozen from the Faubourg Saint-Marcel. Very few came from more than a mile or two from the Bastille: among them were a locksmith from the Faubourg Saint-Honoré and a tinsmith from the Gros Caillou, near the Champ de Mars. And all of these, whether from the Faubourg Saint-Antoine or elsewhere, far from being vagrants or down-and-outs, were men of settled abode and occupation. More surprisingly perhaps, the overwhelming majority of its captors went to the Bastille under arms as enrolled members of their local units of the newly formed *milice bourgeoise,* or Parisian National Guard.[15] This, of course, not only serves further to disprove the legend that the captors were vagrants or social riff-raff—such elements were, of course, rigorously excluded from the ranks of the militia—but it also suggests that the operation may have been a far less spontaneous affair than has usually been claimed.

Yet, in a wider sense, we may agree with Michelet that the capture of the Bastille was not just the affair of those few hundred citizens of the Saint-Antoine quarter who were most immediately involved, but of the people of Paris as a whole. At the peak of the insurrection there may have been a quarter of a million Parisians—some thought more—under arms;[16] and, taking an even broader view, we should not ignore the part played by the great

---

[12] J. Durieux, *Les Vainqueurs de la Bastille* (Paris, 1911), pp. 261ff.

[13] Most of these were from the streets adjoining the Bastille—the rue du Faubourg Saint-Antoine and adjacent streets (245), rue de Lappe (53), rue de Charenton (44), rue de Bercy (12), rue de Montreuil (7).

[14] Fournier l'Américain's claim, therefore, to have led 400 of his band of 800 followers from the Saint-Eustache District to the siege must not be taken too literally (*Mémoires secrets . . . de C. Fournier, Américain,* Arch. Nat., F[7] 6504).

[15] In the case of 6 out of every 7 civilians on Maillard's list the name of the company and/or battalion of the National Guard is indicated. I have assumed that the remaining 1 in 7 (they include a boy of 14, another of 16, and a woman) were not enrolled in the *milice.*

[16] Nicolas de Bonneville, the original promoter of the *milice bourgeoise,* later wrote that, on 14 July, Paris had 300,000 men under arms (S. Lacroix, *Actes de la Commune de Paris* [2nd series, 8 vols.; Paris, 1900–14], V, 31); Barnave, on 18 July, wrote of 180,000 (Arch. Nat., W 12, fol. 105).

mass of Parisian petty craftsmen, tradesmen, and wage-earners, in the Faubourg Saint-Antoine and elsewhere, whose revolutionary temper had been moulded over many months by the rise in living costs and, as the crisis deepened, by the growing conviction that the great hopes raised by the States General were being thwarted by an aristocratic plot. . . .

In a very real sense it may be claimed that the Paris revolution of July 1789 was the work of a great part of the population as a whole: those under arms may, as we have seen, have numbered as many as a quarter of a million. Yet the most active elements in the main episodes of that great upsurge were far fewer and are reasonably well known to us. The immediate assailants of the Bastille, most of whom were members of the newly formed National Guard, were only a few hundred in number. While a handful of these were prosperous merchants or other *bourgeois,* the great majority were craftsmen, shopkeepers, and journeymen, drawn from a wide variety of trades and occupations, though predominantly from the building, furnishing, and luxury crafts of the Faubourg Saint-Antoine and its adjoining districts. At the Bastille, the unemployed country-workers, whose influx into the capital had been one of the more striking manifestations of the economic crisis which heralded the Revolution, played little or no part; and wage-earners in general, even workshop journeymen, appear to have been in a distinct minority. Quite different was the composition of the crowds that burned down the customs posts [toll gates or *barrières* surrounding Paris] between 11 and 14 July and raided and sacked the monastery of the Saint-Lazare brotherhood on the 13th. At the *barrières,* as at the Bastille, there was a small number of *bourgeois*—even of nobles—among the most prominent of the insurgents. The aristocratic adventurer, Musquinet de Saint-Félix, was seen at two of the *barrières* on the approaches to the Faubourg Saint-Marcel. Among the incendiaries of two of the northern *barrières* "there had been two rather well-dressed men." The leader of the rioters at Longchamp "looked like a nobleman"; at Passy, "the leader wore a white redingote." Among eighty persons for whose arrest writs were subsequently issued by the Procureur-Général, one is described as wearing "a blue tail coat and carrying a gold-headed cane" and another as being "mounted on a white horse." Yet these were exceptional and the description most often given of the rioters by eyewitnesses was of roughly dressed men and women of the people—local tradesmen, craftsmen and wage-earners, among whom wine-merchants and allegedly professional smugglers were much in evidence, but also working housewives, water-carriers, building and barrel workers, and unemployed from the neighbouring *ateliers de charité* [public workshops].[17] At the Saint-Lazare monastery, too, the work of looting and destruction seems, in the main, to have been carried out by small tradesmen, employed and unemployed labourers, and local poor rather than by craftsmen and journeymen. This was, of course, unlike the two other episodes, a purely local affair and the persons taking part in it were almost all resident in an area adjoining the junction of the rue du Faubourg Saint-Denis and the rue du Faubourg Saint-Lazare on the northern outskirts of the city.[18]

[17] Arch. Nat., Z[1a] 886.
[18] Arch. Nat., Z[2] 4691.

II

THE CHARACTER
OF THE CONSTITUENT
ASSEMBLY (1789–1791)

*F*rom *1789 to 1791, the National or Constituent Assembly began overhauling French institutions. It worked with such great will that one might wonder if any other legislature ever attempted a similar transformation in so short a period of time. It is not surprising, therefore, that there has been disagreement about the political ability of the Constituents and the wisdom of their reforms. Did these men act sensibly and moderately or were they impractical and fanatical? Were they moved by a humanitarian urge for national regeneration or by personal and class interests? Were their policies mostly blunders or long postponed necessities?*

A classic attack on the deputies appeared during the Revolution itself. Watching from London, Edmund Burke was appalled by the destruction the assembly wrought to French traditions. To replace provinces by departments, to make the legislature almost omnipotent, to abolish the parlements, to issue new currency, to seize Church lands—these were to Burke the most extravagant follies. Men are civilized by their religions, traditions, and prejudices; and to deride these or to seek to change them quickly for the sake of abstract ideals is to cause want and theft, anarchy and brutality. The Constituents were neophytes—incompetent and dangerous neophytes.

There could hardly be a greater contrast than that between Burke's inflammatory excoriation and Jacques Godechot's sober and carefully organized description of the most important re-

forms of the Constituent Assembly. Godechot judges many of them admirable; still he does not praise the deputies to the extent that Burke condemns them, for he thinks narrow bourgeois class interests too often determined their policies.

James M. Thompson also finds the bourgeoisie working for their own ends, but he stresses that we must lift our vision above this and see how the assembly benefited France as a whole: sometimes the deputies' bourgeois interests were identical with the needs of the great mass of the population; and sometimes they acted from liberal motives having little to do with class.

Of the assembly's many reforms, perhaps no other caused more upheaval or had such far-reaching consequences than its attempt to reorganize the Gallican (French Catholic) Church. For this reason, we have included two contrasting views of the Civil Constitution of the Clergy. In his description of the conflict between the revolutionaries and the Church, the Catholic historian André Latreille believes that both sides erred, the Church perhaps less than the State. But he prefers to explain rather than to blame, and his account is quite moderate. It indicates how Church-State relations in mid-twentieth-century France have become much less acrimonious than at any time since 1789. The selection from Jean Jaurès also suggests the atmosphere in which it was written: the beginning of the twentieth century, when Jaurès and others were striving to weaken the political influence of the Catholic Church in France and to separate it from the State. Here one meets a vehement anti–clerical defense of the assembly's religious policies—the deputies succeeded in salvaging as much as possible from an inevitable conflict with a powerful, conservative, and outdated institution. They preserved the Revolution while weakening the Church, and they enlarged man's intellectual freedom while diminishing his reliance on supernatural powers.

One may ask whether the assembly did have the moral or legal right to reform the Gallican Church. Did the Constituents blunder by not consulting Pope Pius VI and by requiring loyalty oaths from clergymen? On the other hand, was the pope so dilatory, inflexible, and unaware of French conditions that he himself precipitated the break? Was the Gallican Church so disunited and unsure of its way that it stumbled into a schism?

A word of caution must end this introduction. The points of view taken in the following five selections are closely entwined with their authors' political and religious beliefs. Is it possible to make an impartial and dispassionate historical judgment on the accomplishments and failures of the Constituent Assembly? Or is this one of those questions where a historian must inescapably be more advocate than social scientist?

The Deputies

IMPRACTICAL ZEALOTS*

Edmund Burke

Edmund Burke (1729–1797), often styled the founder of modern conservatism, was born in Dublin. His father was a Protestant lawyer; his mother was a Catholic; and the boy was brought up as a Protestant. He trained for the law, but found his calling in English politics, where he became a spokesman for the aristocratic Whig magnates in the House of Commons. Unlike most politicians, Burke espoused a consistent political philosophy: the rule of an enlightened aristocracy against challenges from absolute monarchy and democracy. He was also a man of letters. His impassioned Reflections on the Revolution in France, *published in November 1790 in the form of a letter to a Frenchman, was the most influential contemporary indictment of the Revolution.*

You [Frenchmen] might, if you pleased, have profited of our example, and have given to your recovered freedom a correspondent dignity. Your privileges, though discontinued, were not lost to memory. Your [ancient] Constitution, it is true, whilst you were out of possession, suffered waste and dilapidation; but you possessed in some parts the walls, and in all the foundations, of a noble and venerable castle. You might have repaired those

* From Edmund Burke, *Reflections on the Revolution in France, Works* (4th ed.; Boston: Little, Brown, & Co., 1871), III, 276–278, 280, 282–284, 299–301, 331–332, 344–348, 524–525, 560–561.

walls; you might have built on those old foundations. Your Constitution was suspended before it was perfected; but you had the elements of a Constitution very nearly as good as could be wished. In your old states you possessed that variety of parts corresponding with the various descriptions of which your community was happily composed; you had all that combination and all that opposition of interests, you had that action and counteraction, which, in the natural and in the political world, from the reciprocal struggle of discordant powers draws out the harmony of the universe. These opposed and conflicting interests, which you considered as so great a blemish in your old and in our present Constitution, interpose a salutary check to all precipitate resolutions. . . .

You had all these advantages in your ancient states; but you chose to act as if you had never been molded into civil society, and had everything to begin anew. You began ill, because you began by despising everything that belonged to you. You set up your trade without a capital. If the last generations of your country appeared without much luster in your eyes, you might have passed them by, and derived your claims from a more early race of ancestors. Under a pious predilection for those ancestors, your imaginations would have realized in them a standard of virtue and wisdom beyond the vulgar practice of the hour; and you would have risen with the example to whose imitation you aspired. Respecting your forefathers, you would have been taught to respect yourselves. You would not have chosen to consider the French as a people of yesterday, as a nation of low-born, servile wretches until the emancipating year of 1789. . . .

Compute your gains; see what is got by those extravagant and presumptuous speculations which have taught your leaders to despise all their predecessors, and all their contemporaries, and even to despise themselves, until the moment in which they became truly despicable. By following those false lights, France has bought undisguised calamities at a higher price than any nation has purchased the most unequivocal blessings. . . .

Laws overturned; tribunals subverted; industry without vigor; commerce expiring; the revenue unpaid, yet the people impoverished; a church pillaged, and a state not relieved; civil and military anarchy made the constitution of the kingdom; everything human and divine sacrificed to the idol of public credit, and national bankruptcy the consequence; and, to crown all, the paper securities of new, precarious, tottering power, the discredited paper securities of impoverished fraud and beggared rapine, held out as a currency for the support of an empire, in lieu of the two great recognized species [gold and silver] that represent the lasting, conventional credit of mankind, which disappeared and hid themselves in the earth from whence they came, when the principle of property, whose creatures and representatives they are, was systematically subverted.

Were all these dreadful things necessary? Were they the inevitable results of the desperate struggle of determined patriots, compelled to wade through blood and tumult to the quiet shore of a tranquil and prosperous liberty? No! nothing like it. The fresh ruins of France, which shock our feelings wherever we can turn our eyes, are not the devastation of civil war: they are the sad, but instructive monuments of rash and ignorant counsel in time of profound peace. They are the display of inconsiderate and presumptuous, because unresisted and irresistible authority. . . .

This unforced choice, this fond election of evil, would appear perfectly unaccountable, if we did not consider the composition of the National Assembly: I do not mean its formal constitution, which, as it now stands, is exceptionable enough, but the materials of which in a great measure it is composed, which is of ten thousand times greater consequence than all the formalities in the world. If we were to know nothing of this assembly but by its title and function, no colors could paint to the imagination anything more venerable. In that light, the mind of an inquirer, subdued by such an awful image as that of the virtue and wisdom of a whole people collected into one focus, would pause and hesitate in condemning things even of the very worst aspect. Instead of blamable, they would appear only mysterious. But no name, no power, no function, no artificial institution whatsoever, can make the men, of whom any system of authority is composed, any other than God, and Nature, and education, and their habits of life have made them. Capacities beyond these the people have not to give. Virtue and wisdom may be the objects of their choice; but their choice confers neither the one nor the other on those upon whom they lay their ordaining hands. They have not the engagement of Nature, they have not the promise of Revelation for any such powers.

After I had read over the list of the persons and descriptions elected into the *Tiers État,* nothing which they afterwards did could appear astonishing. Among them, indeed, I saw some of known rank, some of shining talents; but of any practical experience in the state not one man was to be found. The best were only men of theory. But whatever the distinguished few may have been, it is the substance and mass of the body which constitutes its character, and must finally determine its direction. . . .

It is said that twenty-four millions ought to prevail over two hundred thousand. True; if the constitution of a kingdom be a problem of arithmetic. This sort of discourse does well enough with the lamp-post for its second: to men who *may* reason calmly it is ridiculous. The will of the many, and their interest, must very often differ; and great will be the difference when they make an evil choice. A government of five hundred country attorneys and obscure curates is not good for twenty-four millions of men, though it were chosen by eight-and-forty millions; nor is it the better for being guided by a dozen of persons of quality who have betrayed their trust in order to obtain that power. At present, you seem in everything to have strayed out of the high road of Nature. The property of France does not govern it. Of course property is destroyed, and rational liberty has no existence. All you have got for the present is a paper circulation, and a stock-jobbing constitution: and as to the future, do you seriously think that the territory of France, upon the republican system of eighty-three independent municipalities (to say nothing of the parts that compose them), can ever be governed as one body, or can ever be set in motion by the impulse of one mind? When the National Assembly has completed its work, it will have accomplished its ruin. These commonwealths will not long bear a state of subjection to the republic of Paris. They will not bear that this one body should monopolize the captivity of the king, and the dominion over the assembly calling itself national. Each will keep its own portion of the spoil of the Church to itself; and it will not suffer either that spoil, or the more just fruits of their industry, or the natural produce of their soil, to be sent to swell the insolence or pamper the luxury of the mechanics of Paris. In this they will see none of the equality, under the pretence of which they have been tempted to throw off their allegiance to their sovereign, as well as the ancient constitution of their country. There can be no capital city in such a constitution as they have lately made. They have forgot, that, when they framed democratic governments, they had virtually dismembered their country. The person whom they persevere in calling king has not power left to him by the hundredth part sufficient to hold together this collection of republics. The republic of Paris will endeavor, indeed, to complete the debauchery of the army, and illegally to perpetuate the Assembly, without resort to its constituents, as the means of continuing its despotism. It will make efforts, by becoming the heart of a boundless paper circulation, to draw everything to itself: but in vain. All this policy in the end will appear as feeble as it is now violent. . . .

It is now sixteen or seventeen years since I saw the queen of France, then the Dauphiness, at Versailles; and surely never lighted on this orb, which she hardly seemed to touch, a more delightful vision. I saw her just above the horizon, decorating and cheering the elevated sphere she just began to move in—glittering like the morning-star, full of life and splendor and joy. Oh! what a revolution! and what a heart must I have, to contemplate without emotion that elevation and that fall! Little did I dream, when she added titles of veneration to those of enthusiastic, distant, respectful love, that she should ever be obliged to carry the sharp antidote against disgrace concealed in that bosom! Little did I dream that I should have lived to see such disasters fallen upon her in a nation of gallant men, in a nation of men of honor, and of cavaliers! I thought ten thousand swords must have leaped from their scabbards to avenge even a look that threatened her with insult. But the age of chivalry is gone. That of sophisters, economists, and calculators has succeeded; and the glory of Europe is extinguished forever. Never, never more, shall we behold that generous loyalty to rank and sex, that proud submission, that dignified obedience, that subordination of the heart, which kept alive, even in servitude itself, the spirit of an exalted freedom! The unbought grace of life, the cheap defense of nations, the nurse of manly sentiment and heroic enterprise, is gone! It is gone, that sensibility of principle, that chastity of honor, which felt a stain like a wound, which inspired courage whilst it mitigated ferocity, which ennobled whatever it touched, and under which vice itself lost half its evil by losing all its grossness! [1] . . .

Thanks to our sullen [English] resistance to innovation, thanks to the cold sluggishness of our national character, we still bear the stamp of our forefathers. We have not (as I conceive) lost the generosity and dignity of thinking of the fourteenth century; nor as yet have we subtilized ourselves into savages. We are not the

---

[1] [This particular paragraph of Burke's has been called a landmark in the beginning of English literary romanticism.]

converts of Rousseau; we are not the disciples of Voltaire; Helvétius has made no progress amongst us. Atheists are not our preachers; madmen are not our lawgivers. We know that *we* have made no discoveries, and we think that no discoveries are to be made, in morality—nor many in the great principles of government, nor in the ideas of liberty, which were understood long before we were born altogether as well as they will be after the grave has heaped its mold upon our presumption, and the silent tomb shall have imposed its law on our pert loquacity. In England we have not yet been completely emboweled of our natural entrails: we still feel within us, and we cherish and cultivate, those inbred sentiments which are the faithful guardians, the active monitors of our duty, the true supporters of all liberal and manly morals. We have not been drawn and trussed, in order that we may be filled, like stuffed birds in a museum, with chaff and rags, and paltry, blurred shreds of paper about the rights of man. We preserve the whole of our feelings still native and entire, unsophisticated by pedantry and infidelity. We have real hearts of flesh and blood beating in our bosoms. We fear God; we look up with awe to kings, with affection to Parliaments, with duty to magistrates, with reverence to priests, and with respect to nobility. Why? Because, when such ideas are brought before our minds, it is *natural* to be so affected; because all other feelings are false and spurious, and tend to corrupt our minds, to vitiate our primary morals, to render us unfit for rational liberty, and, by teaching us a servile, licentious, and abandoned insolence, to be our low sport for a few holidays, to make us perfectly fit for and justly deserving of slavery through the whole course of our lives.

You see, Sir, that in this enlightened age I am bold enough to confess that we are generally men of untaught feelings: that, instead of casting away all our old prejudices, we cherish them to a very considerable degree; and, to take more shame to ourselves, we cherish them because they are prejudices; and the longer they have lasted, and the more generally they have prevailed, the more we cherish them. We are afraid to put men to live and trade each on his own private stock of reason; because we suspect that the stock in each man is small, and that the individuals would do better to avail themselves of the general bank and capital of nations and of ages. Many of our men of speculation, instead of exploding general prejudices, employ their sagacity to discover the latent wisdom which prevails in them. If they find what they seek (and they seldom fail), they think it more wise to continue the prejudice, with the reason involved, than to cast away the coat of prejudice, and to leave nothing but the naked reason; because prejudice, with its reason, has a motive to give action to that reason, and an affection which will give it permanence. Prejudice is of ready application in the emergency; it previously engages the mind in a steady course of wisdom and virtue, and does not leave the man hesitating in the moment of decision, skeptical, puzzled, and unresolved. Prejudice renders a man's virtue his habit, and not a series of unconnected acts. Through just prejudice, his duty becomes a part of his nature.

Your literary men, and your politicians, and so do the whole clan of the enlightened among us [the English supporters of the French Revolution], essentially differ in these points. They have no respect for the wisdom of others; but they pay it off by a very full measure of confidence in their own. With them it is a sufficient motive to destroy an old scheme of things, because it is an old one. As to the new, they are in no sort of fear with regard to the duration of a building run up in haste; because duration is no object to those who think little or nothing has been done before their time, and who place all their hopes in discovery. They conceive, very systematically, that all things which give perpetuity are mischievous, and therefore they are at inexpiable war with all establishments. They think that government may vary like modes of dress, and with as little ill effect; that there needs no principle of attachment, except a sense of present conveniency, to any constitution of the state. They always speak as if they were of opinion that there is a singular species of compact between them and their magistrates [government officials], which binds the magistrate, but which has nothing reciprocal in it, but that the majesty of the people has a right to dissolve it without any reason but its will. Their attachment to their country itself is only so far as it agrees with some of their fleeting projects: it begins and ends with that scheme of polity which falls in with their momentary opinion.

These doctrines, or rather sentiments, seem prevalent with your new statesmen. . . .

It is besides to be considered, whether an Assembly like yours . . . is fit for promoting the obedience and discipline of an army. It is known that armies have hitherto yielded a very precarious and uncertain obedience to any senate or popular authority; and they will least of all yield it to an Assembly which is to have only a continuance of two years. The officers must totally lose the characteristic disposition of military men, if they see with perfect submission and due admiration the dominion of pleaders —especially when they find that they have a new court to pay to an endless succession of those pleaders, whose military policy, and the genius of whose command (if they should have any), must be as uncertain as their duration is transient. In the weakness of one kind of authority, and in the fluctuation of all, the officers of an army will remain for some time mutinous and full of faction, until some popular general, who understands the art of conciliating the soldiery, and who possesses the true spirit of command, shall draw the eyes of all men upon himself. Armies will obey him on his personal account. There is no other way of securing military obedience in this state of things. But the moment in which that event shall happen, the person who really commands the army is your master—the master (that is little) of your king, the master of your Assembly, the master of your whole republic. . . .

But am I so unreasonable as to see nothing at all that deserves commendation in the indefatigable labors of this Assembly? I do not deny, that, among an infinite number of acts of violence and folly, some good may have been done. They who destroy everything certainly will remove some grievance. They who make everything new have a chance that they may establish something beneficial. To give them credit for what they have done in virtue of the authority they have usurped, or to excuse them in the crimes by which that authority has been acquired, it must appear that the same things could not have been accomplished without producing such a revolution. Most assuredly they might; because almost every one of the regulations made by them, which is not very equivocal, was either in the cession of the king, voluntarily made at the meeting of the Estates-General, or in the concurrent instructions to the orders. Some usages have been abolished on just grounds; but they were such, that, if they had stood as they were to all eternity, they would little detract from the happiness and prosperity of any state. The improvements of the National Assembly are superficial, their errors fundamental.

BOURGEOIS REFORMERS*

Jacques Godechot

Jacques Godechot (1907–   ) is one of France's most distinguished historians. The son of a businessman from Lunéville, Lorraine, he studied history at the University of Nancy and at the Sorbonne in Paris. He then taught at the École navale in Brest from 1935 to 1940 and published his important doctoral thesis, Les Commissaires aux armées sous le Directoire *(1937). In 1945, he began teaching at the University of Toulouse, where he is now dean. He has written such significant works on the revolutionary period as* Les Institutions de la France sous la Révolution et l'Empire *(1952),* La Grande nation *(1956),* La Contre-Révolution *(1961),* Les Révolutions, 1770–1799 *(1963), part of which also appeared in his* France and the Atlantic Revolution of the Eighteenth Century, 1770–1799 *(1965), and* La Prise de la Bastille *(1965).*

Godechot is noted for his work on the relations between the Revolution in France and those in other countries during the late eighteenth century. He is also an authority on the reforms of the French Revolution; the following selection is a summary of some of his findings.

The essential goal of the National Constituent Assembly was to construct a new regime which would guarantee to the bourgeoisie the peaceful exercise of power and eliminate the possibility of either a return to absolute monarchy, or rule of the aristocracy, or rule of the mass of the people. They envisioned this regime as a constitutional monarchy established upon the rational basis

* From Jacques Godechot, *France and the Atlantic Revolution of the Eighteenth Century, 1770–1799*, trans. Herbert H. Rowen (New York: The Free Press, 1965), pp. 101–117. Reprinted with permission of the publisher. Copyright © 1965, The Free Press.

proclaimed in the Declaration of the Rights of Man and the Citizen.

The assembly proceeded to destroy the institutions of the old regime as soon as new institutions had been created to take their place. But not all of the old institutions were destroyed; some were continued either in their old forms or somewhat modified. The Constituent Assembly therefore did not build the new France from scratch; yet the Constituents never felt the least compunction about preserving the past and never hesitated to destroy inherited institutions.

The achievement of the Constituent Assembly has many aspects. Its political work, which its members unquestionably considered to be their most important accomplishment, was the least enduring, for it collapsed after two years. Its social, economic, and administrative achievements, on the other hand, left much deeper traces, which still persist in the structure of present-day France. We shall begin our analysis by examining these essential aspects of the work of the Constituent Assembly.

Social Achievements

The society of the old regime was built upon hierarchy and privilege, which is to say upon inequality. Contrariwise, in its first article the Declaration of the Rights of Man proclaimed equality before law. The Constituent Assembly attempted to create institutions to put this principle of equality into practice. Because it attempted to reserve the reality of power for the bourgeoisie, the assembly met major difficulties in this endeavor and was not wholly successful.

Although on August 4, 1789, the Constituent Assembly abolished personal servitude (there were still 1.5 million serfs in France) and the three orders into which Frenchmen had been divided, although it granted civil rights to foreigners and actors, a proposal to give equality to Jews aroused very sharp debate and was only enacted by the assembly on September 27, 1791, three days before its final adjournment. Equality also presupposed the removal of all discrimination between Negroes and whites as well as the abolition of slavery. This was the logical consequence of the first article of the Declaration of Rights. But the French colonists, represented in the assembly by such influential deputies as the Lameths and Barnave, did not even accept civil equality between whites and free "colored men." After some hesitation the assembly finally accepted the position of the colonists. They did so in order to avoid the revolt which was forecast, it was explained. In fact the assembly thereby prepared a later explosion in the colonies which brought far greater harm to the planters than honest application of the principles of 1789 would have done.

The most important immediate consequence of the principle of equal rights was the opportunity for all Frenchmen to be appointed to any position in the state. The nobility thereby lost their monopoly of the higher offices. Actually only the bourgeoisie benefited from this change, for only they possessed the education necessary to hold these posts or the wealth necessary to acquire such education. In the army, however, where courage could still take the place of learning and sons of peasants and artisans could rise to the summit of the revolutionary hierarchy as a result of circumstances (the emigration of noble officers and the long wars of the revolutionary period), it could now be truly said that "every soldier carried a marshal's baton in his knapsack." All in all, upward social mobility became more rapid and more frequent than before the revolution.

Even more important in its consequences, however, was the abolition of the feudal system, adopted amid enthusiasm by the National Assembly during the night of August 4, although under the pressure of the peasant uprising. During the days that followed, the owners of manors strove to limit their concessions as much as possible. The decrees applying the decisions of principle taken on August 4 were only adopted on March 15, 1790, and the peasants found them unsatisfactory. The new decrees drew a distinction between the rights of feudal (manorial) overlordship, which the assembly presumed to have been usurped, and rights of "feudal contract," which it assumed derived from contracts made between the landlords and the peasant tenants. The rights of overlordship included honorific and personal obligations, which were abolished without payment. The tithe, which had been a very heavy burden for the peasants, was also abolished without compensation; but the landowners were the principal beneficiaries of this measure, for they ceased to transmit the tithes to the church although they continued to collect them from their tenants and sharecroppers.

On the other hand, most of the manorial dues, or "real rights," were not actually abolished outright but had to be bought back by the peasants at prices they found difficult to pay. Repurchases were to be made by individuals, not the state or communities, and no system of credit was provided to make the repayments easier to meet. Until the dues were completely repurchased, they still had to be paid, together with the arrears for thirty years. It was obvious that if this law were enforced the feudal system would last for many long years. The discontented peasants rose in rebellion again in many regions. It was only later, in 1792 and 1793, after the fall of the monarchy, that the Legislative Assembly and the Convention which followed it gave satisfaction to the peasants by abolishing all dues of "feudal character" without any compensation. Thereafter no servitudes on either person or land existed within the continental territory of France. The right of property became absolute, in the Roman sense of the term, and the transfer of land was vastly facilitated.

Economic Achievements

Circumstances rather than theories led the Constituent Assembly to make important reforms in the field of economics and finances. The Estates General had been summoned essentially in order to solve the financial crisis. Even before May 1789 many financiers considered that the best way of meeting the governmental deficit would be to sell the property of the clergy for the benefit of the state, which in return would be responsible for payment of the salaries of churchmen and the costs of religious activity.

Abolition of the tithes on August 4 proved that the assembly would not hesitate to follow this path. On August 6 the first proposal to put the property of the clergy at the disposal of the nation was presented from the rostrum. Discussion was long and sharp. Mirabeau and Talleyrand clearly posed the terms of the problem: The wealth of the clergy would be placed at the disposal of the nation in order to pay off the debt of the state; in return the government would provide for the costs of religious worship and pay the salaries of clergymen, although without maintaining the scandalous gap between the incomes of parish priests and bishops. Some deputies argued that it was necessary to take the clergy's wealth in order to remove its status as an estate. At last the wealth of the clergy was nationalized on November 2. The properties appropriated from the churchmen were to be employed to back the assignats, a form of paper money, with which the state would pay its indebtedness. Assignats could be used for the purchase of "national property," as the former ecclesiastical holdings were designated. Assignats so used were to be returned to the treasury and burned.

This decision had a considerable influence upon the history of the French revolution. It resulted in inflation and the devaluation of the assignat, and hence in a rise in prices and a higher cost of living; another consequence was a massive transfer of property, which passed from the hands of the clergy to the ownership of the bourgeoisie and prosperous peasantry.

The sale of "national properties" began in May 1790. Credit facilities were granted to purchasers; they had to pay only 12 to 30 percent of the purchase price in cash, depending on the kind of property; the balance could be paid over twelve years at 5 percent interest. The assembly hoped to assist the peasants by these arrangements. Only a small sum was necessary as a down payment for purchase of "national property," but the landless day laborers had used what little money they had to buy bread at very high prices during the spring of 1789, and many small landowners reserved their savings for the repurchase of feudal dues. Furthermore, although some lots were small and inexpensive, many were vast and the minimum acceptable price was very high. Sales were held at auction and bids on part lots were permitted only if their combined figure was higher than the highest bid offered for the same land as a single lot. The sales were very successful at first, but as we have said, it was especially the bourgeois and the prosperous peasants who profited. Nobles and parish priests were also among the buyers. Poor peasants could make purchases only by forming groups. The distribution of landed property in France was profoundly changed, but to the profit of the prosperous classes. The number of landless day laborers did not decline significantly.

The assignats were put to use at once to pay the government's debt. But the obligations inherited from the old regime were soon swollen by new indebtedness when the Constituent Assembly decided to abolish the former "venal" offices with compensation to the owners. New issues of assignats appeared in rapid succession. But Frenchmen did not accept them without suspicion; they had unhappy memories of the collapse of the paper money issued by Law's bank between 1716 and 1720. By 1791 devaluation of the assignats began. Devaluation would probably have been limited, and to some extent even beneficial (for it was at first a stimulant to the economy), if the financial situation had not forced the treasury to have recourse to new and bigger issues. The fact was that taxes were no longer being collected and the treasury was empty. Instead of being used for reimbursement of the state debt—the purpose for which they had been established—assignats began to be used for payment of current expenses. Inflation and devaluation continued at an accelerating rate. In 1792 the assignat dropped a third in value; when the decline became even more rapid, a grave monetary crisis resulted which did not terminate until 1797, with withdrawal of the assignats and a partial bankruptcy.

The Constituent Assembly did not foresee these difficulties and methodically pursued its economic activities. However, its members were divided on economic policy, and their divisions reflected the actual economic life of the nation. In one camp were the big merchants, the big industrialists, and all who advocated complete freedom of industry and trade, which assured the omnipotence of the employer over his workers and staff; in the other camp were those who were attached to the traditional forms of handicraft production and desired to preserve guild organizations and production regulations, most of which were not in accordance with the principle of economic freedom.

Abolition of feudalism contributed greatly to the emancipation of the land, as we have seen. But there also existed servitudes on the soil—rights of usage, the stubble right, collective communal property—which were not of feudal origin and were not immediately abolished. After long debate the supporters of economic freedom won a partial victory. The freedom for any man to enclose his lands and to till them as he pleased was proclaimed, but the stubble right was abolished only in artificial meadows;[1] a law introducing division of communal lands, to which the assembly was favorable, was drawn up but no decision was taken on it. In practice, landowning farmers found these reforms to their advantage, but day laborers were very strongly opposed to abolition of the common lands and the stubble right, which enabled them to keep a few goats or sheep. Furthermore, the right of enclosure could be exercised only with great difficulty, for in many parts of France the multiplicity of small holdings in the "open fields" made enclosure a practical impossibility. Despite these difficulties, the agrarian reforms of the Constituent Assembly were continued by the Legislative Assembly and the Convention. These reforms resulted in reduction of the average size of holdings and an increase in the

---

[1] [Stubble right is the right of peasants to graze livestock on crop land after the harvest; artificial meadows are meadows that are cultivated rather than allowed to grow wild.]

number of landowners, and greatly strengthened the individualism of the peasantry.

In the areas of trade and industrial production, the Constituent Assembly was even more deeply divided. It did not even
begin discussion of these matters until February 1791. Opponents
endeavored to prove that the guilds enjoyed exclusive privileges
and therefore should be abolished on the basis of the decisions
of August 4. Abolition of the guilds was finally voted, but the
Constituent Assembly also adopted the proposal of deputy Le
Chapelier to maintain in force the old police ordinances which
forbade workers to associate in journeymen's leagues (*compa-
gnonnages*), to form "coalitions" (unions), or to strike. The Le
Chapelier law was voted under the pretext of maintaining freedom of labor, but it was in accordance with the ideas of the
economists and the interests of the capitalist bourgeoisie. It passed
almost without debate; not only was there no representative of
the workers in the Constituent Assembly, but it must be added
that the problem of labor did not arise in 1791 in the same terms
as it did fifty years later, for the Industrial Revolution had hardly
begun in France. Still it is true that in the Le Chapelier law the
interests of employers won out under the pretext of economic
liberalism. It was only repealed in the second half of the nineteenth century, by the law of 1864 which permitted strikes and
the law of 1884 which legalized trade unions.

It was also on the basis of the principles of freedom and free-
hold property that the Constituent Assembly repealed the law
on mines of 1744, which had required prior authorization from
the government to use the subsoil for mining and thus limited
the rights of the owner of the land. The Constituent Assembly
returned full ownership of the subsoil to the owner of the land,
but thereby disorganized operation of the mines and generated
interminable lawsuits.

As for trade, the Constituent Assembly applied the principle
of the economists, *laissez faire, laissez passer*,[2] at least as far as
trade within the territory of continental France was concerned.
All tolls and customs dues on imports and exports collected at
the frontiers, within the country, and at city gates—and in
general the majority of indirect taxes—were abolished. Government revenues were to come essentially from three direct "contributions"—the land contribution, the personal property tax,

---

[2] Loosely, "do not interfere or penalize" or "hands off."—*Trans.*

and licenses on businesses and trades. Jurisdiction over fairs and markets was reduced to the most elementary police regulations; all price-fixing was abolished. This measure encouraged an increase in prices and caused discontent among the poor, who feared famine. New disorders caused by the free movement of grain occurred in different parts of France.

Complete freedom of trade was to be favored by a system of uniform weights and measures, which was approved in principle. Freedom of trade led to development of banks, financial companies, and in general all forms of credit. Trade in securities was made nearly free. The profession of bond and mercantile brokerage was opened to all without restriction.

The Constituent Assembly showed itself to be less liberal with regard to foreign trade. In this area the interests of the big merchants no longer coincided with the principle of free trade. To be sure, the assembly abolished the privileges and exemptions which some ports such as Lorient and Marseilles enjoyed, and it suppressed the monopolist trading companies like the India Company. But it maintained a protectionist tariff and indicated its opposition to the trade treaties with the United States (1778) and England (1786), which had lowered tariff rates.

Colonial trade remained strictly regulated. Despite the violent protests of the deputies from the colonies, who desired freedom to trade as they pleased, the system of "Exclusion," permitting the colonies to trade only with the mother country, was maintained. On the other hand, perhaps in compensation, the Constituent Assembly established colonial assemblies with sole authority to legislate regarding persons and property in the colonies; these assemblies maintained the inequality between whites and "colored people," the slave trade, and slavery.

Most of the economic reforms of the Constituent Assembly endured. They continued to be in force long into the nineteenth century, some surviving even to our own day.

Administrative Achievements

The administrative achievements of the Constituent Assembly were also very enduring. They were indispensable reforms demanded by a majority of Frenchmen, for the complexity and incoherence of the monarchical administration scandalized eighteenth-century men infatuated with rationalism. A large number of the cahiers demanded a thorough administrative reform, such as had been in preparation for some years. The monarchical

administration itself had desired to substitute a sensible organization of the national territory for the hodgepodge of "provinces,"
"bailiwicks" and "seneschalsies," civil and ecclesiastical "dioceses,"
"estate lands" and "election lands," "military governments" and
"commanderships-in-chief," and unequal and illogical judicial
districts.

In 1787, in connection with the establishment of provincial
assemblies, the royal government had also conceived a plan for
special districts for the allocation (in old French, *département*)
of taxes. In 1789 the geographer Letrosne proposed an administrative division of France suggested by the federal system of the
new United States of America; his plan called for 25 generalities,
250 districts, 4,500 wards, all approximately equal in shape. In
approving the design of the project as a whole, Condorcet felt
that it would be necessary to "reconcile changes with local convenience." Mirabeau declared: "I should want a division based
upon geography and facts and adapted to the localities and
circumstances, not at all a mathematical division, which is almost
perfect in theory but in my opinion, would be almost impossible
to put into practice. I should want a division intended not only
to establish proportional representation but also to bring the
administration of men and things closer together and to permit
greater participation of the citizenry in the work of government.
Last, I propose a division which will not seem—shall we say?—
too novel; a division which will permit—if I may be so bold as
to use the terms—a compromise with prejudices and even with
errors, and will be desired equally by all provinces and be founded
upon familiar relationships." The Constituent Assembly accepted
Mirabeau's ideas.

Reorganization was facilitated by the abolition of provincial
and communal privileges during the night of August 4. The
Constituent Assembly divided France into eighty-three "departments," but decided that the "former boundaries of provinces
should be respected whenever there is neither real advantage nor
absolute necessity for discarding them." Brittany was given five
departments, Provence three, but the two small provinces of
Aunis and Saintonge were combined to form a single department.
The departments were given the names of their most characteristic
geographical features, which they still retain. An effort was made
to set the boundaries so that the capital of each department would
be no more than a day's travel from its most distant point.

The departments were divided into up to nine districts. It

was intended that residents would be able to make the round trip from their homes to the capital of the district in a single day. Each district comprised a number of cantons. The primary unit remained the parish, which dated from the early Middle Ages; it was now called the "commune."

Each of these divisions was to be administered by representatives of taxpayers, chosen directly in the commune and by two-stage elections in the district and the department. Councils at the head of the commune, the district, and the department were divided into two sections; one—a directory in the department and the district, a mayor and municipal officers in the commune— was given the executive power, and the other—a general council in the department, the district, and the commune—was deliberative. The king was represented by a procurator syndic, who was elected, not appointed. This was the most complete administrative decentralization which France has ever known. Each department was like a little autonomous republic. If the departments fell into the hands of opponents, the revolution would be in jeopardy. Not surprisingly, centralization had to be reestablished in 1793.

These new divisions had to be provided with courts, all alike and with perfectly defined jurisdictions. The capital of the canton received a "justice of the peace," in imitation of Holland and England. He was more an arbitrator than a judge; his task was to avoid trials rather than to suggest them. Assisted by two other citizens, he presided over the police court of the canton, which had the duty of punishing minor crimes. In each district capital there was a civil court, and in the departmental capital a criminal court. All judges were elected from the ranks of graduate lawyers and were paid by the state. In criminal cases it was the citizens themselves who decided upon indictments and guilt. A jury for accusations was composed of eight citizens drawn by lot from one list, and a trial jury of twelve citizens was likewise chosen by lot but from a different list. The judges, brought in from the district tribunals, merely fixed sentences. All courts were to judge according to uniform codes. The Constituent Assembly began drafting these codes but was able to complete only the penal code. Inspired by the humane ideas of Beccaria,[3] it abolished torture and barbarous punishments and increased safeguards for the accused. Nonetheless, despite a speech by

[3] [Cesare Beccaria, a jurist from Milan, was the author of *On Crimes and Punishments* (1764).]

Robespierre, the death penalty was maintained. Appeals in civil cases went from one district tribunal to another; the Constituent Assembly, not wishing to revive the former parlements, did not create appellate courts. It did establish national tribunals: the Court of Invalidation (*tribunal de cassation*), composed of one elected judge from each department, which had the duty of examining not the substance of cases but only their form; and a High Court which would meet in exceptional cases to try crimes by ministers and high officials as well as crimes against the security of the state. This judicial system was logical, coherent, and humane. It made justice totally independent of the king but, as a consequence of the system of property qualifications for the ballot, it placed justice in the hands of the bourgeoisie. Incontestably one of the most successful reforms, it was the work of an assembly more than half of whose members were lawyers.

In military matters the Constituent Assembly was much more hesitant. The assembly legalized the militia bands which had been formed spontaneously in July and August 1789 by making them a "National Guard." In the minds of the members of the Constituent Assembly as well as of the guardsmen themselves, they were not an army but a force whose sole function was to maintain order within the country and to safeguard the "conquests of the revolution." Despite the appeal of Deputy Dubois-Crancé in favor of universal military service, obligatory and equal for all, the Constituent Assembly retained the professional army, although promotion to even the highest ranks was opened to all soldiers. Nonetheless, the royal army soon began to disintegrate when its aristocratic officers went abroad in emigration. Often the soldiers rebelled against commanders who were hostile to the revolution. The Constituent Assembly became more and more inclined to call upon the National Guard to defend the country and the revolution. After June 1791 it ordered the formation of battalions of volunteers selected from the National Guard; an army of citizen-soldiers wearing blue uniforms, with white jackets and red braid, took shape at the side of the old royal army, which wore white uniforms. The navy was also reorganized, and all naval ranks were opened to every citizen, especially merchant marine officers.

Political Achievements

The fundamental objective of the members of the Constituent Assembly, as we have seen, was to establish a constitutional monarchy, which they hoped would last as long as the ten-centuries-old absolute monarchy. In this endeavor they met almost total failure. The constitutional monarchy organized by the National Constituent Assembly lasted less than a year. Its fragility was a result of the fears of a majority of the deputies, who dreaded both giving the king too much power and entrusting the people with too much authority. The regime which they created therefore lacked strength and soon collapsed.

The Constituent Assembly began by transgressing one of the fundamental principles which it had proclaimed in the Declaration of Rights—equality. At Sieyès's suggestion, it introduced a subtle distinction among French citizens. Only the more prosperous, the "active citizens" (about two-thirds of the total), participated in political life. The remainder, called "passive citizens," enjoyed only civil rights. To be an active citizen one had to pay direct taxes equal to three days' wages. Because of the unequal distribution of taxes, the percentage of active citizens varied very widely; and they were proportionally much more numerous in the countryside than in the towns. The large majority of peasants who owned at least their cottages was included among the active citizens, while artisan journeymen who lived in rented rooms remained passive citizens. It must be noted, however, that the active citizens directly elected only the municipal councils. The Legislative Assembly, the general councils of the departments and the districts, and the judges were named at the second stage by electors who had to be chosen from among the 50,000 wealthiest Frenchmen, who owned or enjoyed the income from property worth from 150 to 400 days' work, depending on the locality.[4]

The Legislative Assembly was elected for two years. It received important powers: the initiative and the passage of laws, the voting of a budget which was not subject to the royal veto, the decision on war and peace, the right to address the people by proclamations. Still the king retained many elements of strength. Although he was no longer "king of France by the grace of God" but merely "king of the French," his person remained "inviolable and sacred." The succession to the throne was still governed by the Salic Law, that is, it was hereditary in the male line by order of primogeniture. The king named and dismissed the six ministers who were responsible only to him and had to be selected outside

[4] [For a differing account of the franchise requirements for electors, see R. R. Palmer, *The Age of the Democratic Revolution* (Princeton: Princeton University Press, 1959), I, 524–527.]

the membership of the assembly. The king continued to lead the army and the navy, since he named the majority of their officers. He was the director of France's diplomacy and proposed the declaration of war or conclusion of peace to the assembly, which had the power of decision. His principal prerogative was the right of suspensive veto. If he refused to approve a law it could become effective only if two successive legislative assemblies confirmed the vote of the first assembly. Thus the king could delay enforcement of a law for a period varying from two to six years. On the other hand, the king could not dissolve the assembly.

This constitution, which presents many analogies to the Constitution of the United States, required profound agreement between the executive and the legislature in order to function successfully. It was not possible to create such agreement because the two branches were deeply distrustful of each other and each desired to utilize to the full, and more, the prerogatives granted it by the constitution. Furthermore, the religious problem, rising unexpectedly, caused significant worsening in the relations between the king on the one hand and the assembly and new authorities of the nation on the other. The religious question deepened the crisis in France. Some historians see in it one of the essential causes of the partial failure of the French revolution.

LIBERAL AND HUMANE REFORMERS*

James M. Thompson

James M. Thompson (1876–1956), a great English historian of the French Revolution, was the son of a cleric. He attended the fashionable Winchester School and Christ Church College, Oxford. For most of the balance of his life, he held various teaching and administrative positions at Oxford University. An Anglican clergyman whose first published works were on the Old and New Testaments, he lost his faith and turned to the teaching and writing of European history. His best-known books on the French Revolution are the popular Leaders of the French Revolution *(1929), the two-volume* Robespierre *(1935), and the encyclopedic and perceptive* French Revolution *(1943).*

On Sunday, September 18th [1791], the king's acceptance of the constitution was proclaimed from the Town Hall, and Parisians gave themselves up to public rejoicings. The *Te Deum* was sung at Notre Dame, and there was a balloon ascent in the Champs Élysées. On the 30th the National Assembly met for the last time, and Louis reaffirmed his loyalty to the constitution, amid cries of *Vive le roi! Vive la nation!* and *Vive la liberté!* But it could not be ignored that, of all the thousand deputies, only two were chaired and crowned by the waiting citizens—Pétion of Chartres and Robespierre of Arras, the most stubborn champions of popular rights, and the most persistent opponents of middle-class privilege.

* From J. M. Thompson, *The French Revolution* (Oxford: Basil Blackwell, 1943), pp. 225–227. Reprinted by permission of Basil Blackwell, Ltd., and Oxford University Press, Inc.

Writing to Robespierre after her return home from Paris (September 21st), Madame Roland drew pessimistic conclusions from the reactionary conduct of the deputies. It proved, she said, that "the least aberration from the orbit of perfect equality and complete liberty necessarily tends to degrade human nature."

It was not unnatural that politicians who had lived in close touch with Paris opinion should sympathize with the point of view of the man in the street, and condemn much of the work of the assembly. They could not easily forget the red flag of July 17th, or the undemocratic revision of the franchise, or the restoration of a traitor king.[1] They could not easily forgive the betrayal of the people's interests by representatives whom the people had saved from disaster at every crisis of the revolution. What was the working man's reward for July 14th and October 6th? What boon had the active citizen received from the lawyers and journalists whom his overwhelming vote had placed in power? A franchise which became less effective as it became more important: a ban upon the only available means of improving the conditions of the worker: a land-purchase scheme whose chief aim seemed to be to save the interests of the landlord: and a bureaucracy which provided thousands of well-paid posts for the sons of middle-class parents.

Men so disillusioned might easily overlook the real and general advantages won since '89—the destruction of an obsolete and arbitrary regime; the enthronement of the nation in place of the king; a new social equality and self-respect; a new responsibility in local government; a new hope of justice; and a new interest in living.

For what was obviously defective in the constitution of 1791 two circumstances were more to blame than the selfishness of the middle class. One was the speed with which the political revolution had been carried through. The other was the completeness of its break with the past.

Mirabeau, writing to a friend in August, '88, had anticipated a gradual revolution. "The first States-general," he said, "will be disorderly, and will perhaps go too far. The second will establish its right of way (*assureront leur marche*). The third will achieve the constitution." Mirabeau's three sessions had been compressed

---

[1] [References to the massacre at the Champ de Mars, to the restriction of the franchise in August 1791 which raised the property qualifications for electors of the second degree, and to the fact that Louis XVI was not deposed despite his flight to Varennes.]

into one. Work that might well have been spread over ten years
had been completed in two. Before one reform was launched,
another was on the slipway.

But this was not all. It is as true of revolutions as it is of wars
that those who have won the victory in the field are not the most
fit to sit round the table at the peace conference. The bitter
memories of the old regime which the deputies brought with
them to Versailles, and the just resentment with which they regarded the conduct of the king during the summer of '89, made
it difficult for them to view the situation realistically. Mallet du
Pan was saying both too much and too little when he declared
that France needed thirty years of preliminary training before
it would be fit to support political liberty—too much, if thinking
of the leaders; too little, if thinking of the rank and file. But
almost every divergence between the revolutions of 1688 and
1789, so often too complacently contrasted by English historians,
may be attributed to the different political antecedents and education of two great peoples.

It has become fashionable to condemn "a bourgeois revolution." There is a sense, and one creditable to the intelligence and
energy of the middle class, in which every revolution is a
bourgeois revolution. The French nation at the end of the
eighteenth century was not exceptional in having to rely on its
professional and propertied minority for liberalism and leadership. It was unusually fortunate in that this minority was too
weak to establish its rule without the help of the majority, and
too patriotic to exploit its private interests until it had carried
through a programme of national reform.

No narrowing of the franchise, no obstacles to the revision of
the constitution, could deprive the mass of the people, the sixteen
millions who were the families of "active" citizens, of the power
to call their representatives to account, or to settle the national
affairs in a national way. They had overthrown the old privilege
of class: they could overthrow the new privilege of cash—if only
by another revolution. Meanwhile a bourgeois constitution was
infinitely better than none. It protected their lives, their labour,
and their land. It prevented the return of the royalist refugees,
and of the ecclesiastical monopolists. It saved the country from
a foreign invasion designed by its own royal and aristocratic
families. It provided for the first time the possibility of an ordered
and peaceful existence.

True, these benefits were not given in full measure to the

"passive" citizens, the disfranchised third part of the people. But what other state in Europe would have enfranchised them? Or in what country, having no vote, would they have received so much consideration? If they were excluded from political responsibility, it was not by the propertied and professional minority only, but by their own comrades of the *petite bourgeoisie* —the tradesmen and artisans who were the bulk of the "active" citizens. If they were benefited, it was not by their own violence, but by the legislative action of deputies drawn from the whole hierarchy of the middle classes, who for a while forgot their class interests and enmities in a genuine zeal for national re-generation. The alliance of the middle and lower classes against tyranny and privilege may have been a *mariage de convenance* rather than a love-match. It did not long outlast their common victory. But its offspring was the liberal-thinking and liberal-living France of 1875–1939.

2   *The Civil Constitution*

of the Clergy

TRAGIC ERRORS*

André Latreille

André Latreille (1901–   ) is Professor of History at the University of Lyon, where his father held a similar position. He studied at the University of Lyon, taught at the University of Poitiers from 1933 to 1944, and then served in Charles de Gaulle's Provisional Government as director of religious affairs in the Ministry of the Interior. In 1945 he returned to the University of Lyon. A specialist in French religious history, he has published Napoléon et le Saint Siège *(1935),* La Révolution française et l'Église catholique *(1948–1950), and, in collaboration with others, the* Histoire du Catholicisme en France *(1958–1962). He is also a regular reviewer of historical works for the eminent Paris daily* Le Monde *and the author of* La Seconde Guerre mondiale, 1939–1945 *(1966).*

The Civil Constitution of the Clergy

On July 12, 1790, the National Assembly approved the measures that formed the *Civil Constitution of the Clergy*. It was called

* From André Latreille and René Rémond, *La Période contemporaine*, Vol. III of *Histoire du Catholicisme en France* (3 vols.; Paris: Éditions Spes, 1958–1962), pp. 83–94, 96. These pages, written by M. Latreille, are printed by permission of the publisher. Editors' translation.

a constitution because it was intended as an essential part of a national regeneration and it was called civil because the assembly wanted to make clear that it dealt only with temporal issues. The idea was not to change the national religion, but to cleanse the ecclesiastical body of those abuses universally censured by the national will.

By-passing the Concordat of 1516,[1] which was the oldest of our treaties and actually represented a bilateral agreement with the Holy See, the assembly decided, by its own authority, to regulate the appointment, functions, and salary of the higher clergy.

The boundaries of the dioceses were altered so that henceforth there would be one diocese for each department. Instead of 135 there would be only 85; their size would be much less unequal than in the past; and they would be grouped in ten metropolitan provinces. In drawing up parish boundaries, the assembly ruled that each one had to contain at least 6,000 souls. A considerable reduction in the number of religious positions resulted from these two principles. In addition, all claims to ecclesiastical incomes other than those for bishops and parish priests were abolished. Consequently, clergymen with administrative functions, but who did not care directly for the souls of the faithful, lost their positions.

In the future all the Church's clergy would be elected. Bishops and priests would be elected exactly in the same manner as deputies and government officials—by the *active* citizens (those who paid the required amount of taxes) in the departmental or the district electoral assemblies. When elected, a bishop would request canonical institution from the metropolitan bishop of his province. As evidence of the unity of faith and communion, he would then notify the pope of his appointment; but he did not have to obtain Rome's confirmation of his powers. In the administration of all diocesan affairs, the bishop would be assisted by episcopal vicars, who would form a council and would have to be consulted before he could take any action based on his jurisdiction.

The clergy's salaries would be the responsibility of the state,

---

[1] [The Concordat of 1516 between Francis I of France and Pope Leo X served as the basis of relations between the French Crown and the papacy until 1789. Among other things, it recognized the right of the king to choose bishops and other officials of the Church, who would then receive canonical institution from the pope.]

which would every year (quarterly) pay in cash 20,000 livres to bishops, 1,200 to parish priests, and 700 to country vicars. In return, religious ceremonies would be performed without charge; special fees would disappear.

Such spokesmen for the assembly's Ecclesiastical Committee as the Abbés Goutte and Expilly (one might note that Protestant deputies refrained from commenting) insisted that they had only obeyed the needs of society without ever going beyond the incontestable rights of state authority. Boisgelin, archbishop of Aix-en-Provence, and the Abbé Maury replied skillfully for the right-wing in the assembly. They carefully pointed out the inevitable dangers: the claim that the cooperation of the spiritual power could be dispensed with when revising ecclesiastical districts; the establishment of a system of popular election of bishops, which would result in allowing non-Catholics to vote for clergymen; and the separation introduced between the bishops and the head of the Church, which "would harm that unity so essential to religion." Despite the conciliatory attitude of Boisgelin, they received nothing from the assembly, but instead aroused some alarming replies. Armand-Gaston Camus [a lawyer specializing in Church matters] declared that the time had come for the French Church to be freed from "its servitude" to the bishop of Rome; and Mirabeau declared that "all the members of the clergy are public officials" and that "performing religious services . . . is a government function."

Controversy Over the Civil Constitution

Ever since the countless investigations and studies which flourished in 1790 and 1791, the birth and significance of the Civil Constitution of the Clergy have been examined frequently. The amount of influence particular groups had in the Ecclesiastical Committee will always be arguable. We agree with Edmond Préclin[2] that the measures were the result of "the not always harmonious efforts of several sponsors": we see first of all the

---

[2] [Some of the works by the historians mentioned in this selection are as follows: Edmond Préclin, *Les Jansénistes du XVIIIe siècle et la constitution civile du clergé* (Paris: Gamber, 1929); Canon Paul Pisani, *L'Église de Paris et la Révolution* (4 vols.; Paris: Picard, 1908–1911); Albert Mathiez, *Rome et le clergé français sous la Constituante* (Paris: Colin, 1911); Dom Henri Leclerq, *L'Église constitutionnelle* (Paris: Letouzey, Ané, 1934); Frédéric Masson, *Le Cardinal de Bernis* (Paris: Plon, Nourrit, 1884); Abbé Fernand Mourret, *Histoire générale de l'Église*, Vol. VII: *L'Église et la Révolution (1775–1823)* (Paris: Bloud, Gay, 1913).]

Gallican and Caesarian legists;[3] also the Richerists (that is, the champions of the movement for the autonomy of the lower clergy) rather than the Jansenists (although these two movements had largely merged); and finally the *philosophes*. In any case, Canon Pisani is right to say that the Civil Constitution did not represent an unnatural conception "springing from the brains of some Jansenists and then violently imposed on a declining France by Machiavellian tactics." It was the inevitable outcome of a religious situation for which no one could find a solution in time, as well as the result of some rather confused and contradictory forces that did not consciously aim at schism. Does this mean (as is still said by modern historians writing since the appearance of Albert Mathiez' work) that it was not unacceptable to Catholics, that the Gallicans recognized this, and that it was Pope Pius VI's malevolence toward the French Revolution that made it unacceptable? Certainly not. What pervades the whole Civil Constitution is the statist postulate that the secular authority alone has the right to make changes which it deems wise not only in ecclesiastical organization but also concerning religious worship. Although there were in the Gallican Church some theologians and canon lawyers quite willing to make any effort to reach a compromise, willing to accept, for example, the changes in the ecclesiastical districts or the election of bishops, they continually warned the assembly that it was necessary to consult with the spiritual authority, according to the prescriptions of canon law, "or else religion would be fundamentally harmed."

Earlier, the first chairman of the Ecclesiastical Committee, Bishop de Bonal, had commented about the monastic reform of 1790: "What I believe to be illegitimate in the exercise of this authority is that the assembly alone tears down obstacles that it has not erected . . . before we hear a pronouncement from the only power in the spiritual realm that has the authority to tie and untie on this earth."

All the bishops who were deputies took the same position regarding the Civil Constitution of the Clergy. Three months after the vote, in a notable pamphlet entitled an *Exposition of Principles Concerning the Civil Constitution of the Clergy,* the thirty bishops who still sat in the Constituent Assembly (except for

---

[3] [A Gallican favored the almost total freedom of the French Church from the ecclesiastical authority of the pope; and a Caesarist espoused the supremacy of the state in ecclesiastical matters.]

Talleyrand and Gobel who had kept apart from the others) made the following declaration:

> If the civil authorities want to make changes in religious matters without the cooperation of the Church, they contradict the principles of the Church, but they do not destroy them; they contradict the principles and destroy the means that could help them carry out their opinions.
>
> We want to know the desires of the Church so as to reestablish a necessary agreement between the civil and religious authorities and by their concord put consciences at rest and maintain public tranquillity. . . .

Where did this religious authority rest? The Gallican bishops could not go astray. Since the high Middle Ages the papacy had never admitted that the secular authority could determine the choice of bishops without its consent. More and more since the Council of Trent [1545–1563], it had required bishops to recognize their subordination to the successor of Saint Peter; and it had established and organized dioceses, sometimes with the approval of secular princes and sometimes on its own. To be sure, Boisgelin urged that the Gallican Church be consulted in a national council, but only because the Gallican bishops considered it a point of honor to state their views before informing the pope of them. The two archbishops who sat in the king's Cabinet advised him to ratify the Civil Constitution, but only because they judged open resistance to be impossible and because they still clung to the hope of a compromise *with* the Holy See. So, before knowing the opinion of either the French episcopate or the pope, Louis XVI ratified the Civil Constitution on August 24, 1790. However, neither the precepts, nor the traditions of the Roman Curia, nor the attitudes of the reigning pope made it likely that the Holy See would acquiesce.

By the end of October 1790 the Gallican bishops had accepted their responsibilities. To the *Exposition of Principles*, which had been the work of the bishops who were deputies, almost all the other bishops (ninety-three to be exact) associated themselves—they explicitly referred the determination of the dispute about the Civil Constitution to the successor of Saint Peter. Placed in the center of Catholic unity and communion, he had to be the interpreter and spokesman of the universal Church's wishes. They had to wait eight months before Pius VI announced his decision on March 10, 1791. Eight interminable months, at a time when his silence left the faithful in France uncertain, at a time when the assembly multiplied the decrees designed to speed up the implementation of the Civil Constitution, eight months of irretrievable delays!

The Constitutional Oath

Fortified by its first victory over the king, the Constituent Assembly quite naturally felt in no way inclined to reduce its claims to legislate independently on religious problems. To rush matters, on November 27, 1790, it decided to require, under the threat of dismissal, that "all bishops, former archbishops, parish priests, and other public officials" take an oath that they would "be loyal to the nation, to the law, and to the king, and would uphold with all their power the Constitution decreed by the National Assembly and accepted by the king." This was the historically famous constitutional oath that unleashed dissension within Church and State and brought about the breakdown of a harmony between the two powers so often extolled as indispensable to the success of the Revolution.

Of 160 prelates, only 7 decided to take the oath; 4 of these— Brienne, Jarente, Savine, and Talleyrand—were heads of dioceses, but because of their disbelief and their morals they were completely discredited. All the other bishops refused to take the oath after a majority of the deputies had killed every proposal that would have definitely allowed the clergy to exclude anything dependent on the spiritual authority from the oath.

But to what extent would the lower clergy and the faithful follow the example of the bishops? The path to take was less clear than it would be for us today. Rome's silence was not the difficulty: the good country priest ordinarily did not look so far, and the voice of the First Shepherd did not reach him easily. Often he was estranged from his own bishop by many legitimate resentments and by a very different manner of understanding the political situation. He looked for "enlightenment from those whose way of life he shared and whose learning he admired, without seeking his doctrines outside the diocese" (Dom Leclerq). He would ask some canon lawyer or some canon from a neighboring city, but very contradictory views were expressed. Even if he ignored the material and spiritual advantages that the ecclesiastical reorganization promised him and even if he ignored the threat of being treated as "a disturber of the peace" and an enemy of national regeneration should he refuse to take the oath, he still hesitated to cut himself off from his flock, to abandon his post, his parish, and his rectory, to which he was bound by so many ties. This was especially true when the local officials, desirous of keeping him, were willing to ignore the reservations that he added to the oath. As well as can be determined from innumerable local studies and general statistical accounts, we can estimate that half of the parish clergy or even a little more than that—in other words, a third of the entire clergy—accepted the Civil Constitution immediately. A high average, but like all averages the result of extreme divergencies on both sides: in the Vendée or Bas-Rhin departments 90 per cent refused to take the oath; in Var 96 per cent accepted it. And the average conceals many inexplicable "cases": in the Haute-Saône department, 4 refused to take the oath and 178 surely took it; but it has been determined that 352 priests in Haute-Saône, two-thirds of the total, took it with reservations or later retracted their pledge.

The adherence of this rather large number of clergymen and laymen thereby allowed the "Constitutional Church" to organize. Every Sunday from the end of January to the end of March 1791, in the capitals of the new departments there were meetings of the active citizens responsible for electing the new bishops who were to replace the "refractory" ones. As no requirement of religious faith was stipulated, unbelievers took part in the elections, while those who were scrupulously faithful abstained. At Le Puy in the Haute-Loire department, 150 active citizens who were Catholics failed to attend the electoral assembly, while Protestants came from Yssingeaux [thirteen miles away]. With some exceptions these electoral activities took place in a calm atmosphere. The voice of the people chose as bishops eighteen of the priests who were members of the Constituent Assembly. When the final stage was reached everything almost came to nought, for someone had to consecrate these newly elected bishops so as to confer the apostolic succession on them, and even the bishops who had taken the oath shunned that task. Talleyrand finally agreed to assume this role: on February 24, 1791, the former bishop of Autun (just fifteen days earlier he had given up his authority there) took up the crosier again to consecrate Expilly as bishop of Finistère and Marolles as bishop of Aisne. Observers noticed that the liturgical ritual was followed exactly except that the reading of papal bulls was omitted as was the oath of loyalty to the pope. Thereafter consecrations occurred in rapid succession, since by April 25 some sixty bishops were at their places in the new dioceses.

Precisely at this point the news began to spread in France that Pius VI had just condemned the Civil Constitution of the Clergy.

The Papal Condemnation

Historians have thoroughly investigated the motives for Pius VI's surprising delay in announcing his decision on the Civil Constitution. Frédéric Masson stresses the forbearance that he showed toward King Louis XVI, whose embarrassing position was explained to him by the French ambassador at Rome, Cardinal de Bernis. The Abbés Mourret and Richard insist on the pope's uncertainty about the intentions of the Gallican bishops. Mathiez and Canon Leclerq emphasize the political considerations behind his delay and in particular his concern with saving [the papal territories of] Avignon and the Comtat Venaissin from the covetousness of the revolutionaries. More attention must certainly be directed toward the customary slowness of the Roman Curia. The cardinals who surrounded Pius VI were highly indignant at the actions of the Constituent Assembly. Its measures exceeded in scope and boldness anything so far attempted by the most radical reformers and enlightened despots—like Joseph II for example. But, for one thing, we must consider the clumsy machinery of the papal government and the traditional prudence of its advisers, elderly men anxious not to commit the "Throne of Truth" rashly. Then, too, there was the feeling that in a European situation where papal authority found enemies everywhere, it had to refrain from providing any pretext for a Gallican schism, something always dreaded by the ultramontanes [those favoring papal supremacy within the Church]. Together, these factors had led and almost always would lead the popes to act slowly and to come to a decision on the fearful problems raised by the Revolution only after great care. From 1789 to 1815, throughout the twenty-five years of almost uninterrupted crisis between Paris and Rome, again and again we gain the impression that the Holy See was falling behind. In reaction to the hasty moves of a young and dynamic political group, it took its positions only belatedly.

The pontifical decision finally appeared, on March 10, 1791, in an important document, the papal brief *Quot Aliquantum,* which was sent to Cardinal de La Rochefoucauld and to the bishops who had signed the *Exposition of Principles.* Pius VI declared that the Civil Constitution had "as its goal and consequence the destruction of the Catholic religion." By its provisions concerning the consecration of bishops, the election of priests, and the operation of diocesan councils, it mortally wounded the divine constitution of the Church. Although it was an article of faith that the Roman Pontiff had the highest authority over the whole Church, the Civil Constitution claimed to upset this fundamental concept. While scrutinizing the doctrinal and disciplinary matters that had been decided illegitimately by the assembly, the Supreme Pontiff took the occasion to pronounce a severe judgment on the principles that this legislature had proclaimed earlier. And so he publicly condemned the Declaration of the Rights of Man. (He had already done the same thing a year earlier in an unpublished consistorial address.) He said that the Declaration was wrong to have granted to the citizen "that unconditional liberty which guarantees not only the right of being left undisturbed for one's religious opinions, but which also grants the right to think, to write, and even to publish with impunity anything on religious matters that may be the product of the most disordered imagination—a shocking right, which the assembly, however, seems to believe is the result of everyone's natural equality and liberty." But what could be more senseless than to establish among men this unbridled equality and liberty which seem to destroy reason? . . . What can be more opposed to the rights of God the Creator—who limits man's liberty by forbidding him to commit evil—than "this liberty of thought and action that the National Assembly grants to man in society as an imprescriptible natural right?" Thus, with a terrible solemnity, the theses of the Roman Church and the principles of modern liberalism confronted each other. We shall see them clash very often after 1789.

Responding to the brief, the Gallican bishops, with much dignity and moderation, tried to explain their conduct; they distinguished between the area of natural law and that of political action. Using the same words as the Holy Father, they condemned a liberty and an equality contrary to the truths of reason and dogma; but as citizens desirous of not opposing popular aspirations in the civil sphere, they had believed it possible to set up the true dominion of public liberty in a hereditary monarchy: ". . . And we recognized without any difficulty that there is a natural equality where no citizen is excluded from the positions to which Providence calls him because of his talents and his virtues.

Political equality can be extended or limited by different forms of government; and we believed that we were free to express ourselves, as was any other citizen, concerning those more or less extensive areas that God himself declares as given over for men to dispute." Having preceded the pope in denouncing the Civil Constitution, the Gallican bishops had no difficulty in following the line of conduct he prescribed for them.

On April 13, 1791, Pius VI declared those consecrations of bishops already carried out to be criminal and sacrilegious, forbade all religious functions to the consecrators and those consecrated, threatened to suspend all priests who had taken the oath and did not retract it, and exhorted the misguided to repent and the faithful to a resolute firmness. It is and always will be impossible to judge the effects of these disciplinary measures. We know that the publicity given to the papal briefs by the loyal bishops brought about in certain dioceses a relatively large number of retractions of the oath, but of course many of these remained secret. The Constitutional bishops, however, were rather persuasive, whether in challenging the authenticity of the papal documents whose circulation was forbidden by the assembly, or in taking shelter behind the Gallican liberties in order to claim that the pope, having no direct jurisdiction over the French people, could pronounce no canonical punishment in this matter.

Soon diplomatic relations between Paris and Rome were broken. When the French government ended Cardinal de Bernis' mission as ambassador, the pope refused to receive a new ambassador. Turbulent demonstrations in Paris (during which the mob burned an effigy of "the Ogre of the Tiber" at the Palais Royal) led to the departure of Dugnani, the papal nuncio. At a time in France when it was especially important for an authorized representative of the Holy See to keep in touch with the loyal clergy, only a semiofficial chargé d'affaires stayed behind, and his position was unclear and indefinite.

The Two Churches

Henceforth there were two churches in the kingdom face to face. There were even frequent instances of two bishops or two priests in the same locality hurling anathemas at each other in front of a divided population which had its own way of interpreting the opposing issues. In fact the public did not understand much about the distinctions concerning ecclesiastical discipline: so long as the Mass was said as usual in the parish church and the sacraments were administered, it hardly cared whether the priest who officiated had legal jurisdiction or whether the taking of a political oath had made him a schismatic. The public was rather inclined to rate priests according to its own personal likes or dislikes and according to its support of the Constituent Assembly and the revolutionary cause. On one side were those clergymen who took the oath [assermentés], on the other were those who refused [insermentés]—contemptuously called jurors or refractories, approvingly called civic priests or good priests. Under such conditions, the antagonists had to fight for the favor of the public authorities and compete, with heated polemics, for the support of the faithful. . . .

Looking at the religious issue from a modern standpoint, it is rather hard to understand why the Constituent Assembly did not stand by its principles on the freedom of religious belief and quite simply adopt total freedom of religion, as it almost did during the last months of its existence. But one must clearly understand that this was impossible to do. All the Constituent Assembly's work had been based on the idea of a national religion serving the new political and social system. It had placed all its prestige behind the formation of the Constitutional Church, which it could not abandon, defenseless, to the relentless attacks of counter-revolutionaries. If the Constituent Assembly at the end of its term forbade refractory priests from preaching or opening new churches, at least it did have the merit of not banishing them.

NECESSARY AND ADMIRABLE DECISIONS*

Jean Jaurès

Jean Jaurès (1859–1914) was one of the most eloquent and influential political figures of his day. A meridional or southern Frenchman, he came from a middle-class family. At the École normale supérieure he studied philosophy and gave promise of a brilliant academic career. But in the early 1890's he left teaching to enter politics full time and for the rest of his life he devoted himself to the cause of democratic socialism. He served as a leader of the Socialists in the Chamber of Deputies and in 1904 founded the French Socialist Party's newspaper, L'Humanité. *He also edited the thirteen-volume* Histoire socialiste *(1901–1908), for which he wrote the four volumes on the French Revolution up to the fall of Robespierre. On the eve of World War I a demented nationalist assassinated him.*

The French Revolution was bolstered by a great increase in wealth. And though the vigor of mind and soul, the passion for liberty and knowledge, the spirit of audacity and inventiveness which great crises produce all contributed a good deal to this growth of national wealth, it had its first and principal source in the revolutionary expropriation of Church property.

But the National Assembly could not restrict itself to seizing and distributing the Church's landed property. It had to regulate all the relations between the Church and the new society created by the Revolution, and we are going to witness the tragic encounter of Christianity and the Revolution.

* From Jean Jaurès, *La Constituante (1789–1791),* Vol. I of *Histoire socialiste (1789–1900),* ed. Jean Jaurès (13 vols.; Paris: Rouff, 1901–1908), pp. 521–522, 532–533, 535, 539, 541, 543–544, 546–548. Editors' translation.

The assembly could not ignore the ecclesiastical organization. In the first place, the temporal power of the Old Regime, the king, played a role in the proceedings of the spiritual power. The pope confirmed bishops, but it was the king who nominated them. To a great extent the Revolution substituted the power of the nation for the power of the king. It therefore had to decide what it was to do with that aspect of royal power. In the second place, a very large number of monks and nuns, who were bound to the cloister by perpetual vows upheld by civil law, petitioned the assembly requesting it to strike off their chains. Finally, by seizing the Church's landed property, the assembly, in order to give a legal pretext for that magnificent revolutionary expropriation, had taken on the responsibility of providing for the administration of the cult and the support of its clergy. The assembly was therefore completely involved in ecclesiastical problems. . . .

A great many details of the Civil Constitution of the Clergy seem bizarre to us, and a great many historians have said that it failed miserably. False. In the first place, it lasted in its original form until February 21, 1795, that is to say four years, and it was, at least for three years, really in operation. The electors charged with choosing parish priests and bishops took their duties seriously. The religious ceremonies which were a part of the electoral procedure were attended without any ill will, even by the freest thinkers among them; and very far from believing that by so doing they compromised themselves with the Church, the electors believed instead that they were acting as good revolutionaries.

But the Civil Constitution survived especially in the Concordat of 1801, although bastardized and debased. There are two great differences between the Concordat and the Civil Constitution: in the first place, the Concordat reestablished the papal right of intervention [in the life of the French Church]. Whereas the Revolution had nothing to do with the pope and confidently affirmed the sovereignty of popular suffrage in the appointment of Church officials as well as other national officials, the Concordat was the result of negotiations with the pope and it restored his supreme right of canonical institution. The other difference is that, according to the Concordat, bishops and parish priests were to be selected by the executive branch of the French government and not by popular vote.

From the Civil Constitution to the Concordat there is, therefore, a diminution of the revolutionary spirit. The Civil Constitution is much more laic, national, and democratic than the Concordat. The Civil Constitution recognizes no foreign power, and, in the last analysis, no theocratic power: it is the nation, in its absolute sovereignty and by means of popular suffrage, that chooses and installs the officers of the Church.

But what is retained of the Civil Constitution in the Concordat is the right of a sovereign with a revolutionary and laic origin to appoint bishops and priests even though it receives its legitimacy not from the Church but from the people. In the Civil Constitution, those electoral assemblies in which everyone—even Protestants, even Jews, even nonbelievers—took part in naming the bishop and the priest seem a little bizarre to us; but in fact the situation is much the same under the Concordat, where the minister of religion in the Cabinet, who might be a Protestant, a deist, or an atheist, chooses the bishops and priests. The essential thing is that a power that does not emanate from the Church and that represents the rights of man—a conception absolutely opposed to that of the Church—takes part in the functioning and recruitment of the Church. This is what survives of the Civil Constitution in the Concordat and this principle is, despite everything, a grave defeat for theocracy.

Those, like us, who desire not only the complete separation of Church and State, but even the disappearance of the Church and Christianity, those who impatiently await the day when the authority of the state will be freed from all contact with the Church and when individual consciences will be freed from all contact with dogma, may believe that the Civil Constitution of the Clergy was an inferior product and a bastardized mixture. Nevertheless, for its time it was basically an act of revolutionary boldness and not, as some have said, an uncertain gesture. In fact, when subjected to the pressure of reactionary and clerical forces, it suffered, as did most revolutionary institutions, a terrible diminution in value; but there still remained in it an intangible part of the Revolution, which survives to this very day. . . .

But why didn't the Constituent Assembly immediately proclaim the separation of Church and State? Why didn't it say that religion was a purely private matter and that the nation should neither persecute, support, pay the salaries, nor regulate any sect? Why didn't it, according to the famous formula of the positivists, bring about then and there the separation of the spiritual and temporal powers? In his very substantial studies of the religious movement in Paris during the Revolution, [Jean-François-Eugène] Robinet vehemently reproaches the assembly for this. . . .

But, actually, taking into account the forces of the year 1790, could the assembly, at that instant, have declared the separation of Church and State? *At that time, the question was not even raised;* it did not exist. None of the legislators, none of the journalists, none of the thinkers or *philosophes* suggested this idea to the assembly. . . .

It was not . . . from the philosophy of the eighteenth century that the politics of separation or of a systematic and immediate dechristianization could reach the Constituents. And the assembly (where Jansenists and legists were much more numerous than *philosophes*) was infinitely more concerned with freeing the French Church from the domination of Rome and with applying the public law of the Revolution to ecclesiastical organization than with intentionally precipitating the dissolution of Christian belief or breaking all legal bonds between Church and State.

Besides, for the state to cut all ties with the Church and proclaim that religion was simply a private matter would not have been tolerated by the overwhelming majority of the people in 1789 and 1790. In religious matters there is a world of difference between the working class today [1901], a part of which is resolutely nonbelieving, and the people of 1789. Not to recognize this vast difference and to be severely critical of the religious achievements of the assembly is to ignore the real significance of the Revolution itself.

The traditions of many centuries had accustomed the people of 1789 to consider public life impossible without the monarchy or religion. It cannot have been expected that the assembly could undo in a moment the results of centuries of servitude and passivity. It took innumerable shocks—the flight to Varennes, the repeated treasons of their leaders, the invasion by foreign hordes requested and aided by the court—to separate the people (I mean the revolutionary people) from the monarchy and the king.

It would take frightful ordeals—the underhanded and violent battle of the clergy against the Revolution, its obvious complicity with the enemies of liberty and the nation, its crimes in the Vendée, its fanatical appeals for civil war—to separate the revolutionary people first from the clergy and then even from Christianity. And still the breach was only superficial. Whoever does not take this into account is incapable of understanding history, incapable also of judging the real stature of those great bourgeois revolutionaries who in four years not only enacted the Civil Constitution, but began the dechristianization of that France so unquestioningly religious for centuries. . . .

One must admire the assembly for its great audacity in bringing the Church within the administrative framework of the Revolution and in placing it under the jurisdiction of popular suffrage, where it became one of many civil institutions.

Furthermore, how would the assembly have been able to separate the Church from the State and refuse all public subsidy to religion at the very moment when it was moving toward the general expropriation of Church property? I do not in the least imply by this that the budget for religion was a debt the state owed to the expropriated Church. There is no debt that the state, the Revolution, owes to the Church. . . .

What most concerned the *philosophes* of the assembly was how to regulate the difficult relationships between the Church and the Revolution without too much commotion and at the least possible risk. They did not abdicate responsibility, they were not indifferent. They hoped that little by little Catholicism as an institution, once taken into the framework of the Revolution, would be permeated by the dissolvent influence of revolutionary thought. And when they pretended to believe that there was no contradiction between the principles of Christianity and those of the Revolution, *in practice* they did not deceive the country, for nations, like individuals, have the admirable faculty of not feeling immediately the contradiction between opposing principles that they sometimes hold.

It took several generations and the painful experience of numerous events before people came to feel that contradiction to the point where it became intolerable; for thanks to the power of the illogical in life, mankind comes under the influence of a new principle without suffering immediately the anguish and sadness of a total and conscious repudiation of the past.

Thus the Constituents hoped that pure reason would little by little free itself from the unnatural compound of Christianity and the Revolution which formed the base of the national consciousness in 1789. At that time the essential thing for them (and they were right) was that the revolutionary stamp be imprinted on the organization of the Church, that the latter not be treated as a special institution, but subject to the same conditions as all civil institutions.

In that way the Church, at the same time as it found its property expropriated, also found its spiritual primacy expropriated. It was above all deprived of its mystery: how long would the people revere as the interpreters of a supernatural power those men whom they chose themselves, whom by their own votes they put into office like any local administrator? . . .

I do not say that this intellectual mixture of Christianity and rationalism is very attractive; furthermore, it is a very mediocre and very unstable philosophical compound. But the people had been kept in ignorance and in Christian dependency as much by the disdain of the *philosophes* as by the Church's will to dominate. And even though they were beginning a Revolution, they could not attain all at once the pure philosophy of knowledge and reason. In the religious sphere, therefore, this first revolutionary period was necessarily a period of compromise. The essential thing once again is that this compromise, while it imposed disagreeable formalities and displeasing attitudes on free thought, did not impair the essential power of reason; on the contrary, by diminishing the masses' spirit of passivity and dependency, it struck at the essence of the Church's power. The four million active citizens who yesterday greeted the bishop as a double incarnation of God and the king now elected that bishop. The Church was in the position of a candidate before the electors. In the last analysis, popular suffrage must decide, popular suffrage becomes pope and to a certain extent, by the transfer of sacerdotal power, popular suffrage becomes God.

Such an exalting of the people causes the abasement of the Church, and dogma loses the halo of power which made it truth. In any case, having lived under the Civil Constitution, the people would find it easier to look point-blank at the altar, where the priest stood thanks to them. I am convinced that the Civil Constitution, so disdained by some haughty spirits, contributed a good deal to the intellectual liberty of the people in religious matters today. It was a first step in the secular accommodation of religion and it accustomed the people to the wide-ranging audacities of free thought.

The Church felt the gravity of the blow; for under the pope's direction it immediately began a furious resistance to the Civil Constitution. It claimed that the new arrangement of dioceses was absolutely counter to canon law. It claimed that the Constituent Assembly could not rightfully avoid consulting the leader of the universal Church. We can dispense with these claims. . . .

In its long life the Church has accepted too many different

constitutions, it has adapted itself to too many diverse political and social conditions for it to be able to oppose revolutionary innovations with the authority of an unchanging tradition. The problem is summed up in a word. The Church aspires to domination; therefore, it declares as contrary to principle anything which hampers its domination, but since it is not obstinate before the inevitable and since it prefers to evolve rather than to disappear, it ends up by resigning itself to what it cannot destroy and by readjusting its principles to what exists.

If the Revolution had triumphed completely, if political liberty and popular suffrage had not been submerged in the despotism of the Napoleonic Empire, if the electoral principle had continued to function everywhere, and if the triumph of the Revolution and democracy had given France a vigorous national purpose, the clergy and the pope himself would have been forced to accept the Civil Constitution. The pope certainly would not have cut off revolutionary France from the universal Church; he would have confined himself as much as possible to maintaining "the unity of the faith" between the elected bishops and the Holy See. Therefore, the controversy did not concern a question of canon law. It was a political question. The issue was whether the Revolution would have the power to prevail in all its works and in the Civil Constitution itself.

I sometimes hear "moderates" regret that the French Revolution created so many enormous difficulties for itself by bestowing a Civil Constitution on the clergy. But truly they reason as if it were possible for the Revolution to ignore the existence of a Church which had dominated and molded France for centuries. They reason as if it were possible for the Revolution, by feigning ignorance, to abolish the profound conflict between the Catholic principle and revolutionary principles. There was not a single question on which the Revolution had to take a stand where it would not meet the Church in its path.

To raise only the question of the dioceses: at a time when the constitution abolished the old provincial boundaries and made France uniform, should it have allowed the dioceses to continue as a reminder of the old France superimposing itself on the lines of the new France and encouraging a universal hope of reaction? At a time when the nation took power from the king, surely it was necessary for it to decide what to do with that part of his authority which concerned the Church; or should it have left the Church for an indefinite period master of everything, of its recruitment, of its preaching, of schools, of the registers of vital statistics?

Again, the dramatic encounter of Christianity and the Revolution could not be postponed. The only task of the Constituent Assembly was to arrange that encounter in such a way that it would wound as slightly as possible the prejudices of the masses who would have turned against the Revolution and also arrange it in such a way that it would give the people new habits of freedom on religious matters. As much as possible, that is what the Civil Constitution provided. In fact the Revolution did find Constitutional priests for every parish, Constitutional bishops for every diocese. It could thus divide the Church against itself; it prevented a unanimous uprising of religious fanaticism in which it would have foundered; and it gave itself time to render the essential part of its work unassailable and irrevocable.

III

THE GIRONDINS
(1791–1793)

*B*y *1791 what was left of the old political order in France was near collapse. The traditional upper class had lost its privileges and most of its prestige. Louis XVI, who had been caught fleeing the country in June 1791, was overthrown and imprisoned in August 1792 and executed in January 1793.*

Who governed in the new political order from 1791 to 1793? Historians agree that most power rested in the hands of the two successive legislative assemblies. But can one say more than that? Was there a party of like-minded deputies, the Girondins, who devised a common parliamentary strategy and attempted, often successfully, to shape and direct policy? Historians disagree.

Alphonse Aulard believes that there was a Girondin party composed of more than 160 deputies, that they grew more and more unified during the course of the Revolution, and that they differed little from the radical Montagnards except in their distrust and even hatred of a Parisian dictatorship.

Like Aulard, Albert Soboul thinks the Girondins resembled a political party, but, unlike Aulard, he thinks they were strikingly different from the Montagnards. The Girondins were much more circumscribed by their bourgeois upbringing and ideas, therefore less aware of the people's needs and less willing to satisfy them. This led to the downfall of the Girondins, because the Revolution needed popular support to triumph over its domestic and foreign enemies.

M. J. Sydenham argues, on the contrary, that no Girondin

party existed. He finds that the Montagnards were fairly well organized, but not the Girondins: no more than fifteen so-called Girondin deputies concerted their actions in the Convention; and more often than not, each of the fifteen went his own way.

Who is right or at least closest to the truth? Before answering this question one must define the word "party" and distinguish it from the terms "faction," "clique," and "collection of men." Then, too, one should pay close attention to the deductions the authors make from the evidence they offer. The "Girondin Problem" is a clear instance where a historian must be part semanticist and part logician.

A PARTY OF ANTI-PARISIAN REPUBLICANS*

Alphonse Aulard

Alphonse Aulard (1849–1928) was one of the first great professional historians of the French Revolution. The son of a secondary school administrator, he came from the provinces to Paris and attended the best French schools—the Lycée Louis-le-Grand and the École normale supérieure. He began his teaching in the field of literature, but his writings on the orators of the French Revolution led to his selection as the first holder of the Chair of the History of the French Revolution at the University of Paris, a professorship which he held from 1885 until his retirement in 1922. For more than forty years he wrote and edited work after work on the religious and political history of the Revolution, and he was especially zealous in publishing such documents of the period as the Acts of the Committee of Public Safety. From 1887 to 1928 he was also editor of the historical journal La Révolution française. *Many twentieth-century historians have questioned some of what Aulard—a bourgeois, anticlerical republican—had to say about the Revolution. Still, he has much to offer the present-day student, as this selection from his most widely read book indicates.*

Historians, rather than contemporaries, gave the collective name of the *Gironde* to the friends and followers of Brissot, Vergniaud, Mme. Roland, and Buzot. In the Legislative Assembly those deputies who sat on the left, below Chabot and Basire,

* Reprinted with the permission of Charles Scribner's Sons from pages 32–40, 42–43, 45–50, 52–55, 57–58, 71, from Volume III of *The French Revolution* (New York, 1910), by A. Aulard, translated by Bernard Miall.

called themselves the *Jacobin Patriots;* and their opponents called them derisively *Brissotins, Bordelais,* or the *Guadet-Brissot gang.* In the Convention they were still *Brissotins,* but *Rolandists, Buzotins* as well. Marat ironically called them the *Statesmen.* By *Girondists* we understand more particularly Vergniaud, Guadet, Gensonné, Grangeneuve, Ducos, Boyer-Fonfrède, Bergoeing, and Lacaze: all deputies of the department of the Gironde. Even at their trial the distinction was maintained between the Brissotins and the Girondists. Officially, their conquerors called them the *Federalists,* in order to justify, by a word, the violent procedure of June 2nd [1793]. I believe that Thiers and Charles Nodier [in the early nineteenth century] were responsible for the custom of calling Girondists the deputies from other departments than the Gironde, such as Brissot, Buzot, Barbaroux, and Petion. Since 1847 Lamartine's *History of the Girondists* has rendered this name so popular that in order to be understood one must use the term *Gironde* to denote the *Right* of the Convention, or even the *Left* of the Legislative Assembly.

The Girondist party dated, in fact, from the Legislative Assembly. It was Brissot who originally brought together Condorcet, Clavière, and Roland, and the deputies of the Gironde, and founded their alliance. "At the time of the convocation of the Legislative Assembly," he said at the Revolutionary Tribunal, "the deputies of the Gironde on arriving in Paris used to seek my friendship on account of my opinions respecting the Colonies.[1] We used to meet three times a week, before the hour at which the National Assembly opened its sessions." Very soon political breakfasts were held; almost daily indeed, at number 5 in the Place Vendôme, a few steps from the Manège, at the house of one Dame Dudon, "an honest woman, rich, who could, without inconveniencing herself, lend them a spacious room of which they were free to make use even in her absence."[2] There Étienne Dumont met Brissot, Clavière, Roederer, Guadet, Gensonné, Vergniaud, Ducos, Condorcet, and others whom he does not name, but among whom was Fauchet. "Roland, whose good sense and integrity were at this time greatly valued, was invited to attend; but he hardly ever did so, on account of the distance." The same cause made Gensonné's visits very irregular. "They came there before going on to the Assembly, argued upon their measures,

---

[1] Paganel says that Brissot and his followers were at first known as the "defenders of the black man."

[2] Mme. Roland's *Mémoires.*

and, as may be supposed, there was more chatter and party gossip than resolutions taken or procedure determined. Brissot was the practical man; his activity was equal to anything." [3]

Although Brissot was actually the leader and business man of this "Committee of the Place Vendôme," which was to provide Louis XVI with the Roland-Dumouriez Ministry, there were, at the time of the Legislative Assembly, other meetings of the same group under another presidency. Thus Gensonné, in his defence before the Revolutionary Tribunal, said that they met at Vergniaud's three times a week; and there, while debating, awaited the opening of the Assembly. Chabot, in his deposition before the same tribunal, spoke of meetings regularly held by "the faction" in the Rue d'Argenteuil, or at the house of Bernard (of Saintes). Again, the "Gironde" used to dine at Clavière's house; but these were literary rather than political meetings, at which the poet Lebrun *Pindarised*.[4] Petion, being mayor, gave dinners to his political friends, at which the company would seem to have been decidedly mixed, according to Étienne Dumont, who was astonished to see the Marquis de Condorcet rubbing shoulders with the *sans-culotte* Chabot.

Thus the Gironde was already a party at the convocation of the Convention. On December 31, 1792, Marat denounced it from the tribune, saying "that the folk of Roland's faction hold secret meetings at the Palais-Royal, number 248, in order to concert the means of dismissing Pache from the Ministry of War." At the beginning of 1793 Bouquey, brother-in-law to Guadet, nominated by Roland steward of the Château of Saint-Cloud, was in the habit of receiving at his house Brissot, Vergniaud, Gensonné, Petion, Buzot, and others. These meetings were held three times a week, according to an accusation signed by Fréron. Brissot had obtained from Bouquey apartments in the granary of the château. Denounced for this reason, he immediately left; but his wife continued to live at Saint-Cloud. It was evidently he who arranged their meetings out of Paris, which were surrounded by mystery by the ingenious caution and suspicion of the times.

At the height of their struggle against the Mountain the Girondists attempted to improve their party organisation. This was the "liberticide conspiracy" denounced by Marat on May 23,

---

[3] Étienne Dumont, *Souvenirs,* p. 374.
[4] *Ibid.,* p. 448.

1793. "The Committee of General Security," he said, "has been impressed by a circular letter, written by Dufriche-Valazé to Jacaze, in which he invites the latter to repair to the Convention with as many colleagues as possible—that is to say, *statesmen*. Every one knows that the directorate of the *statesmen* of the liberticide faction is established at the house of Dufriche-Valazé." To this Valazé replied: "This circular—I have written thirty-eight to forty similar ones—this circular ran as follows: *at the National Convention at ten in the morning with as many colleagues as possible*." And he explained that it was a question of filling the benches on the Right as a provision against an insurrection on the part of the sections. "Many of my colleagues," he added, "animated by the purest love of country, habitually meet at my house.[5] Surely we shall not be forbidden to hold friendly meetings, especially when their object is the defeat of conspiracy."

We find that some forty of the Girondists belonged to this "Valazé Committee"; about fifteen were present at the meetings, which were held nightly, according to Meillan; according to Valazé himself, three or four times a week; sometimes only once. The most assiduous were Brissot, Guadet, Gensonné, Buzot, Barbaroux, Bergoeing, Duprat, Lacaze, Lesage, Mollevaut, Hardy, Salle, Deperret, Chambon, Lidon. Their object was "to prepare the discussions" which were to take place in the Convention. Thus Louvet tells us, in his memoirs, that the "Valazé Committee" entrusted him with the delivery of a speech upon the popular movement of March 10, 1793.

It would seem that we have here one of the most serious attempts made at this period to create a party in the English sense of the word. Yet it was not until Marat came across one of their notices of convocation that the Girondists realised what they were doing. Some few months earlier, Brissot, in one of his pamphlets, wrote:

> No, you do not know those you are calumniating, you who accuse the Girondists of belonging to a faction. Guadet has too proud a spirit; Vergniaud possesses in too high a degree the indifference that goes with talent, and which forces it to stand alone; Ducos has too much wit and honesty; Gensonné is too profound a thinker, ever to stoop to fight under the banner of any chief. Certainly they have a centre, a focus; but it is the love of liberty and reason; they have ties, but they are those which unite fellow-workers

[5] No. 18, Rue d'Orléans-Saint-Honoré.

whose tastes are alike, in their simplicity and purity, and whose opinions are dictated by reflection.[6]

We were so little disposed [*said Meillan*] to form a party,[7] that the mere thought of a concerted measure revolted us. Each of us wished to be independent, and to shape his conduct after his own heart. We always hoped that the wise and truthful writings of some among us would suffice to enlighten the people, and above all we wished to avoid the reproach of forming a party. Instead of mutually binding ourselves together, we seemed to avoid one another; in a word, we had no points of contact but conformity of principle and love of the public good. These motives have necessarily made us act and speak in the same manner, but not in concert. Even at Caen, when we were only a few in number, our conduct had no uniformity except when we had no choice in the matter.

With greater reason they constantly refused to recognise a leader. Valazé himself, the "Cato of the Gironde," was the host and not the director of the Committee. As for Brissot, although he assiduously attended all meetings, from those of the Place Vendôme down to Valazé's political *soirées,* and although he undertook the management of practical affairs, and, at one period, directed his friends as far as they could be directed, his authority was neither avowed by himself, nor recognised by the very men who did nothing without consulting him.

Another influence, one which was continually increasing its hold on the Girondist party, and which finally became preponderant, was that of Mme. Roland. She herself confessed, in her memoirs, that during the two ministries of her husband she was his collaborator.

I did not [*she says*] meddle in administrative matters; but if it was a question of a circular letter, of instructions, of a public and important statement, we conferred on the matter with the mutual interdependence which had become a habit with us; and I, steeped in his ideas and nourished on my own, held the pen which I had more time than he to use.

It was she who drafted the public documents, and was responsible for the general political writings, which emanated in such numbers from her husband, and which may be read as

[6] *À tous les républicains de France,* p. 9.

[7] Boyer-Fonfrède said, in the Convention, on March 15, 1793: "I belong to no party; I refuse to belong to any man; I belong to my conscience and my country."

manifestoes of the Girondist party. Her influence was not merely secret. Twice a week she gave a dinner to Ministers and deputies, as she tells us in her memoirs. She admits that the company addressed themselves to her.

> It often happened that friends or colleagues who required to speak to the Minister in confidence, instead of seeking him at his work, where his clerks and the public surrounded him, would come to me and beg me to send then for him. I thus found myself in the stream of things without intrigue and without idle curiosity. Roland thenceforth had an understanding with me that he would discuss matters with me in private with the confidence which has always reigned between us, and which has made our knowledge and opinions in common. It also used to happen that friends who wished only to give information, to speak a word or two, being always sure of finding me, would come to me and ask me to tell him at the earliest possible moment.

This was well known. When the motion was proposed in the Convention to invite Roland to remain in the Ministry, on September 29, 1792, Danton said: "No one does Roland more justice than myself; but this I will say: If you invite him, invite Mme. Roland also; for every one knows that Roland was not alone in his department. As for me, I was alone in mine (*murmurs*)."

The importance of Mme. Roland's part in the Girondist party was due not only to the fact that she led her husband; it was also, and more especially, due to the fact that she influenced Buzot, to whom she was bound by a passionate love. Through Buzot she influenced Petion, and these two men turned against Robespierre, with whom they had formed a famous trio under the Constituent Assembly. Barbaroux and Guadet were under the spell. Brissot, who at the outset had organised Mme. Roland's influence, remained himself her subject. Vergniaud and Condorcet escaped it to a large extent. But when they considered their friend insulted by Danton, when they heard "Father Duchesne" [8] bullying her, they could no longer hold out against this woman, who inspired them not only with her dislikes and indignations, but also with a heroic stoicism, and the desire and the power to die nobly.

[8] [A reference to the radical journalist Jacques-René Hébert, editor of the newspaper *Père Duchesne (Father Duchesne)*.]

At the end of their career, in the desperate moments of their struggle against the Mountain, when nothing was left for them but a worthy death, they gathered all the more around her who never trembled; who never counselled cowardly, nor even prudent transactions; who, her head full of Plutarch and of Rousseau, taught them to smile at death, and saved them at need from the secret anguish of their hearts. It was for these reasons that in supreme moments the memory of Mme. Roland was for the Girondists a religion which united them; some until the scaffold, some until their final dispersal. They loved one another through her; they call themselves, in their memoirs, *the friends,* as if their association were sentimental rather than political. For posterity, as for contemporaries, the Girondists were a party led by a woman.

Personal statistics of the Girondists are not easy to establish. The roll-calls of the trial of Louis XVI give us no information in this respect, since the Girondists were not agreed upon the penalty to be inflicted, nor even upon the appeal to the people. The roll-call which took place during the session of April 13 and 14, 1793, when the question of Marat's impeachment was before the Assembly, tells us that out of 360 voters 220 voted for the decree of accusation; 92 voted against it; 41 declared they had no feeling in the matter; 7 demanded an adjournment. But are we to conclude that there were 220 Girondists in the Convention? No; for the Centre voted with the Gironde. On the other hand, at this time a large number of members were away "on mission"; so that this roll-call gives us no definitive information relating to the respective strength of the two parties. We find more important data for the statistics of the party in the decree of June 2, 1793, which ordered the arrest of 29 deputies; in that of July 28, by which 20 deputies were declared traitors to the country; and in that of October 3, by which 41 deputies were betrayed to the Revolutionary Tribunal, and 75[9] put under arrest, as signatories to protests against the doings of May 31st and June 2nd. In all 129 deputies were affected by these measures: for many of the names figure in all three decrees. Other deputies were the object of measures of individual punishment, or signed protests, or publicly expressed their sympathy for those proscribed; and it seems to me that these deputies, who numbered some 36, might

[9] On account of two printer's errors in the list of these 75 as published in the journals, these deputies have been called the 73.

and should be classed among the Girondists. To sum up, we find that of 165 deputies we may say, without much chance of error, that they were all members of the Gironde. . . .

As a matter of sober fact the forces of this party were not concentrated in a definite and particular district. In May, 1793, there were Girondists in almost all quarters. They were least numerous in the north-east, and in the ancient Ile de France. They were most numerous in Provence, Guyenne, Limousin, Brittany, Normandy, and Picardy—in the south and the north-west. But in none of these regions (in so far as they were represented by certain groups of departments) did they form the majority of the national representation. They were even in the minority in all the departments save eight; the Gironde, Somme, Seine-Inférieure, Aisne, Haute-Vienne, Ardèche, Finistère, and the Jura. Nowhere, not even in the Gironde, did they number all the representatives; this latter department sent to the Convention, together with eight "Girondists," two Montagnards—Garrau and Jay (of Saint-Foy); and two of indefinite colour—Duplantier and Deleyre. Buzot's department, Eure, was represented by six Montagnards and five Girondists; and Brissot's, Eure-et-Loir, by five Montagnards and four Girondists; Barbaroux', the Bouches-du-Rhône, by seven Montagnards and five Girondists. On the other hand, some Girondists were returned by the Jacobin departments; in Meurthe, the Vosges, Indre-et-Loire, Seine-et-Oise, and in Paris. No Girondist deputy was returned by any of the following twenty-eight departments: Allier, Ardennes, Ariège, Cantal, Cher, Côte-d'Or, Creuse, Dordogne, Doubs, Isère, Loir-et-Cher, Lot-et-Garonne, Lozère, Marne, Haute-Marne, Mayenne, Meuse, Mont-Blanc, Mont-Terrible, Nièvre, Nord, Hautes-Pyrénées, Bas-Rhin, Haut-Rhin, Haute-Saône, Seine-et-Marne, Vendée, and Vienne.

It is not easy to perceive precisely how the Girondists, in the matter of principles and essential ideas, differed from the Montagnards. In reading their speeches, their pamphlets, and their journals, one can distinguish scarcely any difference between their ideals and their respective faiths. In religion, the Girondists were deists; some after the fashion of Voltaire, some after the fashion of Jean-Jacques Rousseau. Nearly all lived the lives of philosophers. Concerning the attitude of many of the Girondists at the moment of death we have the testimony of the Abbé Lothringer, who, in a letter published by the *Républicain français* of the 6th of *Fructidor* in the year V [August 23, 1797], relates how he attended on the Girondists condemned by the

Revolutionary Tribunal. Lothringer confessed Fauchet, who in turn confessed Sillery. Others, Lauze-Deperret, Gardien, Lesterpt-Beauvais, Lehardi, Viger, also confessed; but it was otherwise with the flower of the Girondists, with Brissot, Vergniaud, Carra, Ducos, Boyer-Fonfrède; these did not confess. But, on the other hand, we do not find that the leaders of the Mountain, Danton and Robespierre, had recourse to a priest before death. . . .

Were the Girondists, then, atheists? By no means. Vergniaud, in his speech on the war (January 17, 1792), had urged the patriots "not to neglect the occasion *that Providence afforded them.*" Brissot and Louvet, in their memoirs, incessantly invoke "Divinity," "Providence," and "the just God." Brissot also proclaims himself a deist in his memoirs.

They differed from Robespierre in this: Robespierre accepted intact the "civil religion" of Rousseau, with all its dogmas, and was doubtless already dreaming of making it the national religion of France; the Girondists accepted only the dogma of the existence of God, and it is obvious that their deism was only a denial of the God of the Catholic Church. In this they differed from Robespierre only, and not from the Montagnards, among whom Couthon alone perhaps was addicted to dreams of a State religion, and the cult of the Supreme Being, which haunted the imagination of Robespierre.

One might perhaps say that the Girondists had a religious policy which was more elevated but less impassioned than that of the Montagnards. In the Legislative Assembly Gensonné seemed to own as his ideal the separation of Church and State (see his speech of November 3, 1791), and Guadet stated that it was necessary "to become accustomed to separate religion from the Constitution" (see his speech of November 25th). Ducos had even stated, on October 26th preceding: ". . . I believe I have solved the problem; separate from all that concerns the State all that concerns religion." Bancal des Issards, the friend of Mme. Roland, was an ardent advocate of the secularising of public education, and his proposed decree of December 24, 1792, excluded the clergy and religion from the schools. Generally speaking, perhaps, the idea of a secular State, which so far was by no means popular, was conceived and adopted by the Girondists more unanimously and more promptly than by the Montagnards. But we are dealing here with "fine shades"; in essentials I can perceive no difference between the religious opinions of the Girondists and those of the Montagnards in general; I can only see it between the religious opinions of the Girondists and Robespierre in particular.

Did they differ from their adversaries in matters of politics proper? The Montagnards accused them of royalism. In the accusation which the Committee of General Security launched against them in the person of Amar, on October 3, 1793, we read: "They were republicans under the monarchy and royalists under the Republic." Some of them—Brissot, Condorcet, and Paine—were republicans under the monarchy. Under the Republic it was Buzot who was responsible for the decree of December 4, 1792, which punished with death all proposals to re-establish the monarchy. It is impossible to find evidence of a single word, action, or line written, performed, or spoken by the Girondists in the period from August 10, 1792, to June 2, 1793, which tends, even indirectly, to favour royalty. The Girondists gained over to their party the most illustrious of the founders of the Republic: Condorcet. Even during the time of the civil war, in June and July, 1793, their leaders, as a whole, refused to form a compact with the royalists. At Caen, Petion suddenly broke up the meeting at which General Wimpffen, throwing off the mask, proposed to ask England for a king.

> I could have wished [*he says in his Mémoires*] that the cowards who slandered us so perfidiously, and who, in the depths of their hearts, did us justice, might have been present at this meeting, and indeed at all our conferences, even our most secret gatherings; they would have been able to judge whether the Republic had any more zealous supporters.

As good republicans as the Montagnards, were they less democratic? The projected Constitution presented by Condorcet was fully as democratic as that which was later known as the Montagnard Constitution. It has been said that the Girondins were in favour of an aristocracy of talent. True; it is possible that they hoped to see a dictatorship of persuasion, a Periclean tyranny. But was not this the very idea of Robespierre? They dreamed, it has been said, of an Athenian republic, while the Montagnards dreamed of a Spartan republic. These are phrases: the words and actions of Danton, of Robespierre, of Saint-Just, of Barère, prove that they were all equally anxious to embellish the Republic by means of the arts as were, or had been, Vergniaud, Condorcet, or Mme. Roland. But we must understand that when the people of Paris applauded *Père Duchesne* for representing

Mme. Roland as a toothless hag, when they became sensible that their party was unpopular in Paris because it was directed by a woman, the Girondists came little by little to have a horror of the mob. The populace was pure and intelligent in 1792, when it applauded the Girondists; in 1793, now that it hissed them, "its *morale* had been entirely perverted." [10] They had not the art of leading the people by speaking to its conscience; and one of them spoke more truly than he knew, when he said ironically of his adversaries: "It must be granted that they have understood better than we the mass of the people whom they govern; its character, its particular genius, and the degree of energy and of enlightenment of which it is capable." [11] Save Petion and Brissot, who were perhaps the least aristocratic of them all, contact with the people embarrassed and disgusted them, almost without exception towards the end of their career. See how Buzot, during his proscription, speaks of the popular deputations:

> I know how necessary it was to be patient; but a thousand times I was taken by surprise with the longing to blow out the brains of some of these monsters. Great God, what deputations they were! It was as though some one had searched through all the gutters of Paris and the great cities for all that was most hideous, foulest, and most noisome. Villainous, filthy faces, black, or the colour of leather, surmounted by great mops of greasy hair, with eyes sunk half-way through their heads, they filled the place with their nauseating breath, giving vent to the grossest insults, and screaming like carnivorous beasts.[12]

Doubtless Mme. Roland was in part responsible for, or at least had accentuated, this egoistical delicacy, these shrinkings of a distinguished refinement. She extolled an ideal people, who had nothing in common with the real people, who scoffed brutally at these hyperæsthetic manners. It was easy for the Montagnards (although their manners were as *bourgeois* as those of the Girondists) to represent such people of refinement as enemies of the people. The Girondists were labelled and lost by the aristocratic quality of their attitude, of their tastes, almost of their skins. We may say that although their ideas were as democratic as those of the Montagnards, their manners were not.

It is a commonplace saying that the Montagnards were

[10] Buzot's *Mémoires.*
[11] Buzot's *Mémoires.*
[12] Buzot.

bloodthirsty, while the Girondists were merciful. [The nineteenth-century man of letters] Sainte-Beuve, speaking of the friends of Mme. Roland, salutes "these noble figures; humane, of a fine moral balance; who one and all halted, from a Divine instinct and with a cry of pity, upon the shores of the river of blood." [13] This is a legend. I do not know that the Girondists were not the first to have recourse to the guillotine. It was the Girondist Isnard who, in the Legislative Assembly, on October 31, 1791, expounded the idea that it was necessary to kill the enemies of liberty, and he resumed the subject in these terms on November 14th following: "In matters of political liberty to pardon a crime is almost to share it. (*Applause.*) Such rigour may result in blood being shed, I know; but if you do not employ it, will not still more be shed? Would not civil war be a still greater disaster? The gangrened part must be excised to save the rest of the body." It was Isnard again who, a few days later (November 29th), let fall these terrible words: "By the word 'responsibility' we understand death." On December 26, 1791, Gensonné demanded the maintenance of the Constitution *or death*. It was Barbaroux who sketched the first idea of the law of suspects, when he cried, on September 26, 1792: "I demand that every person who despairs of the safety of the Republic shall be punished by death." On December 4, 1792, Buzot obtained the vote of the death penalty against royalty.

Never did the Girondists propose the true test of clemency: the abolition of the death penalty in matters political. On the contrary: Condorcet declared to the Convention, on January 19, 1793: "Abolish the death penalty for all private misdemeanours, while reserving your decision as to whether it must be kept for offences against the State; because in that case the question is different; considerations enter into it which cannot be weighed otherwise." And in a speech on February 23rd he says that the death penalty is abolished for private misdemeanours, but that it must still be maintained for political offences; and he confines himself to recommending that it should be applied rarely and not unscrupulously. Lastly, Boyer-Fonfrède, on June 17, 1793, while his friends were in prison, demanded the abolition of the death penalty, *except in political matters*.

It was the Girondist Petion who first formally declared that defeated parties should perish. "I wish," he said at the session of

[13] Introduction to Mme. Roland's *Lettres . . . adressées à Bancal des Issards*, p. xxi.

April 12, 1793, "that one might begin by writing accusations, that the replies should be written, and that every one should submit to risk his head that those of the guilty might fall." When, at last, the first to break the *talisman of inviolability*, the Girondists sent Marat before the Revolutionary Tribunal, did they not believe that they were sending him to his death?

There is no doubt that the Girondists execrated the September massacres, which the Jacobin Club and many of the Montagnards justified. But what was the date of this difference of opinion? . . . At the outset their impressions and opinions of the massacres of September were the same as those of the Montagnards; then, by policy, they began to wax indignant over the massacres, and brought them up against their adversaries. These tactics have to a certain extent deceived posterity, which has beheld in the Girondists the party of clemency and humanity. In sober reality the Girondists, face to face with bloodshed, in the presence of the people killing its enemies, felt no more indignation than did the Montagnards.

What was the real object of the quarrel between the Girondists and the Montagnards? You are Federalists, said the Montagnards to the Girondists, while we stand for the Republic one and indivisible. The Girondists protested loudly against this accusation.[14] Was it not one of the most important among them, Barbaroux, who, in the electoral assembly of the Bouches-du-Rhône, had definitely condemned the "federative type of government"? Could we cite a single Girondist responsible for a federalist action, or manifesting federalist tendencies? Who, then, did preach Federalism to France? Was it not two Montagnards, Billaud-Varenne in 1791 and Lavicomterie in 1793? We read in Buzot's *Mémoires*:

> I am not attempting to conceal my opinions. The Republic was only possible in France (supposing we had possessed the moral

[14] In November, 1792, in a pamphlet entitled *Neither Marat nor Roland*, Anarcharsis Clootz declared: "The royalists and the federalists are about to excite the secret jealousy of the principalities against the *great city*, by insinuating that Paris wants to be *King of France*. They conclude therefrom naturally that the House of Bourbon is preferable to a communal building, and that federalism is better than subjection." And he accused, by name, Roland, Kersaint, Guadet, and Brissot of being federalists. Roland, in reply, declared himself an upholder of the "sole Republic." Kersaint said: "I uphold the unity of the Republic." Guadet protested also, almost in the same words. Brissot said: "In two words, my system is this: unity of the departments of France, extension to the limits prescribed by nature; beyond that, a girdle of federative republics, not a universal republic."

qualities we lacked) in a form closely resembling the government of the United States. But never did either our actions or our speeches suggest any attempt to naturalise the American government in France.

That is to say, Buzot had a theoretical preference for Federalism, but he did nothing to realise it. If we are to believe Mme. Roland's *Mémoires,* he owned to this preference in private; and an English friend of the Girondists, Miss Helena Williams, writes as follows:

> I have often been present at conversations between Vergniaud and Lasource on this subject; they saw too late the folly and danger of an indivisible republic composed of a people which professed itself republican the moment it had escaped from slavery. . . . My opinion is that the Girondists hoped for good results from the immediate and local action of small federative republics, hoped to form and elevate the people, to enlighten it, and to inspire it with sentiments more consistent with the duration of its political rights. They often spoke of republics bounded by the course of the Loire and the Rhône, having Lyons or Bordeaux as their centre.

I do not know how much of this is true. But two things are certain: it was at the outset that the Girondists passed as Federalists; it was afterwards that they continually declared themselves partisans of the unitarian Republic.

And this is the essential difference, or rather the only real difference, between the Montagnards and the Girondists: the former wished to see Paris provisionally, during the war, at the head of the united Republic, as the ruling capital; the latter, on the contrary, did not wish Paris to exert any supremacy over the departments, even in war-time. This was the actual cause of the quarrel. . . .

Fear and hatred of a Parisian dictatorship was the ruling characteristic of this group, which differed from the Mountain not in principles, but in its conception of the part that the capital was to play in an invaded and disorganised France. . . .

Such were the organisation, the programme, and the personalities of the Girondist party; a party more or less indefinite about the edges, but which presently grew more definite and more compact; until at the end of its normal career, in May, 1793, it was almost unified. In any case, it was certainly a party.

A PARTY OF INCOMPETENT BOURGEOIS*

Albert Soboul

Albert Soboul (1914–   ), a carpenter's son, was born in Algeria and attended the École normale supérieure in the 1930's. He gained a reputation as the leading French Marxist historian of the French Revolution with the publication, in 1958, of Les Sans-culottes parisiens en l'an II *(of which there is a condensation in English:* The Parisian Sans-Culottes and the French Revolution, 1793–1794). *The result of years of careful archival research, the work is a very long, detailed political and sociological study of this group of wage-earners, artisans, and shopkeepers; and it probes more deeply into their aims and lives than any earlier account. Among his other works are* La Révolution française *(1964) and* Paysans, Sans-culottes et Jacobins *(1966). At present he is Professor of History at the University of Clermont-Ferrand and an editor of the journal* Annales historiques de la Révolution française.

Journalists, lawyers, teachers, the *Brissotins* formed the second revolutionary generation. Most often coming from the middle bourgeoisie, they were in contact with the big business bourgeoisie of the maritime ports—Bordeaux, Nantes, and Marseille—a bourgeoisie of shipowners, bankers, and merchants whose interests they defended. If their origin and their philosophical schooling inclined them toward political democracy, their contacts and their temperament tended to make them respect wealth and serve it. . . .

* From Albert Soboul, *Précis d'histoire de la Révolution française* (Paris: Éditions sociales, 1962), pp. 189, 225–228, 256. This selection is printed by permission of the publisher. Editors' translation.

In the National Convention of 1792, there were no organized parties but rather political groups with imprecise limits which followed two general staffs—the Girondins and the Montagnards. Essentially, differing class interests led them to oppose each other.

On the Right was the Gironde, the party upholding respect for law, which loathed the revolutionary measures initiated by the Paris Commune (staffed by Montagnards and militant activists of the sections). It represented the well-to-do commercial and industrial bourgeoisie who intended to defend property and economic liberty against the restrictions demanded by the sans-culottes. In the political domain, the Gironde continued to oppose all emergency measures which the public safety required. It had triggered the war, but was unwilling to take the steps necessary to win it. Against the concentration of power [in Paris] and the strict subordination of the different branches of administration [to the Convention], the Gironde invoked the support of local authorities among whom the moderate bourgeoisie was dominant. In the economic domain, tied to the business bourgeoisie and distrusting the people, the Gironde passionately upheld economic liberty, free enterprise, and unrestricted profits, while it opposed strict controls, price-fixing, the requisitioning of goods, and the forced circulation of assignats, all measures that the sans-culottes, on the other hand, favored. Imbued with a sense of social hierarchy that they intended to preserve and strengthen, considering the right of property as an inviolable natural right, completely espousing the interests of the bourgeois property owner, the Girondins felt an instinctive dislike for the people, whom they regarded as incapable of governing. The power to govern they reserved for their own class.

On the Left, the Mountain represented the middle bourgeoisie and the lower classes, artisans, shopkeepers, consumers, those who suffered from the war and its consequences—the high cost of living, unemployment, and insufficient wages. Though originally coming from the bourgeoisie, the Mountain understood that France's critical situation demanded extraordinary solutions that could be successful only with popular support. Therefore, it allied with the sans-culottes who had overthrown the monarchy and who had achieved a political role by insurrection. Realistic because it was closer to the people and their needs, the Mountain was less encumbered by theories and knew how to make the public interest come before private interests. In the interest of the people—the only loyal support of the Revolution—it was willing to restrict the free use of private property and curtail individual liberty. The leaders of the Mountain, mostly deputies from Paris, knew the decisive role the people of the capital had played in the first revolution of 1789, as well as in the second revolution of August 10, 1792. They rebelled against the pretensions of the Girondins who, in their fear of the revolutionary masses, wanted to reduce the influence of Paris "to an eighty-third part, like any one of the other departments," which was just what the deputy Lasource had called for on September 25, 1792.

In his *Appeal to all French Republicans, Concerning the Paris Jacobin Society,* dated October 1792, which characterized the Jacobins and the Montagnards as "anarchists who control and dishonor the Parisian Jacobin society," Brissot wrote: "The disrupters are those who want to equalize everything—property, comfort, food prices, the different duties owed to society."

In the first issue of the *Letters to his Constituents,* on September 30, 1792, Robespierre had already replied to this: "Royalty has been abolished; the nobility and clergy have disappeared. The reign of equality begins." He attacked the false patriots "who wish to set up the Republic only for themselves, who intend to govern only in the interests of the rich and the government officials." He contrasted them with the true patriots "who will seek to found the Republic on the principles of equality and the general interest."

The leaders of the Mountain, especially the Jacobins, strove to give the concept of the nation a positive meaning capable of rallying the masses. In this respect, the evolution of Saint-Just is significant. In *The Spirit of the Revolution and the French Constitution,* which was published in 1791, while he was still not quite free from Montesquieu's influence, Saint-Just wrote, "Where there is no law, there is no country. That is why people living under a despotism have no country except when they scorn or hate other nations."

Going beyond this banal eighteenth-century theme of the identity between country and liberty, Saint-Just on November 29, 1792, in his speech about the food supply, identified country and happiness; here again there was no great originality: "An unhappy people has no country." But he went further when he stressed that in order to found the Republic, "the people must be pulled out of a state of insecurity and wretchedness that corrupts them." Denouncing "the haphazard issuance of tokens," that is, of assignats, he said to the deputies of the Convention, "You can in an instant give [*the French people*] a country"—by halting the ravages of inflation, by assuring the people a means of livelihood, and therefore by binding "closely their happiness and their liberty." Robespierre was even clearer in his speech on December 2, 1792, concerning the grain riots in the department of Eure-et-Loir: by subordinating the right of property to the right of existence, he laid down the theoretical foundation for a nation enlarged to include its masses:

> The authors of the [laissez-faire] theory have considered the food-stuffs most necessary to life as merely ordinary merchandise. They have made no distinction between the wheat trade and the indigo trade. They have discoursed more on the grain trade than on the people's subsistence. . . . They laid great stress on the profits of merchants or landholders; they have hardly considered men's lives. . . . The first of all rights is to exist. Therefore the first law of society is that which guarantees every member of society the means of existence. All others are subordinate to that one.

But as the necessities of the war and their national spirit pushed the Montagnards toward the sans-culottes, the class spirit of the Girondins moved them farther away from the latter, all the while entangling them even more in their own contradictions. The Gironde had declared war; but it feared that turning to the people—which was indispensable in combatting the aristocracy and the foreign coalition—would result in compromising the preponderance of the "haves." It refused to offer any concessions. On December 8, 1792, Roland had free trade in grain reestablished after Barbaroux had denounced those "who want laws prejudicial to property." On March 13, 1793, Vergniaud underscored even more strongly the class bases of Girondin politics by denouncing lower-class conceptions on matters of liberty and equality: "The only equality for man in society is that of equal rights." Vergniaud continued: "It no more concerns equality of wealth than that of height, of strength, of the mind, of energy, of diligence, and of work." This was tantamount to maintaining the primacy of property and wealth. Is this Girondin nostalgia for a nation organized according to wealth? . . . At the very least it shows a distrust of the people.

The rivalry between the Gironde and the Mountain therefore took on the appearance of a class conflict. True, most of the Montagnards were, like the Girondins, of bourgeois origin.

But the needs of national and revolutionary defense forced them to follow a political course favoring the masses, a politics of principle for some, a politics of expediency for others. . . .

[In the coup of May 31–June 2, 1793], the Gironde perished. It had declared war, but had not known how to conduct it. It had denounced the king, but had flinched before condemning him to death. It had demanded the people's support against the monarchy, but had refused to govern with them. It had played a part in aggravating the economic crisis, but had rejected all popular demands. Together with the Mountain, for whom the public safety was the supreme law, the sans-culottes achieved power. The Days of May 31 to June 2, in this sense, do not assume simply a political significance: they constitute a national reflex as much as a revolutionary shock, a defensive and punitive reaction against a new manifestation of the aristocratic conspiracy. The development of the *federalist movement* in the departments revealed in advance the significance of these days: under the cover of the Girondin opposition, the aristocratic counter-revolution retook the offensive.

Jean Jaurès, in his *Socialist History,* has denied the class character of the Days of May 31 to June 2. To be sure, if we confine ourselves to their political and parliamentary aspect, the Girondins and Montagnards both came from the bourgeoisie (although the nuances would have to be clarified). But the elimination of the upper bourgeoisie, the entrance on stage of the sans-culottes, gave these days their total social significance: Georges Lefebvre could even speak of the *revolution of May 31 and June 2, 1793.*

INDIVIDUALISTIC
POLITICIANS*

M. J. Sydenham

*M. J. Sydenham is Principal Lecturer in History at the
City of Portsmouth College of Education in Great Britain. He is the author of a monograph,* The Girondins *(1961),
which was originally written as a doctoral dissertation at the
University of London and is an example of the kind of work
such English scholars as Lewis Namier have excelled in: the
study of political history by analyzing the behavior of a large
number of politicians rather than concentrating attention and
research on a few of their leaders. The results often challenge
established points of view. Sydenham has also written* The
French Revolution *(1965), a history for the general reader incorporating much recent research.*

. . . Neither general histories nor monographic studies have
so far produced any adequate investigation of the deputies in the
Convention who are commonly called the Girondins. Those
who have written the history of the Revolution as a whole have
most often been interested in the rise of the Jacobins and the
events which culminated in the triumph of Robespierre in June
1793. This concentration of attention has magnified the distor-
tions caused by the tendency to treat all Robespierre's opponents
as if they were a united party, and to identify them with policies
which are really deduced from the historians' own interpretations

* From M. J. Sydenham, *The Girondins* (London: The Athlone Press, University of London, 1961), pp. 1–2, 39, 43–44, 72–74, 98, 185–192, 198, 205–206,
207–208. This selection has been reprinted by permission of the author and
the publisher.

of the whole course of the Revolution rather than from a study of what the so-called Girondins said or did. On the other hand, for more detailed researchers the career of Robespierre has become so symbolic of the triumph and atrophy of the Revolution that the fate of his opponents has tended to be treated as a side-issue, and therefore neglected.

Successive historians have thus put forward a series of contradictory generalizations about these opponents of Robespierre. Radical writers have regarded them as men who unconsciously served the royalist cause, moderates have seen them as liberal republicans or as constitutional monarchists, and those of royalist sympathies have thought them indistinguishable in violence and ambition from the Jacobins. At the same time, even hostile writers, catching the echoes of the Girondins' oratory and considering the drama of their downfall, have been tempted to colour history with romance and so have made them in some sort legendary figures—symbols, perhaps, of the persistent weakness and repeated failures of moderation in France.

Two consequences have followed from this prolonged variation of view. One is the general acceptance of the belief that the Convention, summoned in the early autumn of 1792 to provide France with another new constitution but primarily concerned with domestic disorganization and the imminence of foreign invasion, was from its inauguration distracted by the strife of two opposing parties, the Girondins and the Jacobins or Montagnards, strife which was only ended when in the spring of 1793 the triumph of the Jacobins cleared the way for the effective reorganization of France. The second consequence is that confusion still prevails about the nature of the Girondin party and the reasons for its conflict with the Jacobins. A complete reassessment of the position through a detailed investigation of the deputies concerned is therefore necessary. . . .

The conception of the Girondins as a large and integrated party, apparently derived in part from Jacobin propaganda, has been fostered also by the deceptive ease with which a list of "party supporters" can be compiled from the names of those whom the Montagnards proscribed. . . .

The use of the proscription lists to establish *previous* party membership is in fact essentially unsound. It either presents a picture of a party at the very time when it had for all practical

purposes ceased to exist—if, indeed, it had ever existed at all—
or it simply confuses opposition to the Mountain at one time
with opposition to it at another. . . .

The first question that ought to be asked is one that has
hitherto been completely neglected in practice: is the fact that
a deputy was proscribed by the Montagnards after 2 June 1793
in itself sufficient proof that he had been a member of a Girondin party before that date? If it is not, then a similar question
must be asked about the particular reasons for his proscription,
and about any other reasons historians have given for his inclu-
sion in their lists.

The answer to the main question is a simple negative. If the
fact that a man was proscribed by the Montagnards is to be
regarded as proof that he was a Girondin, then the word Girondin is nothing more than a term of negation, applicable to all
those who in any way incurred the Montagnards' displeasure.
While this may possibly prove to be the only meaning that can
be attached to the name, it does not provide any reason why the
200 deputies named by the historians should be regarded as a
distinct party. Still less acceptable is the totalitarian doctrine
that all opponents of a dominant party must of necessity be
counter-revolutionaries, whose actions are by hypothesis precon-
certed. That the Jacobins did their best to propagate this idea
cannot excuse its disregard of individuality, of time and of circumstance.

Moreover, the assumption that all who opposed the Revolution of 2 June, by which the twenty-nine deputies were arrested,
must have been their associates and supporters before that date
is also fundamentally unsound. It disregards the essential fact
that a revolution had taken place, in which a minority had
triumphed over a majority and legal forms had been beaten
down by armed might. Many deputies, perhaps even some who
would have welcomed Montagnard leadership if it had been
brought about by other means, may have been alienated from
the Mountain by the methods which were employed on that
occasion. Proscription for subsequent hostility to the Mountain
need not imply previous support for the arrested men: it may
equally well indicate a sincere and disinterested dislike of a
coup d'état and of the violation of the Convention, the sacrosanct
assembly which embodied the sovereignty of the people. After
the insurrection, support for its victims and opposition to those
who had triumphed by force naturally became synonymous,

but resistance after the event is no criterion of earlier association with a hypothetical Girondin party.

For these reasons proscription alone cannot be accepted here as any proof of party membership, and the particular reason for the classification of the 200 deputies must be considered in greater detail. . . .

[It is true that] a group of friends, interested in politics before the Revolution, continued and extended their association in active political life during the days of the National Assembly. In the Legislative Assembly, they formed new friendships and acquired influence, some of their number becoming ministers and others being leaders of debate. In the Convention, many of them were among the principal opponents of Robespierre and the Mountain. Since almost half of those arrested on 2 June were of their number, a "connection" can be said to have existed among the deputies who were purged on that occasion.

This, however, does not necessarily imply that the group formed a considerable body of united opinion, or that it was in any way unusual. . . . The number of those concerned is small in comparison with the 200 names derived from the proscription lists. Amongst these deputies, differing degrees of intimacy and varying periods of association certainly existed, and no common policy towards any specific political problem has yet emerged.[1]

Moreover, the essential unity of the group even in terms of personal relationships is debatable. Where Dulaure, writing in January 1793, considered that the names "girondins," "brissotins" and "rolandins" referred to the same group of deputies, Paganel's historical essay of 1810 distinguished the "Girondins" from the "Rolandins," and Ellery, a recent biographer of Brissot,

---

[1] Cp. Roland's reply to the allegation that he had plotted with the Brissotins: "I have no belief in this supposed faction. I know and esteem Brissot, but his opinions are not always mine" (13 September 1792, *Moniteur*, XIII, 670). [The abbreviations used by the author to designate his sources are the following:

B.M.	British Museum.
Brissot	J.-P. Brissot, *Mémoires*, ed. C. Perroud (2 vols.; Paris, 1904).
Jacobins	Alphonse Aulard (ed.), *La Société des Jacobins* (6 vols.; Paris, 1889–1897).
Journal	*Journal des Débats de la Société des Amis de la Constitution séante aux Jacobins* (Paris, June 2, 1791–December 14, 1793).
La Vie chère	Albert Mathiez, *La Vie chère et le mouvement social sous la Terreur* (Paris, 1927).
Moniteur	*Réimpression de l'ancien Moniteur* (31 vols.; Paris, 1854).]

separates those whom he regards as "Brissotins" from a more active and impetuous group whom he calls the "Buzotins." [2] The evidence . . . seems to show that the mesh of associations between Brissot, Roland, the deputies from the Gironde and those from Marseilles, was so close-woven that no clear distinction can be made between the friends and acquaintances of any of these men, although these four separate nuclei are clearly apparent in the development of the connection.

A further comment, from incidental evidence, is also relevant: even among the 200 deputies . . . there were many other small circles of friends. Several deputies, some of whom have appeared as friends of Brissot or his associates, shared living accommodation with others from the same Departmental delegation as themselves, and in these circumstances there is a strong presumption that common interests and friendships would have united these deputies closely. The existence of other and more important groups is also apparent. One of these probably centred on Grégoire. He was admired by Cazeneuve, by Audrein and by La Revellière-Lépeaux, to name no others.[3] A second group, possibly composed more of admirers than of friends, is apparent around Condorcet. In addition to his relationships with Brissot and Clavière, he was closely associated with Jean Debry and Tom Paine, and probably with Fauchet and Rabaut St. Étienne as well, apart from possible connections with the Montagnards.[4]

The fact that at least one deputy in each of these separate groups was friendly with one or more of Brissot's friends suggests a way in which Brissot could have built up a considerable connection. No evidence has as yet appeared, however, to show that these various groups can be considered as one, or that anyone of importance ever essayed to weld them into a coherent whole. Brissot himself, who said on one occasion that he always loved

[2] Dulaure, *Physionomie de la Convention nationale* (Paris, 1793), B.M., F.R.61.28; Paganel, *Essai historique*, II, 344, and III, 37–8; Ellery, *Brissot de Warville*, p. 420.

[3] T. Lemas, "Ignaze de Cazeneuve," *La Révolution française*, XVIII (1890), p. 332; Hémon, *Audrein, Yves-Marie*, introduction; La Revellière-Lépeaux, *Mémoires*, I, p. 157; Bougler, *Mouvement provincial en 1789 et biographies des députés de l'Anjou*, p. 177 and *passim*.

[4] Pingaud, *Jean de Bry*, p. 9; Conway, *Life of Thomas Paine*, II, p. 48; J. Charrier, *Claude Fauchet*, I, p. 149; Mirabaud, *Rabaut St. Étienne*, pp. 63, 211; Alengry, *Condorcet, guide de la Révolution française*, pp. 174–5, 198–203; Cahen, *Condorcet et la Révolution française*, pp. 457 and 381.

to introduce his friends one to another, yet said later—but before his fall—that he scarcely knew forty members of the Convention and was only intimate with three or four truly enlightened friends.[5] The only legitimate conclusion from the evidence is that, in the absence of organized parties, personal friendships were a common and natural form of political association. What may perhaps best be described as the groups of the Brissotin connection were by no means an isolated phenomenon. It remains to be seen whether they should be regarded as groups of friends in only a personal or the vaguest political sense, or whether they ever endeavoured to formulate and effect any particular policies. An answer to this question may first be sought in an investigation of the "secret meetings" for which they became notorious. . . .

The evidence suggests that the salons and the club [to which the so-called Girondins belonged] existed rather in succession than simultaneously. If their periods of probable maximum importance are considered, a series emerges fairly clearly, i.e., Madame Roland's first salon (February to September 1791), Vergniaud's salon (mid-autumn 1791 to September 1792), Madame Roland's second salon (March to June 1792), the Reunion Club (June to October 1792), Madame Roland's third salon (August 1792 to January 1793) and Valazé's salon (December 1792 to May 1793). Further, analysis of the names of those who can be shown to have been present at these meetings shows that Brissot and Gensonné were present at all four of them, and that a limited but increasing number of deputies met together with these two fairly regularly over a period of about eighteen months. These conclusions are interesting supplementary evidence of the development of a "connection" around Brissot and his closest friends.

The evidence about these "secret meetings of the Girondins" does not, however, afford sufficient ground to show that the connection ever formulated or tried to effect any policy more specific than that of resistance to Robespierre and the Montagnards. This defensive attitude is apparent even in the alleged preparations by Vergniaud and his friends of their attacks upon the "Austrian Committee," and thereafter it becomes ever more obvious. Further, all the evidence indicates that the men who

[5] *Brissot*, I, 176, and *J. P. Brissot . . . sur la dénonciation de Robespierre* (Paris, 1793), B.M., F.675.9.

attended these assemblies remained independent both in thought and in action. Perpetual indecision and persistent individualism appear to be the hall-marks of their private meetings. . . .

The negative conclusion to this attempt to find some distinguishing characteristic or bond of unity among the 200 without reference to ideas seems to force us back to an explanation in terms of policy. Some historians have suggested that the most fundamental distinction between the "Girondins" and the Jacobins was their differing attitudes toward economic and social problems. In Mathiez's view, the former weakly sought in war a solution to all the economic ills of France, and vacillated between the free-trade interest of their own class, the bourgeoisie, and their need to recruit popular support; Robespierre, however, represented the small man, and voiced the popular demand for the only true solution to economic evils, a return to the system of state-control which had been enforced by the old monarchy and destroyed by the Constituent Assembly.[6]

Not only does the indiscriminate use of the name "Girondins" in this argument gloss over many differences of opinion, but the existence of well-defined differences in economic and social policy between the Jacobins and the remainder of either the Legislative Assembly or the Convention is itself questionable.

In the time of the Legislative Assembly, Brissot certainly argued that war would restore the national credit of France, and he was supported on occasion by Gensonné, Condorcet and Lasource.[7] This, however, was only an incidental argument, and the first economic crisis which the Assembly encountered, the sugar shortage of January 1792, reveals those who have been called Girondins as perplexed politicians rather than doctrinaire economists. Fauchet, a preacher of evangelical socialism, urged the Committee of Commerce to draft a scheme "which will reconcile freedom of trade with measures for the prevention of hoarding." Ducos claimed that the shortage would solve itself without state intervention, yet urged careful study so that a law could be drafted which would meet the situation without infringing

---

[6] *La Vie chère*, 29, 67, and *passim;* cp., e.g., Michon, *Robespierre et la Guerre révolutionnaire 1791–1792*, and *La Défense de C. E. Dufriche-Valazé* (Paris, 1793).

[7] *Moniteur*, XI, 118; *Chronique de Paris*, 11 January 1792; Lasource, *Discours tendant à réfuter les orateurs* (Paris, 1791), B.M., F.338.6.

property rights.[8] Lasource echoed this indecision, while exhort-ing the Assembly to act promptly. Réal, at that time sympathetic to Brissot, thought that free-trade must be sacrificed unless the situation improved, and Manuel and Louvet fell back upon the curious expedient whereby all the Jacobins agreed to abstain from sugar and coffee until the shortage was over.[9] This evidence does not suggest more than general irresolution in a situation in which the obvious solution conflicted with a generally accepted belief in economic freedom, nor is there any evidence to suggest that the problem was a party issue at this date.

A second economic crisis later in the year shows the beginning of a distinction between Robespierre and the deputies in the Assembly, but according to Mathiez's own analysis of the situa-tion, Robespierre was almost alone among leading politicians in his economic views. In the late spring of 1792 there was a recrudescence of the local shortages of [grain] which had long troubled France. Two of the more revolutionary sections of Paris presented petitions demanding measures of price-control, and disorders occurred in many places, disorders which Mathiez regards as manifestations of a vast but unorganized social move-ment by the peasantry and workmen. After a brief period of appeasement, the Assembly resorted to repression.[10]

This general crisis was crystallized by the murder by rioters of Simmoneau, the Mayor of Étampes, in March. The Assembly and the Jacobin Club joined in condemnation of this crime. Guadet and Isnard, Chabot and Thuriot, all agreed that counter-revolutionaries were responsible. The Jacobins sent a letter of consolation to the Mayor's son, and Jean Debry proposed that a monument be erected to his memory.[11]

A different attitude was apparent in Robespierre's speeches. On 26 March he opposed a proposal that the Mayor be post-humously awarded a civic crown, and on 9 April the Jacobins ignored, at his instigation, a proposal that a fête should be held in honour of the murdered man. When the Assembly undertook the organization of the fête, Robespierre again opposed the proposal, and censured the policy of repression by saying that

[8] *Moniteur,* XI, 181, 204.

[9] Walter, *Histoire des Jacobins,* 234-8.

[10] *La Vie chère,* 50, 63, 66; Sagnac, *La Révolution,* I, 346 (in Lavisse, *Histoire de France contemporaine*).

[11] *Moniteur,* XI, 557, 563, 566, 573, 578, 666; *Jacobins,* III, 431.

there was one law for the powerful and another for the poor. The importance of his attitude is undeniable, but he was not in this respect representative of opinion in the Legislative Assembly, which, as Mathiez himself says, "remained devoted to the dogma of free-trade with an unshakable stubbornness." [12] No separate Girondin party can be discerned on this issue at this time.

The further economic troubles which occurred in the autumn of 1792 show that the balance of opinion had remained unchanged. In spite of a good harvest and the extension of democratic measures after 10 August, the lower classes of France remained distressed and discontented. Inflation had continued to augment the cost of living, while the invasion and the needs of the army had dislocated the distribution of corn. In these circumstances, the Legislative Assembly authorized local authorities to requisition supplies. Unaccompanied by any central direction or measures of price-control, the legislation proved ineffective in practice, and was eventually replaced by a reversion to free-trade and the repression of all disturbances.

Mathiez has suggested that one reason for the failure of this first attempt to control the economic situation was the fundamental hostility of the Girondins towards any form of state interference in economic matters. Certainly many of the leaders of the Legislative Assembly and the Convention again appeared as convinced free-traders. Vergniaud proposed the introduction of requisitioning as an extraordinary measure dictated by the supreme needs of the army. Roland, although Minister of the Interior, opposed the operation of the law, and repeatedly preached economic liberalism to the Convention. Amongst others, Pétion, Gardien and Serre supported his arguments, and Creuzé-Latouche, speaking for those who wanted "complete freedom for commerce," secured the decree of 8 December 1792 which repealed the earlier regulations and announced that "the most complete liberty will continue." [13]

But again these views do not afford a criterion to distinguish a Girondin party. As always, the deputies spoke as individuals. Where Valazé and Roland urged an increase in foreign purchases by the Government, Boyer-Fonfrède believed that even this would prove injurious, and recommended a mild measure

---

[12] *Jacobins*, III, 452, 477; Sagnac, *op. cit.*, I, 356; Hamel, *Histoire de Robespierre*, II, 276; *La Vie chère*, p. 29.

[13] *La Vie chère*, 100–6; *Moniteur*, XIII, 727, and XIV, 517, 599, 619, 642, 682, 694–6.

of tariff control, while Barbaroux objected to even the limited degree of compulsion which Serre supported. When Roland and Pétion urged repression of disorders in the Eure et Loire, Buzot joined Robespierre in proposing that civil commissioners should accompany the troops in order to prevent injustices. By Mathiez's own account, the only deputy who really understood the situation and favoured price-control was Louis Viger—who has also been accounted a Girondin.[14]

The deputies of the Gironde were no more alone in supporting free-trade in the autumn than they had been in the spring of 1792. The great majority of the Convention took this view, and the Mountain silently disavowed the principle of price-control.[15] The publication of Saint Just's speech in support of free-trade, which began with the words "Violent legislation about trade does not appeal to me," was agreed to without dissent, and both Robespierre and Danton recognized the necessity of restoring order, even by force. It is true that Robespierre again showed himself in advance of other deputies by his insistence that the first duty of the State was to ensure that the means of existence were within the reach of all, but even his attitude was full of caution. In his speech on 2 December he approved of free-trade in principle, limiting his criticism to those responsible for monopolies and exploitation and saying that such men should be forced to be honest; he refused to propose any specific decree, and simply promised to support any measure against exploitation.[16] His views may contain the seeds of later action, but in December 1792 he was decidedly non-committal.

In this matter, as in others, a situation which was not in itself a cause of dissension seems to have been used both by the Montagnards and by their opponents for the purpose of securing political advantage. At first the Montagnards attacked Roland and his friends as the pawns of the financiers and speculators they alleged to be behind the crisis,[17] while the opponents of the Mountain alleged that the disorders were being fomented by the Jacobins, by agents of the Commune or of Orléans, and that

---

[14] La Vie chère, p. 107; Moniteur, XIV, 236, 499, 614, 619–20, 642, 694.

[15] This point is accepted by Mathiez (La Vie chère, p. 103), and indicated by Lefebvre (La Convention, I, 16) also.

[16] Moniteur, XIV, 610, 620, 629.

[17] The account given of Clavière by Jean Bouchary, Les Manieurs d'argent à Paris à la fin du XVIIIe siècle, does not support the view that his relationships with financiers had political significance.

the demand for price-control was part of a plan to establish the dreaded *loi agraire*.[18] Later, as we have already seen, the Montagnards had the political acumen to see that the masses must be rallied to the Revolution if the invader were to be repulsed, and they then, in April 1793, purchased popular support by accepting that price-control from which they, in common with the rest of the Convention, had shrunk in horror only two months before. In this matter it is the Montagnards who are distinct, and that by their political initiative rather than by their economic policy.

The same contention, that the differences which appeared between the Montagnards and their opponents in economic policy were dependent upon and secondary to political developments, seems equally true of Mathiez's assertion that the Girondins can be distinguished by their tendency to support the economic interests of the provincial bourgeoisie.[19] Until price-control had been adopted these interests were favoured by a Convention preponderantly sympathetic to free-trade, and the adoption by both the Montagnards and their opponents of partisan attitudes in the social strife subsequently occasioned by such questions as recruitment had a clear political purpose, that of gaining or retaining effective control of local assemblies, and so ultimately of the Convention. Thus while we can agree that Robespierre was more advanced in his views than most deputies, and that the Mountain was peculiar in adopting a popular policy at an earlier stage than the rest of the Assembly, Mathiez's more general thesis must be considered, at best, unproven. The economic and social problems which confronted the Convention do not furnish evidence to distinguish a Girondin party from the body of the Convention, a distinction which must still be sought elsewhere.

Another assertion is that all the differences between Robespierre and his opponents sprang from a fundamental difference

[18] E.g., *Patriote français*, 17 September 1792, or Brissot, *À Tous les Républicains* (Paris, 1792), B.M., F.353.8. [The *loi agraire* was a proposal by some radical revolutionaries to split up the estates of the rich and give them to the poor.]

[19] *La Vie chère*, e.g. p. 189: "Economic federalism duplicated political federalism," or Mathiez, *Girondins et Montagnards*, pp. 87-90, where the decentralization of Condorcet's constitution is treated as a deliberate attempt to enhance the power of the provincial middle-classes in order to check social changes.

of philosophy.[20] The "Girondins" have been said to represent the critical and pragmatic philosophy of Voltaire and the Encyclopaedists, a philosophy based on the hypothesis that all problems can be solved by knowledge and by reason, and one which had little place for any personal deity, whereas Robespierre is said to represent the more emotional and romantic philosophy of Rousseau, a philosophy which, however theoretical, was nevertheless coherent and constructive, deriving its strength from the conception of a benevolent Deity, the God of Nature and of Natural Man.

Evidence to support this explanation of the difference between Robespierre and his opponents is abundant. In the Legislative Assembly the attitude of the deputies of the Gironde was particularly apparent in their views on the problems created by the hostility of the non-juring priests to the Civil Constitution of the Clergy. In his report on the situation in the Vendée, Gensonné revealed a complete lack of sympathy for the religious issues involved, deploring both the intolerance of the priests and the incipient intolerance of the State and recommending the complete separation of civil and religious affairs as the rational solution of the problem.[21] Later Ducos called upon God and good sense to preserve him from treating the same question from a theological standpoint. His view that a diversity of religious opinions was both inevitable and politically desirable seems a distinct echo of Voltaire. Guadet, too, said that the problem must be approached in the light of reason and not in that of theology, for the one was eternal and the other transient, while Vergniaud expressed the opinion that civil government bore no relation to heavenly dogma, for every man was free to turn East or West, as he chose, to worship the Divinity.[22]

These deputies of the Gironde appear to be of one mind in their vague Deism, in their dislike of dogma and of clericalism, and in their attitude of reasoned secular toleration. They did not however lead anything approaching a party on this issue, for their anti-clericalism did not differ from that of the great majority of their colleagues in the Assembly and in the Jacobin Club. They were not even wholly agreed with those who were associated with them in other matters: Ducos and Gensonné

[20] E.g., Blanc, *Histoire de la Révolution française*, VI, 311 ff.; Aulard, *Orateurs*, I, 172 ff.; Thompson, *Robespierre*, I, 215 ff.; Walter, *Robespierre*, pp. 561 ff.

[21] *Moniteur*, X, 328, 386.

[22] *Moniteur*, X, 215, 471, and XII, 92 and 406.

both rebuked Fauchet for his intemperate and inflammatory language, which was nevertheless voiced as violently by such men as Isnard and Jean Debry.[23]

The distinction between this general cynicism and the attitude of Robespierre became apparent in the Jacobin Club on 26 March 1792.[24] Speaking of the effect on France of the death of the Emperor Leopold, Robespierre said: "The most resolute were beginning to despair, and then Providence, which watches over us far better than our own wisdom, struck down Leopold and disrupted the plans of our adversaries." Guadet seized upon this point, saying that he could see no meaning in such a conception and suggesting that Robespierre, having laboured to destroy the despotism of monarchy, was now resurrecting the despotism of superstition. In a long and unprepared[25] reply Robespierre renounced all sympathy for a corrupt and degenerate priesthood, but proclaimed his heart-felt faith in the existence of God, the Eternal Creator of man and nature, the Providence "which is an essential influence on the destinies of nations and which seems to me to watch over the French Revolution with very particular care."

In sharp contrast to this speech, which Thompson considers to have been "the momentary unveiling of a fundamental difference of mind and outlook" between Robespierre and the easygoing intelligentsia of the Assembly,[26] is Brissot's defence of Condorcet at the Jacobins on 25 April. Brissot attributed the freedom which France had won to the untiring energy and burning genius of Condorcet and his collaborators, Voltaire and d'Alembert: "The most durable monument to our Revolution is philosophy. The patriot *par excellence* is a philosopher." [27]

Three days later Robespierre agreed that "the mathematicians and the members of the Academy that M. Brissot holds up to us as models" had indeed destroyed the credit of the clergy, but he condemned them as sycophants of royalty and persecutors of Jean-Jacques Rousseau, "who in my opinion is alone among

[23] *Moniteur*, X, 252, 308, 389, and XII, 5; *Journal*, 30 October and 7 November 1792.

[24] *Journal*, 26 March 1792.

[25] Blanc, *Histoire de la Révolution française*, VI, 316; Michelet, *Histoire de la Révolution française*, VI, 405.

[26] Thompson, *Robespierre*, I, 217.

[27] *Jacobins*, III, 529; Blanc, *op. cit.*, VI, 323.

the celebrities of his time in meriting public honour, prostituted as it is to political charlatans and trumped-up heroes." [28]

These speeches, with the later conduct of Robespierre in condemning the "philosopher" Helvétius as a persecutor of Rousseau and in promoting the worship of the Supreme Being,[29] justify the assumption that a profound difference of philosophy existed between him and the great majority of the deputies both in the Legislative Assembly and in the Convention. The difference is important, for philosophies may be regarded as the mainsprings of political action, but it does not serve to distinguish a Girondin party in either assembly. The views expressed by Brissot and the deputies of the Gironde were those most commonly held at the time, and those of Robespierre mark only his own isolation from all but a few of his colleagues.[30]

The other characteristic commonly attributed to the supposed Girondin party is that of federalism. . . . That which was manifest, however, was hostility to Robespierre and to the delegation and city of Paris. It is federalism, in this limited sense, which is of all the various characteristics attributed to the supposed Girondin party that which has the greatest verisimilitude. . . .

The Montagnards alone appear as a distinct entity, having a fair measure of unity imposed upon them by the public debates and frequent purges of the Jacobin Club and having their separatism justified in their own eyes by the conviction that they represented, not a party, but the true voice of the sovereign people. The only distinction between them and their principal opponents which has any consistent validity is that of their divergent attitudes towards Paris, and in this essential matter the attitude of the so-called Girondin deputies was that of the majority of the Convention. Had it not been so, the insurrection of 2 June 1793 would not have taken place, for it would not have been necessary.

The attempt that has been made in these pages to draw closer to Brissot and his friends has shown that current generali-

[28] Buchez and Roux, *Histoire parlementaire*, XIV, 153–5.
[29] *Jacobins*, IV, 550; Walter, *Robespierre*, p. 561.
[30] An exception to this generalization may be Bancal des Issarts, who also spoke of Providence as watching over the Revolution: Mège, *Le Conventionnel Bancal des Issarts*, p. 263.

zations on the subject need some revision, and this revision in its
turn is not without importance in the interpretation of the
general course of the Revolution.

The closer approach, originally suggested by the doubts and
differences which are apparent in the historians' views about the
unity and policy of the supposed Girondin party, has revealed
that its very existence is a remarkable historical legend, originating in contemporary propaganda and subsequently accepted by
historians as a matter of convenience. Under examination, the
party disintegrates. Proscription by the Montagnards, which has
long been accepted as a criterion of membership of the party, has
proved to be a fortuitous process from which no valid deductions
can be drawn. In practice, there was neither a recognized party
leader nor an accepted policy. The supposed Girondin deputies
consistently asserted their independence, speaking and acting as
individuals even at the most critical moments of the conflict with
Robespierre. As for the alleged party headquarters, they have
appeared as irrelevant to the main question. When the *Club de
la Réunion* was influential it was as much Robespierrist as
Brissotin in composition, and a subsequent attempt by Brissot's
friends to capture and maintain or develop it was a complete
failure. The *Comité Valazé*, the nearest approach to an attempt
at party organization, represents nothing more than an ineffectual
effort by a comparatively unimportant deputy to rally even more
obscure men against the threat of domination by the Montagnard
minority. In short, the only people in the Convention to bear
any resemblance to a coherent party were the Montagnards, who
were opposed by most of the amorphous majority of the Assembly.

Brissot and his friends should be regarded as a small and
loose-knit group or coalition of individualists who rapidly became representative of the resistance of the majority to Robespierre, their personal independence remaining unqualified. Evidence even of collaboration between them during the time of
the Convention is extremely slight, for the meetings at Madame
Roland's salon lacked any precision of purpose and ended when
her husband resigned his office in January 1793. They appear in
the Legislative Assembly as a fairly coherent group, but one of
only some seven or eight prominent radicals, a coterie which increased little in size in the Convention. Even in May 1793, when
Montagnard pressure was greatest, the "faction" was no more
than a frail alliance of some fifteen deputies, men whose outlook

was so identical with that of the majority of their colleagues that they can be distinguished only as personalities, individuals whose reputation, powers of oratory or personal courage marked them out above others as enemies of the Mountain.

IV

THE WAR OF 1792

*T*he War of 1792 was one of the most momentous and
tragic events of the French Revolution. It lasted for
many years, resulted in the deaths of hundreds of thousands, and
demanded such sacrifices from the French people that it helped
provoke the Terror, counter-revolution, and military dictatorship.

Who was responsible for causing it? Some historians, such as
Albert Goodwin, distribute the blame on both sides: in the
French cabinet and legislature there were influential partisans of
war; on the other hand, the émigrés and some European monarchs were determined to crush the Revolution by force of arms.

Other historians, such as Hippolyte Taine, blame the French
assembly and especially the Girondins for using justified grievances against émigrés and foreign rulers as a pretext for war.

War "guilt" is difficult to assess, as anyone who has studied
the events leading to World War I well knows. Do we hold the
powers who declared war responsible? Or those who had any part
in causing the tension? Or those who uncompromisingly sought
ends prejudicial to their neighbors? Such are the kinds of questions one must ask in analyzing the issue.

Another matter to be studied—an equally complicated one—
concerns France's war aims. Did she have clear ones, and if so
what were they? Jacques Godechot rejects the oversimplified thesis of the nineteenth-century historian Albert Sorel—that France
throughout the Revolution sought to expand to her natural frontiers. Instead he argues that her aims frequently changed: sometimes French leaders indeed sought the conquest of the natural
frontiers; sometimes they wanted to create friendly republics on

France's eastern frontier; and sometimes they favored nothing more than a peace providing for noninterference in the domestic affairs of all states. Godechot thus finds policies changing as men and circumstances changed. Does he overstate the differences between the war aims of the Girondins and those of the Robespierrists? Does he make their differing policies more cohesive and coherent than they actually were? Is he being partial to either group?

Clearly, even after years of historical research, there is still much that is perplexing about the War of 1792.

THE OUTBREAK: BOTH
SIDES RESPONSIBLE*

Albert Goodwin

*Albert Goodwin (1906–   ), Professor of History at the
University of Manchester, has for more than thirty years
been one of the outstanding British historians of the Old Regime
and the French Revolution. He has edited* The European Nobility in the Eighteenth Century *(1953)*, A Select List of Works
on Europe and Europe Overseas, 1715–1815 *(1956) with J. S.
Bromley, and* The American and French Revolutions, 1763–1793
(1965), which is Volume VIII of The New Cambridge Modern
History. *He has also published many articles and a short survey,*
The French Revolution *(1953), notable for its clarity and good
sense.*

The possibility of war with Europe had existed ever since the
king's escape to Varennes, if only for the reason that the stricter
confinement of the sovereigns in the capital confirmed Marie Antoinette in her views that the sole hope of salvation for the
monarchy lay in foreign intervention. The king's acceptance of
the constitution in September [1791] was a formal act, the effective results of which remained to be seen. For the moment, it
merely stimulated further the reactionary fervour of the *émigrés*.
By her continued intrigues the queen early aroused the suspicions
of the Legislative Assembly and provoked a wave of anti-Austrian

* From Albert Goodwin, *The French Revolution* (2nd ed. rev.; London:
Hutchinson and Co., 1956), pp. 112–113, 114–120. Reprinted by permission of
Hutchinson Publishing Group, Ltd.

feeling, which did much to impair good relations with the Emperor and to undermine the influence of the Feuillants.[1]

In contrast with the Feuillants' efforts to reconcile the refractory priests and to conciliate the Emperor, the Brissotins set out to repress the ecclesiastical counter-revolution and to intimidate the *émigrés*. Their first move in this direction was the passing of a decree on 31st October, summoning the count de Provence to return to France within three months, upon pain of forfeiting his rights to the succession. This, however, only produced a belated and evasive reply from the prince in December. The next step was taken on 9th November, when the Assembly decreed that all *émigrés* who had not repatriated themselves by 1st January, 1792, would be treated as traitors. Their goods would thus be subject to confiscation and, if caught, their lives would be forfeit. Though the *émigré* Court at Coblentz, now guided by Calonne, had undoubtedly been partly responsible for the Declaration of Pilnitz, and though the military forces of counter-revolution under the Prince de Condé at Worms were assuming greater coherence, it can hardly be considered that the threat represented by the *émigrés* was in itself a serious one. On the other hand, the effect of the emigration on the financial and commercial situation in France and on the discipline in the army could not be ignored. More disturbing were the administrative and political results of the religious schism. . . .

Though the decrees of 9th and 29th November[2] were vetoed by the king in December on the advice of the Feuillant leaders, the Brissotins continued with their policy of legislating against the agents of counter-revolution. Under pressure from this quarter and on the advice of [the Minister of War] Narbonne, the king announced in the Assembly on 14th December that he would summon the elector of Trêves to disband the armed gatherings of *émigrés* at Coblentz before 15th January, 1792, and that he would declare war on the elector if he refused to give satisfaction. To show that this was not an empty threat, Narbonne announced that three French armies would be formed under the command of Rochambeau, Lückner and Lafayette. The elector of Trêves,

[1] [A loose-knit group of anti-Jacobin deputies and ministers who favored a peaceful foreign policy and constitutional monarchy in 1791. Its leading members included Lafayette, Sieyès, Adrien Duport, Barnave, and Alexandre de Lameth. Their club often met at a former convent of the Feuillants, hence their name.]

[2] [These decrees provided for severe penalties against *émigrés* and those clergymen who refused to take an oath of loyalty to the nation.]

glad of the excuse of ridding himself of his unwelcome guests, and conscious of the Emperor's lukewarm support of the *émigrés*, replied without delay that he was willing to carry out Louis' wishes.

That these events did not bring about a relaxation of the tension between France and Austria may be attributed, on the one hand, to a sudden stiffening of the Emperor Leopold's attitude and, on the other, to the military and political schemes of Narbonne. Even before the French pressure on the elector of Trêves, Leopold had revived the question of the feudal rights of the imperial princes in Alsace. In accordance with the decrees of 4th–11th August, 1789, the feudal dues of the German princes with possessions in Alsace had either been abolished or made subject to redemption. In reply to this unilateral action taken by the Constituent Assembly, the German princes had refused to discuss the matter of compensation and had appealed to the Imperial Diet. After long hesitations, the Frankfort Diet had finally issued, on 21st July, 1791, a decree or *conclusum*, upholding the claims of the princes. On 3rd December the Emperor informed Louis XVI in a dispatch that he intended to ratify the decision of the Imperial Diet, which he did a week later. This issue, which had seemed likely to become extinct, was thus revived. More provocative was an imperial dispatch, dated 21st December, 1791, in which the Emperor, while approving the dispersal of the *émigrés* at Coblentz, announced that he had ordered Marshal Bender, commander-in-chief of the Imperial troops in the Netherlands, to protect the elector of Trêves, if the need arose, from any incursions on his territory by undisciplined French forces. This action was supported by the argument that the French government was no longer master of the situation on its own soil.

That there was some substance in these contentions is shown by the fact that, on 21st December, Narbonne had set out on a tour of the north-eastern frontier districts in order to tighten up the discipline of the troops. In three weeks, Narbonne practically put a stop to emigration in the army, raised its morale and returned to the Assembly with plans for raising 50,000 new recruits by fusing the National Guards with the regiments of the line. These plans, however, proved premature and Narbonne soon concluded that the army could only be cured of the evils with which the revolution had afflicted it if it were tested in a limited war with the Rhineland electors. The protection offered by the Emperor to the elector of Trêves, however, threatened to transform the punitive expedition which Narbonne had in mind into a more general conflict. This situation forced Narbonne into an alliance of convenience with the Brissotins, with whom he had come to agree in thinking that France's real enemy was not the *émigrés* but Austria. It also induced him, at the suggestion of Madame de Staël, to set on foot negotiations with the idea of ensuring Prussian neutrality and an alliance with Great Britain. At the end of December 1791 the count de Ségur was dispatched on an official mission to Berlin with instructions to dissuade the King of Prussia from supporting the Emperor. Meanwhile, the son of Marshal Custine was commissioned to pay a secret visit to Frederick II's great captain, the duke of Brunswick, in order to offer him the post of generalissimo of the French armies. In January 1792 Talleyrand, a personal friend of Narbonne's, was sent on an unofficial mission to London to prepare the ground for a Franco-British understanding. All these overtures were rebuffed. Ségur's mission was wrecked by the agents of the *émigrés* and by Louis XVI's secret repudiation of his envoy, Custine's by the caution of the duke of Brunswick, and Talleyrand's by his intrigues with the parliamentary opposition and by the British Government's mistrust of his proposals.

The secret political design upon which these diplomatic manœuvres hinged was that the constitutional revision envisaged by the Feuillants should be effected by means of an army victorious in war, which could then be employed in the interest of the monarchy. Narbonne was thus the first to contemplate ending the revolution and restoring order by a military dictatorship. These plans, however, involved the minister in a situation which soon got out of control. His scheme for a limited war against the elector of Trêves alienated Barnave, who early in 1792 finally realized the hopelessness of his attempts to guide the queen and retired from the political scene. Narbonne's alliance with the Brissotins also had the effect of stimulating the rising demand in the country, not for a military promenade in the Rhineland, but for a fullscale war with Austria. Ever since October 1791 Brissot had been preaching an ideological war of peoples against sovereigns, and the war with Austria was envisaged as one in which France would be assisted by the subject races of the Habsburg dominions. In this illusion the Brissotins were encouraged by refugee patriots from Belgium, Liège, Holland and Switzerland. In January 1792 Robespierre, at the Jacobin club, did his best to expose the preparations for a military dictatorship made by Narbonne and to dissuade the war-mongers from becoming "armed missionaries," but he only succeeded in widening the breach between the Brissotins and his own followers. It is perhaps worth noting, in passing, that Robespierre, at this point, was neither an unqualified pacifist, nor a covert collaborationist. He was merely contending that counter-revolution should be defeated in France before its protectors abroad were assailed. Marat, too, argued in the same sense, but his influence was diminished by the fact that his popular newspaper, *L'Ami du Peuple,* had temporarily ceased to appear in the middle of December 1791.

A fresh stage in the events leading to war opened in the middle of January 1792 when Gensonné, in the name of the diplomatic committee of the Assembly, raised the question whether the Emperor's orders to Marshal Bender could be reconciled with the Franco-Austrian treaty of 1756. On 25th January, the Assembly decided to challenge the Emperor on this point. It invited Louis to ask Leopold whether he still regarded himself as an ally of the French nation and whether he renounced all engagements directed against French sovereign independence and the stability of the French constitution. If no answer were received to this inquiry before 1st March, France would feel compelled to declare war on Austria. From this point, all de Lessart's efforts, as Foreign Minister, to tone down the asperity of the notes which subsequently passed between Paris and Vienna only played into the hands of the Brissotins, who now determined to overthrow the Feuillant government by exposing the almost criminal weakness of its diplomacy. Meanwhile, on 7th February, the Emperor had succeeded in procuring the King of Prussia's signature to a treaty of defensive alliance, the preliminaries of which had been concluded in the previous July. In this treaty the two powers agreed to afford each other mutual aid and assistance and to promote a concert of other powers for the settlement of French affairs. Though the question of a possible further partition of Poland continued to divide the allies, and though the treaty did not protect the most vulnerable parts of Austrian and Prussian territory, it persuaded the Austrian chancellor, Kaunitz, that France could safely be hectored into submission. Hence it was that Franco-Austrian diplomacy in February and March of 1792 consisted merely of an exchange of mutual recrimination and abuse.

The final phase of these rapidly deteriorating relations opened on 10th March, when Louis XVI abruptly dismissed Narbonne and news was received in Paris of the death of the Emperor Leo-

pold. Narbonne had virtually brought about his own fall by in-
triguing against the king's favourite minister, de Molleville, and
by threatening Louis with the combined resignations of Rochambeau, Lückner and Lafayette. The king's action, however, provided the Brissotins with the excuse for impeaching de Lessart,
and for denouncing the other members of the Feuillant administration. In this way, the ministry was overthrown and the Brissotins were left to construct one of their own. The Department
of Foreign Affairs was given to Dumouriez, that of Finance to
Clavière, a Swiss banker and former collaborator of Mirabeau,
the Ministry of the Interior to Roland de la Platière, a civil servant, the Navy and Colonies to Lacoste, and the Ministry of Justice to Duranthon. Narbonne's place was taken by de Grave—a
nonentity. The chief figure in the new government was Dumouriez, a fanatical opponent of Austria, ambitious and determined on war. The change of Austrian rulers also brought war
nearer, for the successor of the cautious and pacific Leopold was
Francis II, young, impetuous and with a taste for military adven-
ture. His very youth threw him into the hands of the Imperial
Chancellor Kaunitz, who was determined to humiliate France by
threatening her with the newly concluded alliance with Prussia.
It soon became clear, moreover, that Francis had made up his
mind to champion the cause of the Alsatian princes and of the
Pope, and to secure some guarantee of strong government in
France.

In some respects, the policy of Dumouriez proved to be identical with that of his predecessor. He had the same conviction
that Austria could be isolated by means of understandings with
Prussia and Great Britain, and hoped that he might even be able
to induce the German princes not to elect Francis as emperor.
Like Narbonne, he secretly regarded war as an effective means of
restoring the monarchical authority of Louis XVI. As a former
agent of Louis XV's secret diplomacy, however, Dumouriez inherited from the *ancien régime* a bitter hatred of the Austrian
alliance, and was convinced that the German powers intended
to treat France as a second Poland. As soon as he became Foreign
Minister, Dumouriez adopted a challenging and uncompromising attitude towards Vienna and pushed on with active preparations for war. Whereas, however, Narbonne had contemplated a
French offensive on the Moselle and the Rhine, directed on
Trêves and Mayence, Dumouriez laid plans for overrunning the
Low Countries. His object there was not formal annexation, for

that would have antagonized Great Britain, but the establishment of a Belgian federal republic. The attack was to be justified to the British ministers on the ground of military necessity, and it was intended that the French armies should live on the country and thus relieve the pressure on French finances. One of Dumouriez's first acts was to dispatch Maret—the future duke of Bassano—as an agent to incite the Belgians to revolt. Custine was once again charged with the duty of separating Prussia from Austria, and Talleyrand was entrusted with the task of preparing the way for a prospective alliance with England. The suggestions which were put to the British Government were bold and imaginative. As the basis of the alliance, Dumouriez offered to draw up a new commercial treaty, to surrender Tobago and to co-operate in the liberation of the Spanish American colonies. Great Britain, France and possibly the United States were together to share the opportunities for great commercial ventures, which would thus be opened up. The aggressive continental ambitions of Austria, Prussia and Russia could be checked, and the peace of Europe guaranteed by means of a balance between the liberal powers of the West and the autocratic monarchies of the East. It was the same policy which Talleyrand was to champion with success after a quarter of a century of conflict at the Congress of Vienna in 1815.

These grandiose plans and calculations, however, soon came to grief. Custine's mission in Berlin was futile from the start, since the King of Prussia was obsessed with the danger from revolutionary France. Throughout Europe, Dumouriez's diplomacy was frustrated by the secret agents employed by the baron de Breteuil, who was now working in close association with Fersen and the count de Mercy-Argenteau.[3] The Austro-Prussian combination proved unbreakable, while the duke of Brunswick showed his real sympathies by accepting the post of commander-in-chief of the combined anti-French forces. As the interchange of notes between Paris and Vienna degenerated in the course of March into a series of ultimata, war became inevitable. On 20th April, 1792, war on the "King of Hungary and Bohemia" was declared on the proposition of Louis XVI in the Legislative Assembly, before Talleyrand had set out for London. Only seven votes were cast against the motion.

[3] [Breteuil, Louis XVI's unofficial adviser; Fersen, Marie Antoinette's Swedish admirer; and Mercy-Argenteau, the Austrian Ambassador to France, were all three avowed counter-revolutionary confidants of the royal family.]

THE OUTBREAK: THE FRENCH
PRIMARILY RESPONSIBLE*

Hippolyte Taine

Hippolyte Taine (1828–1893) was one of France's most well-known men of letters in the second half of the nineteenth century. He built his reputation with works of literary criticism and philosophy. Then, deeply affected by the "année terrible" of the Franco-Prussian War and the Commune of 1871, he turned his powerful intellect toward history and published his multivolume Origines de la France contemporaine *(1875–1893). Although Taine has been severely criticized by professional historians for a biased presentation of evidence, his* Origines *nevertheless has had a broad and continuing influence in France and elsewhere, especially among those who deplore the Revolution.*

War, like a black cloud, rises above the horizon, overspreads the sky, thunders and wraps France filled with explosive materials in a circle of lightning, and it is the Assembly which, through the greatest of its mistakes, draws down the bolt on the nation's head.

It might have been turned aside with a little prudence. Two principal grievances were alleged, one by France and the other by the Empire. On the one hand, and very justly, France complained of the gathering of *émigrés,* which the Emperor and Electors tolerated against it on the frontier. In the first place, however, a few thousands of gentlemen, without troops or stores, and nearly without money, need not excite much fear, and, be-

* From Hippolyte Taine, *The French Revolution,* trans. John Durand (2nd ed. rev.; New York: Henry Holt and Co., 1892), II, 96–102. Some of the footnotes have been omitted or clarified.

sides this, long before the decisive hour came these troops were dispersed, at once by the Emperor in his own dominions, and, fifteen days afterwards, by the Elector of Trèves in his electorate. On the other hand, according to treaties, the German princes, who owned estates in Alsace, made claims for the feudal rights abolished on their French possessions and the Diet forbade them to accept the offered indemnity. But, as far as the Diet is concerned, nothing was easier nor more customary than to let negotiations drag along, there being no risk or inconvenience attending the suit as, during the delay, the claimants remained empty-handed.

If, now, behind the ostensible motives, the real intentions are sought for, it is certain that, up to January, 1792, the intentions of Austria were pacific. The grants made to the Comte d'Artois, in the Declaration of Pilnitz, were merely a court-sprinkling of holy-water, the semblance of an illusory promise and subject to a European concert of action, that is to say, annulled beforehand by an indefinite postponement, while this pretended league of sovereigns is at once "placed by the politicians in the class of august comedies." [1] Far from taking up arms against new France in the name of old France, the Emperor Leopold and his prime minister Kaunitz, were glad to see the constitution completed and accepted by the King; it "got them out of trouble," [2] and Prussia likewise. In all state management political interest is the great mainspring and both powers needed all their forces in another direction, in Poland, one for retarding, and the other for accelerating its divisions, and both, when the partition took place, to get enough for themselves and prevent Russia from getting too much. The sovereigns of Prussia and Austria, accordingly, did not yet entertain any idea of delivering Louis XVI, nor of conducting the émigrés back, nor of conquering French provinces,

---

[1] Jacques Mallet du Pan, *Mémoires et correspondance . . . pour servir à l'histoire de la Révolution française* (Paris: Amyot, 1851), I, 254 (February 1792). Mirabeau and the Comte de La Marck, *Correspondance . . . pendant les années 1789, 1790, 1791 . . .* (Paris: Vᵛᵉ Le Normant, 1851), III, 232 (Note of M. de Bacourt). On the very day and at the moment of signing the treaty at Pilnitz, at eleven o'clock in the evening, the Emperor Leopold wrote to his prime minister, M. de Kaunitz, to this effect: "The agreement he had just signed does not really bind him to anything. The declarations it contains, extorted by the Count d'Artois, have no value whatever." He ends by assuring him that "neither himself nor his government is in any way bound by this instrument."

[2] Words of M. de Kaunitz, Sept. 4, 1791, as quoted in Alfred von Vivenot, *Recueil*, I, 242.

and if anything was to be expected from them on account of personal ill-will, there was no fear of their armed intervention.

On the side of France it is not the King who urges a rupture; he knows too well what mortal danger there is to him and his in the chances of war. Secretly as well as publicly, in writing to the *émigrés,* his wishes are to bring them back or to restrain them. In his private correspondence he asks of the European powers not physical but moral aid, the external support of a congress which will permit moderate men, the partisans of order, all owners of property, to raise their heads and rally around the throne and the laws against anarchy. In his ministerial correspondence every precaution is taken not to apply the match or let it be applied to gunpowder. At the critical moment of the discussion[3] he entreats the deputies, through M. Delessart, his Minister of Foreign Affairs, to weigh their words and especially not to send forth a challenge on a "fixed term of delay." He resists to the very last as far as his passive will lets him. On being compelled to declare war he requires beforehand the advice of all his ministers, over their signatures, and, only at the last extremity, utters the fatal words "with tears in his eyes," dragged on by the Assembly which has just cited M. Delessart before the supreme court at Orléans, under a capital charge, and which qualifies all caution as treachery.

It is the Assembly then which launches the disabled ship on the roaring abysses of an unknown sea, without a rudder and leaking at every seam; it alone slips the cable which held it in port and which the foreign powers neither dared nor desired to sever. The Girondists are the leaders and hold the axe; since the last of October they have grasped it and struck repeated blows. As an exception, the extreme Jacobins, Couthon, Collot d'Herbois, Danton, Robespierre, do not side with them. Robespierre, who at first proposed to confine the Emperor "within the circle of Popilius," [4] [that is, to give him an ultimatum] fears the placing of too great power in the King's hands, and, growing mistrustful, preaches distrust. But the great mass of the party, led by

---

[3] *Réimpression de l'ancien Moniteur* . . . (Paris: Plon, 1847–1850), XI, 142 (session of January 17, 1792). Speech by M. Delessart. Decree of accusation against him March 10, 1792. Declaration of war, April 20, 1792. . . .

[4] B.-J. Buchez et P.-C. Roux, *Histoire parlementaire de la Révolution française* . . . (Paris: Paulin, 1834–1838), XII, 402 (session of the Jacobin Club, Nov. 28, 1791).

clamorous public opinion, impels on the timid marching in front. Of the many things of which knowledge is necessary to conduct successfully such a complex and delicate affair, they know nothing; they are ignorant about cabinets, courts, populations, treaties, precedents, timely forms and requisite style.

Their guide and counsellor in foreign relations is Brissot whose pre-eminence is based on their ignorance and who, exalted into a statesman, becomes for a few months the most conspicuous figure in Europe.[5] To whatever extent a European calamity may be attributed to any one man, this one is to be attributed to him. It is this wretch, born in a pastry-cook's shop, brought up in an attorney's office, formerly a police agent at 150 francs per month, once in league with scandal-mongers and black-mailers,[6] a penny-a-liner, busybody, and intermeddler, who, with the half-information of a nomad, scraps of newspaper ideas and reading-room lore, added to his scribblings as a writer and his club declamation, directs the destinies of France and starts a war in Europe which is to destroy six millions of lives. From the garret in which his wife washes his shirts, he enjoys the snubbing of potentates and, on the 20th of October [1791], in the tribune,[7] he begins by insulting thirty foreign sovereigns. This keen, intense enjoyment on which the new fanaticism daily feeds itself, Madame Roland herself delights in, with evident complacency, in the two famous letters in which, with a supercilious tone, she first instructs the King and

---

[5] Gustavus III, King of Sweden, assassinated by Ankarström, says: "I should like to know what Brissot will say."

[6] On Brissot's antecedents, cf. Edmond Biré, *La Légende des Girondins* (Paris: V. Palmé, 1881). Personally Brissot was honest, and remained poor. But he had passed through a good deal of filth, and bore the marks of it. He had lent himself to the diffusion of an obscene book, *Le Diable dans un bénitier*, and, in 1783, having received 13,355 francs to found a Lyceum in London, not only did not found it, but was unable to return the money.

[7] *Moniteur*, X, 174. "This Venetian government, which is nothing but a farce . . . Those petty German princes, whose insolence in the last century despotism crushed out. . . . Geneva, that atom of a republic. . . . That bishop of Liège, whose yoke bows down a people that ought to be free. . . . I disdain to speak of other princes. . . . That King of Sweden, who has only twenty-five millions income, and who spends two-thirds of it in poor pay for an army of generals and a small number of discontented soldiers. . . . As to that princess (Catherine II), whose dislike of the French constitution is well known, and who is about as good looking as Elizabeth, she cannot expect greater success than Elizabeth in the Dutch revolution." (Brissot, in this last passage, tries to appear at once witty and well read.)

next the Pope.[8] Brissot, at bottom, regards himself as a Louis
XIV, and expressly invites the Jacobins to imitate the haughty
ways of the Great Monarch.[9]

To the mismanagement of the interloper, and the sensitive-
ness of the upstart, must be added the rigidity of the sectary. The
Jacobins, in the name of abstract right, deny historic right; they
impose from above, and by force, that truth of which they are
the apostles, and allow themselves every provocation which they
prohibit to others. "Europe must know," exclaims Isnard,[10] "that
ten millions of Frenchmen, armed with the sword, with the pen,
with reason, with eloquence, might, if provoked, change the face
of the world and make tyrants tremble on their thrones of clay."
"Wherever a throne exists," says Hérault de Séchelles, "there is
an enemy." [11] "Honest capitulation between tyranny and liberty,"
says Brissot, "is impossible. Your Constitution is an eternal
anathema against absolute monarchs. . . . It places them on
trial, it pronounces judgment on them; it seems to say to each—
to-morrow thou shalt pass away or shalt be king only through the
people. War is now a national benefit, and not to have war is the
only calamity to be dreaded." [12] "Tell the King," says Gensonné,
"that war is necessary, that public opinion demands it, that the
safety of the empire [France] makes it a law." [13] "The state we
are in," concludes Vergniaud, "is a veritable state of destruction
that may lead us to disgrace and death. To arms! to arms! Citi-

[8] Letter of Roland to the King, June 10, 1792, and letter of the executive
council to the Pope, Nov. 25, 1792. Letter of Madame Roland to Brissot, Jan.
7, 1791. "Briefly, adieu. Cato's wife need not gratify herself by complimenting
Brutus."
[9] Buchez et Roux, XII, 410 (meeting of the Jacobin Club, Dec. 10, 1791). "A
Louis XIV declares war against Spain, because his ambassador had been
insulted by the Spanish ambassador. And we, who are free, we give a moment's hesitation to it!" [Until late 1792 Brissot and many of his followers
were members of the Jacobin clubs. That is why Taine can speak of them
as Jacobins.]
[10] Moniteur, X, 503 (session of Nov. 29 [1791]). The Assembly orders this
speech to be printed and distributed in the departments.
[11] Moniteur, X, 762 (session of Dec. 28 [1791]).
[12] Moniteur, XI, 147, 149 (session of Jan. 17 [1792]); X, 759 (session of Dec.
28 [1791]). Already, on the 16th of December, he had declared at the Jacobin
Club: "A people that has conquered its freedom, after ten centuries of
slavery, needs war. War is essential to it for its consolidation." (Buchez et
Roux, XII, 410). On the 17th of January [1792], in the tribune, he again
repeats: "I have only one fear, and that is, that we may not have war."
[13] Moniteur, XI, 119 (session of Jan. 13 [1792]). Speech by Gensonné, in the
name of the diplomatic committee, of which he is the reporter.

zens, freemen, defend your liberty, confirm the hopes of that of the human race. . . . Lose not the advantage of your position. Attack now that there is every sign of complete success. . . . The manes of past generations seem to me crowding into this temple to conjure you, in the name of the evils which slavery has compelled them to endure, to preserve future generations from similar evils, the generations whose destinies are in your hands! Let this prayer be granted! Be for the future a new Providence! Ally yourselves with eternal justice!" [14]

There is no longer any room for serious discussion with those Marseilles orators. Brissot, in response to the claim made by the Emperor in behalf of the princes' property in Alsace, replies that "the sovereignty of the people is not bound by the treaties of tyrants." [15] As to the gatherings of the *émigrés,* the Emperor having yielded on this point, he will yield on the others.[16] Let him formally renounce all combinations against France. "I want war on the 10th of February [1792]," says Brissot, "if we do not receive advices of this renunciation." No explanations are to be listened to; we want satisfaction; "to require satisfaction is to put the Emperor at our mercy." [17] The Assembly, so eager to start the quarrel, usurps the King's right to take the first step and formally declares war, fixing the date.[18]

The die is now cast. "They want war," says the Emperor, "and they shall have it." Austria immediately forms an alliance with

[14] *Moniteur,* XI, 158 (session of Jan. 18 [1792]). The Assembly orders the printing of this speech.

[15] *Moniteur,* X, 760 (session of Dec. 28 [1791]).

[16] *Moniteur,* XI, 149 (session of Jan. 17 [1792]). Speech by Brissot.

[17] *Moniteur,* XI, 178 (session of Jan. 20 [1792]). Fauchet proposes the following decree: "All partial treaties actually existent are declared void. The National Assembly substitutes in their place alliances with the English, the Anglo-American, the Helvetic, Polish, and Dutch nations, as long as they remain free. . . . When other nations want our alliance, they have only to conquer their freedom to have it. Meanwhile, this will not prevent us from having relations with them, as with *good-natured savages.* . . . Let us occupy the towns in the neighborhood which bring our adversaries too near us. . . . Mayence, Coblentz, and Worms are sufficient." *Ibid.,* p. 215 (session of Jan. 25). One of the members, supporting himself with the authority of Gelon, King of Syracuse, proposes an additional article: "We declare that we will not lay down our arms until we shall have established the freedom of all peoples." These stupidities show the mental condition of the Jacobin party.

[18] The decree is passed Jan. 25 [1792]. The alliance between Prussia and Austria takes place Feb. 7. (François de Bourgoing, *Histoire diplomatique de l'Europe pendant la Révolution française* [Paris: Lévy, 1865–1885], I, 457.)

Prussia, threatened, like herself, with revolutionary propaganda.[19]
By sounding the tocsin the Jacobins, masters of the Assembly,
have succeeded in bringing about that "monstrous alliance,"
and, from day to day, this tocsin sounds the louder. One year
more, thanks to this policy, and France will have all Europe for
an enemy and for an only friend, the Regency of Algiers, whose
internal system of government is about the same as her own.

Behind their *carmagnoles* we can detect a design which they
will avow later on. "We were always opposed by the Constitution," Brissot is to say, "and nothing but war could put the Constitution down." Diplomatic wrongs, consequently, of which they
make parade, are simply pretexts; if they urge war it is for the
purpose of overthrowing the legal order of things which annoys
them; their real object is the conquest of power, a second internal revolution, the application of their system and a final state of
equality.

[19] Albert Sorel, "La Mission du Comte de Ségur à Berlin" (published in the
Temps, Oct. 15, 1878). Dispatch of M. de Ségur to M. Delessart, Feb. 24,
1792. Count Schulenburg repeated to me that they had no desire whatever
to meddle with our constitution. But, said he with singular animation, we
must guard against gangrene. Prussia is, perhaps, the country which should
fear it least; nevertheless, however remote a gangrened member may be, it
is better to cut it off than risk one's life. How can you expect to secure
tranquillity, "when thousands of writers every day . . . mayors, office-holders,
insult kings, and publish that the Christian religion has always supported
despotism, and that we shall be free only by destroying it, and that all
princes must be exterminated because they are all tyrants?"

FRENCH WAR AIMS (1792–1794): SHIFTING POLICIES*

Jacques Godechot

> *For biographical information on Jacques Godechot, see the section entitled "The Character of the Constituent Assembly (1789–1791)."*

The French became involved in the War of 1792 without clearly defining their aims. The Girondins had been its strongest proponents, expecting rather irresponsibly to gain personal advantage by tightening their hold on power. To be sure, they anticipated helping peoples who wanted to change their political systems, but nothing had been carefully worked out. . . .

The war did not develop as the Girondins had hoped. It had begun with some serious defeats, which brought on a new and important political revolution in France—the fall of the monarchy on August 10, 1792. Only after the victories of Valmy, September 20, 1792, and Jemappes, November 5, 1792, did France, now a Republic, take the offensive. Its victorious armies went on to conquer Belgium, a part of the left bank of the Rhine, Savoy, and Nice. What policy should France follow in these conquered regions?

Suddenly presented with an unexpected problem, the Convention was hesitant and divided. A debate began on September 22, 1792, when it was learned that the people of Savoy wanted union with France. In support of their petition, the Savoyards

* From Jacques Godechot, *La Grande nation: L'Expansion révolutionnaire de la France dans le monde de 1789 à 1799* (Paris: Aubier, 1956), I, 76–77, 77–87. This selection is printed by permission of Éditions Montaigne. Editors' translation.

cited the right of peoples to self-determination and the precedent of Avignon. But many deputies feared that a policy of conquest would endanger the young Republic. "We should be careful," exclaimed Camille Desmoulins, "not to imitate kings, by binding Savoy to the Republic." The debate resumed a month later, and the deputy Lasource criticized General Anselme for having introduced French laws into Nice without waiting for a decision from the Convention. "To give laws to other people is to conquer," he said. The Minister of Foreign Affairs Lebrun[1] expressed the views of a majority of the Convention when he wrote to Noël, France's representative in England, "We do not want to get involved in giving any people this or that form of government. The inhabitants of Belgium are to choose the kind that they find most suitable; we will not get mixed up in it."

But the Girondins, who dominated the Convention until June 2, 1793, soon managed to win approval for another point of view. Among their friends were political exiles, such as the Genevan Clavière and the Prussian Anacharsis Cloots, who could hope to return to their own countries and to obtain power only with the protection of French bayonets. In 1785 Cloots had published his *Prayers of a Gallophile,* in which he urged French annexation of the left bank of the Rhine: "This river is the natural limit of the Gauls," he said. Here we see the *début* of that famous phrase.

It appears that the "policy of the natural frontiers," which the Girondins and their successors under the Directory were to adopt, was not, as Albert Sorel has tried to prove in his large work, an old and firmly established tradition in French diplomacy. M. Zeller has studied its origin.[2] In his view the concept of a *natural frontier* was formulated first neither in France nor by Frenchmen. It was a foreign idea, originally from the Rhineland. In the sixteenth century, allusions to the Rhine as a natural frontier can be found only in a small number of unimportant pam-

---

[1] [He held this office from August 12, 1792, to June 14, 1793. Other foreign ministers mentioned later in this selection are the Marquis d'Argenson (1744–1747), the Comte de Vergennes (1774–1787), Delessart (November 28, 1791–March 17, 1792), Dumouriez (March 17, 1792–June 14, 1792), and Deforgues (June 14, 1793–April 3, 1794).]

[2] [The references are to Albert Sorel, *L'Europe et la Révolution française* (8 vols.; Paris: Plon, Nourrit, 1895–1904), and Gaston Zeller, "La Monarchie d'ancien régime et les frontières naturelles," *Revue d'histoire moderne,* VIII (1933), 305–333.]

phlets. Although the historian Mézeray mentions the "natural frontiers of Gaul," neither Richelieu's *Political Testament* nor his *Memoirs* speak of them except in a few cautious allusions. Under Louis XIV the natural frontiers were never an issue. The consistent aim of French foreign policy during the sixteenth and seventeenth centuries was to annex part or all of the Low Countries so as to push the frontier farther away from Paris. The idea of a *natural* frontier appeared only in the eighteenth century in line with the general infatuation with *nature*. Still, it clashed with official diplomacy, which found any conquest repugnant. "France has enough to make it content with its present size and boundaries," wrote the Marquis d'Argenson; and Vergennes even added, "France would do better to be wary of territorial expansion rather than seek it."

On the other hand, out of fear or out of desire, it was believed in the Rhineland that French diplomacy aimed at gaining for France its "natural frontiers"—those of Gaul in the Roman era. The notion of the *natural frontier* spread to France from Germany by means of Cloots's pamphlets in 1785, then even more forcefully through the writings of Georg Forster of Mainz in November 1792. Most of the Girondins accepted the idea; and at the end of November 1792 Brissot wrote to Dumouriez, "I want to tell you about an idea that is spreading somewhat here—that the French Republic should have no territorial limit but the Rhine." General Custine, for his part, stated in a letter to Minister Lebrun dated December 22, 1792, "The Republic will perish if the Rhine is not its frontier." Finally, on January 31, 1793, Danton officially announced to the Convention what has been called the "doctrine of natural frontiers": "Nature has marked out the limits of France; we shall reach them in every direction, the Rhine, the Atlantic, and the Alps. The boundaries of our Republic should extend that far." And Carnot specified on February 14, "The ancient and natural limits of France are the Rhine, the Alps, and the Pyrenees. . . . The areas that have been detached were lost only by usurpation."

The Girondin Convention adopted this new doctrine of natural frontiers, which seemed so rational and conformed so well to the new institutions that France was adopting. It accepted a plan to annex all territories lying between the old frontiers of 1789 and the new goals, the Rhine and Alps. Therefore, it is not surprising that when the Savoyards made another request for annexation, it was received favorably. On November 27, 1792, the annexation of Savoy won unanimous approval except for two votes and with the proviso of ratification by those concerned.

On December 15, the Convention decided to set up political procedures in the occupied countries that inevitably would lead to their annexation. It provided that the generals would destroy the Old Regime and replace the princely officials by provisional administrations "from which the enemies of the Republic would be excluded." The new administrators would be elected, but only those citizens could vote who took an oath "renouncing privileges and swearing allegiance to liberty and equality." By virtue of this decree and after handpicking members, assemblies were convoked in the occupied territories—Belgium, the Rhineland, the Porrentruy region [on the Swiss frontier], and the county of Nice. They proceeded to elect officials, then generally requested union with France. In the Rhineland, a "Rhenish Convention" which gathered at Mainz included only "patriots" chosen by a very small number of the inhabitants. On March 21, 1793, it voted for union with France.

The French National Convention itself decided to make some annexations: the county of Nice on January 31, 1793; Belgium, in fifteen different decrees published between March 1 and 30; the principality of Salm (in the Vosges mountains) on March 2; thirty-five communes of the Palatinate and of the Zweibrücken region on March 14 and 20; the "Rauracian Republic" (that is, the Porrentruy region) on March 23; Montbéliard, a year later, on February 11, 1794; and all the territory between the Rhine and Moselle rivers on March 30, 1793.

Perhaps the Convention believed itself to be the faithful interpreter of a majority of the population's desires, which had been the case for Avignon. In fact, except in Savoy, Nice, and Montbéliard, the inhabitants opposed union with France. In addition, these large-scale annexations, along with the execution of Louis XVI, contributed to the formation of the First Coalition. In a short time the defeated French forces had to evacuate most of their conquests and retreat to the national frontiers.

The Sister Republics

Some of the Girondins did not want to restrict France's expansion to the "conquest of the natural frontiers." They intended to go much farther. Influenced by "patriot" émigrés from the United Provinces, Germany, Switzerland, and Italy, they advocated the formation of "sister republics." These would in some way come under France's protection, would form a buffer on the frontiers, and would extend France's influence even farther.

Dutch patriots—or Batavians, as they began to be called—were the first to advocate such a policy. This was so because they were numerous in France, over five thousand, and also because they were solidly organized and their desires were not at all utopian. They wanted to carry their own Revolution of 1783 to its logical conclusion and push the Dutch Republic in a more democratic direction. Still, the first proposals of the Dutch "patriots" had received a cool reception. On May 15, 1791, a delegation of these patriots showed up at the Jacobin Club. "Their sudden appearance surprised the politicians," one newspaper reported, "but what really astonished them was the reading of a very long petition in which the patriots asserted that the time had definitely come for the French to support the oppressed Dutch refugees and to supply them with help in fomenting a revolution in Holland." The very embarrassed chairman of the Club discouraged the Dutch somewhat. "We are not going to set forth on crusades against Holland and Prussia," he said; "we will be satisfied with expressing hopes for universal liberty and for the true happiness of the human race."

A year later the situation had changed. France had declared war on Austria only, but Prussia joined the Emperor. The Girondins, now in power, remained cautious about Holland. In the instructions that Foreign Minister Dumouriez sent to de Maulde, France's representative at The Hague, he advised "prudence and circumspection." De Maulde was to establish "close relations" with the Dutch patriots, but he was cautioned to stir up an "outbreak" only if the government of the United Provinces abandoned its neutrality and took a strong position against France. Only if this situation developed should he "encourage a change in the form of government."

But at the news of the war there was a revival of hope among the Batavian patriots in Paris. Since December 1791 they had requested permission to form a "Batavian Legion," which would fight alongside the French Army for the victory of the Revolution in France and in the United Provinces. On May 29, 1792, they not only established a committee to recruit this legion, but also to create a "unitary and constitutional kingdom" of which William V of Orange would be king, so as "not to antagonize England." It was only on July 8, however, that Louis XVI made it known, in a letter to the Legislative Assembly, that he agreed to the creation of the legion. There was some resistance. Brissot opposed it, fearing to antagonize England. But the Batavian Legion was established at the end of July, and the Batavian Committee worked to win over the Jacobins. The military defeats of August and the fall of the monarchy slowed down its activity, but after Valmy and the proclamation of the Republic by the Convention, the Batavian Committee entered a new phase of feverish activity. The "Batavian Revolutionary Committee" of Paris officially constituted itself on October 22, 1792. Its most influential members were van Hooff, Colonel Daendels, and Dumont-Pigalle, a Frenchman who for a long time had edited the *Gazette de Leyden*. The Committee saw its aim as "the abolition of the stadholders' despotism" and replacing them by a "Batavian Republic" under a "constitution similar to that which the French are drawing up." Now the Committee's activities multiplied. Its minutes include a long list of visits to French officials and politicians, especially to the Minister of Foreign Affairs, Lebrun, who had lived in Belgium for a long time and who was still undecided on whether to annex Belgium to France, create a Belgian Republic, or form a new state comprising the United Provinces, the Austrian Netherlands, and Liège.

Little by little the Batavian Committee won support. It obtained some money and then it received the right to send agitators to Holland. Finally, on November 19, 1792, La Revellière-Lépeaux, deputy from Angers, proposed a decree which the Convention adopted and which had wide repercussions outside France. It delighted the patriots and it threw the monarchs and aristocrats into consternation. "In the name of the French nation, the National Convention declares that it will extend fraternity and aid to all peoples who wish to recover their liberty; and it charges the executive authority to give the generals the necessary orders to help such peoples and to defend those citizens who have been, or may be, harassed because of their actions in the cause of liberty."

This decree was significantly altered by that of December 15, which has already been mentioned: in any enemy country occupied by French forces, the new authorities set up by the generals could establish "new constitutions." Actually, this decree cleared the ground less for emancipation than for annexation to France. On January 8, 1793, careful instructions on how to apply these decrees were sent to the generals and French commissioners in the occupied areas. They pointed out in particular that the inhabitants of the regions conquered by the French armies were "to liberate themselves, . . . to erect, since they were now the legitimate sovereigns, free governments . . . invigorated by a thoroughgoing transformation in conformity with the principles of equality and liberty."

What new republics would be created in this fashion? It does not appear that the Convention or the ministry had precise ideas, except concerning the creation of the Batavian Republic, already anticipated at this point. The Swiss "patriots" were not yet very active. A very small number of Italian "patriots" were refugees in southern France—Buonarroti in Corsica, Ranza in Monaco, while Laurora, Matera, and Saoli were in Nice. They spoke of "liberating Italy," but this proposal still remained quite vague.

Nevertheless, the idea of "sister republics" had been suggested. It entered the minds of French politicians, especially the Girondins. The system of "sister republics" not only flattered the national and revolutionary pride of the French, by spreading the influence of the new France with the help of "patriots" from all countries, but it would also clearly bring strategic benefits, by protecting the recently expanded frontiers. And there would be economic advantages as well. The last were especially welcome at a time when the war imposed enormous financial sacrifices and when the assignats were rapidly losing their value. At the Jacobin Club on January 25, 1793, the deputy Chabot exclaimed, "Where will we find the money to make war?" He answered, "In Amsterdam and Madrid. . . . Bring freedom to Holland. It will open its arms to you; it will offer you its gold and its ships." To this, a soldier who was present added, "I have just come from the front. In Brussels I met a Dutchman. He told me that tons of gold were awaiting the French in Holland." This myth spread quickly. To the gold of Amsterdam was added that of Milan, Rome, Venice, and Berne. The decree of December 15, 1792, described above, explicitly specified that French assignats would circulate as money in all areas occupied by French armies.

The system of "sister republics," therefore, aimed not only at improving the condition of the French treasury, it would also promote an improvement in the country's entire economy. The desire for economic expansion had been the only expansionist sentiment expressed in the cahiers of 1789. Manufacturers and merchants wanted to export goods so as to destroy English competition, or at least to eliminate it from a part of Europe. Would not the sister republics serve as a sure market?

On November 16, 1792, in a resolution that also had broad repercussions, the Provisional Executive Council decided, in support of a proposal of the Minister of Foreign Affairs, Lebrun, to open the Scheldt to maritime trade. The mouths of this river had been closed by the Dutch since the sixteenth century, an action that had brought prosperity to Amsterdam and Rotterdam, while ruining Antwerp. The French government opened the Scheldt not only to provide an outlet for the industrial products of northern France and to satisfy the big French manufacturers, but also to win over the Belgians, to embroil them forever with England, Holland, and Prussia, and to get them to vote in favor of annexation by France. While supporting free navigation on the Scheldt, the Executive Council also raised some "general principles": obstacles to shipping on this river, it argued, are "against natural law; and they are a remnant of feudal servitude, or at least an odious monopoly established by force alone."

It was clear, however, that such a step could be accepted only by a Holland that was conquered or under French influence as a "sister republic." Several months later, on September 21, 1793, the Convention passed a "navigation act" inspired by English precedents. All French foreign trade was reserved in principle for French ships. Its application implied an extension of France's political, and then economic, influence in the maritime countries. But this measure, as much as the opening of the Scheldt and the new annexations, was to exasperate England and the old powers of Europe.

The condemnation of Louis XVI, as we have pointed out, served as a pretext that led to the formation in February 1793 of a great coalition directed by England and Austria against France. From April 1793, it will be recalled, the French armies had evacuated the largest part of their conquests, primarily those in the Rhineland and Belgium. The Girondin plan for expansion seemed to have failed.

The Plan of the Robespierrists

During the spring of 1793, the Girondins gradually were evicted from political leadership and were replaced by the Mountain. In July Robespierre and his friends took control of the Committee of Public Safety. Robespierre had been a bitter opponent of

Brissot on the war issue. He had pointed out how dangerous war would be for the Revolution, and events had proved how right he was. During the fall of 1792 Robespierre continued to oppose the Girondins. He was hostile to the conquest of the natural frontiers and even more strongly to a war of liberation and to the creation of sister republics. "Liberty," he frequently said, "does not come on the points of bayonets." Besides, the real problem facing the country between April 1793 and June 1794 was no longer to decide whether it should "liberate" peoples or conquer territories. And even less was it to decide the future of these conquests. It was above all to defend the fatherland, menaced at home and attacked on all its frontiers, at times even invaded. The "great" Committee of Public Safety had to concentrate all the country's energy so as to "organize" victory.

In the famous and carefully documented report that he presented to the Convention on November 17, 1793, Robespierre described the foreign policy that the Mountain expected to follow: close friendship with the "free" countries—the United States and Switzerland; loyalty to France's traditional alliances with small countries—Turkey, Genoa, Venice, and Denmark; and the renunciation of any policy of conquest and liberation. The following day a decree put the essentials of this speech into precise terms: the French Republic disavowed the war of propaganda and conquest. It would faithfully observe the treaties that bound it to Switzerland and the United States. It would guarantee that its soldiers would respect the territory of allied and neutral nations.

At the time, Barère [a member of the Committee of Public Safety] considered Robespierre's report "wise and sensible." The historian Albert Sorel (with a hostility to Robespierre that today strikes us as somewhat ridiculous) judged it "a needless elaboration," the work of "a small mind"; and he contrasted this speech of November 17 to a diatribe that Robespierre pronounced against the monarchies on December 5. Albert Mathiez, absorbed in the study of French internal affairs, mentioned Robespierre's speech in passing and praised its skillfulness, but he did not raise the question of its sincerity. However, neither of these historians concerned himself much with the effect that this speech had abroad, which was its main significance. In Holland the stadholder's government exulted. In a dispatch dated January 10, 1794, Caillard, a French secret agent in Amsterdam, wrote to Deforgues, the French Minister of Foreign Affairs, that Robespierre's report produced a tremendous sensation there. It had been translated into Dutch and printed in the newspapers. Then it was published separately and distributed by the thousands to convince the Dutch "patriots" that France was not going to intervene in their favor. The latter were indeed concerned and forwarded a note to Caillard. They wanted to know what policy France expected to follow concerning Holland. "Will it," they wrote, "carry out the long-standing declarations of peace and fraternity to free nations and of war against the tyrants and oppressors of the people?" What attitude would France adopt if the "Dutch people brought about a revolution"? But on February 25, 1794, or over three months after Robespierre's speech that Albert Sorel has called hypocritical political oratory, Deforgues sent a reply to the Dutch patriots that conformed to the policy defined by Robespierre. "The Republic's ambition," he said, "is not to make conquests; its chief aim is to live in peace with its neighbors and to contribute to their happiness. If a revolution by the people *were begun* in Holland, the French government certainly would support it; but it is essential that it be underway." This is, as one can see, a doctrine quite different from that of the Girondins.

In France foreign patriots were under suspicion. Many of them had been too closely associated with the Girondins. Some even were implicated in the "foreign plot," [3] tried by the Revolutionary Tribunal, condemned to death, and executed. The Batavian Revolutionary Committee stopped holding meetings. The premises of its secretary, Dumont-Pigalle, were searched. On November 6, 1793, Deforgues even declared that he knew absolutely nothing about such a committee. Dumont-Pigalle wrote to his former colleagues on November 13, "It seems to me somewhat dangerous to preserve the name of an association which, at this time, the government is no longer willing to acknowledge or recognize. In the present situation . . . even true patriots should be very circumspect in their actions, their speeches, and their writings. . . . Until further notice, I no longer wish to be involved in anything."

Nevertheless, at a date not revealed in the documents, the Batavian patriots did sound out Robespierre. His reply agreed closely with what we know of his policy. "When we possess Belgium," he said, "we'll see what we can do." In fact, after the vic-

[3] [A complicated series of intrigues late in 1793 involving some Frenchmen and aliens.]

tory of Fleurus on June 26, 1794, and before the fall of Robespierre on July 27, contacts were resumed between members of
the old Batavian Committee and the Committee of Public Safety.
On July 6 Dumont-Pigalle had an interview with Carnot.[4] They
considered a possible campaign in Holland and the political
consequences that might arise from it. From this point on, Dumont-Pigalle's datebook mentions more and more frequent meetings with Carnot and contains copies of correspondence with the
Organizer of Victory. But on 9 Thermidor (July 27), Robespierre
was overthrown and arrested; he was executed the next day. His
opponents, the Girondins or their friends, quickly regained
power; and with them the plans devised in 1792 returned to the
agenda of the Thermidorian Convention.

[4] [The Committee of Public Safety's chief specialist on military affairs, later
called the "Organizer of Victory."]

V

THE CAUSES OF THE
VENDÉE REVOLT
OF 1793

*A*mericans can recognize, as much as any people, the
*fascinating yet tragic nature of a civil war. The Ven-
dée uprising in western France was a civil war in the midst of a
revolution, a struggle that began on a large scale in 1793 and
continued sporadically until early in the Consulate.*

*Historians as well as such novelists as Balzac, Victor Hugo,
and Alexandre Dumas have been attracted to this dramatic episode. They have asked, and one may still ask, why the revolt took
place. Religious fanaticism, monarchical loyalty, treasonous conspiracy, the defense of ancient traditions, social conflict, opposition to military conscription—what was it that brought tens of
thousands of men out to fight against the Revolution?*

*Émile Gabory thinks religious feeling among the peasants
was the main underlying cause for a revolt triggered by other
provocations. Charles Tilly has found a history of social and economic antagonisms among the various people of the Vendée—
generally those from the cities against those from the countryside,
those engaged in commerce and manufacturing against those re-
lying exclusively on agriculture. These differences underlay the
religious antagonisms, and he believes that they generally determined which side people joined once they felt they had to make
a decision for or against the Revolution. Jacques Godechot considers that both religious and social differences played significant
parts in causing the revolt, and he also stresses other causes including that bête noire of republican historians, the aristocratic
conspiracy.*

*A definitive explanation seems as difficult to achieve for the
complex Vendée insurrection as for the American Civil War.*

A RELIGIOUS EXPLANATION*

Émile Gabory

*Émile Gabory (1872–1954) was born in the Vendée. While
serving as a professional archivist in this region, he devoted much time to writing about its colorful history. His major
works include* Napoléon et la Vendée *(1914),* Les Bourbons et la
Vendée *(1923),* La Révolution et la Vendée *(1925–1928), and*
L'Angleterre et la Vendée *(1930).*

The Uprising

The civil war in the Vendée broke out when the Convention
called up 300,000 men to protect the *patrie en danger*. The death
of Louis XVI [January 21, 1793] had brought about a general
coalition. After Austria and Prussia, the English, Russians, Spanish, and Dutch had struck at the frontiers with waves of soldiers.
In three decrees issued between February 20 and 24, 1793, all single Frenchmen from the age of eighteen to forty were declared
eligible for military service, and then 300,000 were called to the
colors. Eighty members of the Convention were ordered to over-
see these operations in the provinces. For the patriotic republicans this provided a new opportunity for emotional demonstrations. But among embittered souls, whose highest aims in life
were far beyond personal and mundane goals, there arose a unanimous feeling of protest. However, the draft quota fixed for each
department of western France was very small: for the department
of the Vendée, 4,197 men out of a population of 305,610; in
Maine-et-Loire, 6,202 men, of which 752 were to come from the
Cholet district and 701 from that of Saint-Florent; and in Loire-
Inférieure, 7,327 from a population of 430,000.

* From Émile Gabory, *La Révolution et la Vendée* (Paris: Librairie aca-
démique Perrin, 1925), I, 146–148, 195–199, 201–206, 214–217. Printed by
permission of the publisher. Editors' translation. Wherever possible, the
author's citations of sources in footnotes have been clarified.

If there had been time to prepare the public and to explain the decrees, opposition certainly would have been less vehement; but the orders had to be carried out immediately. . . .

One detail of the draft procedure was especially exasperating. Article 20 of a decree dated March 4 exempted most public officials from military service. To be sure, the militia of the Old Regime had also exempted royal officials, as well as most manorial officials. Moreover, those peasants who were at all well-to-do had known how to slip through the net. But in the new regime, where that glorious word equality rang out in every sentence, why, exclaimed the peasants, were these old distinctions kept for the benefit of the privileged class? When all this was added with electrifying rapidity to the underlying causes, one of the most awful political tempests in human memory was unleashed throughout a part of the West. It was like a sudden growth of every bad seed, like the unexpected sprouting of gigantic plants under a tropical sun. . . .

The Circumstances of the Uprising Clarify Its Causes

In the crackling of volleys, the thunder of cannon, the incitements to massacre, and the imploring wails, one can recognize the signs of all the remote and immediate causes that provoked and then launched the uprising. The rebels shouted their various rancors and individual resentments; they insistently proclaimed their motives. One cannot misread them.

What does not appear is "the plot," the celebrated and legendary plot that several writers have seen as the origin of the movement. No doubt, it would take a bold man to deny any significance to the instigations of the nobility and especially the clergy. To deny the existence of agitation by these suspected persons would be to misunderstand the situation. After having desired a new order or at least acquiesced in it, they had come to loathe a regime of which they had much to complain; and they did not hide their opinions. But no tie among all these dissatisfied people can be found, nor can any expressed or secret intention to overthrow the government by force of arms be found. Although some blood had flowed since 1791, there was no general pattern. In many other departments, the installation of Constitutional priests had also been carried out by gunfire; yet no plot or concerted plan is suggested.

In an oppressive atmosphere the storm could be felt building up: "We are having disturbances in our district, and we are afraid of seeing the germs of a general insurrection develop here," said a report from the town of Montaigu in the Vendée department. A dispatch dated March 10, 1793, from Chapelle-Heulin in Loire-Inférieure, noted the arrival "of men known to be disloyal; they have influenced the citizens to such a point that most of the commissioners of the sections [elected officials of small administrative units] have resigned." But these individual agitators obeyed no single watchword—they were moved to action by their own passions. The officials of the Maine-et-Loire department wrote to the Convention, "The servants of clergymen and of former nobles were the first agitators and many of them are leading crowds."[1] Could it have been otherwise? Was it not natural that the leaders of the movement would be those whose masters had suffered the most, those who had listened to their masters utter the most violent recriminations? These servants were the best prepared and often were former noncommissioned officers. The plot? It was denied even by those supporters of the revolutionary government who were intimately acquainted with the disorders. One of them wrote, "I realized that these events could not be considered the result of a concerted plan."[2] Later, the republican General Travot, always so acute and fair in his judgments, asserted that although the peasants had to be forced and coerced to march in the year VIII [fall 1799], the movement of March 1793 was spontaneous.

Some authors have tried to connect the pseudo-plot to the real one of Armand, Marquis de La Rouairie, in Brittany,[3] but the facts shout out against such an assertion. No one has been able to uncover the mysterious network which was supposed to have joined Brittany to the other provinces of the West. If some nobles in Anjou or Poitou were acquainted with the schemes of

---

[1] François Grille, *Lettres, mémoires et documents . . . sur . . . l'esprit du 1er bataillon des volontaires de Maine-et-Loire . . .* (Paris: Amyot, 1850), IV, 215, 218, concerning March 17, 1793; F.-A. Aulard (ed.), *Recueil des actes du comité de salut public avec la correspondance officielle des représentants en mission . . .* (26 vols.; Paris: Imprimerie nationale, 1889–1923), III, 432; the plot is mentioned in *Mémoires d'un ancien administrateur,* p. 10; on the causes cf. Dom François Chamard, *Les Origines et les responsabilités de l'insurrection vendéenne* (Paris: Savaète, 1898); and Henry Jagot, *Les Origines des guerres de Vendée* (Paris: Champion, 1914).

[2] Célestin Port, *La Vendée angevine* (Paris: Hachette, 1888), II, 202; Desmazières, *Précis des évènements dans le district de Cholet.*

[3] Charles-Louis Chassin, *La Préparation de la guerre de Vendée, 1789–1793* (Paris: Dupont, 1892), III, 285. [For biographical information on La Rouairie, see the selection on the Vendée revolt by Jacques Godechot.]

La Rouairie, which is possible, none were caught having any direct or indirect relation with him. No letter gives proof of such an association, no revelation to a friend, no admission before a court of law. Not one emissary of the Bourbon princes was arrested at this time while making his way toward the Vendée. There is total agreement in the statements of Vendean nobles carried along, despite themselves, by the popular flood and in the statements of peasants whose tongues were undoubtedly loosened by being so near the scaffold. All denied any prior agreement and insisted on the spontaneity of the movement's outbreak.

It has been asserted that d'Elbée[4] knew of the Breton plans, but neither at meetings nor among close friends did he ever mention them. "If the Vendeans had taken part in La Rouairie's plot," Madame de La Bouère has wisely pointed out, "they would have obtained weapons and ammunition; they did not do so; instead they had to fight with sticks." [5]

The insignificant part played by those Vendeans who, according to the scheme of the Breton plotter La Rouairie, were to lead his artificial uprising, is quite revealing. The region had been split up and assigned to various leaders. If we can trust the historian Alphonse de Beauchamp[6] (who, as an employee of the Ministry of Police under the Napoleonic Empire, had access to documents that have since disappeared), the principal agents of La Rouairie in the Nantes region were Palierne and Gaudin-Bérillais. Palierne, however, appeared on the scene only after the uprising had occurred—he asked for a military post under General Bonchamps. Gaudin-Bérillais showed himself to be mainly interested in calming the fervor of the insurgents. In Poitou Prince de Talmont was supposed to be the head of the uprising. But Talmont had emigrated to Germany. He joined the rebel army at Saumur only after the tumult of the Vendean hurricane attracted him. Paris was not fooled: on May 30, 1793, the Provisional Executive Council, which the deputies accused of not having foreseen the revolt, drew up a brief account of the measures taken to deal with the disturbances in the Vendée. It flatly

---

[4] [Maurice Gigost d'Elbée, a former army officer, emigrated in 1791, returned to France in 1792, became a leader of the Vendeans in 1793, and was executed in 1794.]

[5] Comtesse de La Bouère, *Souvenirs* (Paris: Plon, Nourrit, 1890), pp. 30–31; also see M.-J.-N. Boutillier de Saint-André, *Mémoires* (Paris: Plon, Nourrit, 1896), p. 51.

[6] Author of *Histoire de la guerre de Vendée* . . . (Paris: Giguet and Michaud, 1806).

declared that the La Rouairie affair had no connection with them. . . .

The peasants, and not the agents of La Rouairie, succeeded in igniting the general conflagration. The Breton agitator thought the nobles would begin and the peasants would follow, but in fact it was the peasants who led and the nobles who obeyed. This was the reverse of the plan. As soon as the first shots were fired, the rustics recognized the seriousness of their action. If they gave up, it meant the gallows. Fighting was their safest bet, but they lacked leaders. The republicans were commanded by career officers; they had to have some also. Logic clearly pointed to the manor houses. "If we had some nobles to lead us," one of them cried out, "we could march on Paris." [7] The nobles had served in the army; they had learned strategy and tactics. Because of their social standing, they had gained an authority which they would know how to exercise and which could quiet the rivalries among the commoners who were vying for leadership. Finally, the rebels had the very natural thought—almost instinctive among peasants who had fallen into an unfavorable situation—that of appealing to those more powerful than themselves, to those whose châteaux had stood for centuries amidst their cottages, protecting or menacing them. . . .

Nor did the black robes of the clergy appear in front of the red glare of the early fighting. Can one seriously believe that they contrived a plot, but discreetly left it to the peasants to carry out? The clergy had suffererd even more than the nobles. Outlawed in 1792 for refusing to take a schismatic oath, individual priests stirred up their faithful and fought back at the thresholds of their churches. But it is a long step from this kind of resistance to a general conspiracy. The day that the uprising broke out, the priests were not to be found amidst the crash and thunder leading the insurgents. No hidden thread bound the rectory to the parishioners. Studying the investigations made of those dramatic days, one can find no instance of a group led by clergymen. The priest of Saint-Martin de Beaupréau, tears in his eyes, rushed in front of his parishioners and begged them to return to their homes. It was too late, for they had already manhandled the gov-

---

[7] Port, III, 271, the words of Julien Chauvat; C.-L. Chassin, *La Vendée patriote, 1793–1800* (Paris: Dupont, 1893–1895), I, 209, where Guerry du Cloudy wrote to Boulard, "Soon . . . the people felt that they had to organize; willy-nilly, they chose peaceful men and forced on them the difficult and paramount duty of command."

ernment's recruiting agents. The bridges were burned between them and repentance. . . .

The older, underlying cause of the Vendée revolt, that of religion, was soon evident. Though rebels in the districts of Challans, Savenay, and Ancenis mentioned the call up of the 300,000 men in their manifestoes of March 14, 15, and 19, they especially emphasized their desire for the old religious arrangements and their vision of liberty. They complained of the many kinds of oppression. They boasted of bringing back "the good priests." They forced republicans to shout "Long live the pope, down with the nation." "God will end up being stronger than the devil," asserted the young women of the village of La Chèze. On March 24 Joly's insurgent army issued a declaration of justification while en route to Les Sables-d'Olonne. It sought to reestablish, so the army said, the throne and religion, order and peace. In this declaration the military draft was no longer an issue.

"Yes, we are defending the religion of our forefathers," declared the leaders of the Vendean army a little later, "and we shall defend it to the last drop of our blood, as did our divine Master, who did not fear to give His own life to establish it among us." And General Bonchamps, in the peroration of a speech, vehemently criticized republican officials for religious persecution, for hunting down priests, and for profaning churches. He did not refer to military service. Still later, replying to requests contained in M. de Gilliers' dispatch, sent by the Bourbon princes, the leaders of the revolt said the same thing: "The peasants took up arms mainly to reestablish the Catholic and Roman religion." Nothing about military service. Some rebels are even supposed to have said—and we learn this from the republican General Kléber: "Give us back our good priests and we will let you have the king." They were supposed to have added, "And we will let you have our nobles too." But that was not the way a Vendean thought.[8]

All the peasants who were arrested insisted on their Catholicism before their judges. Their enemies called this attitude a delirium: "They are really fanatical, as in the fourth century. Every day they are executed and every day they die while singing hymns and professing their faith. The use of capital punishment . . . only has the effect of rendering odious the power that

---

[8] *Kléber en Vendée (1793–1794). Documents publiés . . . par Henri Baguenier Desormeaux* (Paris: Picard, 1907), p. 29.

employs it." This comes from a statement by the deputy Volney, on mission from the Convention in Loire-Inférieure. The republican General Berruyer wrote, "Death is the beginning of happiness for them." Turreau [on mission from the Convention] compared them to crusaders.[9]

No doubt, some nobles did say that they wanted to restore the king. The Vendean leader Sapinaud died crying out, "I die happy, for I am dying for my king." When the Vendean General Beauvollier was asked by his judges, "What was your aim?" he replied, "My aim was to have a king." On August 18, 1793, the Vendean generals wrote to the Comte d'Artois [brother of Louis XVI], "We have revolted in the defense of Louis XVII, a child so worthy and so unfortunate." But all these people had forgotten the truth. They were plunged into the struggle by the sinewy arms of the peasants and only later did they recognize the interests of the monarchy.

Not all of them so misrepresented the real cause of the revolt. While dying, d'Elbée confessed, "I swear on my honor that although I sincerely and truly wanted a monarchical government, I had no specific plan in mind, and I would have lived as a peaceful citizen under any regime as long as it assured my tranquillity and the free exercise of the religious beliefs that I have always practiced." On the republican side, Choudieu [a deputy on mission in the Vendée] asserted that the monarchical cause had no effect on the revolt. An Angevin, Joseph Clemenceau, insists in his *History of the Vendée War* (1909) that the military draft simply provided an opportune excuse. The views of the deputy Turreau do not differ from this.

The ridiculous has even been claimed—that the Vendeans wanted to revive the feudal dues. Why should they? In their cahiers they had requested abolition of these payments. Immediately after the abolition of these dues, why would they feel regret? What they really wanted was the restoration of property to its former owners—to churches, to monasteries, and to individuals; but they were not so stubborn as to want it returned

[9] Port, II, 330, statement of Pierre Davy and similar accounts, pp. 232 *et seq.*, and p. 260; Vicomte B. d'Agours (ed.), *Documents inédits pour servir à l'histoire des soulèvements de mars 1793* . . . (Saint-Nazaire, 1883), p. 123; Chassin, *La Vendée patriote*, I, 358, a report to Minister Lebrun dated May 20; Jean Savary, *Les Guerres de Vendéens* . . . (Paris: Baudouin, 1824–1827), I, 170, dated April 28; Louis Turreau, *Mémoires pour servir à l'histoire de la guerre de la Vendée* . . . (Paris: Baudouin, 1824).

still covered with the feudal moss that these properties had accumulated over centuries.

Such interpretations of the causes are errors made by republicans. Now to deal with a royalist error that can be quickly refuted in the light of events: some writers, more interested in edifying their readers than in instructing them, have characterized all the insurgent peasants as men of angelic sweetness. But this was a war, a religious war, not a war of religion—a religious war upholds liberties, a war of religion tries to impose beliefs. This was a war, and no war, even if made by the best of Christians, can be won by the cross alone without other weapons. The crusaders also used swords, and the old chronicles tell us how terribly they used them on entering Jerusalem. In the fire of battle the ethereal zephyrs of Christianity are not always enough to temper hatreds—icy breaths which rise from the inner depths of men. This is even more true in civil wars, so open to the interplay of resentment and hatred. The uprising was a peasant revolt, as were previous uprisings against the nobles in other provinces. The insurgents wore their rosaries around their necks, but they carried their scythes with them. Woe to the one who refused to join their ranks! The popular flood uprooted by brute strength anyone who hesitated.

Insurgent parishes forced their neighbors to march with them. Peasants placed convinced republicans at their head when they recognized their abilities. Menaced by grape pickers' knives, Citizen Gelligné, a well-known patriot of Saint-Aignan, was forced to command the rioters. They needed not only leaders but also rank and file. This caused recruitment to be extremely brutal. The rebels "scoured the countryside, forcing all the inhabitants to join them—everyone marched, even ten- to twelve-year-old boys." [10] Unless the peasant could furnish proof of a severe wound making it impossible for him to march, he was liable to be recalled. If he could not fight, but was able to do such work for the army as kneading dough, then he was forced to do so. If he could perform no service, he had to give money. Often curiosity led the peasant to follow the crowd. Once committed, he rallied to succeeding musters without difficulty. Woe to those who were known to oppose this conscription against conscription! . . .

[10] Henri Gibert, *Précis historique de la guerre de Vendée, publié par Baguenier Desormeaux;* see also Boutillier de Saint-André, p. 48; and the *Documents inédits* of Vicomte d'Agours.

It should not be imagined that the two sides in the war corresponded without exception to particular social classes: all peasants did not become insurgents; all nobles were not carried away by the uprising; nor were all bourgeois favorable to republican ideas. In the most patriotic cities, such as Cholet and Segré, there were strong movements against national conscription. On the other hand, one has only to glance through the lists of refugee patriots (to be found in the Archives in Nantes) to be struck by the preponderance of peasants. While many petty bourgeois from rural areas marched at the heads of rebel groups, nobles could be found in the front ranks of the republican forces in the Vendée or on the national frontiers. . . .

From the same peasant family some went to the Right, others to the Left. The two Bernard brothers from Vézins turned up in opposing camps: one was a city official who saw his workshop burned by rioters; the other joined the Vendean army and was shot after the battle of Savenay. Charles Davy des Nauroy, a surgeon at Saint-Étienne-du-Bois, took part in the insurrection and became a major in General Charette's army; his brother stoutly proclaimed his republican sentiments. One bloody example of family hatreds deserves special notice. At the taking of Legé, Joly, commander of one of Charette's divisions, learned that one of his sons had just received a mortal wound. He ran to him; just then he was told that his other son, who was fighting on the republican side, had been captured. "What shall we do with him?" he was asked. "Shoot him," spat out the inexorable father. The two sons died at the same moment.

[The nineteenth-century republican historian] Edgar Quinet posed this question: if the land of the nobles and priests had been divided among the peasants, would they have revolted? He did not think so. But this is still an open question. For one thing, human self-interest seemed to be minimal in the uprising—rewards in the next world predominated over material desires. Some well-to-do peasants and some rich bourgeois, who would have been able to draw up chairs at the huge banquet of national property taken from the Church and the *émigrés,* refused to increase their fortunes by acquiring these confiscated properties. We do not hear from the mouths of rebels any regrets that they did not receive the government's manna in return for a little handful of depreciated assignats. But another point has to be made: those who are acquainted with the greediness of the farmer and his frantic desire for land would naturally think that a free gift, a total partitioning of the land, as was to be carried out in Russia, would have won over enough peasants to hinder the others, the great majority, from acting.

There are other unanswerable questions. Would the uprising have broken out without the draft of 300,000 men, that drop of water in a pitcher filled to overflowing, that spark in a building crammed with combustible materials? We do not know. Perhaps another cursed event would have occurred to unite all the discontented in one unanimous act. Or if religion had not been a factor, would the Vendée have obeyed the draft call? All we can say is that when complete religious liberty was granted under the Consulate, the conscription issue lost its sharp edge. A valuable piece of evidence, but in this kind of speculation, analysis loses its power and any attempt to see through the shadows is only vanity.

A SOCIOLOGICAL ANALYSIS*

Charles Tilly

*Charles Tilly (1929–   ), Professor of Sociology at the
University of Toronto, was born near Chicago and received his Ph.D. from Harvard University. In several articles and
a book,* The Vendée *(1964), he has carefully studied the Vendée
revolt from a sociologist's point of view.*

Those who have retold the epic of the Vendée have often given
the great counter-revolution of 1793 only two characters: a
steadfast, unified Vendée and a terrible, encircling Revolution.
Whether they have considered its source of power angelic or
demonic, they have often pictured the Vendée as rising to full
strength spontaneously, in an instant. Yet the Vendée was divided, and the division appeared long before the counter-revolution. It was divided not only into territories whose people supported the Revolution and territories whose people struck out
against it, but also—even in the heart of the section that resisted
the Revolution—into local groups of revolutionaries and counter-revolutionaries.

The most judicious historians of the Vendée have, of course,
recognized the major regional variations in the West of 1793,
seen the contrast between city and country, and observed the
alignments of social classes for and against the Revolution.[1] Yet

* From Charles Tilly, "Local Conflicts in the Vendée before the Rebellion of
1793," *French Historical Studies*, II (Fall 1961), 209–215, 230–231. Reprinted
by permission of the author and the editor of *French Historical Studies*.
[1] Charles-Louis Chassin, *La préparation de la guerre de Vendée* (3 vols.; Paris,
1882); Léon Dubreuil, *Histoire des insurrections de l'Ouest* (2 vols.; Paris,
1929); Émile Gabory, *La Révolution et la Vendée* (3 vols.; Paris, 1925);
Pierre de la Gorce, *Histoire religieuse de la Révolution française* (Paris, 1910),
vol. II; Célestin Port, *La Vendée angevine* (2 vols.; Paris, 1888). The term
Vendée includes all the sections of Brittany, Poitou, and Anjou that joined
the insurrection south of the Loire.

their traditional concerns—tracing the noble-clerical plot that they have often presumed to lie behind the counter-revolution, assigning the credit or blame for the counter-revolution to some particular segment of the population, or identifying the sort of mentality that could lead peasants into counter-revolution— have turned their eyes from the relationship between the essentially local party conflicts of 1791–92 and the essentially local beginnings of the counter-revolution in 1793. They have therefore not seen how far the party divisions reached into the countryside, in how many rural neighborhoods a tiny but determined and officially dominant pro-revolutionary minority struggled with an angry but disorganized anti-revolutionary majority, and how many troublesome incidents of 1791 and 1792 were local party clashes that anticipated the furious encounters of 1793.

The existence of local party conflict cannot in itself explain the counter-revolution. That enterprise requires a detailed examination of the Old Regime and implies a comparative study of revolutionary and non-revolutionary sections of the West as well as of individual supporters and opponents of the Revolution. The aim of this article is not so grand as that: it is to trace the formation, the composition, and the conflict of the two parties in the territory that was swept by counter-revolution in 1793. . . .

There are three essential points to local party conflict before the Vendée: (1) The parties of revolutionaries and counter-revolutionaries—"patriots" and "aristocrats," in the terminology of the time—formed along fairly regular lines of class and locality which divided even the rural areas into contending factions. (2) The parties formed early in the Revolution and eventually left almost no one uncommitted to one side or the other, with a small but energetic and self-conscious patriot group forming first, and a much larger, awkward and uncoordinated aristocrat party forming later, largely in opposition to the patriots rather than in pursuit of any specific program. (3) The years 1791–93 witnessed a long series of increasingly violent struggles between the parties, during which the patriots gained control of the governmental machinery and lost control of the population; the counter-revolution of March, 1793, was the last and deadliest of these party conflicts.

The boundaries of class and locality that separated the adherents of the Revolution from their opponents followed lines of cleavage that were already prominent in western France before the great political upheaval began. The eighteenth-century stirring of industry, the expansion of the market, the extension of urban influence, the penetration of the state into local affairs had all affected the West, but had not touched all its segments equally. In general, it was the areas and the elements of the population which these processes had affected most deeply that supported the Revolution.

The patriots were predominantly bourgeois, in the sense of the term which includes not only rentiers, but also professionals, administrators, merchants, and entrepreneurs. The predominance of one class among the patriots fostered communication, coordination, and a sense of common purpose, but it also set up rugged barriers to cooperation with wavering or even sympathetic members of other social classes. The opposition was much more diffuse, disparate, and disjointed: peasants, nobles, priests, and substantial numbers of artisans.

There are three ways in which locality entered into party alignments. First, each of the departments stricken by the counter-revolution (Vendée, Deux-Sèvres, Loire-Inférieure, Maine-et-Loire) included large territories that were faithful to the Revolution. Those territories were, generally speaking, the vicinities of large cities and those areas which combined considerable peasant property and the production of cash crops such as wine or flax with the presence of wealthy monasteries or chapters. Second, throughout the region city-dwellers were more likely to be patriots than were their rural neighbors. This generalization applies even to the "cities" of a few thousand souls, which dotted the countryside. As rural as such settlements would have appeared to modern eyes, they were filled with people who were detached from agriculture and engaged in trade, manufacturing, and administration. Their citizens were more often literate, more often mobile, more often hostile to the established church, more often politically skilled, more often aware of national affairs, more often capable of envisaging the reforms that would better their lot. Each of these would lead us to expect more support for the Revolution in the cities.[2] Finally, even in the countryside itself, it was the most citified segments that were the revolutionary outposts.

[2] For some indications of the "urban" character of the Revolution as a whole, see Georges Lefebvre, "La Révolution française et les paysans," in *Études sur la Révolution française* (Paris: Presses Universitaires de France, 1954), and Crane Brinton, *A Decade of Revolution* (New York: Harper, 1934), pp. 23–26.

The most important division in this respect was between the *bourgs* and the open country. A *bourg* was a small center of population which ordinarily contained a church, an inn, shops and offices, the homes of a few merchants, notaries or doctors and of most of the local weavers, dyers, and other craftsmen. There was at least one *bourg* in every commune, but the majority of the population usually lived outside it, in tiny hamlets and isolated farmsteads. The *bourg*-dwellers, in general, were the element of the rural population most favorable to the Revolution, and the larger commercial *bourgs* the principal centers of pro-revolutionary activity in the countryside. The important difference between their situation and that of the cities is that the patriots of country communes were in direct everyday contact with their political enemies, and were frequently the weaker party.

A case in point is Le May, not far from Cholet, where "the *bourg* . . . formed the center of a concentration of merchants, clothiers, wool-spinners, tanners, and smiths, having a sort of monopoly on the special, and then quite important, manufacture of spindle liners. . . ." [3] At the beginning of the Revolution, the *bourg* contained the exceptionally high proportion of about 2000 of the commune's 3500 people. The bourgeois of Le May shared the outlook of their urban confrères, demanding roads above all else in 1787, later supporting the Revolution, organizing a National Guard, and providing a number of army volunteers. Yet even in Le May the patriots were an uncertain minority. The old curé, who had refused the oath relative to the Civil Constitution of the Clergy, had such a following that it was extremely difficult to remove him from his post as *procureur de commune*. The patriotic successor to the curé that the local bourgeois proposed was hooted, cursed, threatened, chased, and finally stoned. Even though the patriots of Le May eventually took over the local offices that the Revolution had to offer, up to the very counter-revolution the commune was split into two factions, an "urban" minority and a "rural" majority.

As the case of Le May suggests, it was the inhabitants of the *bourgs* and particularly the bourgeois, who were more likely to be both patriots and supporters of the Constitutional clergy,[4]

---

[3] Célestin Port, *Dictionnaire historique, géographique et biographique de Maine-et-Loire* (Paris and Angers, 1878), II, 630. References for the following account: A. D. Maine-et-Loire C192, 1 L 202, 1 L 357, 1 L 357 bis, 1 L 364, 1 L 365.
[4] I.e., the priests who were willing to hold office under the conditions set by

and the outlying residents of the commune who were more likely to be the enemies of that clergy. This fortified the otherwise insecure position of the Constitutional curé in the Vendée, since he generally lived and worked in the *bourg*. However, it also increased the emotional distance between the *bourg* and its surroundings. The same barrier that separated city and country divided *bourg* and hinterland.

On the other hand, some *bourgs*—particularly those that lacked commerce or industry and had been the seats of important noble houses—were counter-revolutionary.[5] This fact indicates that sheer concentration of the population was not the most important matter. Rather, it was the appearance of manufacturing, commerce, and their typical personnel in the *bourgs* that counted. One might say in general that where commerce and manufacturing had penetrated the West, there were supporters for the Revolution. This statement applied not only to regions, not only to cities, but also to the segments of individual communes. Even though the West remained one of the most rural sections of France, commerce and manufacturing had reached the countryside and placed their agents there. As a consequence, there were tiny patriotic nuclei scattered throughout the Vendée, each surrounded by an anti-patriotic mass, in continual, enervating collisions with that mass.

Obviously, the parties that shed each other's blood in 1793 were already present and angry long before the counter-revolution. The revolutionary party appeared first, in the form of small groups of bourgeois who wished to encourage and profit by the reforms of the Revolution. By the time of the local elections of February, 1790, a great many communes already contained two factions, one supporting the curé for the post of mayor, and the

---

the Civil Constitution of the Clergy. In the West, support for the Constitutional generally implied "patriotism," and patriotism implied support of the Constitutional. Cf. the report of Gallois and Gensonné, *Réimpression de l'Ancien Moniteur*, X, no. 314 (10 novembre 1791), 332.

[5] In southern Anjou, some of the most striking cases of geographic division of the revolutionary and counter-revolutionary parties appeared where a commune contained two rival *bourgs*. Often, one of these was an agricultural center, and the other a commercial center. This was true at Villedieu-la Blouère, where the church, and therefore the official seat of the commune, remained in the small *bourg* of la Blouère, but where manufacturing and commerce flourished in the larger center of Villedieu, and where two factions struggled during the Revolution, the defenders of the new regime established at Villedieu, and the adherents of the old centered at la Blouère.

other opposing him. Nevertheless, it was not until the beginning of 1791, with the application of the Civil Constitution of the Clergy and the first sales of church property, that identification with one faction or the other became general. In January of 1791 began a multitude of incidents like the one that brought 60 or 70 men from the parish of St. Aubin de Baubigné to the offices of the District of Châtillon (Deux-Sèvres). "If you don't pay our curé," they objected to a member of the Directory, "and if you take everything away from our seigneur, how will we get work, and what will we live on?" They complained that the execution of the law would deprive them of their priests, threatened to "cut the administrators in two and pull out their innards," then shouted that the officials weren't wasting any time selling the church properties.[6]

Religious administration was the great public issue that divided the two parties. This fact has led most historians of the Vendée to see in it either the struggle of religion and irreligion or the conflict of free thought and fanaticism. This simplification of matters is misleading because it ignores the fact that the religious issues, like all great public issues anywhere, permitted local and personal rivalries to align people with one party or the other, and the fact that the choice of sides men made on this issue followed fairly well-defined lines of class and locality.

In describing the composition and formation of the two parties I have also necessarily discussed their conflict, which became open, fierce, and general in 1791. During 1791 and 1792, the patriots were fortifying their control over the governmental machinery, as the aristocrats disappeared from office through a process of exclusion and voluntary withdrawal. It was therefore mainly the patriot minority that was charged with keeping revolutionary order, collecting taxes, and introducing the reforms of the Revolution to their hostile compatriots.

All the important events in the Vendée between 1790 and the outbreak of the counter-revolution found the two parties opposed to each other, and almost all of them involved attempts of the patriots to enforce the laws of the Revolution. These were the events that most frequently aroused violent incidents: the in-

[6] Archives Nationales F⁷3690¹. St. Aubin (which was, no doubt significantly, the seat of the famous counter-revolutionary La Rochejacquelein family) was a continuous source of trouble for the District of Châtillon for at least two years before the insurrection.

stallation of a Constitutional curé, the closing down of a super-
numerary church, the policing of a religious pilgrimage, the organization of the local National Guard troop, the holding of local
elections, and the recruitment or conscription of soldiers for the
national army. It was precisely in the districts where incidents of
these kinds were most common in 1791 and 1792—the districts of
Montaigu, Challans, Clisson, Marchecoul, St. Florent, Cholet,
Châtillon—that the counter-revolution took hold first and with
greatest force. That is hardly surprising; the counter-revolution
was simply the last and most disastrous clash of the series. Many
historians have explained the generality and effectiveness of the
rebellion by means of a noble-ecclesiastical plot, with a bewil-
dered and subservient peasantry as its instrument. This unproved
hypothesis hardly seems necessary, when one considers the years
of wrathful relations between the very parties that were to make
war in 1793. . . .

In its heyday, the counter-revolution so successfully swept the
patriot minority from the Vendée that it almost seemed there
had been no patriots there at all. The struggle began with a multitude of local attacks on the patriots of country *bourgs,* and developed into a war against the patriot cities that remained. Within
ten days after the invasion of Chemillé by the *gars* [young fellows]
of St. Georges, Melay, and other nearby communes, a group of
representatives had to report to the Convention:

> What we have here are not simply local disturbances which are
> easy to break up, but almost the whole countryside marching in
> battle order, led by able chiefs, with some firearms and munitions,
> and placing themselves to attack and massacre the cities. It is ig-
> norance and fanaticism, become the blind instruments of the aris-
> tocracy, which is working with it to destroy the more enlightened
> cities, which, if destroyed, will leave nothing on the earth but
> despotism and slavery.[7]

In a more homely style, a favorite verse of the Vendéans reveals
how much of their war was directed against the urban bourgeois
patriots. The epithet *pataud,* applied to the enemy, combined
the concepts of city-dweller, bourgeois, and patriot:

[7] Alphonse Aulard (ed.), *Recueil des actes du comité de salut public* (Paris,
1889), II, 468.

Vous créverez dans vos villes,
maudits patauds,
tout comme les chenilles,
les pattes en haut.[8]

In the long run, it was the counter-revolution that "broke" because it was unable to subdue the cities and the armies of the Convention. It reached its most furious and effective force on its own territory, while striking at its own local enemies. This in itself is simply one more reflection of the importance of essentially local conflicts, beginning long before March, 1793, in the development of the terrible counter-revolution.

[8] Dubreuil, *op. cit.*, I, 94.
        [You will croak in your cities,
          cursed *patauds*,
          just like caterpillars,
          flat on your backs.]

A SYNTHESIS*

Jacques Godechot

For biographical information on Jacques Godechot, see the section entitled "The Character of the Constituent Assembly (178_-1791)."

The peasant insurrections in western France were but the first of their kind among the numerous counter-revolutionary insurrections. In the course of the period with which we are concerned [1789–1804], there were many other peasant insurrections directed against revolutionary leaders or institutions. For example, the Vendée insurrection revived after 1795, then reappeared in 1799, and again even as late as 1830. The peasants of Normandy, Brittany, and of the western fringes of the Paris basin took up arms against the Revolution from 1793 to 1799. This movement was called the *Chouannerie*. In southwestern France peasants rose up in the name of the king in 1799. Several peasant insurrections took place in Italy from 1796 to 1799, especially in Calabria [the "toe" of the Italian boot], in the Papal States, and in Tuscany. In Belgium there was a "peasant war" in 1798, which was also a counter-revolutionary insurrection. German and Swiss peasants took up arms against the Revolution on several occasions between 1796 and 1799. After 1800 numerous peasant insurrections of a counter-revolutionary nature broke out in different areas of Europe. The most famous such uprising, and the one which had the most important consequences, was that of the Spanish peasantry, known as the Spanish War of Independence. The German wars of "liberation" in 1813 and 1814 also were, in part, peasant insurrections.

* From Jacques Godechot, *La Contre-Révolution: Doctrine et action, 1789–1804* (Paris: Presses Universitaires de France, 1961), pp. 216–229. Printed by permission of the publisher. Editors' translation.

All these insurrections belonged to the same family, and we can ask if they sprang from similar causes. Historians disagree considerably about the causes of the insurrections in western France. There are a great many books dealing with the subject, but most are apologetic and hagiographic works written by royalists who eulogize the Vendeans or *Chouans*.

In their studies of the causes of the insurrections in western France, historians are divided between two points of view, depending on their political sympathies. Those hostile to the Revolution favor the thesis of a spontaneous uprising: the Constitution of 1791 and the institutions of the Revolution contradicted the natural order of things; and so the peasants, shocked by the aberration, revolted spontaneously. They also rebelled against atheism, against all religious innovations, and against unjustified reforms. On the other hand, historians favorable to the Revolution support the thesis of an insurrection incited either by the actions of the clergy and the nobility, or by the agents of the *émigrés*, or by the countries at war with France.

Because of insufficient research, we do not know enough about the economic or social structure of the insurgent areas in either western France or the other regions where peasant uprisings occurred. Only two works have sketched the social structure of the insurgent regions—for France, Léon Dubreuil's book, *Histoire des insurrections de l'Ouest*, and for Italy, that of Gaetano Cingari.[1] Other works are more anecdotal, describing the course of events without really analyzing their causes. Moreover, Dubreuil's study of the social structure of the insurgent regions is quite brief. But at the present moment, new research is attempting to add to our knowledge of this question.

General Characteristics of Counter-Revolutionary Peasant Insurrections

We may ask if the peasant insurrections can be explained by geographical determinism. Upon examining the insurrections in western France, we see that they occurred in the *bocage* areas, where small fields were surrounded by hedgerows through which winding roads ran and where it was easy to hide. The peasants'

[1] *Giacobini e sanfedisti in Calabria nel 1799* (Messina, 1957). [Marcel Faucheux's *L'Insurrection vendéenne de 1793: Aspects économiques et sociaux* (Paris: Commission d'Histoire économique et sociale de la Révolution, 1964), as well as most of Professor Tilly's publications on the Vendée, have appeared since the present selection was originally published.]

fields were scattered, and they lived in isolated hamlets. But, an analysis of other peasant insurrections reveals that they took place in regions of a different character. In southern Italy, Calabria was an area of rather wild scrub land where the peasants lived in very large villages, actually rural cities which sometimes contained more than twenty thousand inhabitants. Yet, communications were as difficult as in western France. In Spain the 1809 insurrection occurred on the Castilian plateau as well as in the *huerta* [irrigated fruit lands] of Valencia and in the Aragonese plains. Communications were difficult in the Spain of the Old Regime too. Therefore, it is hard to identify a geographical determinism underlying the peasant revolts.

Can we speak of a sociological determinism, of a certain social structure which predisposed people to revolt? We must mention that in all insurgent areas during the revolutionary era, in France, Italy, Spain, and elsewhere, insurrections occurred most often in regions where the peasants were very submissive to their lords and landowners. Even today in the Vendée the peasants speak of the landowner as "our master," perhaps a vestige of their former submissiveness. In these areas the peasants either respect the landowner, the lord, and submit to him, or they hate him. The landlord exercises his authority in the secular sphere by collecting the rents due him, and in the religious sphere by requiring his peasants to attend mass, receive the sacraments, and send their children to Catholic school.

It has been pointed out that in these areas, the authority of the clergy, especially that of the local priests, was very great. In the Vendée as well as in Calabria, when the priest was a partisan of the new regime the local population followed him; when, on the contrary, he opposed it, so did the population. The influence of the clergy appears to predominate in all the areas where peasant insurrections have been observed, whether in western France, southern or eastern Italy, Spain, Belgium, or Switzerland.

Are we dealing here with a matter of religious faith or of custom? It is difficult to say. In these regions where communication was difficult and where formal education was rare and hardly developed, superstition was widespread. It appears that the clergy incited the peasants to resist changes in religious ritual rather than arousing them to fight for basic tenets of faith. We also can wonder about the role played in the preparation and development of the insurrections by a secret religious organization, the Aa, a group still very little understood. This association, growing out of the Congregation of the Holy Sacrament, which in turn was linked with the Society of Jesus, grouped together refractory priests, especially in southwestern France. It is possible that it also promoted the Vendée rebellion.[2] Signor Cingari states that in Calabria there were believers and nonbelievers in both the revolutionary and the opposing camps.

It appears, therefore, that the peasant insurrections were caused to some degree by geography—the difficulty of communication that hindered new ideas from spreading. Peasant insurrections were also a consequence of the social structure. They developed in regions where the peasants—sharecroppers or tenants—were very dependent on the landlords, as well as frequently in areas where the peasant was hostile to the bourgeois. The peasant was best acquainted with the bourgeois in his capacity as a tax collector, either for the state or the lord, or as a merchant exploiting the countryside and often lending money at usurious rates of interest. In addition, the effect of religion, of religious practice, is undeniable; the influence of the clergy is certain.

Turning to the particular conditions that affected the insurrections in western France, we must first point out the attitude of the peasants toward the Revolution. At the beginning of the Revolution the regions that were to rebel so extensively and violently were not hostile to reforms. The peasants, on the contrary, favored them. In 1789 they greeted the abolition of tithes and feudal dues enthusiastically—they already had requested such actions in their cahiers of grievances. In the Old Regime the salt tax had aroused much discontent among the peasants and they were happy that it was abolished. They also had been very hostile to the drawing by lot for *militia service,* even though this did not weigh very heavily on them.

There were some peasants, however, whose demands were not satisfied by the reforms of the revolutionary era. In western France there were tenant farmers in a special category—tenants on cancellable leases or *colons partiaires* [a type of sharecropper]. These particular kinds of land tenure existed only in this region.

[2] On the Aa, see B. Faÿ, *La Grande Révolution* (Paris, 1959), as well as P. Droulers, *Action pastorale et problèmes sociaux sous la monarchie de Juillet chez Mgr d'Astros, archevêque de Toulouse* (Paris, 1954). Consult also the article on the Aa in the *Dictionnaire de spiritualité.* More probing studies of the Aa are in progress.

Peasants who were fettered by these especially onerous types of land tenure generally were loyal to the Revolution; in spite of everything, they hoped for changes in their land tenure.

Therefore, the peasant did not, a priori, oppose the revolutionary regime. On the other hand, he was frequently hostile to the bourgeois. He knew the bourgeois only as an employee of the lord, an agent of the noble. It was the bourgeois who collected feudal dues for the lord. It was the bourgeois who sold essential goods to the peasant, and the peasant believed that he was being exploited. Among the peasants, the bourgeois had a reputation for being miserly, grasping, and selfish. Peasants generally were hostile to him. The same attitude can be seen in Italy, Belgium, and Spain. The alliance between the bourgeoisie and the peasantry allowed the Revolution to succeed, but in France, as elsewhere, in those regions where this alliance could not be achieved, the Revolution miscarried.

The religious attitudes of the peasantry of western France have not yet been examined by recently developed methods of sociological analysis. But, in general, the peasant of the West was very attached to religious practices, if not to religion itself. He was very loyal to the forms, rituals, and ceremonies, to which he tended to attach a magical value. The closing of churches and the interruption of normal religious practices certainly caused discontent. He would not tolerate such innovations. In Calabria and Spain there were similar reactions.

The peasantry in western France was subject to the clergy's leadership. Before the Revolution, the clergy was divided into two categories. The lower clergy, poorly educated and very close to the common people, were obliging, charitable, and loved by their flocks. The upper clergy were usually very haughty. In sharp contrast to the poor parish priests, they were recruited from the nobility, often belonged to Masonic lodges, and were wealthy. The richest bishop was that of Bayeux. He had an income of 90,000 livres. The poorest bishop, that of Saint-Brieuc, had an income of 12,000. The lower clergy in western France warmly welcomed the meeting of the Estates-General. In the elections very few bishops were chosen. Only two out of seven bishops were elected from the archdiocese of Rouen; from that of Tours, only two out of twelve; and Brittany sent no bishops to the Estates-General. But from Bordeaux, seven out of ten were elected (the Bordeaux archdiocese was the one least troubled by revolutionary insurrections).

We see, then, that the clergy welcomed the Revolution enthusiastically. But, after the very first measures, they grew dissatisfied. Although pleased with the abolition of the old method of paying priests, they opposed the abolition of tithes, which was decided during the night of August 4, 1789, and they opposed even more the nationalization of Church property, which was voted November 2, 1789. Religious liberty, as set forth first in the Declaration of the Rights of Man and later even more clearly by various laws, also offended this region that was almost entirely Catholic (there were only a few Protestants). The clergy was irritated above all because the revolutionary reforms placed religion and its ministers in a subordinate position instead of keeping them in the top rank, as was true before 1789. On September 12, 1789, Bishop Le Mintier of Tréguier, Brittany, published a statement very hostile to the Revolution. It attacked the thought of the Enlightenment, condemned freedom of the press, warned the faithful against dangerous innovations which put "the essence of royal authority in the hands of the multitude." He deplored "the weakened military discipline and the fact that citizens were taking up arms against each other. . . ." "The Church," he said, "is falling into degradation and servility; its ministers are threatened with being reduced to the status of appointed clerks. Also, the highest courts are ignored and humiliated." Le Mintier went on to protest against the substitution of state welfare for charity and against the abolition of certain very wise old laws. Finally, he warned the peasant against buying nationalized Church lands, even though they had not yet been put on sale. Le Mintier's statement had a very great impact. All the nobles of the region approved of it, and it marked the beginning of the break between the people of the western area and the Revolution.

The publication of the Civil Constitution of the Clergy heightened the discontent, especially because it reduced the number of dioceses. Seven dioceses were abolished in the western region, and in an area of such poor communications this could have resulted in very serious inconveniences. Many priests, perhaps encouraged by the Aa, refused to take the oath required by the Civil Constitution. In the diocese of Angers over 50 per cent of the priests were refractory; in the Vendée and in Brittany more than 80 per cent. Nevertheless, this was not the major reason for the outbreak of the insurrection; for there was an equal or even a greater proportion of refractory priests in other areas of France where insurgency did not develop. For example, around the Massif Central over 80 per cent of the priests were refractory and in the departments of Moselle and Bas-Rhin, 92 per cent.

The replacement of refractory priests by those who took the oath and who were alleged to be bad priests began to arouse some opposition. Arrests of refractory priests made matters worse. Refractory priests then held clandestine services, and religious processions marched at night. Such nocturnal ceremonies awakened the mystical spirit characteristic of the people of western France. The Bretons, who believed in goblins prowling the moors at night, were attached to their legends. Their fears and superstitions were aroused, and this created an attitude hostile to the Revolution. Hatreds were inflamed.

The bourgeoisie's attitude, on the other hand, was generally favorable to the Revolution. The bourgeoisie in western France, as everywhere else, was a composite class—it included merchants, lawyers, and lower government officials. But added altogether, the bourgeoisie was less numerous in the West than elsewhere. In 1789 it actually was large only in Nantes.

From the beginning of 1789 the bourgeoisie gained entry into the municipal councils of the large cities. When Church property went on sale, most of the purchasers were bourgeois. We should not believe, however, that all the bourgeois had the same point of view. Though many of them supported the Revolution, others were quite hostile. An entire group of the bourgeoisie had connections with the nobility by family ties and aspired to noble rank. Nobles and bourgeois mingled in the "literary societies" and Masonic lodges. For example, the lodges of Le Mans included nobles, merchants, and government officials.[3] Yet, in general, the bourgeoisie went along with the revolutionary movement. The majority of the western peasantry, on the contrary, grew more and more hostile to the reforms.

The Origins of the Insurrection

Certainly, the general conditions just analyzed played a very important part in the origin of the western insurrections, but a catalyst was necessary. The thesis of republican historians—that the insurrection originated in plots organized either by refractory priests or by the nobility—cannot be dismissed out of hand. Clearly, the actions of the nobility and the clergy played a deci-

[3] A. Bouton, *Les Francs-maçons manceaux et la Révolution française* (Le Mans, 1958).

sive part in the preparation of the insurrection. In this regard, it appears that a plot organized by a noble, the Marquis de La Rouairie, had a great impact.[4]

The Marquis de La Rouairie was born at Fougères, Brittany, in 1750. He had a wild adolescence, with numerous duels and remarkable love affairs, and gained notoriety by an attempt at suicide. He took part in the American War for Independence: under the name of Colonel Armand he led a band of irregulars, which made him a celebrity. He came back from America very enthusiastic for liberty, but he had neither the intelligence nor the social rank of Lafayette; on his return to France, he was received rather coldly. It appears that the comparison between his reception and that given to Lafayette displeased and embittered him.

In 1788, during the agitation which preceded the calling of the Estates-General, he passionately favored the Parlement of Brittany and he was chosen to transmit to Paris the grievances of the Breton nobility, who were hostile to the recent decisions of the king. La Rouairie was arrested and thrown into the Bastille. Released at the fall of the Brienne ministry, he returned in triumph to his birthplace, Fougères. He protested against the ordinance regulating the methods of election for the Estates-General because it disregarded the laws and customs of Brittany. He was particularly hostile to the doubling of the Third Estate, and when the Constituent Assembly was created, he opposed the first reform measures. It appears that by the beginning of 1790 he was thinking of organizing a counter-revolutionary movement: he gathered a number of his aristocratic friends in his château near Saint-Brieuc; and at this time some of them already suggested appealing to England for aid in supporting a counter-revolutionary movement.

La Rouairie left France in May 1791. Furnished with an ordinary passport, he reached Coblenz. There he claimed to represent the Breton Association, which was composed of *émigrés* from this region. The Association had as its aim a restoration of a monarchy "checked" by the ancient constitution of France, a monarchy respectful of the traditional Breton liberties and of "the religion of our forefathers." As a striking force, La Rouairie

[4] See on this subject A. Goodwin, "Counter-Revolution in Brittany: The Royalist Conspiracy of the Marquis de La Rouërie, 1791–1793," *Bulletin of the John Rylands Library*, 1957, pp. 326–355. The name can be spelled either La Rouairie or La Rouërie.

hoped to provide the Association with guerilla bands similar to those he had led in the United States. The Breton Association soon established branches in all the provinces of the West— Brittany, Normandy, Anjou, and Poitou. It was based on a whole series of committees organized in every city that had been an official seat of a diocese before the Revolution. Each committee was composed of six members and a secretary. There were less important committees in other cities. The committees received orders from their leader, the Marquis de La Rouairie himself. Article 6 of the manifesto distributed to the committees defined the Association's object: to contribute with "the least possible violence" to the restoration of absolute monarchy and to the recognition of "the prerogatives of provinces, landowners, and Breton honor." Association members were urged to do their best to win over National Guardsmen. Article 11 stated, "The military organization will be established later." Clearly, the Association was preparing to create a true counter-revolutionary militia.

In June 1791, the Comte d'Artois recognized La Rouairie as the head of the Breton Association. For financing he went to see Calonne,[5] but received only a small subsidy in the devaluated paper currency of the Paris Discount Bank and in counterfeit assignats. Later, the Comte de Provence confirmed La Rouairie's powers. La Rouairie had many supporters in Brittany, among them his mistress Thérèse de Moëlien, his brother Gervais de La Rouairie, and other nobles, including Boisguy, the soon-to-be-notorious Pictot de Limoëlan, as well as the Chevalier de Tinténiac, a cashiered naval officer. It appears that the Breton Association also included Jean Cottereau, who would soon take the pseudonym Jean Chouan, from which the word Chouannerie seems to be derived.

The rank and file was made up of former salt-smugglers who had lost their livelihood now that the salt tax had been abolished; Breton émigrés who had gone to England, the island of Jersey, or Germany; those who had lost their jobs as a result of revolutionary reforms; and some members of the staff of the National Guard.

Large cities, such as Nantes and Brest, lent little support to the Association, but it had some success in the small ones. The Association charged the members of the conspiracy dues equal to a year's income, but many members did not pay them. It was

[5] [The former Controller-General of Finances from 1783 to 1787 became a leader of the émigrés early in the Revolution.]

never financially well-off. Nevertheless, at the beginning of 1792 the Association possessed over six thousand guns, some powder, and four cannon.

The plotters of the Breton Association hoped to seize Rennes at the same time as an *émigré* corps landed in Brittany and counter-revolutionaries aroused opposition in the Cévennes, Lozère, and Ardèche departments in southcentral France. But the coordination of all these movements could not be fully assured. In addition, the victory of the Revolution at the battle of Valmy disconcerted the plotters. They had expected to revolt at the moment when the Prussian and Austrian armies approached Paris. The defeat of the invaders completely changed their plans.

As early as May 1792 the revolutionary authorities learned of the plot. On the night of May 31–June 1, 1792, one of La Rouairie's secretaries, as well as several other plotters, were arrested and their papers seized. Others talked, especially a man named Chévetel. Still, before the fall of the monarchy, the authorities dared not act against the conspirators. Only after August 10, 1792, did the new Minister of Justice, Danton, order an urgent investigation of the plot. The order to arrest the leading members of the conspiracy was issued. La Rouairie managed to escape the police, but he fell seriously ill and on January 30, 1793, he died in a château in the Côtes-du-Nord department.

Some of the plotters were arrested. Twelve were tried, convicted, and on June 18, 1793, guillotined. So the conspiracy failed. Yet it appears to have played an important role in preparing the insurrection of the West. It trained leaders and organized counter-revolutionary committees; it established contacts among those who were or might become the principal leaders of the counter-revolutionary movement.

The Breton Association sought, it appears, an insurrection not only in Brittany, as its name suggests, but also throughout the West between the estuary of the Gironde and the estuary of the Seine. The conversations of the Vendean leader d'Elbée with General Turreau on Noirmoutier Island shortly before d'Elbée's execution seem to reveal the aim of the Breton Association. In fact, d'Elbée said to Turreau, "Since the Vendée insurrection had broken out ahead of the time set for a general uprising, I did all I could to restrain and prevent any premature action because the whole organization was not completely set up and I foresaw the danger of a piecemeal movement."

In addition, among the documents about the *émigrés* in the

Archives of the Ministry of Foreign Affairs in Paris, there is a paper containing the following question written by an agent of the Comte de Provence: "Who decided the moment for the Vendeans to revolt?" and the response, "Jeopardized by the death of M. de La Rouairie and the seizure of his papers, the coalition of counter-revolutionaries was forced to take action and its first move was to gather 150 men and disarm the National Guard of a small village." These documents prove that there were indisputable connections between La Rouairie's plot and the Vendée insurrection, which in turn marked the beginning of the general insurrections in the West. In fact, it even appears that the seizure of the papers of the Breton Association at the time of its leaders' arrest brought on the Vendée insurrection. The Vendean leaders, already compromised by their part in the Breton Association, feared arrest; and to forestall it, they decided to revolt in early March 1793.

Such was the immediate origin of the Vendée insurrection. But it profited from a whole series of earlier armed uprisings. Some small riots and insurrections already had occurred in the region. In the tiny village of La Croix de la Viollière, in the Vendée department, the peasants took up arms during a village fête in September 1790, but this riot was easily quelled. A government official wrote in October 1790, "The aristocrats have bent all their efforts . . . to bring on a civil war and they have hired men to take up arms against the friends of the people." Near Les Sables-d'Olonne a peasant riot broke out in February 1791, and local officials were roughly handled. On March 1, 1791, armed peasants attacked gendarmes at Saint-Christophe-de-Ligneron. Dumouriez, commander of the military district, was charged with reestablishing order. Again in 1791 another lord, the Marquis de La Lézardière, joined with other notables of his area to organize a plot. The authorities were informed. Before the uprising could break out, it was stopped. The plotters, meeting at La Lézardière's château, were imprisoned; while the peasants, on their way to assemble at the château, were dispersed. Thirty-six persons were prosecuted in the court at Les Sables-d'Olonne and were convicted. But since these actions were soon followed by the amnesty of September 15, 1791 (declared after the king had accepted the new constitution), this plot was not so severely repressed as that of the Marquis de La Rouairie. Nevertheless, the plot of the Marquis de La Lézardière played a part in unleashing the Vendée insurrection.

In 1792 there was another uprising in the Vendée. On August 20, a few days after the fall of the monarchy, the former mayor of Bressuire, Delouche, organized some peasants and occupied the small city of Châtillon. These peasants came from eighty different villages and were led by such nobles as La Béraudière and de Béjarry, who later headed the Vendeans. The National Guard of Bressuire managed to arrest the armed peasants and their leaders. If the Vendeans had been able to take Bressuire at this time, their insurrection might have begun in August 1792 rather than in March 1793. After their march on Bressuire, most of the nobles and peasants were arrested, but then released. No one was punished.

Such were the plots and riots that preceded the Vendée revolt. They seem to have been fostered by the social structure of the region, by the poor communications, by the influence of landowners, nobles, and clergy, by the discontent resulting from the Civil Constitution of the Clergy, and by the actions of refractory priests.

But one more factor played a decisive part. At the end of February 1793, the Convention decided on a levy of 300,000 men in order to resist the military coalition which now included nearly all the countries of Europe. But the peasants of western France always had been very hostile to military service. In the Old Regime volunteers filled the regular army, but it was supplemented by a militia comprised of peasants chosen by lot. This was not a heavy burden for them; only a small number were drawn, and they were subject to just a few training periods a year. Still, the militia was very unpopular throughout France and especially in the West. The peasants always made great efforts to escape being drawn for militia service.

The volunteers raised by the Constituent and Legislative Assemblies in 1791 and 1792 had really joined the colors spontaneously, but by 1793 the number willing to volunteer had been exhausted. The Convention was forced to decide that if there were not enough volunteers to fill the quota of 300,000 men, additional soldiers would be chosen by local authorities or by any other means. In practice, local officials could either designate those whom they wished or choose them by lot. So, the militia reappeared under another form. There can be no doubt that the 300,000-man levy considerably aggravated the discontent in the western region.

The insurrection's chronology is quite clear. The decree

ordering the levy of 300,000 men was dated February 24, 1793. It was known at Angers on March 2 and published in the communes of the western region on March 10. On March 11, to the cries of "No conscription!" and "Down with the militia!" insurrection broke out along the left bank of the Loire. On March 12, peasants shouting these slogans seized Saint-Florent-le-Vieil, an especially important town on the left bank of the Loire, a crossing point that allowed one to go from the Vendée to Normandy and Brittany.

What tends to prove, however, that the insurrection was not spontaneous and not caused by conscription alone, was that nobles assumed leadership and organized the peasants from the very beginning. For example, d'Elbée led a band of peasants and occupied Beaupréau. Lescure and La Rochejacquelein took the leadership of peasant bands. However, peasant leaders also appeared, for such men as Cathelineau and Stofflet emerged during the Vendée War. But, at the beginning, on March 12, 13, and 14, noblemen were the most effective leaders.

Actually, the Vendée War presented two distinct features from the start. On the one hand, it was a peasant insurrection. Caring little about forms of government, the peasants wanted to keep their religion and their "kindly priests"; and they especially disliked the militia, the draft. On the other hand, it was a counter-revolutionary movement. The nobles wanted to profit from the peasant revolt; to use a contemporary phrase, they wanted "to restore the throne and altar."

VI

WHY TERROR IN
1793–1794?

"*Make terror the order of the day!*" "*Deliver a last blow against the aristocracy of merchants!*" "*Punish not only traitors, but even the indifferent!*" *These slogans were proclaimed in 1793 by Barère, Collot d'Herbois, and Saint-Just, members of the most powerful executive body in France.[1] It was clear that France had now entered the period called "The Terror."*

The Committee of Public Safety had been created in April 1793. At first it guided the National Convention by issuing provisional regulations and by overseeing ministers. But during the next seven or eight months, it acquired new and vast powers: to make arrests, to staff parts of the bureaucracy, to name and remove generals, and to control the government's emissaries to the troops and the provinces. The legislators of the Convention, jealous of their powers and prerogatives, only reluctantly delegated this authority. But could the unwieldy assembly itself direct the armies combatting most of the countries of Europe? Could it quash the many revolts in the French provinces? In Paris, could it hold prices down, feed the starving, and restrain, if not satisfy, the disaffected?

There can be little doubt that, at least from September 1793 to July 1794, the Committee with its emissaries and supporters resorted to a policy of intimidation and political executions. Why it did so, however, is a matter of much controversy.

Some historians, such as James M. Thompson, argue that

---

[1] The nine other members of the Committee of Public Safety from September 1793 to July 1794 were Billaud-Varenne, Carnot, Couthon, Hérault de Séchelles, Lindet, Prieur of the Côte-d'Or, Prieur of the Marne, Robespierre, and Saint-André.

political coercion is a tradition in France and that it was less severe in 1793–1794 than at various other times.

Some defenders of the Revolution stress that terrorism was the product of conditions—especially civil and foreign wars—and that most terrorists were neither bloodthirsty brutes nor impractical theorists. Albert Mathiez is concerned with how events affected the revolutionary leaders, and Richard Cobb describes the impact of circumstance on the rank and file.

Other historians are less favorably disposed to the revolutionaries of the year II. Crane Brinton finds that the leaders of the Terror, the Jacobins, were misguided humanitarian idealists. They attempted, under trying circumstances, to create a kind of heaven on earth; rigid and puritanical in their faith and zeal, they imprisoned or killed those whom they could not convert. Pierre Gaxotte believes that a more important reason for the violence was that the Revolution was captured by a clique seeking to equalize wealth by means of force.

There have also been several notable attempts to suggest a combination of motives—some reasonable and some base—for the actions of the terrorists. The selection by Georges Lefebvre is an example of such a synthesis.

Living in the twentieth century, we have grown accustomed to violence and bloodshed, to foreign and civil wars. It should be possible for us to read dispassionately what leading historians say about the psychology of the terrorists and the circumstances of the Terror. Perhaps we can then decide whether the Terror was largely justifiable or reprehensible. Or perhaps we can only marvel at the complexity of events and see how gifted men interpret them in different ways.

A FRENCH TRADITION*

James M. Thompson

*For biographical information on James M. Thompson,
see the section entitled "The Character of the Constituent
Assembly (1789–1791)."*

It is perhaps a pity that this *régime* has come to be called "The
Terror." The word suggests a whole population living in fear,
and no occasion is lost by picturesque writers of representing
Paris as a city of the dead, cowed by the tyrants of the Committee [of Public Safety], and silent save for the clatter of the
tumbrils and the thud of the falling knife. But, in fact, it is
doubtful whether the provisional government of 1793 and 1794
was a heavier tyranny than the government under which France
carried through the Great War 120 years later. Its policy was
intimidation, but its result was not terror. It was a war government, and therefore punished spies, and those who carried on
unauthorized correspondence with foreigners and refugees. It
was a national government, and therefore punished aristocrats,
royalists, non-juror priests, and other counter-revolutionaries. It
was a government of virtue, and therefore punished profiteers,
food-hoarders, dishonest or corrupt officials, and treacherous or
cowardly generals. In its campaign against these classes it was
guilty of many injustices, many cruelties, and many absurdities.
Nobody would care to defend its Law of Suspects, by which all
crimes were confounded in a vague *incivisme* [lack of patriotism],
and it became a duty to the country to denounce one's neighbour; or the excessive powers given to irresponsible local committees; or the procedure of the Revolutionary Tribunal. But

* From James M. Thompson, *Leaders of the French Revolution* (Oxford:
Basil Blackwell, 1929), pp. 197–200. Reprinted by permission of Basil Blackwell, Ltd., and Barnes & Noble, Inc.

there were not many, in a nation of twenty-five millions, or even in a capital of 700,000, who felt themselves seriously threatened by these measures. The very guillotine, which so lent itself to wholesale executions, was chosen for humanitarian reasons, and to popularize the aristocratic privilege of decapitation. The publicity and heartlessness of its use were largely an inheritance from the old *régime,* when fashionable crowds used to gather to see bandits broken on the wheel, or regicides torn to bits by red-hot pincers. There is, in fact, little evidence that Paris as a whole was either shocked or frightened by the Terror. It seemed the natural outcome of the Revolution.

Why was this? The answer lies in French history. "France," says [the historian] Lecky, "was a highly centralized despotism . . . and a great military monarchy. The habits and ideals of military life coloured the whole thought of the nation, and the lines of national character were still further deepened by the unifying, organizing, and intensely intolerant spirit of the Catholic Church. The result of this combination of influences has been that the French political ideal has remained substantially unaltered amid the most violent changes of government. Alike under the despotism of Louis XIV and under the despotism of the Convention it has been the great object of French statesmen to attain a complete unity of type: to expel or subdue all interests, elements, and influences that do not assimilate with the prevailing spirit of the government: to mould in a single die, to concentrate on a single end all the forces of the nation." In the light of such a policy minorities have few rights in time of peace, and none in time of war. Failure to conform to the type becomes, in face of a national crisis, unpatriotic and seditious, and may be deserving of the only punishment fit for crimes against the country—that is, death. If anyone doubts whether this is the way in which the French argue, let him look at what happened, not only in 1793-4, but also in 1852 and 1871. In 1852, during the *coup d'état* that inaugurated the Second Empire, 32 *départements* of France were under martial law; at least 27,000 arrests were made in Paris, and more than 150 people killed in street-fighting. The prisoners were tried by special tribunals, which sat in private, which allowed no witnesses to be heard, and no counsel to be called, and from whose decisions there was no appeal. These courts condemned over 15,000 people, of whom 10,000 were deported to Algeria and Guiana, whilst 84 deputies were also expelled from the country. In 1871, after five weeks' siege of Paris by a French army, and a week's street-fighting, incendiarism, and massacre, in which many public buildings were burnt down, the casualties, admitted to be 6,500, were probably 17,000. When it was over, 13,000 prisoners were condemned to deportation or to hard labour. But why go back even fifty years? Is it generally known what happened in France during the Great War? "When the catastrophe of 1914 was let loose on the world," writes M. Mathiez, "our Republican Government proclaimed *l'état de siège* [a state of siege] throughout the whole of France. It gave to courts-martial sovereign jurisdiction not only over military men but also over civilians. Every liberty was suspended, even that of privacy (*domicile*), for in virtue of *l'état de siège* private persons' houses could be searched by day or night. For many months the law-courts ceased to sit at all, and when they resumed work all serious cases were withdrawn from national consideration, to be dealt with behind closed doors by commissions that were often ill-informed. The censorship imposed a tyrannical restraint on thought, and was extended not only to papers and books, but also to private correspondence. It is enough to recall this stifling dictatorship, to which a calm and united France was subjected during five long years, in order to be fair to the terrorists of 1793. It is not too much to say that they showed themselves liberal, compared to our modern-day statesmen. They never proclaimed *l'état de siège* without limits: they never organized a preventive censorship: they never handed over civilians to the mercy of courts-martial: they never destroyed the right of free speech in the Convention, or even in the clubs. The Revolutionary Tribunal of Paris, of sinister memory, pronounced about 2,500 condemnations up to the ninth Thermidor. There were, alas! in that number too many innocent people; but there was also a great majority of guilty persons, who had really been in communication with the enemy, and conspired against the Republic. When the history of the war councils and courts-martial that functioned during the great torment which has just ended is better known, more indulgence will perhaps be shown towards the repressions of the Year II. Hardly a week passes without one's being informed of the names of condemned persons who were shot by mistake, and whose memory is rehabilitated by the Court of Appeal. I read recently in a journal (*Le Progrès Civique* for February 14, 1920) that the number of those rehabilitated already stands at 2,700, that is, a total greater than that of the condemnations pronounced by the Revolutionary Tribunal."

One crime does not excuse another: but all are better understood when traced to the same source. And it is clear that both the theory of the Terror, as expounded by St. Just, and the practice of it, as illustrated by the Vigilance Committees and the Revolutionary Tribunal, were nothing unique in French history, but instances of an outlook and a temper which may fairly be called national.

A REALISTIC NECESSITY*

Albert Mathiez

Albert Mathiez (1874–1932) came from a peasant family in eastern France. He combined great ability with energy and aggressiveness to gain entrance to the École normale supérieure and eventually to become one of the leading authorities on the French Revolution. A student of Alphonse Aulard and strongly influenced by the historical works of the great socialist Jean Jaurès, Mathiez first began writing about the religious history of the Revolution. Eventually he went on to study its political and, to a limited extent, its economic and social aspects. His attempt to rehabilitate the character and policies of Robespierre and to denigrate those of Danton launched a famous quarrel with his former teacher, Aulard. In addition to writing many monographs and a survey of the Revolution, Mathiez started publishing the journal Annales révolutionnaires *in 1908. The journal's name was changed to* Annales historiques de la Révolution française *in 1924, and he continued to edit it until his death.*

The Montagnards, a minority in the National Convention, based their power on the big city governments and on the Jacobin clubs from which they quickly expelled their rivals. Since the Montagnards had opposed the War of 1792, the common people could not blame them for the frightful economic crisis the war caused; and they kept in contact with the masses by their social welfare program. The military defeats in the spring of 1793, General Dumouriez's treason, and the revolt of the Vendée finally allowed

* From Albert Mathiez, "La Révolution française," *Annales historiques de la Révolution française*, X (1933), 13–18. Printed by permission of the editor of the *Annales historiques de la Révolution française*. Editors' translation.

them to take power. This was done by force of arms during the three days from May 31 to June 2, 1793. They purged their adversaries from the Convention and very soon organized a dictatorship, a collective dictatorship by two committees—the Committee of Public Safety and the Committee of General Security—both supported by a Convention temporarily in the hands of the Mountain. These events constituted a new revolution. . . . The dictatorship by the committees was really a dictatorship by the Montagnard party and to some degree by the sans-culottes.

This dictatorship, which lasted a little more than a year, was much less the result of a well-thought-out ideology than of inescapable pressures brought on by civil and foreign war. The enemy had to be repulsed, the royalist and Girondin revolts crushed. The cities and the armies, starving because of the English blockade, had to be fed, while the million soldiers going to the frontier needed supplies and arms. Terror became the order of the day, and the regime set up the guillotine to deal with its enemies. It suspended elections and sent emissaries with full powers to crush resistance in the provinces. The watchword went out to the generals—victory or death! The statue of liberty was veiled, and authority replaced it in ascendancy. The revolution of the Mountain rested on premises opposed to the individualistic revolution of 1789. In the name of public safety, as formerly in the name of the king, conformity was enforced and property rights were limited when circumstances required. To further the defense of the nation and the Revolution, all provisions were pooled and all kinds of merchandise and food requisitioned. The regime established price ceilings on the most important commodities and opened municipal bakeries and butcher shops. In short, a sort of forced experiment in collectivism was set up. I say a forced experiment, since even those who attempted it considered it only temporary and hoped that it would soon disappear without leaving a trace.

The new dictatorship differed greatly from that of the Constituent Assembly of 1789–1791. The people had accepted and had even desired the earlier one; they merely submitted to this one and even detested it. Public opinion, while supporting the deputies of the Constituent Assembly, pushed them into taking more and more severe actions against the enemies of the Revolution. The assembly's committees were obeyed docilely by elected officials who accepted their authority. But now there was a marked shift, with a civil war to match a foreign war. The Vendée and federalist revolts, the execution of the king, the military defeats, the requisitions, the impoverishment caused by inflation, as well as the dechristianization campaign and the closing of the churches, the arrest of suspects, and the continuing use of the guillotine—all these formidable manifestations of crisis discouraged a large number of Frenchmen and created an opposition that desired peace at any price, even at the cost of restoring the Old Regime.

It was no longer possible to justify this new dictatorship, as the Abbé Sieyès had the earlier one, simply by referring to the theory of constitutional authority. It was only too noticeable that the new dictatorship was no longer an application of the sovereignty of the people but rather its opposite. Therefore, responding to an attack by the Dantonists, Robespierre justified the dictatorship by making the significant distinction between a state of war and a state of peace, a revolutionary government and a constitutional government. His two speeches, of 5 Nivôse [December 25, 1793] and 17 Pluviôse [February 5, 1794], based on this theme, express the theory of revolutionary government that foreshadows the future Marxian Dictatorship of the Proletariat. Constitutional government can function, he said, only in peacetime. It has to be suspended in wartime—otherwise it would cause liberty to perish. "The aim of constitutional government is to preserve the Republic, that of revolutionary government is to establish it. The Revolution is liberty at war against its enemies; the Constitution is the regime of a victorious and peaceful liberty." The Revolution is essentially a civil war; and therefore "its government has to be extraordinarily active precisely because it is at war . . . because it is forced to employ unremittingly new and speedy measures so as to meet new and pressing dangers."

Whereas the theory of constitutional authority established dictatorship solely on the basis of the will of the people, the theory of the revolutionary regime based dictatorship on political and patriotic necessities stemming from the war!

Besides, Robespierre himself had seen and admitted the dangers of such a regime. What would become of the state if the dictators used their omnipotence to gain their own ends? A single remedy, a moral one, suggested itself—the dictators must be virtuous.

The French revolutionaries had believed that seizing political power would be enough to resolve the economic and social problems. Rather quickly they perceived their error. Their work crumbled under the weight of the wealthy. The rich, united against the revolutionary laws, made them inoperative. However, the revolutionaries did not think of modifying their principles. It did not cross their minds to found society on a consistent and permanent limitation of property rights, and they continued to regard individual property as untouchable. Their only intent was to correct momentary abuses, and they considered the revolutionary dictatorship merely a temporary expedient. They imagined that all they had to do to resolve the social problem— which in their eyes remained a political issue, a moral issue— was to frighten the aristocrats, imprison them, or exile them. This attitude can be understood if one bears in mind that a large number of the revolutionaries were landowners, well-to-do bourgeois, merchants, professional men with some landed property. The terrorist dictatorship was meant to answer the needs of the people, but it was run by bourgeois.

Only a small minority of the bourgeoisie learned from experience and understood that the continuation of the sans-culottes in power would be possible and durable only at the cost of a gradual and permanent limitation of individual property rights. Robespierre, Saint-Just, and Couthon sought in the Ventôse Laws to expropriate the property of suspects and to distribute it to the poor. But their colleagues secretly resisted these efforts. The Committee of Public Safety had already been unwilling to nationalize civilian food distribution. Carnot had opposed government operation of factories, even those created by the representatives on mission. The Committee of General Security, with the concurrence of some members of the Committee of Public Safety, blocked the operation of the Ventôse Laws, and their sponsors were overthrown on 9 Thermidor.

The great majority of the deputies to the Convention were individualists, very hostile to anything resembling communism. The true communists, those who believed that the Fourth Estate [the common people] could reign only by the suppression of private property, were isolated and without influence; in any case, most of these men thought only of a collectivization of food and consequently of collectivizing only the land which produced the food. When Babeuf, after Thermidor, sought to unite them into a strong party, it was too late. The dictatorship had collapsed, and Babeuf was powerless to reestablish it. His attempt, which cost him his life, was both behind and ahead of its time. Behind its time because it occurred after the Montagnard party had been thrown out of power and had been already decimated by the proscriptions of Thermidor; ahead of its time because society was not yet prepared for communist ideas.

The revolution of July 1789, which had brought the bourgeoisie to power, was the offspring of the philosophy of the eighteenth century, a philosophy fundamentally liberal and individualistic. The revolution of June 1793, which raised the Montagnards to dictatorial power, was the product of circumstance and necessity. It was not the result of either intellectual training, systematic thought applied to the principles of government or society, or a profound investigation of economic development. And how could it be otherwise when machine production was only coming into being, when industrial concentration (which is the inevitable consequence of it) was not yet apparent? The boldest of the revolutionary thinkers, Babeuf himself, conceived only of agricultural communism. Most of the communists of the time made a careful distinction between industrial property which, having been the product of work, was worthy of respect and agricultural land, the only property that they wanted to collectivize.

One must keep this situation in mind to understand how the Jacobin dictatorship fundamentally differs from more recent dictatorships and to comprehend the underlying reasons for its failure.

If the Bolshevik dictatorship, like the Jacobin dictatorship, sought to justify its conduct by the necessities of war, it was, unlike the Jacobin, at least based on a coherent doctrine, Marxism, which it tried to put into practice. The Bolsheviks were quick to abolish not only private ownership, but even the very structure of the state which they had seized. The Jacobins, on the other hand, only with trepidation and reluctance touched the regime established by the Constituent Assembly. They superimposed their economic dictatorship on the individualistic legislation without destroying the legislation. Their requisitions and their price controls did not abolish private property rights, but only hindered their exercise. Their communism, temporary and incomplete, was only an expedient for which they felt they had to apologize.

In the political domain, the same differences appear. The Russian Communists, faithful to Marx's thought, sought from their first days to give all power to the proletariat. The government they formed is basically a government of one class. On the contrary, the Jacobin Montagnards, although they had to rely on the sans-culottes, to govern in their name, and to benefit them, never arrived at the concept of class. They pursued the royalists, the Feuillants, and the Girondins not because they thought them class enemies, but because they were considered to be political adversaries and accomplices of the enemy. The reason for this is clear. The leaders of the Mountain sitting in the committees and in the Convention were not proletarians, but only the friends and allies of the proletarians. They had not rejected the philosophy of the eighteenth century. Its political aspect, which continued to inspire them, is the negation of the existence of classes—it ignores social groupings and stresses the individual.

That is why, unlike the Bolshevik dictatorship (which is based on class antagonism), the dictatorship of the Mountain (which remained fundamentally individualistic) was never a total or full-scale dictatorship. Lenin and his associates understood that in order to establish a dictatorship of the proletariat and to make it permanent, the separation and division of the state's powers would act as an impediment. The Council of People's Commissars legislates and administers at the same time. Such was not the case during the Terror in France, for unity was never entirely achieved within the revolutionary government. No doubt the Convention was purged and in theory it combined legislative and executive power. But actually the Committee of Public Safety took charge of the war effort, diplomacy, and administration, while the Committee of General Security took charge of the repression of plots and the secret police. Thus in France the legislative and executive powers were separated—the Convention retaining the one and the Committees the other. And there was even a separation within the executive branch, since two distinct committees shared its powers. The revolutionary machine of the Montagnards was infinitely more complicated and therefore its operation more delicate than the revolutionary machine of Soviet Russia.

A MENTALITY SHAPED BY CIRCUMSTANCE*

Richard Cobb

Richard Cobb (1917–   ) teaches history at Oxford University. He has characterized his own family background and schooling as typical of the English upper middle class—his father was a colonial civil servant, and Cobb himself was educated at private schools and at Oxford. As a historian he has attempted to break with the conventional history that he learned as a student. Instead he writes impressionistic accounts, largely drawn from archival material, of the effects of the Revolution on the lives of ordinary people. In his two-volume Armées révolutionnaires *(1961–1963), and in other books, he has studied the paramilitary forces whose main task was to insure that the cities of France were adequately provisioned and whose reputation for bloodthirstiness and rapine he denies. Many of his articles have been collected in a volume entitled* Terreur et subsistances, 1793–1795 *(1965).*

We have spoken elsewhere of the revolutionary sans-culotte during the period of his greatest activity, between April 1793 and Germinal year II [March–April 1794], and we have been especially interested in describing his personal attitudes and his emotional life.[1] These men were puritans for whom vice went hand

* From Richard Cobb, "Quelques aspects de la mentalité révolutionnaire," *Revue d'histoire moderne et contemporaine,* VI (April–June 1959), 86–87, 96–104, 116–120. Printed by permission of the author and the Secretary General of the Société d'histoire moderne. Editors' translation.

[1] Richard Cobb, "The Revolutionary Mentality in France," *History,* XLII (1957), 181–196.

in hand with counter-revolution. They therefore condemned celibacy, gastronomy, gambling, prostitution, obscenity, finery, and luxury; but on the other hand, they showed a marked indulgence for drunkenness. Such then was the essence of their private behavior. It now remains to describe some aspects of their collective behavior, their "public" life. . . .

The revolutionary was not an evil man, still less a professional informer or writer of anonymous letters. So if he occasionally did denounce someone, the main reason was his political credulity . . . caused by his belief in the dangers, the plots of all kinds, which he continuously saw about him. It must be said that the enemies of the regime certainly managed to strengthen his sense of always being "in danger of an assassin's sword"; for they were incredibly indiscreet, and this was certainly not because of drunkenness alone. The evidence is unmistakable: in spite of the Terror, in spite of the sight of the guillotine prominently displayed in the busiest places, in spite of the informers who might be anywhere, and especially in the cafés and the public squares, those Frenchmen who disliked the revolutionary regime had no qualms about expressing their dissatisfaction as loudly and publicly as possible, reproaching the Revolution and its works in the most vulgar language. They were the Pères Duchesne[2] in reverse, as noisy as street vendors. Even very young women in Lyon, waitresses in the cafés patronized by the troops of the garrison, did not hesitate to justify the [counter-revolutionary] events of May 29 [1793] right in front of the government soldiers; and they added that they were proud to have helped the federalist troops by bringing them food and ammunition and that if the insurrection were to resume, they would again aid "our brave lads of Lyon."[3] Common people and fashionable people alike were not satisfied with muttering to themselves, and if the men from Paris trusted only what they heard, they would not have had any difficulty in persuading themselves that they were in a completely royalist region. It was not in Lyon alone that people were so indiscreet in what they said; a similar gar-

---

[2] [A reference to the inflammatory revolutionary newspaper edited by Jacques-René Hébert.]

[3] Archives départementales, Rhône 42 L 149 (Commission temporaire, série alphabétique, dossier de Franchette Mayet, an eighteen-year-old girl whose fiancé had been killed during the siege of Lyon). She was denounced by the artillerymen of the Paris Revolutionary Army. See also 42 L 151 (concerning the woman Miou).

rulousness is to be noted among the enemies of the regime and the discontented at Nantes, Brest, Rouen, and especially in the countryside, where farmers did not hesitate to say what they thought about a Republic they viewed mainly in the forbidding light of price controls, requisitions, and the closing of churches. Avowed counter-revolution marched in the open; royalism was on display; and even at the height of the Terror, federalism still sought converts, especially in such areas as Lyon, where it could be identified with local patriotism.

A denouncer on occasion, a denouncer in spite of himself, the average revolutionary supported the great measures of repression; he had, besides, called for them insistently in the political clubs during the autumn of 1793. At least in his public statements and collective actions he was even harsher on domestic enemies than was the government itself. In particular, he demanded that it legalize the Terror. Repression in the year II followed the rules of "revolutionary legality"; but repression in the year III [the anti-Jacobin terror after the fall of Robespierre], even when carried out by criminal courts, was largely a matter of undisguised murder, individual violence, and class vengeance. The revolutionary of 1793 wanted to punish domestic enemies according to the rules of a justice that was summary to be sure and that was administered of course by the sans-culottes. This was therefore a political justice, but it was justice which nevertheless permitted certain rights to the accused. In the year III there was a reversion to [acts like the massacres of] September 1792, the difference being that this time the terrorists were the victims; for even in the courts, justice revolved around class and social background. In 1795, in the Midi [southern France], people claimed that the "bloodthirsty sans-culottes" could be recognized by their dress; that is, they were clothed like artisans, like workers. The repressive justice of the year III was marked therefore by a class bias scarcely present in the revolutionary repression of the preceding year.[4] In the year III a goldsmith of Salon-de-Provence was accused "of having called for the death of citizens who

---

[4] Arraigned before the tribunal of Aix, some terrorists from Marseille, accused of having participated in the riot of Vendémiaire year III [September–October 1794], challenged some of the jurors: "In behalf of his codefendants, one declared that they did not want merchants, clerks, and property owners as jurors, but workers like themselves . . ." (Archives nationales de France, D III 31 (3) (405), Comité de Législation, Marseille; report made by the criminal tribunal of Bouches-du-Rhône, Ventôse year III [February–March 1795]).

powdered their hair and wore shirt cuffs with ruffles," [5] which is also a way of making justice a class matter; but we think this was mostly just talk. Certain frivolous dress had been much denounced by the sans-culottes, but bewigged members of society did not persecute them because of this.

These *buveurs de sang*, these *mathevons*,[6] were they therefore so fierce? Their language certainly was. Here, for example, is what they said and wrote about Lyon and the Lyonnais. Marcillat, a former parish priest of Jaligny in Allier and a member of the Temporary Commission [set up to pacify Lyon and punish the rebels there], wrote the following to his colleagues on the Revolutionary Committee of Moulins: ". . . Our Commission has sworn to revive public spirit; but what am I saying, comrades, there isn't any, it is gone. Ville-affranchie [the name the revolutionaries gave Lyon] is composed of aristocrats and the selfish: the former we will send to the guillotine; we will make the latter pay and we will make them recognize that poor unfortunates are their equals." We notice, in passing, this didactic aspect of the repression, a repression which people at the time also called a "regeneration." The former priest went on to say, "Blood must be shed in order to consolidate the Republic and to have it recognized in the city where we are living." And he concluded rather unexpectedly: "The people of this city (which had once been called Lyon) are fools. . . ." [7] A member of the Society of Valence [a revolutionary political club] even proposed that all federalists be expelled from Commune-affranchie [Lyon] and from Ville Sans Nom (Marseille), which would really mean the expulsion of nearly all the inhabitants, and that the two cities be repopulated with sans-culottes who would move into their homes. A statement to this effect was sent to the National Convention.[8] Rather often similar sentiments came from the pens of Parisian revolutionaries when referring to Lyon, whose population was accused of being both counter-revolutionary and "crassly mercenary." [9]

[5] Archives nationales, D III 29 (2) (61), Comité de Législation, Aix; sentence handed down 3 Thermidor, year III [July 21, 1795], against twenty-four terrorists from Arles and Salon.

[6] [Two terms of disparagement directed against militant revolutionaries.]

[7] Archives départementales, Allier, L 879, Comité de Moulins, correspondance (Marcillat to the Committee, 29 Brumaire, year II [November 19, 1793]).

[8] Archives départementales, Drôme, L 1086*, Société de Valence; meeting of 5 Pluviôse, year II [January 24, 1794].

[9] See, for example, Friedrich Christian Heinrich Laukhard, *Un Allemand en France sous la Terreur*, trans. Wilhelm Bauer (Paris, 1915), p. 267: ". . . They

In public and, more important, in private, they, like Marcillat, approved of rigorous repression that struck, with little regard for social distinctions, sometimes nobles, sometimes the upper middle class, and sometimes silkworkers. A proprietor of a gift shop on the Rue Saint-Denis in Paris, a loyal republican who was to be outlawed twice (after the affair at the Camp de Grenelle and again in the year IX),[10] wrote to his section: "In my last letter, I told you that the guillotine is taking care of some *dozens* of rebels every day, and that about the same number are shot. Now I want to inform you that several *hundreds* are to be shot every day so that we will soon be rid of those scoundrels who seem to defy the Republic even at the moment of their execution. . . ." [11] Officers from Montpellier, at the time also stationed at Lyon, revealed the same kind of unqualified approval; and since their sentiments were expressed in letters to their personal friends, they are all the more reliable as evidence of sincerity. One of them noted that "every day the Holy Guillotine cleanses the soil of liberty of all federalists in the department of the Rhône and Loire; so it goes, so it will continue. . . ." Another officer from Montpellier, in an almost jovial tone, wrote to someone back home that "everything continues to go well here, all rebels are being guillotined and shot. . . ." [12]

However, these men were neither professional executioners, nor naturally bloodthirsty. But they felt no pity for the people of Lyon, federalists who attacked the indivisibility of the Republic, an unpardonable crime deserving capital punishment. Their hatred for the population of Lyon, already strongly conditioned by a Parisian press that unanimously called for quick reprisals against federalists, was undoubtedly reinforced on the spot by the state of isolation imposed on them by a silent and hostile people. A tour of duty at Lyon in the year II was not a laughing matter, and the troops complained bitterly about the ill-will and

---

claim that almost all the people of these areas are crassly mercenary and shamelessly rob poor artisans, workers, and laborers of their pay. . . . Here the aristocracy of money rides high. . . ."

[10] [These two events concern abortive plots against the government, the first quelled by the Directors in 1796 and the second by Napoleon and his Minister of Police Fouché in 1800–1801.]

[11] Archives nationales, F7 4767 d 2, Lassagne (Réaume to the president of the Revolutionary Committee of the Bonne-Nouvelle section).

[12] Archives départementales, Seine-et-Oise, IV Q 187 (confiscated material, papers of Mazuel) (Fayet à Mazuel, 2 Pluviôse, year II [January 21, 1794]; Penelle à Mazuel, 27 Frimaire, year II [December 17, 1793]).

the unfriendliness of the city. Whether Parisians or men of Nivernais and Allier, they were disliked even though *they* were the good sans-culottes, the real revolutionaries. This is therefore one more piece of evidence that "the stupid Lyonnais" lacked the republican spirit. It is true that a few soldiers, on seeing the extreme poverty of the inhabitants and on talking to some women of the lower classes, did feel compassion; and there was one revolutionary officer who even dared to denounce the repression by declaring that "in a Republic no one should be singled out for proscription." [13] But these examples are rare. Most soldiers did not mingle with a population they distrusted—the bodies of soldiers were sometimes fished out of the Rhône River—and the local imitators of the *Père Duchesne,* Dorfeuille and Millet, made it their business to encourage the zeal for repression by sounding the trumpet for revolutionary vengeance.[14]

It is very easy to condemn the repression at Lyon straight off. Not only can it be considered a horrible crime, but also an incredible political blunder which succeeded only in turning all Lyon against a Republic that, in its eyes, seemed inseparable from the guillotine and the firing squad. Couthon saw this quite clearly. But we must also recapture the life of the year II; do not forget the great federalist revolts of the summer and how they had almost swallowed up the Republic in a terrible civil war. No doubt little effort was made to understand the causes of these revolts, but what was remembered was the critical situation in which they had placed France by June and July 1793. That is why the revolutionary, whether he was a small shopkeeper, a professional soldier, a former priest, a physician, or an artisan, approved the use of force against the people of Lyon, Marseille, the Vendée, and Toulon. He favored it also when it struck at refractory priests and more generally when it struck at those whom he accused of being "fanatics," for he could not forgive the latter for having caused "small Vendées" in various regions. Moreover, the soldiers, who had everywhere helped de-

---

[13] See my study *L'Armée révolutionnaire parisienne à Lyon et dans la région lyonnaise* (Lyon, 1952), p. 31. Also Archives départementales, Rhône 31 L 50, Société de Lyon; meeting of 16 Frimaire, year II [December 6, 1793].

[14] *Le Père Duchesne* [of Lyon] (Dorfeuille and Millet), No. XX (17 Pluviôse, year II [February 5, 1794]) and No. XXVIII (14 Ventôse, year II [March 4, 1794]). Referring to the "embroidery merchants," they said quite delicately: "We are going to send over our dragoons . . . to make them dance the carmagnole to the tune of the commander of the garrison, and he will, with all due respect, shoot their faces to bits."

velop a definite revolutionary mentality, were especially hostile to the Catholic people of the countryside, whom they regarded as allies of the *Chouans* and the other avowed enemies of the regime. In their hatred of the "fanatics," there was also something more personal; for many of the soldiers had witnessed atrocities committed against republicans by the peasants, both men and women, of the Vendée.

But the revolutionary demanded even harsher measures against the hoarder, the economic criminal, and the disobedient, "selfish" farmer and tried to show that these acts of repression had an economic basis. If the Parisians and the little people of Moulins and Nevers so favored the use of force in Lyon, it was primarily because they saw the city as that "big business capital" where even the workers were unworthy of liberty.[15] For similar reasons, Hébert and members of the Paris sections demanded that the machinery of terror and the temporary commissions of popular justice be sent to that other business capital, Rouen; for the revolutionaries also had a very low opinion of the population there.[16] Some people even wanted to extend repressive measures to every rural area and terrorize the farmers, but on this occasion government policy did not go so far as the one advocated by the urban sans-culottes.

This approval of force and the Terror was therefore the result of a combination of very diverse elements. With regard to the measures taken against the people of Lyon and Marseille, there were intermingled the economic prejudices of the small shopkeeper and the small merchant against the big merchants, the shipowners,[17] and the big firms; there was the condemnation of the "special interests" who had placed themselves between the citizen and the sovereign people and who had dared to strike a sacrilegious blow against the Convention; and of course there

[15] Dorfeuille and Millet, editors of the Lyon *Père Duchesne*, wrote on the 17 Pluviôse [February 5, 1794]: "The workers of Lyon seem to think they have lost everything because they have lost their rich merchants." Almost all the men from Paris were indignant about the "federalist" spirit of the entire population of Lyon (article "Grande colère," *Père Duchesne* of Lyon, No. XX).

[16] See my article, "La Campagne pour l'envoi de l'armée révolutionnaire dans la Seine-Inférieure," *Annales de Normandie*, August 1952.

[17] Thus at Le Havre the merchants and shopkeepers who composed the Committee of Surveillance pursued the shipowners with special vigor, so much so as to hinder their business dealings with the shipowners of Lübeck, Altona, and Copenhagen, even though these had been undertaken for the Food and Supply Commission.

was the desire to conform to the customs of the time, as well as a vivid memory of what dangers the federalist crisis had inflicted on the Republic. Moreover, the press was ingenious in keeping public opinion at a fever pitch favorable to severe acts of repression; and the revolutionaries themselves, living as if in combat, as an occupation army, as strangers amidst hostile populations, were easily persuaded that only terror and repressive force saved them from the blows of their enemies. If they did not strike first, they would be "struck down by the assassin's sword." Such was the part fear and credulity played, and it was amply fed by the unbelievably imprudent remarks of the enemies of the regime, who did not hesitate to shout at Parisians their hatred for the Republic and the capital.

A taste for blood and vengeance does not seem to have played an important part; still it is very difficult to distinguish between what may have been a political and group attitude and what reveals a personal bent for violence and brutality. In the affair of the *noyades,*[18] some members of the Marat Company and of the Revolutionary Committee of Nantes were extremely cruel. They persecuted their prisoners, chased the wives of the *Chouans* while clubbing them with their musket butts, pulled girls by the hair, and shoved and cursed everyone. But according to witnesses, drunkenness could explain this especially odious example of brutality, just as it had fortified so many of the murderers at the Carmes prison in September 1792. To be sure, at the trial of Carrier, there was one witness, a young man of twenty, who not only admitted taking part in the "drownings," but who added that he had no regrets, and that if he had it to do over, he would again volunteer to carry out similar acts. But he was a young soldier of the first Nantes battalion and he had seen his comrades tortured by the wives and daughters of Breton peasants when the soldiers were captured by the *Chouans* in the countryside around Nantes; and he had himself escaped torture and mutilation thanks to a wound that was more horrible to look at than it was serious.[19] During the trial, most of the witnesses almost became sick while recalling the horrible scenes that had taken place on the small boats when the trap doors installed in the

[18] [The *noyades* of Nantes were mass executions by drowning conducted by the deputy on mission Jean-Baptiste Carrier, who had been sent to the city in October 1793 to suppress the revolt there.]

[19] Archives de la Préfecture de Police, Paris, A A 269; notes of Topino-Lebrun on the trial of Carrier.

holds were opened. The men of the eighteenth century were somewhat accustomed to brutality, but this did not make them sadists. It is true that the revolutionary regime did allow some sadists to use their deplorable talents under exceptionally favorable circumstances, and everyone has heard of Mathieu Jouve Jourdan [called Jourdan the Decapitator] and other bloodthirsty brutes of his ilk, but these monsters were, we think, the exceptions. The revolutionaries were often violent, especially in speech; they were hot-tempered and fanatical; when they drank to excess they must have appeared at times terrifying and obscenely brutal in the manner of the *Père Duchesne*. Some civilian officials were hotheaded and violent, their fiery temperaments being most apparent in the years of proscription after the fall of Robespierre. No one would be so bold as to claim that a Collot-d'Herbois and a Javogues[20] were normal, sensible men, and many must have resembled them. But even this sort of violence was to be temporary; it was connected with the recent dangers brought on by the federalist crisis. The Revolution had its professional fiends, its murderers, its sadists; and in the cities of the Midi, some of the assassins of the years II and III were also to be the perpetrators of the bloody brutalities of 1814 and 1815. But the average revolutionary was neither a sadist nor a brute.

Finally, there was an educational aspect: the work of "regeneration" had to be undertaken, and the use of force was a part of a general program of civic education. A revolutionary in the Yonne department insisted that "all youths from seven to ten be brought together in order to watch all public punishments, including executions." [21] Now this *Émile* of repression was not a *buveur de sang*; and neither were the revolutionaries of the year II, despite all efforts of Thermidorian propaganda to identify them with the murderers. Actually, the epithet is much more appropriate for those young dandies of the year III who attacked individual terrorists or men of modest appearance and poor dress and who could not even claim that they acted from fear. It is just as wrong to label the revolutionary a killer as it is to call him a denouncer. Because of certain circumstances, to be sure, at times he had to be both, but the revolutionaries with

[20] [Claude Javogues, deputy of the Convention, was an ultra-revolutionary who accused the Committee of Public Safety of counter-revolution and when on mission used terror against the rich, the priests, and others.]

[21] Archives nationales, D III 306, Comité de Législation, Yonne; petition to the Convention by Héry, 1 Pluviôse, year III [January 20, 1795].

whom we are familiar—shopkeepers, small merchants, physicians, former priests, lawyers—do not resemble in the slightest those "sanguinary brutes" of Thermidorian and royalist iconography.

It would be equally wrong, I believe, to try to explain the origins of the Terror and the revolutionaries' approval of the great repressive measures by stressing hidden psychological motives in the traditional mentality of the common people, a mentality in which the fear of plagues aroused a climate of panic and mutual fear in bourgeois and artisan alike.[22] The revolu-

---

[22] René Baehrel, "Épidémie et terreur: histoire et sociologie," *Annales historiques de la Révolution française*, April–June 1951, pp. 113–146, and "La Haine de classe en temps d'épidémie," *Annales: Économies, sociétés, civilisations*, July–September 1952. The first of these studies provides very interesting information on the spread of the great plague of 1720 in Marseille and on the social and "terroristic" consequences of other plagues in French cities during the sixteenth, seventeenth, eighteenth, and nineteenth centuries. In particular, the author has analyzed the reactions of the common people to the measures taken by health officials and by "Boards of Health" to halt the spread of epidemics and to isolate the victims, measures which the poor especially—the probable sources of the infection—had to bear, while the well-off frequently went to their country homes. But doubtless Monsieur Baehrel is a little hasty when he identifies these measures and the very violent social conflicts they provoked with the executions and the Great Terror of the year II. Surely these two series of events had in common only the fear they aroused (fear of "conspiracies," fear of the spread of infection) and the rumors and panic they also aroused, especially among the common people of the cities and countryside. Fear, panic, and rumor are, however, evident throughout the history of the common people, but they do not always cause the same reaction. The people are often afraid, but only in 1792, 1793, and 1795 did fear set off a great outburst of anger and popular violence resulting in massacres, drownings, and mass shootings. And the great institutions of terror in the year II, the special commissions responsible for carrying out the repressive policies, were in no way instruments of any one class or any very distinct social group. The Terror was directed against almost every group that composed French society during the revolutionary period. To claim, as does Monsieur Baehrel, that "Frenchmen in 1792 inherited a long tradition of terrorism" and that the memory of the great plague of 1720, of the periodic famines during the eighteenth century, of the epidemics—the most recent occurring in 1775—helped create a climate of terror and helped inculcate among the French common people a class hatred, a use of terror against other social groups, is to argue abstractly and to advance some very speculative theories. We prefer to say that the Terror of the year II sprang from the special circumstances of that year—the civil war, the foreign war, the treasons, the victories of the coalition, the common people's suspicions of prison plots, the fear of prison breaks, federalism, etc. These seem to us to explain adequately why a terrorist mentality appeared that was as brief and fleeting as the revolutionary man himself. To suggest that there is no need to look for the origins of the terrorist mind in the memories of the plague of 1720 in no way detracts from the originality of Monsieur Baehrel's thesis. As for the rest, the author is certainly right to stress the importance

tionary of the year II did not have the slightest need of very old historical memories in order to demand a pitiless outlawing of all those who, at the time, menaced the existence of the Republic. It was not a question of proscription based on class or even of a tradition of violence. The danger was there, it was obvious, and when the danger passed, it had to be prevented from recurring by "striking a mighty blow." From the year III on, all this seemed quite unreal even to the revolutionaries themselves when they recalled the crisis. This is so because the atmosphere had already changed, the time of extreme measures had passed. The justification for the Terror is that it was a response to circumstance, not a permanent state of mind or one act of a naturally violent temperament. It was just as transitory as the revolutionary man himself. . . .

Our "revolutionary man," if he existed at all, is only known to us by a kind of historical documentation unique to the revolutionary period, and it reveals at least the public attitudes of a whole social group, a complete cross section of the common people of the cities and even of the towns. All of this is entirely hidden from us in other periods of history. It is therefore difficult for us to distinguish clearly between the public and the private man, since we know him only at that one time, and then only for one year or eighteen months, a unique time in the life of the individual and in the history of France.

Let us try nevertheless to draw the essential features of our portrait. I believe we are concerned especially with a matter of temperament; and it seems to me that to rely solely on studies of social structure will not furnish us with the basis for a satisfactory answer. The revolutionary man seldom behaved the way he did because of social struggles, except to the extent that he typified the world of the small property owner, the small tradesman, and the artisan. His predominant characteristics were incontestable political and physical courage, strong beliefs, also of course a certain love for power, and finally an undeniable fondness for speech-making and display. Public life in the year II, we must remember, was an opportunity for many of these small tradesmen to play the role of men of importance, of "politicians," of Roman Senators, while at the same time meddling in their neighbor's affairs. The rewards? Well, they were not to be

of plagues and epidemics in the development of class hatred and sometimes in the outbreak of insurrectionary events. But such considerations are not relevant for 1793.

sneered at: first of all there was the presidency of a political club, or much more influential though less conspicuous, a position on its executive committee. Any prominent place in one of these clubs could sometimes provide excellent free publicity for one's business. Think for example of the club member at Vaison, a painter by trade, who when asked to paint the tree of liberty in three colors, declined the honor. (He was not to be paid for the job.) But after the society had asked another of the local painters, the first changed his mind and declared that he would be delighted by the club's confidence.[23] These posts and honors, furthermore, caused bitter personal strife and dispute often having nothing to do with republican propriety, but this proves that they were worth a lot of effort and ingenuity. We know little about the elections of officers and noncommissioned officers in the National Guard stationed in the cities, but we surely can guess that the competition was just as acrimonious.[24] The revolutionary was all the more avid for honors, sashes, and stripes, since they compensated for years of obscurity and insignificance.

But in the final analysis, in spite of these material incentives, the revolutionary temperament was mostly a product of faith, enthusiasm, and generosity. The poet Coleridge was not the only one who, recalling the enthusiasms of his youth, remarked how glorious it was to be alive at that time. How many mature men, settled in occupations as obscure as they were honorable, recalled in their old age the *Radiant Days of '93*! For the revolutionaries were mostly young men or men in the prime of life, and their enthusiasm must have been in part the enthusiasm of youth.[25]

In the birth of such a mentality of battle and crisis, the role of the war must also be stressed. The revolutionaries thought of themselves as always standing in the breach, and this was not merely a figment of the imagination. Those at Nantes knew

[23] Archives départementales, Vaucluse, L VI 12; Register of the Société populaire de Vaison.

[24] My friend Rémi Gossez has told me that during the Revolution of 1848 there was fierce competition for promotions in the National Guard. Unfortunately we know little about the way such elections were conducted during the period of the French Revolution.

[25] A general study of lower-echelon revolutionary personnel would certainly demonstrate that men between twenty-five and forty were in the majority. Regarding the famous Temporary Commission of Lyon, thirty was the average age among some forty members. Revolutionary France was a country offering innumerable opportunities to young men of talent.

that they were surrounded by almost universal hatred; those in
Lyon, even more isolated, could never forget the head of Chalier,
and most of the *mathevons* were to die in the terrible massacres
of the year III.[26] Like the leaders of the great revolutionary
committees, they were absolutely sure that Pitt had put their
names on his death lists. It is true, in general, that nothing happened to them in the year II, but the Thermidorian proscription, owing to its blind vengeance against anyone, without exception, who had held power in the year II, certainly played a
large part in causing this revolutionary temperament to survive
somewhat, thanks to persecution. A political club in Vaucluse
asked the following question when screening candidates for
admission: *What have you done for which you would be hanged
if the counter-revolution should triumph?* [27] This was not simply
rhetoric. The revolutionaries had to face such an eventuality,
especially in a region like the former Comtat Venaissin where
they constituted a very small minority isolated from the rest of
the people.[28] They were, in every sense of the word, embattled.

Yet to maintain this spirit of combat, danger had to be constant. But beginning in Floréal year II [April–May 1794], it
receded more and more from a France which until then had
been besieged and invaded. The great victories of the summer
of 1794, which made the threat of invasion and the military
triumph of the counter-revolution more remote, inevitably resulted in some relaxation of tension. The feeling of urgency
waned. It was also at this very time that the Robespierrist government chose to attack the political institutions of the common
people. And then with the coming of summer, daily affairs de-

[26] Renée Fuoc, *La Réaction thermidorienne à Lyon (1795)* (Lyon, 1957).
[Marie-Joseph Chalier was the leader of the Jacobins of Lyon. During the
city's counter-revolution, he was arrested, tried, and on July 16, 1793, guillotined. After the revolt was quelled, he became a martyr; and a model of
his decapitated head was publicly displayed, even carried to Paris where it
was presented to the Convention.]

[27] Archives départementales, Vaucluse, L VI 12; Register of the Société
populaire de Vaison, meeting of 28 Messidor, year II [July 16, 1794].

[28] Archives nationales, D III 292 (2) (4), Comité de Législation, Vaucluse,
Avignon: ". . . The department of Vaucluse, which is largely inhabited by
men who lived under the domination of the Roman priesthood, has a great
number of those opportunists . . . who call themselves patriots so that they
will be able to get rich with impunity at public expense . . ." (To the
Committee of Public Safety from Barjavel, Public Prosecutor of the Revolutionary Tribunal of the department, 25 Frimaire, year II [December 15,
1793]).

manded attention, and a great deal of it, since they had been
neglected for so long. This was not only true for the country
people whose revolutionary temper did not usually survive the
resumption of work in the fields. The urban sans-culotte also
had to make a living, to think of his business. His wife kept re-
minding him of that. But the political clubs met almost every
evening from five to ten o'clock, sometimes until midnight; and
his life as an active revolutionary, which included guard duty
and many other obligations, encroached not only on his leisure,
but also resulted in long absences from his shop, which, however,
still had to be kept open sixteen hours a day. Such obligations,
of course, also took time from billiards. Thus gradually normal
life, banal existence, regained the upper hand. We can see quite
well what constituted the drama in these men's lives. One from
Anduze said in protest, *The bow breaks if bent too far.*[29] In fact,
for most of the club members, politicians only for the moment,
the bow did break; revolutionary enthusiasm and activity ended.
In general, their billiards and wives had the last say.

Furthermore, the Robespierrist Republic was far from amus-
ing. It oozed boredom and virtue, just like the insipid and
pedantic speeches of Robespierre the Incorruptible. Think of
those vapid and interminable celebrations of the Supreme Being,
after which one sat down to eat the "republican plate," a single
course, sometimes served without wine! It was useless to say to
these men, *Look out; don't slacken; above all, don't miss club
meetings; we still need you; the hidden enemies have not been
defeated; victory is not yet won.* It was a waste of words if all
they were called upon to do was vote on congratulatory speeches
delivered in a bombastic and trite style. One grew weary. This is
proven by the sharp drop in attendance at meetings of provincial
clubs beginning in Germinal year II [March–April 1794]. Long
before the fall of Robespierre, the revolutionary man began to
fade away, to resume his anonymity. The time "to make revolution" was already long past.

To summarize, the revolutionary man was only a temporary
phenomenon. A product of exceptional circumstances, he did
not resist time, wear and tear, fatigue, and boredom. He was not
a professional in the art of revolution. Anyway, what is a professional revolutionary if not a bureaucrat like all the others, a
bureaucrat solidly installed in a petrified Revolution; or else a

---

[29] Archives nationales, F7 4609 d 2, Borie (letter of Cavalié from Anduze to
the Committee of Public Safety, 25 Pluviôse, year II [February 13, 1794]).

half-baked conspirator, a romantic, a "cardboard revolutionary." Except in the imagination of the policemen and the informers reporting to the Ministry of Police, the followers of Babeuf had very little in common with the revolutionaries of the year II. Our men of 1793 were neither "cardboard revolutionaries," nor ideologists and professors of revolutionary theory. And the very moment they put on their slippers and relaxed, their role as politicians ended. Thus, after the great hopes and dangers had passed, they returned to their everyday banal existence. In the year III, when inequality became more marked and one's daily bread became the biggest problem, the matter was settled. The revolutionaries were less the victims of the *muscadins,* of those young assassins in fine shoes, than of an economic crisis and a food shortage which struck their families and which, in many cases, reduced them to wretchedness, to the anonymity of the beggar.

Something survived of the revolutionary mentality, of course, especially in the army where it often took the form of violent anticlericalism. It also was to reappear in the political sphere beginning with the elections of the year IV, which saw numerous attempts at regroupment among the former terrorist cadres. But these efforts were confined to a handful of leaders. As for the conspirators among the revolutionaries, they constituted a very small minority—the tough and pitiless, the totally convinced, perhaps also the *violent;* for the revolutionary temperament certainly included a dash of violence. Among the others, silence descended as before 1789. The revolutionaries vanished along with the extraordinary circumstances that had given them an intense but fleeting existence; so did those institutions whose extant records allow us to uncover a few months of the submerged history of the common people and thus to see the attitudes and prejudices of a world of stores and workshops. These voices would be heard again only through the very distorted screen of police reports.

A KIND OF RELIGIOUS
FAITH*

Crane Brinton

Crane Brinton (1898–   ) is one of America's most distinguished historians. He received his A. B. from Harvard University and his Ph.D. from Oxford University, and since 1923 has taught at Harvard. He has written many books on European intellectual and political history in a spritely, urbane style. His works on the French Revolution include the admirable survey Decade of Revolution *(1934) and* The Jacobins *(1930), an original and learned attempt at historical sociology.*

The Jacobins unquestionably held their political philosophy as a matter of faith. It is possible to sketch from the proceedings of the clubs the outlines of a polity held together by concepts primarily theological. Grace, sin, heresy, repentance, regeneration have their place in these records. Of course, no one individual is assumed to go through this cycle. The theological parallel is not a literal one; but it is not a forced nor an imaginary one.

That Robespierre and his more sincere followers conceived themselves to be the small band of the elect is of course a truism. The conception of election, however, like so much else in the Terror, goes back surprisingly far in the Revolution. Desmoulins speaks at the Jacobin club in Paris in 1791 of "the very small number of those *to whom only the witness of their conscience is necessary*, the small number of men of character, incorruptible

* From Crane Brinton, *The Jacobins: An Essay in the New History* (New York: Macmillan Co., 1930), pp. 218–222, 231–242. Reprinted by permission of the author. A Harper & Row Torchbook edition of *The Jacobins* appeared in 1968.

citizens." [1] This insistence on an inner, emotional conviction or righteousness rather than on external rules—the very old opposition of faith and works—comes out again in the proceedings of the Paris club. "One must distrust," says the speaker, "liberty unaccompanied by virtue"; and by virtue he understands "not the mere practice of moral duties, but also an exclusive attachment to the unalterable principles of our constitution." [2] The club at Limoges was told: "It is not enough, in order to belong to a truly republican society, to call oneself republican, to have done guard duty, to have paid one's taxes; one must have given sure indications of hatred for kings and nobles, for fanaticism; one must have passed through the crucible of perilous circumstance." The idea of grace is actually complemented, in this same club, by the addition of a new Jerusalem, the city of the elect. Paris, for its work in the revolution, is to be "that holy city." [3]

There are also the damned. The Jacobins did not feel of their opponents merely that they were wrong, or inconvenient; but that they had sinned. A member at Rodez recalled to the society that just a year before, a deputation from the Tarn had "soiled the precincts of the society with the venom of federalism." The society therefore decided "as *expiation* for that scandalous session, to consecrate a portion of the present session to patriotic songs." [4] At Bergerac the society burned the papal bull condemning the civil constitution of the clergy, in order to purify the paper from "the outrageous blasphemies which insult our sublime Constitution." [5] The club of Toulouse delegated six members, and asked the "peuples des tribunes" [the spectators in the public gallery] (always that distinction, so out of place in an ideal republic!) to delegate six more, to help burn and lacerate certain evil journals.[6] At Beauvais, the club was delighted with a circular from the Committee of Public Safety asking for lists of Jacobins eligible for government places, and especially at the words, "Keep from these lists all these cold, selfish, or indifferent men. . . . The law of Athens would have inflicted death upon

[1] A. Aulard, *La Société des Jacobins* (Paris, 1889–1897), II, 103.

[2] *Ibid.*, II, 235.

[3] A. Fray-Fournier, *Le Club des Jacobins* (Limoges, 1903), pp. 246, 169.

[4] B. Combes de Patris, *Procès-verbaux de la Société populaire de Rodez* (Rodez, 1912), p. 347.

[5] H. Labroue, *La Société populaire de Bergerac* (Paris, 1915), p. 118.

[6] Archives départementales, Haute-Garonne, L 746, April 19, 1793.

them. National opinion among us inflicts upon them political death." [7] The club of Le Havre was told by that of Harfleur "not to receive in its bosom a certain Duclos, priest of the protestant religion. He tried to compromise this society with that of Gaineville, and to ruin the reputation of several patriots." [8]

Some aristocrats at Vesoul having kissed the tree of liberty in mockery, the local club decided to purify it. So, with the president at its head, and with four members carrying vases of pure water and braziers of incense, the club marched in procession to the tree, where, after everyone had sworn to preserve it forever after from all contamination, "the tree was purified with the lustral water, and the president threw on the heated tripods generous handfuls of the most exquisite perfumes." [9] The club at Auch had so strong a conviction of sin that it adapted for its own use the attitude of the Church toward burial in consecrated ground. It proposed to have two town cemeteries, one for good citizens, the other for bad.[10]

Heresy is, of course, one of the easiest ways of falling into sin. The word itself was by no means shunned by the Jacobins. Even under the monarchy, Brissot is found at the Paris club objecting that an opinion of Barnave's is "a great heresy." [11] The rejections of members at the various *épurations* [weeding-out sessions] are, of course, usually for heresy of some sort. One man was excluded at Thann because, although at first he had been a good *patriote,* "the corrupting contact of his brother-in-law had completely perverted him"; another, though himself pure, because his maid was not.[12] At Carcassonne one of the questions put was: How long did you lack confidence in Marat and the Mountain? Several were excluded for honestly confessing that they had had a period of doubt on this subject.[13] The pressure of foreign and civil war made the Jacobins more than usually exacting to-

[7] Archives départementales, Oise, L IV, unclassified papers of the club of Beauvais.

[8] Archives départementales, Seine-Inférieure, L 5647, 24 Germinal, year II [April 13, 1794].

[9] *La Vedette, ou journal du département du Doubs,* No. 68 (June 29, 1792).

[10] F. Brégail, "La Société populaire d'Auch," *Bulletin du comité des travaux historiques* (1911), p. 152.

[11] Aulard, II, 189.

[12] H. Poulet, "L'Esprit publique à Thann pendant la Révolution," *Revue historique de la Révolution française,* XIII (1918), 544.

[13] J. Mandoul, "Le Club des Jacobins de Carcassonne," *Révolution française,* XXV (1893), 326.

wards their proselytes. One society at least penalized those converted after 1792 by not allowing them to hold office.[14] That of Moulins decided in the spring of 1794 never to admit a new member, except from other towns, and then only when such persons could prove membership in some club before September, 1793.[15] Heretics were apparently not even allowed to repent. Collot d'Herbois at Paris was seeking to get readmitted to the society some of those who had followed the *feuillants* in the schism. "Many of these," he said, "are exceedingly repentant, and would like to efface from their lives the days they spent at the *feuillants*." Yet at Robespierre's insistence they were rejected.[16] And, along with heresy, there is the concept of blasphemy. This is from a report of a session of a Paris club: "An officer, an exchanged prisoner, gives an account of the condition of the French and Austrian armies. But as he reports some violent words used by the enemy general, he is interrupted. Billaud-Varenne reminds the orator that he is repeating expressions which ought not to soil the mouth of a republican." [17]

A little club in Savoy took a milder, and perhaps more modern attitude towards those who disagreed with it. The majority of their fellow citizens they called "the sick ones we have to treat." [18] The club of Toulon, withdrawing its affiliation from the heretics of Pignans, wrote and warned other clubs of this *brebis galeuse* [black sheep].[19] But the best indication of the theological state of the Jacobin mind is to be found in a circular of the club of Montauban. The class of *émigrés* is to be composed, not merely of those who have gone off, *émigrés de fait,* but also of *émigrés d'opinion.*[20]

No less thoroughly religious a concept than that of regeneration is evident in these proceedings. The taking of the Bastille became the symbolic date, the moment when man was born anew, washed clean of the evils of the old régime. A little provincial society, accordingly, when it celebrates the "holy festival" of July

[14] A. Fray-Fournier, p. 243.

[15] Archives départementales, Allier, L 901.

[16] Aulard, III, 313.

[17] *Ibid.,* V, 618.

[18] A. Gros, *Le Club des Jacobins de St. Jean-de-Maurienne* (St. Jean-de-Maurienne, 1908), p. 70.

[19] H. Labroue, "Le Club jacobin de Toulon," *Annales de la Société d'Études provençales* (1907), p. 45.

[20] J. Bellanger, *Les Jacobins peints par eux-mêmes* (Paris, 1908), p. 123.

14, refers to it as the day "when man is resuscitated and born anew in his rights." [21] The society of St. Jean-de-Luz held a festival to celebrate the "abolition of royalty and the *resurrection* of the republic." [22] It is hard to see how the word resurrection can here be taken in any but a theological sense, as the French Republic had never existed on this earth. Finally, the society at Saverne gave proof of the most extraordinary faith in the completeness of the rebirth brought about in 1789, for its secretary refers to "les ci-devant Juifs" [the former Jews].[23]

The Jacobins, then, were a band of the elect, thoroughly aware of their election, and determined to rule on earth as well as in heaven. The club of Ervy was told, "You must suffer but one caste of men, that of Republicans, Sans-culottes, Montagnards." [24] At Le Havre, the club voted that those of its members who belonged to any kind of corporation or brotherhood must choose between the Jacobin club and such other corporations.[25] The club of Besançon indignantly refused to open its doors to all, as "the wicked, mixed with the good, would predominate." [26] The club of Chablis hesitated before accepting affiliation with the club of the Ursulines at Tonnerre, and then turned it down on the grounds that there couldn't possibly be two clubs in a small town like Tonnerre.[27] The secretary at Gerberoy apologized to the club of Beauvais, because everybody passed the *épuration*. Three—their names are duly sent on to Beauvais—should have been expelled. But the mayor formed a party among the "little enlightened," packed the club, and notwithstanding their vices, these three were passed "by the multitude." The whole letter is filled with a consciousness of being right and being few.[28]

Finally, it was evident even to some of their number that the Jacobins were a sect. A member at Ars-en-Ré remarked that "the

[21] H. Labroue, "La Société populaire de la Garde-Freinet," *Révolution française,* LIV (1908), 155.
[22] J. Annat, "La Société populaire de St. Jean-de-Luz," *Revue du Béarn* (1910), 170.
[23] D. Fischer, "La Société populaire de Saverne," *Revue d'Alsace,* XX (1869), 181.
[24] H. Destainville, "Les Sociétés populaires du district d'Ervy," *Annales historiques de la Révolution française,* I (1924), 446.
[25] Archives départementales, Seine-Inférieure, L 5644, September 19, 1793.
[26] *La Vedette,* No. 54 (May 11, 1792).
[27] Archives départementales, Yonne, L 1140, August 18, 1793.
[28] Archives départementales, Oise, L IV, unclassified papers of the club of Gerberoy.

moral discourses delivered on *décadis* [every tenth day of the French republican calendar] are so many dogmas, and consequently, so much religion." He was, it is true, immediately suspended.[29] The Jacobins held firmly to their final superiority; theirs was no fanaticism. . . .

The fall of Jacobinism . . . can be quite plausibly accounted for; an explanation of its rise is a far more difficult matter. It is not that the actual triumph of the Jacobins over other groups during the Revolution is at all hard to understand. Given Jacobin organization and Jacobin faith, their triumph was almost inevitable. . . . Indeed, it is tempting to assert that the ultimate, if brief, victory of well-organized extremists can be accepted as a kind of sociological law applicable to all great revolutions. The really interesting and subtle problem is, how did the Jacobins themselves come to be what they were? . . . The Jacobins were not predominantly failures before 1789, frustrates, victims of maladjustment; nor were they members of a lower class struggling against oppression by their masters, and held together by economic solidarity. They were in the main ordinary, quite prosperous middle-class people. And yet they behaved like fanatics. The Reign of Terror was marked by cruelties and absurdities which the greatest of misanthropes will hardly maintain are characteristic of ordinary human beings. The heart of our problem then, is this: how did the Jacobins come to produce, at least to accede to, the Terror?

Augustin Cochin saw with admirable clearness that all explanations of the Terror have fallen into two classes: that represented by Taine, which Cochin calls the *thèse du complot* [the conspiracy thesis], and that represented by Aulard, which he calls the *thèse des circonstances* [the circumstance thesis].[30] Taine in a famous metaphor asks what a spectator must think if he sees a man in apparently sound health take a drink, and suddenly fall down in a fit. The drink, obviously, contained a poison. The drinker was the Jacobin, and the poison was the philosophy of Rousseau. The Jacobins, then, were a group of madmen bent on realizing an impossible Utopia. The Revolution was plotted by these men, made irresponsible by fanatic devotion to their ideal.

---

[29] M. de Richemond, "Délibérations de la Société des Amis de la Liberté et de l'Égalité d'Ars-en-Ré," *Archives historiques de la Saintonge et de l'Aunis,* XXXIV (1904), 205.

[30] A. Cochin, "La Crise de l'histoire révolutionnaire," in *Les Sociétés de pensée et la démocratie* (Paris, 1921).

Their lack of principle made it easy for them, though in a minority, to overcome the good sense of the majority, and establish themselves in power. Once in power, they could maintain themselves only by the Terror. Cochin himself accepts a variant of this explanation. According to him, the Jacobins formed a "petite ville," a society of unpractical idealists, fanatics bent on imposing upon their fellows of the "grande ville" a rigid code governing all human actions, a code quite inconsistent with normal human conduct, as we know it from tradition and from observation.[31]

Now it is impossible not to accept much of this explanation. The Jacobins were certainly fanatics of the religion of humanity. It is tempting to maintain that the acceptance of certain tenets of eighteenth-century philosophy—the essential equality of men, the natural goodness of men—lead in action straight to the Terror. The trouble is that the acceptance of just these tenets by Thomas Jefferson, for instance, led to consequences so very different from those following their acceptance by Maximilien Robespierre. Moreover, granting to Cochin that the Jacobins formed a "petite ville," where are we to look for the "grande ville"? Cochin himself probably thought of decent, non-socialist Frenchmen of the Third Republic as the citizens of the "grande ville." But even in the fairly stable nation-state of the nineteenth century, the realist will discern numerous "villes," numerous groups of men with different aims and different ways of life struggling to maintain themselves, and achieving only a precarious equilibrium. And during the Revolution, when this equilibrium was completely destroyed, this "grande ville" did not exist in France. Surely it was not the royalists, nor the Catholics, nor the Feuillants, nor the Girondins. And if the citizen of the "grande ville" is simply the ordinary man who acts reasonably, and in accordance with traditional ways, then he hardly exists in the French Revolution. Any study of the various groups just mentioned should convince the impartial observer that their state of mind was almost as abnormal, as much inclined towards extremes of cruelty or absurdity as the Jacobins'. The White [counter-revolutionary] Terror was as real as the Red.

It is perhaps too easy here to make a synthesis of Taine and Aulard. The Jacobins were an organized minority bent on imposing their way of life on their fellow Frenchmen; so much for the *thèse du complot*. But circumstances—the inheritance of the

---

[31] Jacobin virtue, for instance, is not attainable by ordinary human beings.

ancien régime, the pressure of war from without, of civil disturbances and food scarcity from within—put such obstacles in their
way that they were driven to extremes. In order to exist at all,
they were obliged to be cruel and intolerant. Even in their fac-
titious ritual, their republican catechisms and decalogues, the
Jacobins appear beleaguered; the touch of Hebraic fury one finds
from time to time in their records is not wholly artificial. The
revolutionary government was a government of national defense.
No fair-minded person need deny the value of Aulard's life-work.
The war, at least as much the product of traditional European
high politics as of anything Jacobin, made the Jacobin more
righteous, and more bitter, and saved him from any chance of
appearing ridiculous in his own eyes. Moreover, the introduction
of circumstances at least disposes of the difficulty with Thomas
Jefferson. But it gives little comfort to the sociologist seeking
from history laws permitting human beings to adjust their actions
to conditions in the present—little comfort, in short, to the new
historian. For the circumstances of a great event like the French
Revolution are unique—unique, if not to omniscience, at least
in their extreme complexity unique to the historian. The fatal
"ifs" of history in the conditional—if Mirabeau had not died, if
the king had not fled to Varennes—enter in, and make scientific
induction impossible. Men's beliefs are, for a given group, held in
common and relatively easy to arrive at; so too a given group may
have certain similar and perfectly describable characteristics in
common—rank, occupation, social standing, wealth. Yet we have
no right to assume that their actions can be predicted from these
data.

For the whole point of our study is just this: when one considers the material facts about the Jacobins—their social environment, their occupations, their wealth—one finds sufficient evidence of their prosperity to justify predicting for them quiet, un-
eventful, conservative, thoroughly normal lives. When one studies
the records of their proceedings, one finds them violent, cruel, intolerant, and not a little ridiculous. The antithesis, it must be
insisted, is real. Where material evidence indicates normality, we
find abnormality. Rightly enough, no doubt, this material evidence seems real and important. Therefore the Jacobins present
a genuine paradox. Their *political* being seems quite inconsistent
with their *real* being. Their words and their acts *qua* members
of the clubs are not what we should expect from them *qua* members of civil society. Or to put it as crudely as possible, the Jaco-

bins present for a brief time the extraordinary spectacle of men acting without apparent regard for their material interests.

This, of course, will never do. The economic interpretation of history would tell us that we are either mistaken in our facts (which is always possible) or that there is an explanation which will show men properly and decently following their material interests. Yet perhaps after all the economic interpretation of history is not the whole explanation of the Terror. We are in a realm of thought where the professional psychologist could no doubt add greatly to the precision of our argument. But to a layman it would appear that voluntary human action must have either a more or less directly physical, bodily source (desire, habit, desire partly intellectualized into interest) or a more or less immaterial and intellectual source (principle, idea, desire thoroughly intellectualized into ideal) or finally, must have its source in mere chance. Now if certain important Jacobin actions did not originate from interest, they must have originated from principle or from chance. The first alternative suggests the old-fashioned belief that men act on principle, and leads us back to the school of Taine. If it can be shown that Jacobin ideas logically produce Jacobin actions in 1794, then we need not worry because Jacobin interests and Jacobin habits would not produce such actions. There is just the possibility that the old-fashioned belief about the importance of ideas is justified, at least for certain historical crises, and for certain groups of men. It is not even necessary to refer to such examples of corporate madness as the Children's Crusade; one need only reflect on how much the *interests* of the average man were at stake in the late highly popular war [World War I]. But to accept this explanation would lead to the restoration of ideas to their active rôle in human life, and would put the history of ideas, at least during times of crucial change, on a level with the history of institutions, customs, commerce, and the rest of man's material environment. This will hardly content the new historian, for whom intellectual history is largely a reflection of social history, for whom ideas are most decidedly born of, and consistent with, material interests.

There is the final possibility of accepting chance as the determining factor in human conduct. This need not be as shocking as it seems. Chance may merely stand for a complexity unfathomable to human beings; or it may mean that historical events—that is, of course, human actions—are really unique and exempt from the play of cause and effect as nineteenth-century science understood it. That would still leave the play of cause and effect as the artist, and perhaps even the philosopher, have always understood it. It would still leave narrative history; it would merely destroy the new history.

Our enterprise in retrospective sociology has not perhaps been altogether satisfying. The kind of information about the Jacobins available to the social scientist has not provided us with any fashionable explanation of why men take part in revolutions. The Jacobins seem not to have been crudely at odds with their environment before the Revolution; they certainly were not starving; they were hardly a social or an economic class. They were certainly a collective body—a group—of more than ordinary cohesion, reasonably well disciplined, active, with a definite program, a ritual of their own, a faith charged with emotion, and a pertinacity, a vitality that has enabled the group to survive under changing forms into the Third Republic. Yet so disparate were the social and economic origins of these revolutionaries that we have been driven to the conclusion that large numbers of them, by espousing the Jacobin cause, acted against what they must have been aware were their true selfish interests. Before so surprising a conclusion sociology rightly recoils. The exploded intellectualist fallacy is obviously trying to creep in, and we had better not open the door any wider.

But if we have not got far with applications to the French Revolution of a science of social dynamics, can we not at least give a clearer definition of Jacobin at the end of this enquiry than at the beginning? Here, however, as with so much of modern history, the trouble is that we know too much. A fragment of the rules of one of the clubs would be illuminating to the historian at work in the dark; the records of hundreds of them are blinding. Where statistics fail—and they fail very soon—there is no way of arriving at what is common to the Jacobins. No classification of the complete records of these clubs can be so made that the members of each class can be counted. One might count the number of references to Rousseau; but would such a count serve to weigh the influence of Rousseau on the clubs? The historian must fall back on the normal functioning of his mind, which classifies loosely and pragmatically enough what he experiences in daily life, and which with urging can so classify the matter of his historical studies. But no matter how honest he is, into the making of this classification will come much of his own personal history. What one finds in the Jacobin clubs is what one finds important; and importance, when it is not mathematical, is as subjective as good and bad or sweet and sour.

And yet perhaps the true Jacobin is the rare and perfect Jacobin of the imagination—the Jacobins, let us say, of Anatole France's *Les Dieux ont soif*. One rarely meets an American like Uncle Sam or an Englishman like John Bull, and never a Frenchwoman like the cartoonist's Marianne. Indeed, just as a mass of unbarbered and untailored human animals, Englishmen, Frenchmen, and Americans are probably more alike than we are apt to think. Yet national types do exist, if only in our minds and aspirations. To define them is in a measure to create them; whether we create scarecrows or flesh-and-blood will perhaps not suffer ultimate determination.

This true Jacobin, who may be a scarecrow, but who we hope will be of flesh and blood, is then of no one occupation, of no one social class, of no determinable rank and wealth. He has no ordinary, daily, selfish human interests. He is a religious fanatic, a man inspired and possessed, a man bent on changing overnight this earth into his heaven. What his notion of heaven was we have tried to learn. It was not an uncommon notion of heaven, not one that many men of modern times, if they entertained at all the notion of heaven, would reject—a place where pain and strife could not exist, where the traditional Christian virtues had banished forever the traditional Christian vices, where men were free and equal, and contented with their freedom and equality. The Jacobin was not a revolutionary in that he believed in heaven, or even in that he believed in a special kind of heaven, but in that he attempted to realize his heaven here on earth. That attempt led to the Terror. You cannot have disagreement in heaven. When the Jacobin found he could not convert those who disagreed with him, he had to try to exterminate them. *La sainte guillotine* was not so christened in the spirit of Villon or of Rabelais, but in the spirit of Calvin.

Now common sense, to say nothing of the social sciences, would tell us that most of our five hundred thousand Jacobins were not of this heroic mold. Yet the Terror was a reality, a reality not to be diminished by statistical proof that even in 1794 violence was the exception, not the rule. The slightest document of the period—a theater program, a fashion plate—is no ordinary document, but a sign from another world. Most men in 1794 no doubt ate, drank, slept, and went about most of their business as they had in 1784; most men were no doubt as stupid, as selfish, as kindly, as good in 1794 as in 1784. But into the whole lives of some Frenchmen, into some part of the lives of all Frenchmen, had come this indefinable, incredible pattern of action and feeling we have called Jacobinism. Very real, very earthly grievances had gone into making the pattern; wise, selfish, ordinary men had helped make the pattern to achieve wise, selfish, ordinary purposes. But a few foolish, unselfish (as the world uses the term) and extraordinary men—with circumstances aiding—had by 1794 turned the pattern into the madness of true Jacobinism. Yet still most Jacobins were normal men. They were still of respectable middle class origins. What had happened to them? Were 499,000 of them hypocrites, trembling before a thousand fanatics? Probably not. It seems more likely that, for a few short months, these ordinary men were possessed by a faith, a contagion, an unearthly aspiration. Jacques Dupont, the man in the street, the economic man, the sociological man, the psychological man, ceased for a brief while to behave in the orderly fashion laid out for him by these sciences, and took instead to the ways of Carlylean heroes or Emersonian representative men.

Jacobinism is, then, first of all a faith. Were they not believers, the Jacobins would be unintelligible to us. As it is, the Jacobin may be strong or weak, tall or short, rich or poor, gentleman or vagabond; what makes him a Jacobin is none of these varying and individual attributes, but a fixed faith. "Liberty, Equality, Fraternity," as words, may be subject to definition and contain the seeds of infinite dispute; as symbols, they were to the Jacobins a common property above logic. The emotions which they evoked allowed the Jacobins to form, for the moment, one body; they provided a common fund of pooled emotions, an inexhaustible and immaterial fund.

Now, in time, this very immateriality of the fund began to pall on many Jacobins. Tough-minded philosophers who, from the utilitarians to the economic interpretationists have perhaps thought a little too highly of their fellow men, would of course maintain that the fund must have been material, or held out the promise of materiality, ever to have held human beings at all. To them, there must somehow be a connection between the individual's standing, and the position he takes in politics. Perhaps they are right as a general rule, right in the long run and in normal times. Yet our study of the Jacobin clubs has failed to establish such a connection for the French Revolution. Neither the class struggle theory nor the maladjustment theory seems in itself to account for the extraordinary diversity of membership in the clubs, nor for the extraordinary variety of things the clubs endeavored to do.

What was meant sincerely as a study in the new history has come to a conclusion strangely like that of very old-fashioned history indeed. If the subject matter of the social sciences be natural man, then the Jacobin appears to have a touch of the supernatural. The French Revolution appears, as it did to Maistre, to Wordsworth, and to Carlyle, as utterly inexplicable in terms of daily life, of common sense, of scientific causation. Yet perhaps we need not call the Revolution a miracle. Only if man is wholly at the mercy of his simpler appetites need we have recourse to the miraculous to explain Jacobin aberrations. If the incredibly complex world which human thought has added to the world of our simpler appetites can at times give ordinary men motives for action even stronger than these simpler appetites, then the French Revolution is explicable. It seems too bad to have to conclude that sometimes some men—or even many men—believe for no more apparent reason than that they want to believe, that their beliefs have, at least in part, independent and immaterial lives. Yet, if only in his capacity for adjusting his conduct to illusion and not to fact, man is most obviously an animal apart. Surely there is nothing surprising if a study of the Jacobins forces us to the conclusion that man cannot live by bread alone?

THE DESIRE TO
COMMUNIZE*

Pierre Gaxotte

*Pierre Gaxotte (1895–) has been a member of the
Académie française since 1953. After attending his coun-
try's finest schools, the Lycée Henri IV and the École normale
supérieure, he taught for a short while before becoming a journal-
ist. He has written many books on French and German history.
The selection which follows is from his earliest historical work,
La Révolution française (1928), which is still very popular among
French conservatives.*

The more firmly the Revolutionary Government was established,
the more sanguinary it became, and the more actively the guillotine was kept at work. Those historians who are anxious at all
costs to represent the hecatombs slaughtered by the Montagnards
as regrettable excesses in what were perfectly legitimate reprisals
find themselves in considerable embarrassment when they come
to deal with the year 1794. Moreover, in their blind desire to
exonerate the system, they find themselves forced to lay the blame
for all the crimes which they cannot otherwise explain at the
door of one man, Robespierre. Robespierre's ambition, Robespierre's hypocrisy, Robespierre's cruelty . . . these words appear
on every page. Such excuses are as puerile as they are false. The
Terror was of the very essence of the Revolution, because the
Revolution was not merely a change in the system of government, but a social revolution, an attempt at expropriation and
extermination. . . .

* Reprinted with the permission of Charles Scribner's Sons from pp. 288–
289, 291–292, 298–303, of *The French Revolution* (New York, 1932) by Pierre
Gaxotte, translated by Walter Alison Phillips.

The Mountain was manœuvred by its extreme Left, known as the party of the *Enragés*. It is hard to say where this party began or ended, or to assign it any definite limits. There was mutual hatred and much squabbling among its members, and excommunications were prompt. But, with these reservations, it may be said that the movement sprang from the communistic preaching of Jacques Roux and his rivals, Varlet and Leclercq. It was they who launched the idea that the political revolution ought to be completed by a social revolution, and that equality of civil rights would be useless without equality of fortunes. Snubbed by the revolutionary leaders, they found a hearing among the poorer classes in the towns, whom the inflation of the currency had plunged into the most appalling distress. By May [1793] they were so strong that Marat and Robespierre had to buy their assistance against the Girondins, and up to September their influence was constantly on the increase. . . .

The first decree fixing the price of wheat was passed . . . on the 4th of May, 1793, in return for the alliance of the *Enragés* against the Girondins. It was, however, very badly applied. The departmental authorities charged with the duty of applying it purposely dragged out the preliminary operations and used the obscurities and omissions in the law as a pretext for allowing it to be evaded in nine cases out of ten.

In July there was a drastic change; for Communist pressure was becoming more and more violent. On the 27th, after listening to the report presented by Collot-d'Herbois, the Convention passed, almost without debate, a law on the hording or forestalling of supplies which, according to [the French historian] M. Marion, "amounted to no less than treating as a public enemy anyone who should still have the courage to trade in those things the dearth of which caused the greatest complaint." Forestalling (*accaparement*) was defined as the fact of holding stored up in any place, without publicly exposing them for sale day by day, food-stuffs and articles of prime necessity, to wit: flour, bread, meat, wine, vegetables, fruit, butter, cider, vinegar, brandy, honey, fats, tallow, fish, wood, coal, oil, soda, soap, salt, sugar, hemp, wool, paper, hides, iron, copper, lead, steel, cloth, linen and stuffs generally. Those who were holding back these commodities were directed to declare them within eight days to the municipalities, which would nominate commissaries to verify the declarations, and, in case of need, to proceed to the sale of the goods. Those who should make false returns were to be punished with death, and those who denounced such frauds were to be rewarded with a third of the property confiscated.

The law did not affect the producer, nor did it interfere with prices. A great step had, however, been taken towards general confiscation. There were no longer any trade secrets. The *commissaires aux accaparements* were empowered to enter all premises, examine account-books and invoices, dispose of stocks, and visit barns and granaries. When once this road is started upon there is no stopping. It was not long before the idea took shape that the law of the 27th of July was only a preliminary, and that the State had the power to exert pressure on prices and lower them. From time to time a few tentative experiments were made in fixing the prices of some commodities. Finally, on the 29th of September, the Convention passed a decree fixing a maximum price for all commodities of prime necessity. This was known as the Law of the Maximum.

In addition to the things enumerated in the decree of the 27th of July, the sale of which was already under control, the new law mentioned grain, forage, tobacco, boots and wooden shoes (*sabots*). In the case of some articles the maximum price fixed was the same for all France; in the case of others it varied in different communes. Those engaged in agriculture were obliged more especially to send in returns of the yield of their harvest, and were forbidden to sell their wheat anywhere save in the public market or at any except the official price. If they refused, the authorities were to supply the markets by force, requisition the standing [wheat], and have it reaped and threshed by labourers mobilized for this purpose. The transport of [wheat] was made subject to an official permit, while the millers and their equipment were requisitioned, their function being regarded as a public service. Finally, since the currency had already fallen to half its face value and the process of devaluation was becoming accelerated every day, *the maximum was fixed at only one-third above the prices current in* 1790. The law, in short, was not only tyrannous, but a measure of expropriation. Those who contravened it were threatened with the severest penalties: a year's rigorous imprisonment for bakers who should cease work, ten years in irons for millers who bargained over the sale of grain or flour, ten years in irons for farmers who sent in false returns, and death for those who tried to obstruct the requisitioning.

Having assumed control of internal trade, it now only remained to the State to assume that of foreign trade. This was the object of the decree of the 30th of May, 1794, which placed at its disposal all commodities, raw materials or goods imported either by land or sea. Agencies were established at the ports and on the frontiers for requisitioning what they saw fit, leaving to the owners nothing but the surplus, so that to all intents and purposes the State became the sole importer. As for export trade, this was forbidden so far as a large number of articles were concerned, and in the case of the others could only be carried on under strict control. Finally, the whole of the mercantile marine was requisitioned.

Goods having been requisitioned, it was next the turn of the men. The decree, passed on the 23rd of August, 1793, which ordered the *levée en masse* had sent to the front only young men from eighteen to twenty-five years of age, but placed the whole population of France, women included, at the service of the State. It was a logical consequence that the State, being now the only master and the only shopkeeper, should also become the only employer. The law of the 29th of September, which prescribed a maximum price for commodities, also prescribed maximum wages. It was, however, a little more generous to the workmen than to the tradesmen, for, instead of only a third, it allowed them to be paid half as much again as in 1790.

The requisitioning of workpeople, in 1793 and 1794, was carried out by categories, according to the needs of the moment. First came the journeyman bakers, followed by printers for the manufacture of *assignats,* of cartwrights, metal-founders, turners, tailors, tanners, etc., for war supplies, and of carters and raft-men for the transport of fuel and grain. The whole of France was transformed into a vast barracks; and since a law [of June 14, 1791], passed on the motion of Le Chapelier, had deprived proletarians of the right to combine and strike, the burden of the Communist policy weighed as heavily on the working classes as on any other. Then, on the 4th of April, 1794, the Convention proclaimed a general requisition of all who could serve the State, whether with hand or brain, and threatened to hale before the Revolutionary Tribunal those who should try to evade this duty.

And now arose the real difficulty, namely, how to apply laws which were impossible to execute. The moment the maximum was promulgated the shops were emptied, for everyone hurried to buy at an artificially low price what had cost two or three times as much the day before; and when the stocks were exhausted no one was willing to renew them. In a single day there would be no sugar, oil or candles in Paris. Wine was still to be had, but it was doctored and undrinkable. In the provinces the country people rushed to the towns to exchange their notes for clothes, boots, pieces of stuff or groceries, which the law forced the tradesmen to sell at a ruinous price, and then hurried back to bestow their [wheat] in hiding-places which none could discover. In fact everyone wanted the maximum for his neighbour and liberty for himself. "Brothers and friends," said Frécine, a member of the Convention, to some workmen who had revolted against the maximum wage, "I learn with sorrow that there are individuals among you who are obstinately bent on obtaining an increase of wages which would be a charge on the Republic. What, citizens? Can it be that the detestable spirit of greed which the national justice has just destroyed in the case of the forestall-ers has insinuated itself into the pure soul of the *sans-culottes?* . . . You ask that the law shall be rigorously enforced in respect of what you buy, yet you refuse to obey it in respect of everything you sell to others! . . ."

The resistance of the peasants soon assumed formidable pro-portions. It was clear that they would use every possible means of making the legislation which despoiled them a dead letter. Wherever they were in a position to evade search they under-stated the yield of their crops and only sold them clandestinely, at the price that suited them. When they could not safely do this, they let the crops rot on the ground on pretext that they had not enough labour to gather them. In other places, since the maximum price for wheat had been imposed before that for oats, they consented to sell the oats, but fed their horses on the wheat. When the retail price of meat was fixed, they refused to supply the butchers. When the price of cattle on the hoof was fixed, they let their beasts perish.

Smuggling assumed enormous proportions on the frontiers. A quintal (200 lbs.) of wheat fetched 40 *francs* in gold at Geneva, while in France it had to be sold for 14 *francs* in paper money. However strict a watch might be kept, it would have been im-possible to prevent so lucrative a trade.

In the Department of Haute-Saône, about which M. Mathiez has given us so much valuable information, the immediate effect of the promulgation of the maximum was to aggravate the crisis in the supply of food. The farmers stopped threshing; the bakers ceased to bake; the innkeepers refused to serve guests; the workmen who had no work in the towns refused to undertake work in the country where it was needed. A young volunteer, whose correspondence is in the possession of M. Marion, wrote to his family from Pfalzburg: "The fixed prices of commodities have been promulgated here, but since then it is almost impossible to get anything to eat." From Toulouse the Committee of Public Safety received the following report: "The city seems as though it had been cut off by a hostile army; food-stuffs have ceased to reach it, and the inhabitants of the countryside only visit it in order to clear out the shops." And from Bergues came a note which sums up all the rest: In this part of the country "the Law of the Maximum has had the effect of a liberticide plot hatched by Pitt."

Communism was inconceivable without an unexampled display of coercion and force, and it was this which was the real significance of the Terror, and explained its development and duration. The terrorist dictatorship was connected with the social laws, and not with military events. Debated in the Convention on the 5th of September [1793], after the great Hébertist demonstration, the Terror was organized at the very time when the danger from abroad was diminishing. It was reduced to a code when the frontiers had been cleared of the enemy, and it reached its high-water mark when the French arms were victorious and Belgium had been reconquered.

A SYNTHESIS*

Georges Lefebvre

*For biographical information on Georges Lefebvre, see
the section entitled "The Outbreak of the Revolution
(1787–1789)."*

In the revolutionary mentality, as has been noted,[1] the punitive
will was associated from the beginning with the defensive reaction against the "aristocratic plot." They were inseparable
elements, although one might predominate and the behaviour
that resulted might differ greatly as the result of circumstances
and individual temperaments. Repressive action arose as early
as July, 1789. The permanent committees confined themselves
to surveillance and to investigations made on suspicion, but in
a few cases summary executions by the aroused mob occurred.
The deployment of the police force was not always enough to
prevent these, and it was necessary to check the agitation through
the all-out pursuit of conspirators and by prompt and severe
penalties. The assemblies instituted committees of investigation
or of general security, and referred crimes against the nation
(*lèse-nation*) to a special jurisdiction, first Le Châtelet, then the
High Court, and finally the tribunal of August 17, 1792.

During this first period, however, repression was not made
uniform. In times of calm, with the danger fading and the
bourgeoisie disliking hasty procedures that threatened individual
security, the penalties seemed absurd; but a local incident was

* From Georges Lefebvre, *The French Revolution from 1793 to 1799*, trans.
John Hall Stewart and James Friguglietti (New York: Columbia University
Press, 1964), pp. 116–125. Copyright © 1964 Columbia University Press. Re-
printed by permission of Columbia University Press, Inc., and Routledge &
Kegan Paul, Ltd.

[1] [For Lefebvre's description of what he means by the revolutionary mentality
see pp. 27–29.]

enough to cause renewed popular executions. With the war and invasion these multiplied, and in Paris they culminated in the September Massacres. The response of the Girondins, far from bringing about the reinforcement of governmental action, was to suppress it. The High Court disappeared, then the tribunal of August 17, so that political trials returned to the jurisdiction of ordinary courts.

The crisis of 1793 posed the problem once again, for the punitive will was joined with the defensive reaction to give birth to the revolutionary government. It aroused its leaders as much as its partisans. The September Massacres had nearly destroyed them, however, and resolving not to tolerate a repetition they undertook to organize the Terror. By so doing they opened a second period. At the lowest level, the watch committees, created on March 21, 1793, assumed the power to arrest suspected persons; and after the law of September 17 they were left full discretion, under the control of the Committee of General Security. If there were grounds for indictment, the Revolutionary Tribunal (instituted on March 10, reorganized on September 5, and appointed by the Convention) intervened. For some crimes the criminal court of each department, sitting "revolutionarily," followed the same methods. Finally, in the areas of civil war, military commissions became active. Procedure was simplified in all cases. The grand jury was replaced by judges, and recourse to appeals disappeared. Moreover, the Convention reduced trials to a simple verification of identity and pronouncement of the death penalty for individuals who had been outlawed, rebels, émigrés, and deported priests who returned to the territory of the Republic.

In reality the government lost some control over the repression. Like administration, it was decentralized by the emergency. Nothing could serve better than local committees, because of the information which their members had long since acquired. The centrifugal tendency was curbed in principle by the deputies on mission. For months concentration of powers was displayed chiefly at this regional level, but in many communes the revolutionary committees were established solely for appearances, or never existed. Having difficulty in recruiting competent and reliable administrations in the villages, the deputies often preferred to leave political policing either to the committee of the chief town of the district or canton, or to the committees of public safety created spontaneously by the revolutionaries of the locality. By virtue of their full powers, however, the deputies on mission claimed to direct the Terror as they pleased. At times they collaborated with the local terrorists; at times they opposed them. The result of this inconsistency was that the scope of repression was expanded, but its severity varied greatly.

Suspicion was directed not only towards probable authors of acts already committed, on grounds of definite circumstances susceptible of discussion and of proof, but also towards the possible perpetrators of eventual crimes, who were believed capable of them because of their opinions or even their real or simulated indifference. The margin for uncertainty and the risk of arbitrary action, which normal judicial procedure reduced only slightly (because of its attention to detail and its slowness), increased enormously. The dangers were multiplied in a singularly perilous fashion when it came to arraignment. In investigating the past of persons concerned, acts or declarations that were irreproachable in their time (such as the petitions of the "8,000" and the "20,000" [2]), or that were justified according to law (notably the protests against August 10, 1792, or June 2, 1793), were introduced. Although no subsequent opposition could be charged to these Feuillants or federalists, many of them were imprisoned and even guillotined.

Yet the "aristocratic plot" was not the sole factor involved. The economic situation and its social consequences now revealed other "enemies of the people"—the rich who hid their money or sent it abroad, the producers who evaded the Maximum, and those who refused assignats. The Terror thus became the prop of the controlled economy on which the sans-culottes depended for their own existence. Undoubtedly crimes of an economic nature did not all fall within the special jurisdiction. Still, they exposed their authors to detention as suspects; and if their opinions and circumstances tended to impute counter-revolutionary intentions to them, their lives were at stake.

Nevertheless nothing contributed as much to spreading the Terror as dechristianization. Former clergy, constitutional priests, and practising faithful were treated as dangerous or culpable. Thus conceived, the terrorist repression was unquestionably effective, because it intimidated, reduced to impotence, or sup-

[2] [The first of these petitions (June 10, 1792) opposed the stationing near Paris of 20,000 National Guardsmen from the provinces. The second (July 1, 1792) protested the indignities the king suffered during the demonstration of June 20, 1792.]

pressed many enemies. Yet it was no less responsible for injuring, or far more frequently, for disturbing and vexing a host of people who, although hostile to the revolutionary government for various reasons, were resigned to obeying it, and who, in any case, dreamed neither of conspiracy nor of revolt.

Even making great allowances for the opinions of those who applied the Terror, its harshness depended upon their character and upon circumstances. Personal hatreds, the desire for vengeance that had permeated the punitive will from the outset, and particularly the impulsive authoritarianism of certain individuals occasionally aggravated its severity or rekindled it after a period of calm. Conversely, forbearance, friendships, and political spirit often tempered it, and numerous deputies on mission confined themselves to setting a few examples or making a few imprisonments. Likewise, the commissioners of the committees varied in their behaviour: in the district of St.-Pol one arrested 141 persons in the canton of Frévent, while his colleagues elsewhere apprehended only one or two.

Yet circumstances exerted a more considerable influence. An estimate of the relative danger, and not temperament alone, prompted some deputies to assume responsibility for establishing revolutionary tribunals or popular commissions. These, ignoring the Paris tribunal, precipitated executions. In the matter of suspects, mass arrests coincided with specific events: those of August, 1793, period of the greatest peril and the levy *en masse*; those of the autumn, when terror had just been made the "order of the day"; and those of Ventôse [March 1794], at the opening of the campaign. The role of circumstances is more clearly evident from the statistical analysis of death sentences made by Donald Greer.[3] Seventy-one per cent occurred in the two areas of civil war—19 per cent in the south-east and 52 per cent in the west—as against only 15 per cent in Paris. Moreover, this agrees with an examination of the motives for these condemnations: in more than 72 per cent of the cases they were due to rebellion. Six departments, on the other hand, had no executions, thirty-one had fewer than ten, and fourteen fewer than twenty-five.

Of course it is not percentages but the figures themselves that account for the impression made on public opinion. Greer's statistics are limited to death sentences, which he estimates at almost 17,000; but the number of deaths was far higher. Apart

[3] [*The Incidence of the Terror* (Cambridge, Mass.: Harvard University Press, 1935).]

from rebels who fell in combat, it is necessary to add the executions without trial, whether by order, as at Nantes and Toulon, or by refusal to grant quarter on the battlefield, in pursuit, or in police roundups. Besides, conditions in the prisons caused a high mortality. Since an exact computation is impossible, Greer suggests an estimate of 35,000–40,000 dead. It is well to recall that the property of condemned persons, of émigrés, and of deported priests was confiscated, and that of relatives of émigrés was sequestered until the inheritance belonging to the fugitives was deducted. Finally, suspects should not be forgotten. The district of St.-Pol confined 1,460 of them, and the total number of 300,000, although hypothetical, is not improbable. The fright and rancour of contemporaries, and the indelible memory which they handed down to posterity, are quite understandable.

Greer's findings are important particularly because they confirm the nature of the Terror. It was in the two areas where counter-revolutionaries took up arms and committed open treason that it raged with the greatest fury. Despite the elements that spread it thoughtlessly or abused it, it remained until the triumph of the Revolution just what it had been at the outset—a punitive reaction indissolubly linked to the defensive spirit against the "aristocratic plot." Some will object that 85 per cent of the known dead—bourgeois, artisans, peasants—belonged to the Third Estate, while the clergy accounted for only 6.5 per cent, and the nobility 8.5 per cent; but in such a struggle, turncoats were treated more harshly than original enemies.

Yet to a large extent this is merely the outward aspect of the Terror. Another may be revealed within if it is observed that, associated with the revolutionary government, it conferred upon the latter the "coercive power" that restored the authority of the state and allowed it to impose upon the nation the sacrifices indispensable to public safety. If the majority of Frenchmen clung to the Revolution and detested foreign intervention, their civic education was not enough to repress selfishness and make them all submit to discipline. The Terror forced it upon them and contributed greatly to developing the habit and feeling of national solidarity. The Montagnards undoubtedly shared the punitive will of the sans-culottes, but the fact remains that from this point of view the Terror became an instrument of government that regimented the nation, without making even occasional exception for the sans-culottes themselves. This was, so to speak, its internal aspect.

Henceforth, as the dictatorship of the Committee asserted itself, a third aspect was revealed. Some Montagnards condemned the harshness of the system, and some sans-culottes reproached it for not doing enough for them. This time the Terror was turned against those who had created it. The drama of Ventôse and Germinal [March–April 1794] thus marked a new stage in its history. It appeared destined to maintain in power the small group of men who, entrenched in the committees, embodied the revolutionary dictatorship.

Still, its earlier characteristics persisted during this third period. Centralization had progressed slowly. The Committee of General Security required justificatory reports on imprisonments, the Committee of Public Safety sent agents here and there to investigate (Jullien of Paris to Nantes and Bordeaux, and Demaillot to Orléans), and the most notable terrorists (Carrier, Barras, Fréron, Fouché, and Tallien) returned one after another. Now the decree of 27 Germinal, Year II (April 16, 1794), ordered the suppression of revolutionary tribunals in the provinces, and most of them were terminated on 19 Floréal (May 8).

Once more, circumstances produced exceptions. In the north the campaign took a turn for the worse: Landrecies surrendered on 11 Floréal, Year II (April 30, 1794), and Cambrai was threatened. Dispatched to the army, Saint-Just and Lebas appealed to Lebon,[4] who established a branch of his Arras tribunal, which was then allowed to remain until 22 Messidor (July 10). In Provence, when [the deputy on mission] Maignet declared it impossible to transfer thousands of prisoners to Paris, the Committee, on 21 Floréal (May 10), created the popular commission of Orange, which was still functioning on 9 Thermidor. On the other hand, with the Committee of Public Safety and that of General Security both directing the repression, centralization drove the former to dispossess the latter; and at the end of Floréal it established a Bureau of General Police. Its rival did not give way, and . . . this rift within the revolutionary government hastened its downfall.

As an instrument of government, the terrorist methods might have given the victorious committees cause for reflection. All authoritarian regimes, and others, too, resort to them in time of war or insurrection. But it is a rule among politicians to

---

[4] [One of the Convention's deputies on mission who headed a Revolutionary Tribunal in Arras.]

confine themselves to setting a few examples that assure the submission of the multitude without reducing it to desperation.
There were signs that some members of the Committee perceived
the danger. Robespierre had opposed the trial of the deputies
arrested following their protest against the "day" of June 2
[1793]; and thanks to Lindet, a general proscription of federalists
was avoided. The vain efforts against dechristianization, and the
recall of the worst terrorists, were steps in the same direction.

On 5 Nivôse, Year II (December 25, 1793), it was agreed to
"perfect" the Revolutionary Tribunal. Did this mean that the
crimes to be repressed would be precisely defined, that guarantees for the defendant would be increased, and that arrests would
be reviewed? Such was not the case. Once more, circumstances
were decisive. Until the end of June, victory remained doubtful
and required an all-out effort. The moment did not seem ripe for
any slackening of energy. On the contrary, the decree of 27
Germinal, Year II (April 16, 1794), expelled nobles and foreigners
from Paris and the fortified towns. In proscribing Indulgents and
extremists, however, the committees had no intention of sparing
the counter-revolutionaries. They shared the sans-culottes' urge
to punish, and had no desire to risk being accused of treason.

In Paris, in Floréal, notable trials—those of the deputies
compromised by their attitude in 1789, of the farmers-general
(who included Lavoisier), and of Madame Elisabeth [Louis XVI's
younger sister]—proved that the Terror, faithful to its origin,
had not become simply an instrument of government. The widespread belief in the "aristocratic plot," extended to all those accused of hostility towards the regime, explains the increasing
practice of the "amalgam." This, by denying all truly judicial
procedure, threw together under the same sentence accused
persons who did not know each other, and whose deeds or words
had nothing in common other than their supposed solidarity in
the "conspiracy against the French people." Finally, with this
state of mind exaggerated because of attacks threatening the
personal safety of revolutionary leaders, terrorist procedure was
altered, but only to be even more greatly simplified.

Late on 3 Prairial, Year II (May 22, 1794), a certain Admirat
fired his pistol at Collot d'Herbois, but missed his target. On the
evening of the 4th, Cécile Renault, who insisted upon seeing
Robespierre, was arrested. She refused to reveal her intentions,
but voiced her hopes of victory for the Coalition. Earlier that
day Barère had denounced Admirat as the agent of the plot,

financed by Pitt, against the Republic. On the 7th (May 26), the Convention forbade the granting of quarter henceforth to British and Hanoverian soldiers. This was an unprecedented step, and the army could scarcely apply it; but it attested the emotion aroused by the memories of the assassination of Lepeletier and Marat. This feeling was again expressed in the appeal from the Committee of Public Safety to Saint-Just, on the 6th, in the midst of the campaign: "Liberty is exposed to new dangers. . . . The Committee needs to unite the knowledge and energy of all its members."

Obviously, in the eyes of the revolutionaries these assassination attempts, which they linked (without any convincing proof) to the intrigues of the elusive Baron de Batz,[5] foreshadowed some attempt to disorganize the national defence on the eve of decisive battles. Saint-Just arrived on the 10th, but discussions (of which we know nothing) and preparations for the Festival of the Supreme Being (set for the 20th) delayed the result. This took shape on 22 Prairial (June 10), when Couthon presented the famous law, the draft of which is in his handwriting. Robespierre, who was presiding, stepped down to the tribune to secure the approval of the Convention. Later, when threatened by the reactionaries, the members of the Committee of Public Safety ascribed the initiative for the law to their vanished colleagues, and declared that they themselves had not been consulted. But the Thermidorians did not believe them. It is at least certain that the Committee of General Security was not called upon to give its opinion, and that it did not forgive this oversight.

Suppressing all preliminary questioning, leaving the summoning of witnesses to the discretion of the court, and refusing the accused the aid of counsel, the law succeeded in destroying the judicial guarantees for the defence. Furthermore, the court was left with no choice but acquittal or death. Considered as an instrument of government in the service of revolutionary defence, the Terror did not require such reinforcement. Besides, Couthon had said, "It is not a matter of setting a few examples, but of exterminating the implacable henchmen of tyranny." This was scorning the point of view of a statesman, a yielding completely to the passion for repression, which the threat of assassination tinged with personal animosity.

In the Convention, on the other hand, the law brought a

[5] [Baron de Batz (1760–1822) was a royalist plotter involved in many counter-revolutionary conspiracies but never apprehended.]

long-felt uneasiness to its height. The opponents of the Committee claimed, on the 23rd, that the law implicitly authorized it to arraign deputies without referring the matter to the Assembly. On the next day, not without difficulty, Robespierre secured the repudiation of such a charge; but doubts persisted. For this reason the conviction spread that the Committees were accelerating the Terror in order to maintain themselves in power. So the new trend, which had been foreseen on the day following the deaths of Hébert and Danton, now prevailed.

The Law of 22 Prairial, Year II (June 10, 1794), gave birth to the "Great Terror." As early as the 29th it was applied to a "batch" of 54 persons who had been implicated in the assassination attempts and the Batz conspiracy. Yet it was the anxious attention paid to the prisons which extended its scope. This was nothing new: it had been admitted in July, 1789, and September, 1792, that a prisoners' revolt was part of the "aristocratic plot." The great number of imprisoned suspects—now more than 8,000 in Paris—could only increase this fear. The prison system justified it. A report in Prairial acknowledged, in short, that the prisoners were virtually free to revolt. Such a plan had been charged to the Hébertists, and later to Dillon and Lucille Desmoulins.[6] In June, after a planned escape was denounced at the Bicêtre prison, three "batches" were brought before the Revolutionary Tribunal on these grounds.

Since the attacks of Prairial were linked to the counter-revolutionary conspiracy, it is not astonishing that the prisons were again made the order of the day. But the intention to "exterminate," expressed by Couthon, also explains why denunciations by informers were welcomed complacently. With the approval of the Committee of Public Safety, and under the direction of Herman, the head of the Commission on Civil and Judicial Affairs, seven "batches" were taken from the Luxembourg, Carmes, and St.-Lazare prisons between 19 Messidor, Year II (July 7, 1794), and 8 Thermidor (July 26). ([The poet] André Chénier was included in one of them.) In all, the "Great Terror" cost the lives of 1,376 persons, while only 1,251 had been executed in Paris from March, 1793, to 22 Prairial.

Public opinion was shaken, and the practices of the repression abetted the fear. The tumbrils slowly transported the condemned

---

[6] [Comte Arthur Dillon, a French general, and Lucille Desmoulins, the widow of the guillotined Camille Desmoulins, were convicted and executed on the basis of this accusation.]

across the Faubourg St.-Antoine as far as the Trône-Renversé gate, the new emplacement for the scaffold. The executions were public, and the guillotine, cutting off heads and spattering blood, struck the imagination. But precisely because the victory of the Revolution no longer appeared in doubt, fear of the "aristocratic plot" faded, the punitive will was dulled, and the popular fever subsided.

The Terror was a method of settling a fear of losing the Revolutionary government. It was a Security blanket which appeased the people.

VII

THE SANS-CULOTTES

RECENT RESEARCH

DESCRIBED AND CRITICIZED*

Robert R. Palmer

*The eminent American historian Robert R. Palmer
(1909–) was born in Chicago. He received his Ph.D.
from Cornell University and taught at Princeton University from
1936 to 1963. After having served as Dean of the Faculty of
Arts and Sciences at Washington University in St. Louis, he
returned to Princeton in 1967 as Dean of the Faculty. Among
his works on the eighteenth century are an exciting study of
the Committee of Public Safety,* Twelve Who Ruled *(1941), and
his two-volume masterpiece,* The Age of the Democratic Revolution *(1959–1964), in which he sets forth the nature and extent
of the democratic revolutionary movement throughout Europe
and the United States from 1760 to 1800.*

*Professor Palmer excels at comparing the histories of various
countries; he is a fine critic who writes in a lucid style that has
gained him an audience among the general public as well as
among his university colleagues. These qualities are evident in*

* From Robert R. Palmer, "Popular Democracy in the French Revolution:
Review Article," *French Historical Studies*, I (Fall 1960), 445–469. The entire
article is reprinted by permission of the author and the editor of *French
Historical Studies*.

*the following survey of an important new area of research—the
revolutionary role of the urban common people, the sans-culottes,
during the French Revolution.*

All who wish to keep informed on new work on the French
Revolution will owe a great debt to Professor Jacques Godechot,
who has taken over, for the *Revue historique,* the preparation of
the review-articles which Georges Lefebvre used to publish at
five-year intervals. Godechot's first "bulletin" appeared in the
Revue during 1959. It records and comments upon almost two
hundred books and articles dealing with the Revolutionary-
Napoleonic period since the early 1950's. To attempt the same
here would be useless, and impossible for the present writer; it
is enough, for bibliographical purposes, to refer to Godechot's
report, and to the reviews and news currently published in the
Annales historiques de la Révolution française.

Fortunately there are a few works which can be singled out.
Their publication is the real "news" in the field. They undoubtedly represent the most significant contributions to the
study of the French Revolution in many years, with the exception of Godechot's own book of 1956 [*La Grande Nation*] on
revolutionary expansion in the 1790's. The authors may be said to
constitute a school, since they have a common theme, appear to
be in frequent touch with each other, and collectively represent
the most authentic and acknowledged discipleship to Lefebvre.
Their chief work, after years of fundamental research in the
archives, came almost simultaneously to publication in 1958 and
1959. Probably these years will long be seen in retrospect as an
important date in the long history of historical writing on the
French Revolution. It will be the date of the full emergence of
the urban lower classes, the people called *sans-culottes* during
the Revolution, at the center of attention on the historical stage.

The new school shares with Lefebvre a preference for seeing
the Revolution "from below." It is felt that Mathiez was too
preoccupied with events at the national level, with leaders whose
names were and are publicly known, such as Robespierre, and
with decisions made in legislative chambers, or committee offices,
or the Jacobin Club. It was the gist of Lefebvre's work to go into
the country, to discover the peasants, to explore the complex
differences among the peasants themselves, to argue that the
Revolution, while always remaining essentially bourgeois, was

successful against the privileged orders because of a bourgeois-peasant alliance, in which some peasants were, so to speak, admitted to the advantages of bourgeois civilization, but others, very numerous, were not; so that the Revolutionary Government of the Year II, *i.e.,* the Jacobin dictatorship and rule of the Committee of Public Safety, was seriously weakened by its inability to satisfy, or even comprehend, the true needs and wishes of the rural mass. The gist of the new school is to go into the street, to discover the city people, especially those of Paris, to explore the sociological and economic differences among them, to argue that the Revolution, though always essentially bourgeois, owed its success against absolutism and aristocracy to the support of these working classes; but the new school finds less advantage from the Revolution for the city people than Lefebvre found for the peasants, except for the overthrow of the Old Regime; and it tends to conclude, more emphatically than Lefebvre, that the Revolutionary Government of 1793–94 was mortally wounded because it gave offense to the true popular revolutionaries.

The pattern is much the same in both cases, although, as an Italian observer has remarked, "what was in Lefebvre a pure and objective historical finding takes on in his disciples the aspect of a condemnation, or at least of a negative judgment on Robespierre and the Montagnards.[1] The ebb of the true Revolution is placed some months before Thermidor, and marked by the execution of the people called Hébertists by Robespierre. The new school, like Lefebvre when he was thinking about this subject, stresses the degree to which great numbers were left unsatisfied, and so sets the stage for, or legitimates, the resumption of revolutionary activity in the nineteenth and twentieth centuries, and of a revolutionary activity aiming for more than the Jacobin dictatorship of 1793–94 would ever have countenanced.

The leading figure in the school [2] is Albert Soboul of Paris,

---

[1] Franco Catalano, "Sanculotti e contadini nella Rivoluzione francese," in *Nuova rivista storica,* XLII (Sept.–Dec., 1958), 546.

[2] Albert Soboul, *Les sans-culottes parisiens en l'an II: Mouvement populaire et Gouvernement révolutionnaire, 2 juin 1793–9 thermidor an II* (Paris: Clavreuil, 1958), 1,168 pp. with appendixes. [An English translation and abridgment has been published as *The Parisian Sans-Culottes and the French Revolution, 1793–4* (Oxford: Clarendon Press, 1964).]
George Rudé, *The Crowd in the French Revolution* (Oxford: Clarendon Press, 1959), 267 pp. with appendixes.
R. C. Cobb, "Quelques aspects de la mentalité révolutionnaire, avril 1793—thermidor an II," in *Revue d'histoire moderne et contemporaine,* VI (Apr.–

whose major thesis for the French doctorate, a huge and definitive study of more than a thousand pages, was published in 1958. There are two Englishmen: George Rudé of London, whose book came out in 1959; and R. C. Cobb of Manchester, who has published almost entirely in French, with his findings most effectively summarized in a brilliant article of 1959. To these may be added the Norwegian, Kåre Tønnesson, whose book appeared in 1959. The group is represented in East Germany by Walter Markov, and in Italy by Armando Saitta. Saitta, with Soboul, brought out in 1959 a new edition of Lefebvre's classic of 1924, *Les paysans du Nord et la Révolution française*.[3] In 1958 he sponsored Italian translations of short pieces by Lefebvre, Soboul, Cobb, and Rudé.[4] Markov has sponsored similar translations in German, and has also published the best available collection of documentary sources on the Paris sans-culottes, presented in both French and German on facing pages. In addition, for the bicentennial of Robespierre's birth, Markov assembled some twenty articles on revolutionaries both of France and of other countries in the 1790's. The list of contributors offers a roll-call of the new school; it includes, besides Lefebvre who wrote a short introduction, the names of Soboul, Rudé, Cobb, Tønnesson, B. Lesnodorski for Poland, K. Benda for Hungary, and Samuel Bernstein for the United States.[5]

Two facts stand in the way of a proper absorption of this new work in America. First, it is far better known in French, German, and Italian than in English. Nothing has been trans-

June, 1959), pp. 81–120; "The Revolutionary Mentality in France, 1793–94," in *History*, XLII (Oct. 1957), pp. 181–96; "L'armée révolutionnaire parisienne (composition sociale et politique)," in *Bulletin de la Société d'histoire moderne*, 11th ser., No. 3 (June–July, 1952), pp. 4–12; *L'armée révolutionnaire parisienne à Lyon et dans la région lyonnaise* (Lyon: Éditions de la Guillotière, 1952).

Kåre D. Tønnesson, *La défaite des sans-culottes: Mouvement populaire et réaction bourgeoise en l'an III* (Oslo: Presses universitaires, and Paris: Clavreuil, 1959), xix plus 456 pp.

[3] See my review-article, "Georges Lefebvre: The Peasants and the French Revolution," in *Journal of Modern History*, XXXI (Dec. 1959), 329–42.

[4] G. Lefebvre, A. Soboul, G. E. Rudé, R. C. Cobb, *Sanculotti e contadini nella Rivoluzione francese* (Bari: Laterza, 1958), 387 pp.

[5] Walter Markov, ed., *Jakobiner und Sans-culotten: Beitrage zur Geschichte der französischen Revolutionsregierung 1793–94* (Berlin, Rütten and Loening, 1956); *Die Sans-culotten von Paris: Dokumente zur Geschichte der Volksbewegung 1793–94* (Berlin, Akademie Verlag, 1957); *Maximilien Robespierre 1758–1794: Beiträge zu seinem 200ten Geburtstag* (Berlin, Rütten and Loening, 1958).

lated into English, and since Cobb has published in French, Rudé's book stands almost alone in this respect. The second fact, which seems to be indeed a fact, is that this re-examination of the "lower" classes in France during the Revolution, based though it is on the most admirable and thorough archival researches, is closely identified with the European Left, and in the case of some writers with avowed Communism. The incentive, sympathy, and purpose sustaining the years of exacting work in difficult sources have been to a degree Marxist, and the cordial reception of the new writings in some quarters reflects the same affiliations.

In short, there is a strong ideological element in the picture. History, as usual, is reflecting the present. These books are part of the cold war; so is their present reviewer. I do not believe that they are vitiated by this fact, as the bulk of what follows will show. We must learn what they have to teach. It would be a disaster if no one but Marxists had any knowledge or understanding of the common people of France during the French Revolution. But if ideology can be largely disregarded, it cannot be ignored; and a word may be said on it.

Soboul, Rudé, and Cobb are responsible and capable historians, given, as civilized men, to a good deal of qualification in their statements. With them the ideology seldom becomes explicit. Elsewhere it can be very shrill. For example, a long review published in East Berlin hails Markov's volume mentioned above in which pieces by Lefebvre, Soboul, Cobb, and Rudé are included. The reviewers are outraged that the West-German, Martin Göhring, should have been admitted as one of the contributors. I have myself the honor to be mentioned with Crane Brinton among "reactionary bourgeois ideologists, who, as spiritual followers of H. Taine, give historical sanction to the hatred of the imperialist bourgeoisie for the people." [6] The work of "the French Communist, Albert Soboul," is praised as the kernel of Markov's book. It shows, we are told, when compared with the work of Karl Kautsky, the progress of Marxist historical writing in forty years. (This is true.) The reviewers reveal, in a special paragraph, the true meaning and value to them of these scientific studies. These studies, they say, show that the Jacobin dictatorship, the national Revolutionary Government of 1794, fell because it lost the support of the working people. (This is also true; the new studies do emphasize this

---

[6] H. Heitzer and B. Weissel, reviewing the two first of Markov's collections mentioned above, in *Zeitschrift für Geschichtswissenschaft*, VI (1958), 912.

among the causes of Robespierre's fall, but the same had been said before, with less evidence.) "In contrast to bourgeois-revolutionary dictatorship the dictatorship of the proletariat is free of the objective antagonism between leadership-strata and working masses. It is in consonance with historical law both that Jacobin dictatorship should have fallen in the process of founding bourgeois society, and that proletarian dictatorship should become stabilized through the planned upbuilding of socialist society. In the building of socialism an accentuation of class conflict *within* the forces representing the proletarian dictatorship is impossible. . . . The 'Thermidorians' of today might live a hundred lives, and yet wait in vain to see the proletarian dictatorship go the same way as the Jacobin." [7]

It would be misleading to make too much of such pronouncements. The works reviewed here are solid and pioneering. That their net conclusions are not strikingly new is in their favor; the French Revolution is not a new or unexplored subject. What they do is important. They fill a void, they supply evidence, they turn conjectures and opinions into something like certainty. They make us see what ordinary men and women in the French Revolution were like. They give faces to what has been a faceless multitude, and raise the common people, who have not been too well known in academic circles, to the level of human dignity and understandable behavior.

II

The writings in question all deal with the *sans-culottes*. It is unfortunate that no satisfactory English word for them has ever been agreed upon. To go on using a foreign technicality keeps up a barrier to perception, since it suggests that the thing signified is untranslatable, or quite unknown in English-speaking countries. The word, of course, means only that the persons thus designated were without knee-breeches. It is not that they *rejected* them; they simply had none. In all countries at the time different social classes wore different costume. Some men wore breeches, others trousers. The sans-culottes were simply those below a certain level of income and social standing, people normally confined to their work, of limited education, debarred from the refinements and from the "culture" of their own country. There is also a second meaning. The sans-culottes were

[7] *Ibid.,* p. 909.

people of this kind in a special state of political action and excitement. This state of excitement existed briefly in France in 1792–1794, and nothing quite like it existed except in France. In the work of Soboul, Cobb, and Tønnesson the second meaning predominates; the end of popular agitation in 1794–95 sees the end of the sans-culottes, though not of course of the individuals or the social classes who made them up. In the work of Rudé the first meaning predominates; he is interested in people of this kind so far as they caused disturbances, especially in France from 1788 to 1795.

Soboul's book is incomparably the most important. It meets the highest standards of the French *doctorat ès lettres,* being based, for the most part, on assiduous, long, and exhaustive study of the papers of the "sections" of Paris, the chief pertinent documents to survive the fire of 1871. The "sections," the forty-eight subdivisions of the Paris municipality, with their neighborhood assemblies and committees, were the centers of spontaneous combustion for popular revolutionary zeal. The book is about what happened in these sections, the kind of people who frequented their meetings and what they wanted. It is written with the loving care of one to whom every street and quarter of the city are known and important. Hence there is a good deal of detail and repetition, which however are very skillfully managed, with summaries at the beginning and end of chapters to carry the development of the thought. Since the book is so long that few will read it, an extended résumé may be useful.

The sans-culottes, according to Soboul, who is entirely convincing on this matter, were in effect popular democrats, who applied the great concepts of liberty, equality, and the sovereignty of the people to themselves and to the concrete circumstances with which they were personally familiar. They strove to maintain the autonomy of their section assemblies against control by the Commune, the Convention or the national government. They believed that they themselves were sovereign, in face-to-face contact in their section meetings; and that distant elected persons were only their delegates, often not to be trusted. They favored what a later generation in America would know as the referendum and recall. "Consent of the people" meant their consent in their own assemblies. The right to bear arms meant that they should carry pikes in their own streets. The judgment of the people meant that they should denounce their own neighbors for suspicious behavior or unsuitable sentiments, and that their own committees should put them under arrest.

If they thus presumed to exercise sovereignty, they accepted the corresponding responsibilities; they were ready to give their time, to act and to fight. They spent long hours at meetings, and in the work of committees, or on the exposure of suspects, or on errands and missions and patrols about the city, or in exchange of delegations with sister groups, or in the *armée révolutionnaire* in which city men went into the country to find food, or to bring patriotic pressure to bear in other communities.

In the collapse of old institutions and habits, they represented an enormous wave of citizen self-help. The military and governmental crisis of the summer of 1792 had brought them forward. At that time, in July 1792, they had swarmed into the section assemblies, and with the Prussian enemy at the gates, the émigrés gloating, the Assembly distracted, the king under suspicion, and the generals unreliable, they had announced that they would take matters in hand themselves. They remained a source of spontaneous political energy for about a year, until the summer of 1793. The following year, the period to which Soboul's book is actually devoted, the year of the Committee of Public Safety, saw the gradual subordination of the sans-culottes to the authority of a national government as represented by the Committee.

The conflict between direct democracy, as affirmed by the sans-culottes, and what is variously referred to as bourgeois democracy, or constitutionalism, or the Jacobin dictatorship, or the needs of centralization, production, and authority in time of war, is the main theme of Soboul's book. It is a great theme never before adequately treated. Soboul has a sense of tragedy, which gives his work depth, and raises it far above the level of crude historical partisanship. Direct democracy, as understood by the sans-culottes, was a natural application of the principles of the Revolution, especially in time of breakdown, crisis, excitement, dedication, and sacrifice. But the direct democracy of neighborhood meetings was anarchic in tendency, and unworkable. The Robespierrist Committee had to resist it. Tragedy followed for both sides, since each was ruined by something in its own nature. The Revolutionary Government had originally owed its existence to sans-culotte pressures. In ending sans-culotte spontaneity and autonomy, it killed the thing by which it lived.

PALMER: RECENT RESEARCH 287

The sans-culottes, on the other hand, "had demanded a government strong enough to crush the aristocracy; they did not realize that, to conquer, this government would have to force them to obey." [8]

The sans-culottes were composed of all kinds of people below the well-situated upper and upper-middle classes. They included shopkeepers, merchants, traders, artisans, small manufacturers, wage-earners, porters, water carriers, domestic servants, café waiters and proprietors, barbers, wig-makers, etc. They were the people of Paris without the frosting—and generally without the dregs, since the vagrant, the shiftless, the idle, the criminally inclined, the delinquent, and the excessively stupid did not become true sans-culottes.

They burned with a new sense of equality, which Soboul finds to be their main characteristic. They wanted respect and recognition. They "no longer accepted a subordinate position in social relations." [9] On holidays they flocked to the fashionable boulevards which in the past they had avoided. "Citizens of poor outward appearance," in the words of an approving contemporary, "and who in former times would not have dared to show themselves in these places reserved for more elegant company, were going for walks along with the rich, and holding their heads as high." [10]

They could not bear arrogance and disdain. Irony and elaborate speech aroused their hostility. All above their own level they came to regard as "aristocrats." "Gentlemen" (*les honnêtes gens*) became a term to be used with sarcasm. They made a virtue of their long trousers, and a vice of breeches, and at the height of excitement they advertised a few other peculiarities of dress, such as the red or "Phrygian" cap. Since the difference between *vous* and *tu* was a genteel affectation, used to connote class relations, they favored honest *tutoiement* by all persons— like the Quakers in the use of English a century before.

These popular democrats had no developed economic ideas, but they took a negative attitude toward the wealthy, and while not objecting to private property believed that a more equal division of it was desirable. It is notable also, and more new, that Soboul finds in the documents repeated demands for public

[8] *Sans-culottes parisiens en l'an II*, p. 1026. For other statements of this main theme see pp. 11–12, 187, 238–39, 503–4, 546–47, 699, 703.
[9] *Ibid.*, p. 408.
[10] *Ibid.*, p. 660.

schools, more education for all, and vocational training. In general, in economic ideas, the popular democrats looked backward rather than forward. They came to demand more "equality of enjoyments," but never thought in terms of higher production or rising material standard of living. Though perhaps as much as half the Paris working class were wage-earners, attitudes were shaped by the artisan-shopkeeping outlook. The sans-culottes favored small property, small business, small employers, small workshops. They objected to business men, big merchants, financiers, commercial capital, and stock companies. They wished to preserve an older economic system against new forces by which they felt threatened. As Soboul says, they were unprogressive in economic ideas; they were opposed to the actual course of economic development, whether it be called bourgeois capitalism or modernization. An American is bound to feel that these French popular democrats had much in common with their contemporaries the Jeffersonian democrats, except that the former were not agrarians, and were prepared to see more powers in the hands of the state. Their ideal, in common with that of the Robespierrist wing of the Mountain, says Soboul, was "a community of independent producers among whom the State, by its laws, should assure an approximate equality." [11]

Such were the attitudes and ideals, and the popular democrats were highly political; but the one thing that could arouse them to mass action, to take part in demonstrations and make demands on the public authorities, was hunger and the fear of hunger. The price of bread, even in normal times, in the amount needed for a man with a wife and three children, was half as much as the daily wage of common labor. A rise in its price brought disaster. At times, from 1793 to 1795, there was positive scarcity, to the point where bread and other foodstuffs became unobtainable at any price. The effects became grimmer as one descended the income scale. The fear of hunger colored all sans-culotte politics. It motivated their demands on the Convention to obtain price controls, or repression of hoarding and profiteering; it made the popular democrats favor the bourgeois leaders who were willing at least temporarily to agree with them, and force the expulsion of those who did not; it made them hate the "rich" and the "aristocrats" because they ate better, or abhor and fear them, in the belief that the rich might use popular starvation for their own political advantage. It was hunger, ac-

[11] *Ibid.*, p. 473.

cording to Soboul, more than idealism or exaltation or ideological fanaticism, that made the sans-culottes violent.

Violence, which has seemed to some an essential characteristic of the Paris populace during the Revolution (and will deter comparison with the milder Jeffersonian democrats) seems to Soboul a natural by-product of real events. Violence, *exaltation terroriste* [fanatical terrorism], *buveurs de sang* [bloodthirsty men] there were. But overwhelmingly the sans-culottes were not violent men—or women. They were "often rough men, without education, their souls inflamed by poverty." [12] Their violence was not wanton. It had an understandable aim. It was directed against the use of force by the counter-revolution. There was fear, but it was well-grounded fear. The idea of an aristocratic conspiracy was not baseless. There was the crisis of war and civil war, betrayal and secret conspiracy and the fear of the unknown. The guillotine was welcomed and idealized; it was the "popular ax," the "scythe of equality," and it was believed to promote the supply of bread.

Soboul's book is organized primarily on chronological lines, so that it is possible to follow the actual course of events. In the insurrection of May 31, 1793, the popular democrats forced the liquidation of the Girondists from the Convention. There followed a conflict in which popular democrats agitated for economic controls, while bourgeois democrats (Montagnards and Jacobins) tried to put them off with the vote and with a new constitution. In September the Convention yielded, enacting general price controls, and authorizing new machinery for the official Terror, but at the same time it struck back, by prohibiting the *permanence des sections*. The section assemblies had been "in permanent session" since July 1792. Henceforth they met only twice a week. To make this restriction more palatable, the Convention also ruled that poor citizens should receive forty sous (two livres) for each meeting attended; but in fact few poor citizens applied for this compensation in the following months, in part because the section assemblies disliked the expense. With restrictions thus imposed on the assemblies, which were constituted bodies dating from the constitution of 1789–91, the militants took to forming clubs, or "popular societies," in general one for each section. The same men went to the *assemblées* on two days a week, and on other days to the *sociétés,* which were free, "private," non-constitutional, or as George Washington said

[12] *Ibid.,* p. 577.

of American clubs, "self-created" bodies. The societies became a network of activists, who dominated the assemblies and their committees.

On attendance at the assemblies and societies, and on the personnel of the assembly-committees, we are offered some highly valuable (if unavoidably imprecise) statistics. In the Year II, at which time all adult males were qualified voters, attendance at section assemblies ran between 5 and 20 per cent, with an average around 10. A good attendance would be from one hundred to three hundred persons in a section—sometimes more. This suggests a figure somewhat exceeding 10,000 as the number of active popular democrats in the city. In a way the number is small; but actually, at the level of political participation which the meetings represented, a proportion in the neighborhood of 10 per cent of adult males seems high—at least it was high enough to be disconcerting not only to conservatives but to the Revolutionary Government. In any case it was not very different, in size, from the attendance at section assemblies in the earlier years of the Revolution. In 1790–92, at which time only "active" citizens, somewhat over one half the adult males, were qualified to sit in the assemblies, the attendance had run far below 20 per cent of the *actifs*. If in 1793–94 the sections were more "democratic," it was not because they were more numerously attended than in 1790–92, but because they included broader and lower segments of the population.[13]

Figures for attendance are harder to obtain for the *sociétés populaires*, since these were unofficial.[14] The societies charged dues, which varied from one to another, but might involve something like a 3-livre entrance fee or ten sous a month. Sometimes the poorest members were excused from paying. In the Year II between 25 and 55 persons habitually attended the Society of the Section Révolutionnaire, which consisted of the half of the Ile de la Cité at the end toward the Pont Neuf. This was out of a total of 1,264 qualified voters in the section. Clearly the societies drew a smaller number of more zealous militants than the assemblies. Something of their social status is suggested by the fact that their dues if anything were higher than for the London Corresponding Society [a British club advocating political democracy] at the same time, and if there were 5,000 members in Paris,

[13] *Ibid.*, pp. 588–99 and tables on pp. 1091–1102.
[14] *Ibid.*, p. 640 and table on p. 1104.

the membership was about the same as that of the Corresponding Society in London.

Deep in the middle of Soboul's book are some enlightening figures, based on the identification of 1,311 individuals, but neither tabulated nor included in the appendix, perhaps because the author regards them as too uncertain.[15] As he says, the names of occupations mean little: a "carpenter" could be a simple workman or the owner of a large enterprise. Again, one is reminded of parallels—Francis Place, who began as a poor youth in the London Corresponding Society in 1794, became the owner of a manufacturing establishment and retired on a competence at the age of forty, but remained a "tailor" to the British governing classes long after 1832.

The 1,311 individuals were members of the civil committees and the "revolutionary" committees of the sections, plus others whom Soboul calls simply "militants." The civil committees, though busy, were unpaid; members of the revolutionary committees received five livres a day after September 1793, many of them being of luxury trades ruined by the Revolution. The social position, and presumable income and kind of income, as among the three categories, are suggested as follows:

Social Classes in Section Assemblies[16]   (PERCENTAGES)

	CIVIL COMMITTEES	REVOLUTIONARY COMMITTEES	MILITANTS
Living on income from property	26	4	2
Liberal professions	12	10	7
Heads of businesses	2	3	1
Merchants, shopkeepers, artisans, etc.	59	64	57
Wage-earners	0	10	20
Salaried employees [of the government, the post office, etc.]	0	5	8
Total numbers	343	454	514

These figures are compiled from lists of men arrested in the Year III as dangerous sans-culottes of the Year II. There was

[15] *Ibid.*, pp. 439–51.

[16] [The terms in this list have been translated by the editors.]

a dyer with a fortune of 21,600 livres, and others with shops employing sixty men. "The sans-culotterie was indeed a coalition of heterogeneous social elements." [17]

It seems likely that many or most of these men must have qualified as active citizens under the constitution of 1789–91, and so been able to attend the section assemblies continuously since 1790. The withdrawal of upper-income groups, as much as the inrush of lower, made the difference between the two phases of the Revolution. It appears that men of the master workman and shopkeeper level, present throughout, but expected in 1790–92 to accept the lead of those socially above them, in 1792–94 assumed the lead, welcomed the support, and enjoyed the confidence of those below them. The poorest sans-culottes obtained their revolutionary ideas from their own employers, in the shops in which they worked side by side, or from the neighborhood tradesmen with whom they dealt.

To resume the narrative: The Revolutionary Government continued to encroach on section autonomy, and by about March 1794 was successful. Robespierre denounced a direct democracy which made representative democracy unworkable. "The revolutionary committees, elected by section assemblies in the spring of 1793, re-elected in September, purged in the autumn by the General Council of the Commune, fell during the winter under control of the Committee of General Security, and by the spring of the Year II were to be appointed by the Committee of Public Safety." [18] Militants were set to such humdrum operations as collecting saltpeter for the war effort. Secret voting was imposed on the assemblies. The ardors of the popular democrats were cooled by the authority of the government.

To keep their support, while ending their independence, Saint-Just proposed the laws of Ventôse. These provided that the property of suspects should be confiscated, and the proceeds distributed to the "indigent." The Ventôse laws were made famous by Mathiez, in the 1920's, as evidence that the Robespierrist group was now coming to take the lead of a popular or social democratic movement. Soboul believes that Mathiez was entirely mistaken in thus identifying Robespierre with the sans-culottes.

He considers the laws of Ventôse a mere maneuver or sop.[19]

[17] Soboul, *Sans-culottes*, p. 449.
[18] *Ibid.*, p. 515.
[19] *Ibid.*, pp. 681–717.

The popular democrats were unimpressed. It had long been accepted that persons disloyal to the Republic had no right to own property within its borders. There was nothing new in further confiscations. In any case, what the sans-culottes really suffered from was scarcity of food, and what they really wanted was more economic controls, with punishment for profiteers and other offenders. They also wanted work, low prices, schools, and public relief for the disabled. They were too intelligent to be mollified by vague promises of distant future rewards from problematical confiscations. They rightly sensed the Ventôse program as mere "moderatism."

So the estrangement between popular democracy and bourgeois democracy grew worse. The ruling Committee of Public Safety sent Hébert and others to their deaths. Control of the sections tightened. Men under forty were drawn off into the army. Section committeemen, with their five-livre wage, turned as the months passed from zealots into bureaucrats, accepting and expounding the views of the Committee of Public Safety. The popular democrats became passive and apathetic. They did not disagree with Robespierre's cult of the Supreme Being; they simply could feel no enthusiasm for it.

Then came the new maximum-wage scale proclaimed on 5 Thermidor.[20] So long as the commune and sections had remained strong, there had been no actual control of wages in most lines of work in Paris. Prices of consumers' goods had been held in check, but wages under war-time conditions had considerably risen. Now the Committee of Public Safety meant to control wages also. The scale of 5 Thermidor, if enforced, would abruptly cut some wages by as much as half.

The sans-culotte movement, now nearing its end, suffered fatally from two "internal contradictions," which are noted repeatedly throughout Soboul's book, and together constitute his main conclusions. There was a contradiction between sans-culottes and Jacobin-Montagnards, between direct democracy and bourgeois democracy, between the *droit du peuple* [rights of the people] and the needs of national defense. The wage-scale of 5 Thermidor was only the last of many signs that the gov-

[20] Mathiez knew of the existence of this wage-scale of 5 Thermidor, but never found the document, which was discovered and reported on by Soboul and Rudé in "Le maximum des salaires parisiens et le 9 thermidor," in *Annales historiques de la Révolution française*, No. 134 (Jan.–Mar., 1954), pp. 1–22; it is included also in German in Markov's *Jakobiner und Sansculotten*, pp. 167–181.

ernment had to side with the business classes. And there was an inner contradiction among the sans-culottes themselves: wage-earners stood to lose, others to gain, if wages were controlled as well as prices. Application of the wage-maximum "broke open this contradiction" also.[21]

The popular democrats, Soboul concludes, were a class in a sense, but not really. They were a mixture of wage workers, artisans, and traders, of proletarian and petty bourgeois types. So an ideological message becomes clear at the end. "Not constituting a class, and so without class-consciousness," the sans-culottes lacked "an effective instrument of political action: a strictly disciplined party, which, to that end, should rest upon class recruitment and severe purging. The same was true of the Revolutionary Government. The Jacobins were not a class either. The whole régime of the Year II rested on an idealistic (*spiritualiste*) conception of political democracy. Hence its weakness." [22]

These observations are the most explicitly Marxist in the book. One does not see how the preceding thousand pages necessitate them. We can take the book without those parting shots. It is not clear what is meant by *spiritualiste*, except as an affirmation of a materialism which is itself undefined. Certainly the book is full of the thoughts, hopes, feelings, beliefs, and aspirations of the popular democrats, and shows that though their most pressing needs were economic their ideas, aims, and actions were intensely political. That there were conflicts of interest among them, and between them and the government, was only natural; the reverse would be truly astonishing, and would suggest the unanimity, or identity of interest between people and government, which are said, in the *Zeitschrift für Geschichtswissenschaft*, to exist nowadays in Eastern Europe. It is evident that the conflicts were basic, difficult to reconcile, and impossible to compromise in the short run, but it is not clear what is

[21] Soboul, *Sans-culottes*, p. 1029.

[22] *Ibid.*, p. 1030. Soboul's general conclusions, pp. 1025–35, are reprinted verbatim as an article in *La Pensée*, a communistically inclined periodical of which Soboul is one of the editorial board (Jan.–Feb., 1959), pp. 65–73. On the sans-culotte lack of real class identity see also, for example, p. 427: "The sans-culottes stood out by their opposition to the aristocracy, to wealth, and to business. These antagonisms demonstrate the lack of precise class lines within the old Third Estate and the impossibility of defining the sans-culottes as a social class. They are clearly distinguished from the aristocracy; with respect to the bourgeoisie, class lines are imprecise. It was a coalition of socially disparate elements. . . ." [Editors' translation.]

added, except philosophy of history, when they are called internal contradictions. It is undeniable that the popular democrats did not get what they hoped for from the Revolution. They have never had it, and do not have it in France today. Had there been, then or since, more equality of mutual respect, of educational opportunity, of income and of "enjoyments," the history of France would doubtless have been less troubled. Whether the purged and disciplined party, alluded to by the author, would be an acceptable or effective means to these ends, particularly in France, is a matter of political judgment. It is certainly open to question.

III

Space is lacking to deal at similar length with the work of Cobb, Rudé, and Tønnesson, which resembles and reinforces that of Soboul. Cobb's seems the best; it is to be hoped that he will soon bring it together in a book in English.[23] His studies of the paramilitary *armées révolutionnaires* carry the subject beyond the bounds of Paris. His account of the sans-culotte state of mind should be read by all concerned. It is a convincing psychological description of men in action, not as mere bearers of "ideas" presumably derived from Rousseau or other writers, but as human beings with personalities and recognizable personality traits. His sans-culottes, like Eric Hoffer's "true believers," are keyed to a high pitch by the hope of introducing a better society, and are thus enabled to maintain a spirit of solidarity and self-sacrifice. Their attitude is moral and civic. If they want a republic of virtue, it is not for ideological or even political reasons but because men in their circumstances live plainly anyway. They dislike the frivolity and pretentiousness of the upper classes. They are credulous and naive, eager to denounce, and readily believing in every conspiracy that they hear of. Here Cobb seems to depart a little from Soboul and the others. Soboul's sans-culottes, for example, feel dismay and skepticism at the trial and death of Hébert. Cobb's, who have hitherto favored Hébert, accept the absurd charge that he is really a conspirator against the Republic, and indignantly add him to the long list of false leaders by whom they have been betrayed.

Their revolutionary state of mind, according to Cobb, was

[23] [His major works since 1960 have been *Les Armées révolutionnaires* (2 vols.; Paris: Mouton, 1961-63), and a collection of articles, *Terreur et subsistances* (Paris: Clavreuil, 1965).]

temporary exaltation, humanly impossible for large numbers of normal men to maintain for long, and impossible ever to recapture. Its abatement was due, not only to political reaction, but to the demands of real life, especially upon men of limited means and outlook. The wife, the job, and the café after a year or two simply got the better of political activism. Not that the popular democrats were not forcibly repressed; Cobb thinks, with good reason, that the repression of popular agitation in the Year III, carried through by the kind of people who kept servants and wore ruffles, showed more class consciousness and class conflict than the view of the sans-culottes themselves in the Year II, which had only reflected the plain man's unsystematized aversion to the well-to-do. He distinguishes sharply between the sans-culotte movement of 1792–94, and Babeuf and the Babouvists of 1796. The former was really revolutionary, Babouvism only conspirational. The popular democrats were part of a real elemental deluge, the Babouvists hoped to provoke a new deluge by pulling some kind of a cork. The resemblance of Babouvists to sans-culottes, says Cobb, hardly existed except in the imagination of the police, to which may be added the imagination of some recent historians.

Kåre Tønnesson of Oslo has worked closely with Albert Soboul, and his *Défaite des sans-culottes* is a sequel to Soboul's book. It traces events in the Year III, with their climax in the Germinal and Prairial uprisings of 1795. These it interprets as primarily hunger riots, brought on by the starvation conditions that followed the fall of the Revolutionary Government and the end of economic controls; but it also brings a new emphasis to political matters, giving details on the one hand for "de-sans-cullotisation," by which moderates replaced extremists in the Paris sections, and on the other hand describing a revival of popular political life in the sections, with new demands for direct democracy against the bourgeoisie now triumphant in the Convention. As with other writers of the school, sans-culottes and Jacobins are sharply distinguished. The popular movement of the Year III owed nothing to the Jacobins, and the surviving Montagnards were of no importance among the organizers of the Prairial insurrection, though some hoped to benefit by it. The significance of the Prairial rising, as Tønnesson sums it up, is that it was the first great popular insurrection to fail, and it failed because it was more clearly anti-bourgeois than its predecessors, and because now for the first time in the Revolution, with the war crisis eased and the danger of counter-revolution receding, no significant groups among the bourgeoisie felt the need of alliance with the common people. The demonstrators of Prairial were the popular democrats as described by Cobb and Soboul, but the planning of the uprising is traced by Tønnesson to the activists who in 1795 were imprisoned at Plessis. The fact that the leaders were in prison naturally weakened the effect. Through the Plessis prison Tønnesson sees a prefigurement of the Babeuf conspiracy of 1796, which, however, like Cobb, he regards as something very different from true sans-culottism, since the Babouvists were unable to win any mass following. After Prairial 1795 there were no more popular insurrections until 1830.

Rudé, in *The Crowd in the French Revolution,* deals with the Revolution from 1789 to 1795, not merely with the period of the Convention. The "crowd" really means what has more uncharitably been called the "mob." It refers to swarms of people coming together with hostile intent. The author is not concerned with more peaceable popular demonstrations, as in the *fêtes de la fédération* of 1790, or the various civic and propagandistic festivals of the following years, even though these affairs may have involved the same kinds of people as took part in the riots, or exhibited the phenomena of a collective or crowd behavior equally well. The book, after preliminary remarks on the bread riots of the Old Regime, proceeds to examine, in turn, the Réveillon riots of April 1789, the action leading to the fall of the Bastille, the march on Versailles of October, the "massacre" of the Champ de Mars, the uprising leading to the fall of the monarchy in August 1792, the bread and food riots of 1793, the popular role in the expulsion of the Girondists, the same in the fall of Robespierre, the uprisings of Germinal-Prairial of the Year III [April 1 and May 20–23, 1795], and finally Vendémiaire [October 4–6, 1795]. These are followed by four chapters of a more analytical character, and by valuable statistical tables, in which numbers of wage-earners and of employers for the forty-eight sections of Paris are given, and the occupations of persons known to have participated in ten demonstrations are set forth. Some interesting working-class budgets are also included.

Rudé finds that (except for the Vendémiaire uprising, a counter-revolutionary affair in which popular elements had little part) his crowds were generally made up of "workshop masters, craftsmen, wage-earners, shopkeepers, and petty traders." He is at pains to distinguish them from the leaders who made political use of crowd demonstrations—the bourgeois "Paris Electors of May–July 1789, the revolutionary journalists, the leaders of the Paris Commune, or the members of the National Assembly, of the Cordeliers and the Jacobin Clubs." [24] The growing conflict between these two groups is stressed. In short, the findings and the ideas in Rudé's book are much the same as in Soboul's, with more emphasis on economic motivations and insurrectionary activity. According to Rudé's conclusions, the disturbance in the Champ de Mars of June 1791 was the only one having a primarily political cause. The Réveillon riots were the only case in which grievances over wages were paramount, although fear of reduced wages added to the disaffection preceding Robespierre's fall. In all other cases the impelling force was economic, not in the sense of trouble between labor and capital, or complaint over wages, but in that the fear of hunger, aroused by scarcity and rising prices, was decisive. It was the solid working-class citizenry of Paris, including the women, who naturally felt this fear.

Rudé is so intent on proving that the revolutionary crowds were not riff-raff that he soon seems to be beating a dead horse. He is forever refuting Taine, for whose name there are sixteen references in the index, as against five each for Lefebvre and Mathiez, and none for any American writer on the subject, although two articles by H. E. Bourne, from 1917 and 1919, are mentioned in a footnote on page 129. To do battle with Taine in a popular work is always to serve the cause of enlightenment, but in a scholarly monograph, addressed to historians, it hardly seems necessary, at this date, to prove that the demonstrators of the French Revolution were not "the lowest populace, living by infamous callings . . . bullies and haunters of evil places, habituated to blood . . . bold and ferocious adventurers from everywhere, foreigners and ruffians from Marseilles, Savoyards, Italians, and Spaniards driven from their own countries." [25]

It may be that the horse is less dead in England than in the United States, at least if we can believe the report of a conference

[24] *The Crowd in the French Revolution*, p. 177.
[25] *Ibid.*, p. 3, quoting Taine, *Origines de la France contemporaine* (Paris, 1876), I, 18, 53–54, 130, 272.

held in London in 1958.[26] Here Rudé and Cobb spoke to some two hundred sixth-form pupils and their teachers. The audience of seventeen-year-olds found the talks a "veritable revelation." They were "much astonished" to learn that the "Paris mob" was not composed of "the dregs of the people," worked upon by "mysterious personages." One wonders what the youth of England can have been reading. The easily maligned American college textbooks do not teach this doctrine, and even the high-school text most accessible to this reviewer, Ethel Ewing's *Our Widening World,* published in Chicago in 1958, gives a brief but perfectly acceptable account of the French Revolution.

The point is of some relevance in view of a little dispute into which Cobb entered with three American historians, Frank Manuel, Stanley Idzerda, and Robert Holtman, in the pages of the *Journal of Modern History* in 1958.[27] Cobb here laments that American historians do not do more research in the French archives, in which of course he and Rudé excel. He even seems to equate historical work with the use of unpublished materials. But he also declares that "our main function," for us who are not French, "is to explain the Revolution in terms that will be understandable to our own countrymen." Cobb himself has published largely in French, and on very special topics. Spending years in foreign archives can have results other than making history understandable to one's countrymen.

I should like to close with some remarks on the role of classes and class conflict in history. It will be clear that the substance of the books reviewed here seems to me important and valuable. Their authors would agree that we must be on guard against over-simplifications. Much of the argument turns on reactions to price inflation and scarcity. Persons of small incomes are supposed to have urged controls and requisitions and "managed economy," those of higher incomes to have resisted.

The truth of any such dualism is far from absolute. Rudé gives examples of well-dressed women taking part in the march to Versailles, or sending their servants to join in demonstrations. A good deal is made in Rudé's book of the disorders caused in 1793, after the war cut down colonial imports, by the rising prices of coffee and sugar. I have never quite understood how the

---

[26] *Annales historiques de la Révolution française,* No. 153 (July–Sept., 1958), pp. 89–91.

[27] XXX (June 1958), pp. 129–30.

availability of coffee and sugar could be a truly inflammable popular issue, at a time when, even normally, the price of bread alone might take half or more of an ordinary workman's wage, and when the price of a pound of sugar or of coffee might be half the daily wage of a journeyman carpenter. One suspects that it was the better-dressed people who were most used to these items of diet, and most annoyed by having to do without them. For Rudé, however, the sugar riots "marked the basic conflict of interests between the *menu peuple* [common people] and the possessing classes, including the extreme democrats that spoke or applauded at the Jacobin Club." [28] When Robespierre and Barère dismiss sugar and coffee as "luxuries," causing needless trouble, they are, according to Rudé, simply talking like bourgeois, insensitive to the needs of the people. Were they really wrong?

The truth is that annoyance at rising prices and scarcities is not a good index to class position. Even George Washington, in 1778, expressed a desire to have a few profiteers on the gallows. He showed an almost sans-culotte vindictiveness: "No punishment, in my opinion, is too great for the man who can build his greatness upon his country's ruin." When a member of Congress hoped to profit by cornering the market in flour, one of Washington's officers was beside himself with rage. He wrote of "another class, equally criminal . . . that tribe who have carried the spirit of monopoly and extortion to an excess . . . dishonest artifices of a mercantile projector . . . traitor . . . despised profligacy . . . scandalous perversion . . . enormities . . . mask of patriotism." The author of these words was Alexander Hamilton.[29]

On the other hand, the importance of social class in the French Revolution was very great, as the present books demonstrate, though in an embarrassed way. Our authors declare repeatedly that the sans-culottes were "not a class," and had at most a rudimentary class consciousness. They all reject the work of the unorthodox Marxist, Daniel Guérin, who in 1946 tried to show the beginnings of a proletarian-vs.-bourgeois struggle in the

[28] Rudé, *Crowd*, p. 114, 118, 201.
[29] See Washington's letter of Dec. 12, 1778, to the President of the Congress, *Writings* (Ford ed.), VII, p. 189; Hamilton's "Publius" letters in the *New York Journal* of Oct. 19 and 26, 1778, *Works* (ed. 1851), II, pp. 156–63. I am indebted for these leads to Richard B. Morris, "Washington and Hamilton: A Great Collaboration," in *Proceedings of the American Philosophical Society*, CII (Apr. 1958), 107–16.

First Republic.[30] At the same time they agree with Guérin that Mathiez was mistaken, that Robespierre and the Montagnards did not stand for the real common people, that in fact it was these bourgeois Jacobins who first put restraints on the popular democrats, and that in 1793 a revolutionary force well in advance of bourgeois democracy was already strongly in evidence.

When our authors say that the sans-culottes were not a class, they mean that they were not a class in the Marxist sense. When they say they had little or no class consciousness, they mean that they were not conscious of belonging to objective classes as defined by Marx. They make it clear that the popular democrats lived by different relations to production, some by a daily wage, some by the sale of articles of their own manufacture, some by the proceeds of shopkeeping, and some even by the extensive use of hired labor. But the evidence of these books themselves, especially the work of Soboul and Cobb, supplies a rich picture of the class status and class consciousness of the popular democrats. It seems absurd to hesitate to call them a class, when we are shown so convincingly how they felt estranged from the middle and upper classes, and were marked off from their social superiors by differences of dress, manners, mode of speech, eating and drinking habits, amusements, living quarters, use of servants, availability of leisure, awareness of family background, degree of schooling, and general expectations in life—not to mention the differences in actual income and in the kind of work in which their days were passed. If there were more interest in class sociology other than Marxist in French and British universities, we might find other interpretations of the facts so abundantly now brought before us. It need not be a choice between Marxist classes and no classes, nor between Marx's economically grounded and dialectically operating classes, and Michelet's big, beautiful, vague, and undifferentiated People.

What the books show is the democratic revolution of the eighteenth century at its most extreme moment, in its most extreme form, at its vital center, which was Paris.

It will never again be possible for a serious historian to explain Robespierre and the Jacobins in terms simply of their own ideas. It will be necessary to allow for the enormous popular pressures under which they worked. If it was Robespierre's hope

[30] *La lutte de classes sous la première République: Bourgeois et bras-nus* (*1793–97*), 2 vols. (Paris, 1946), and the long review in *Journal of Modern History*, XIX (Dec. 1947), 324–33.

to establish a workable and constitutional democratic republic, it will be seen that he had not only to face the needs of war, and the problem of counter-revolution, but to deal with aroused men and women, unknown on the grand stage of history, for whom "democracy" meant that they should do it themselves.

VIII

THE DIRECTORY
(1795–1799)

*A*fter the fall of Robespierre, the Convention continued to rule for another fifteen months. Then it gave
way to the government known as the Directory, which placed
power in the hands of a five-man executive and a bicameral legislature.

The dramatic events and personalities before and after the
Directory have tended to minimize its attractiveness and reputation. This is clearly shown in the selection from Albert Vandal.
In an effort to justify the work of Napoleon Bonaparte as First
Consul, he finds it necessary to unleash considerable passion in
condemning the preceding regime. We are left to decide exactly
which of Vandal's strictures come from an impartial analysis of
fact. Albert Goodwin argues for a less one-sided view of the Directory. The difference in interpretation can be attributed in
part to new research carried out since Vandal wrote, to a detach-
ment that may come from a vantage point across the Channel,
and to an intense and steady scrutiny of the Directory rather than
of what came before or after it.

Who is right? Perhaps one can only say that more facts are
needed before reaching a conclusion. Or one can argue that all
the facts are never in, and that it is time to judge whether the
Directory came close to any satisfactory standard of what constitutes good, or even acceptable, government. Or one may ask
what the realistic alternatives to the Directory were and whether
their triumph would have resulted in a better regime.

AN ATTACK*

Albert Vandal

Albert Vandal (1853–1910), whose father directed the French Post Office during the Second Empire, originally trained for the law, then entered public service. Teaching and writing history attracted him, however, and he eventually became a professor at the École libre des Sciences politiques in Paris, one of the few institutions of higher education in the Third Republic that flourished under the aegis of neither the government nor the Church. His great work in diplomatic history, Napoléon et Alexandre Ier, *appeared in the 1890's and was followed by his* Avènement de Bonaparte (1902–1907), *which extolled the beneficent work of Napoleon as First Consul.*

The old order had collapsed; the new order had not yet been established. On domestic matters the Directory had inherited all the faults of the Revolution. Beset by immense difficulties, it found a lasting solution for none. Its burden was heavy, but it was lamentably incapable of bearing it. It could neither restore nor establish anything. It gave to the French neither order nor liberty. . . .

In the spring of 1799, when the direct causes of the *coup d'état* of 18 Brumaire appeared, the chief officials of the revolutionary group were the five Directors—Reubell, La Revellière-Lépeaux, Barras, Merlin, and Treilhard. The well-known corruption of this government has tended to overshadow the violent nature of its rule. After the purging of the great and upright Carnot and of Barthélemy—who had been expelled by their colleagues [in

* From Albert Vandal, *L'Avènement de Bonaparte* (Paris: Plon, Nourrit, 1902), I, iv, 9–13, 16–18, 21–22, 26–28, 33–34, 70–73, 77. Editors' translation. Wherever possible, the author's citations of sources in footnotes have been clarified.

1797]—the Directory appeared "unspeakably corrupt." [1] This
was due to the squalid intrigues swarming around it and to the
brazen peculation of its most notorious member [Barras]. Other
Directors displayed the traits of dishonest servants rather than of
outright robbers. Some did not lack ability. Merlin (of Douai), a
remarkable jurist and a very clever prosecutor, excelled in making crime legal; his enemies declared that he was most suited to
be "a minister of justice under Louis XI." [2] Treilhard might have
rendered valuable service to another regime. La Reveillière, completely honest, a visionary bigot, was as weak in mind as he was
deformed in body; but the Alsatian Reubell, hard, greedy, cun-
ning, a glutton for work, seems to have been the aggressive leader
of the crew.

Although decked out in theatrical costume and provided with
a military guard, the Directors usually displayed little extrava-
gance; neither "their mistresses" nor "their carriages" excited
comment.[3] They lived side by side in the Luxembourg Palace,
which had been divided into five apartments for their use and
decorated with carpets, tapestries, and gilt furniture taken from
royal palaces. In these sumptuous surroundings, the Directors
lived like bourgeois. Carnot's habits were simple; he invited
friends familiarly "to take pot-luck; we sit down between four-
thirty and five and never eat out." [4] Evenings, La Revellière and
his daughter would go to the home of friends, the Thouïns, "to
spend a couple of hours in their simple kitchen." [5] Reubell had
a reputation for stinginess and a taste for sordid pilfering.[6] Mer-

---

[1] Eric Magnus Staël-Holstein and Baron Brinkman, *Correspondance diplomatique du Baron de Staël-Holstein et de son successeur . . . le Baron Brinkman . . .* (Paris: Hachette, 1881), p. 369, Brinkman to Sparre.

[2] From a session of the Council of Five Hundred, 30 Prairial, year VII
[June 18, 1799]. [Louis XI, King of France from 1461 to 1483, was noted
for his Machiavellian methods in the pursuit of power.]

[3] *Lettres de Charles de Constant*, p. 63.

[4] Letter to Le Coz, quoted in Alfred Roussel, *Un Évêque assermenté (1790–
1802); Le Coz: Évêque d'Ille-et-Vilaine* (Paris: Lethielleux, 1898), p. 259.

[5] Louis-Marie de La Revellière-Lépeaux, *Mémoires* (Paris: Plon, Nourrit,
1895), II, 411.

[6] When Reubell retired from the Directory and when the press became free
again, the newspapers wrote: "The former Director Reubell, on leaving office,
took everything with him—furniture, effects, china belonging to the nation,
including a service worth 12,000 francs." The following correction was later
inserted: "Citizen Reubell has had those things returned which had been
removed from the Luxembourg Palace upon his departure, things which
did not belong to him, and of which he had only the temporary use. We

lin's wife was a frightfully common housewife, as Bonaparte said, a *Madame Angot*.[7] At first the Directors, by an annual deduction from their salaries, set up a fund to be given to the one who had to retire from office each year—the "kitty" of the Directory. Later, they worked out less legal methods so as not to leave office with empty hands. They also claimed the right to take with them the bourgeois carriages provided for their official use and which would have been too painful to relinquish.

Only Barras showed himself to be ostentatious and magnificent; he was the peacock of the Directory. With flair, he wore the outfit designed by [the painter] David—a full red cloak with a lace collar, a Roman sword, and a hat overladen with plumes. When not at an official function, he usually wore a large blue frock coat and boots.[8] With his chest thrown out and his shoulders back, he resembled, as Bonaparte put it, a "handsome fencing master." [9] His voice was strong and well modulated; in the tumult of the Convention it had rung out like a bell.

He knew how to entertain and to put on a good show. When he threw open his rooms at the Luxembourg Palace the rather mixed company that gathered, moving among "the large armchairs of red velvet trimmed in gold," [10] were surprised by the series of brilliantly lit gilt rooms. Once again they were happy to encounter luxury, as well as women dressed in filmy elegance and displaying delicate flesh. They believed themselves transported to an Olympus where Mme. Tallien[11] and her rivals played the roles of goddesses in suitable costumes. Barras also entertained in his château of Grosbois, his country house in Suresnes [near Paris]. When he went there in his carriage drawn by cream-colored horses[12] with silver-inlaid harnesses, Parisians re-

---

are assured, furthermore, that the removal came about neither by his doing nor his orders, but by the action of his sons and the orders of his wife and his sister-in-law." See especially the *Gazette de France*, 5 and 6 Messidor, year VII [June 23 and 24, 1799].

[7] Gaspard Gourgaud, *Journal inédit, de 1815 à 1818* (Paris: Flammarion, 1899), I, 468. [A Madame Angot is a lower-class woman suddenly enriched who retains the coarse traits of her previous condition. From a comic opera by Ève popular during this period.]

[8] Victorine de Chastenay, *Mémoires* (Paris: Plon, Nourrit, 1896–1897), I, 359.

[9] Gourgaud, I, 468.

[10] Chastenay, I, 360.

[11] [The leader of a social set during the Directory noted for its rejection of the prudishness of the earlier years of the revolutionary period.]

[12] Edmond and Jules de Goncourt, *Histoire de la société française pendant le Directoire* (Paris: Charpentier [1880]), p. 300.

marked that he must have stolen a lot to be able to show off in such splendor. His usual circle included big financiers and speculators, promoters of all types, parasites, questionable people, well-born women with bad reputations, and nobles brought low by the Revolution. He strutted about amidst this corruption and deluded himself that this demi-monde was really high society. He was corrupt to the very core, rotten with vice, unbridled and consummate in his pleasures, a connoisseur of wine, women, and elegance. All the perfumed profits and the pleasures of power he kept for himself.

A rather easygoing temperament, a taste for munificence, some flexibility of mind, and a rather remarkable political flair distinguished him from his narrow-minded colleagues. But whenever his interests and his pleasures were disturbed, he became capable of anything. Ordinarily lazy and sluggish, he regained his native energy for the occasional violent acts which had made him the supporter and the strong man of that faction in the Councils composed of former deputies of the Convention. The shady game of intrigues pleased him even more. Fundamentally treacherous, selling himself to each and deceiving all, a man who enjoyed lying, he had the soul of a whore in the body of a handsome man. La Revellière considered him "ill-bred," [13] because one could surely see in him the speech and manner of a man who had always lived among bad company. Nevertheless, he retained a certain air, a certain demeanor, that he owed to his origin. No matter how deeply degraded he was, he never departed from "some of the manners customary among men of quality." [14] He gladly played the part of a soldier—it pleased him to be called *citizen general.* Posing as being on extremely friendly terms with the other Directors and eagerly using the intimate form of address with them, he really scorned their pettiness. This déclassé, this gentleman from the Midi [southern France] who had gone bad, disdained the upstarts that the accidents of annual elections gave him as colleagues.

The distinctive feature of all these men was their moral baseness. In them, there was no elevated conception of their duties and rights, no generosity of heart or mind, no willingness to pacify or rally the nation, no compassion for an unhappy France which was enduring so many evils. They governed meanly, stu-

[13] La Revellière-Lépeaux, I, 337.
[14] MS Document by Cambacérès. The present Comte de Cambacérès has been so kind as to allow us to consult this valuable document.

pidly, crudely. Their policy consisted in slashing out sometimes at the Right, sometimes at the Left, and retaining power by these alternate blows. This was the famous seesaw system, which humbled one party only to raise the other. . . .

How did France live under this shameless regime? All the wounds made by the Revolution continued to bleed, and the violent actions of the Directory reopened those that had begun to heal. A France, no longer revolutionary, remained revolutionized, that is, in a state of complete subversion from which a great many evils followed. All of them can be attributed to certain general causes of suffering that were constant and endemic and that oppressed the various regions of France more or less severely.

First, there was the physical disorder. Actually, at the beginning of 1799, some months before the obscure beginnings of the Consulate, large-scale seditious movements were not evident. There had hardly been a time during the Revolution when the government had been held in such contempt and the whole of the country been so manageable. But it was apathy rather than calm, apathy still troubled by thousands of fears, unceasingly assailed by the vexations caused by those in power and by the violence of extremist groups. Although the Directory posed as a government defending the social order and the middle of the road, it could not stop the guerillas, men of blood and pillage, from oppressing many areas and terrorizing their inhabitants. As late as 1798 there were cruelties in Tours reminiscent of the Terror.[15] And even when the left-wing anarchists, the *sans-culottes* or *bonnets rouges,* seemed for the moment under control, their presence could still be felt, and people trembled at the thought of a repeat attack. In the bowels of a great many cities and small towns, groups of malevolent men, human slime, secretly plotted a thoroughgoing revolution, a universal abolition of order, babouvism[16] in action. Panic-stricken landlords told each other that sooner or later the agrarian law [splitting up large rural holdings] would come.[17]

---

[15] Jean-Nicolas Dufort, Comte de Cheverny, *Mémoires sur les règnes de Louis XV et Louis XVI et sur la Révolution* (Paris: Plon, Nourrit, 1886), II, 376.

[16] [A reference to the radical revolutionary Babeuf, a proponent of economic equality who was guillotined in 1797.]

[17] Dufort, II, 365. Dufort de Cheverny lived in Blésois. His *Memoirs* are valuable. Written by a man free of strong passions, they are almost a day-by-day history of the Revolution in an average department.

At the other extreme swarmed right-wing anarchists, genuine, active anarchists. For the moment, the royalists had given up large-scale armed uprisings, real insurrections. Civil war was splintered into individual actions. Its current form was political brigandage. If Jacobinism was one career for scoundrels and desperate men, highway robbery by royalists was another. . . .

Although this kind of rural terrorism was more or less the common fate of all France, political brigandage centered in certain areas. In the West, *Chouannerie* spread again through nine or ten departments. This large ulcer kept all the surrounding areas irritated and feverish. If we cut obliquely across central France to its southeastern limits, the Bouches-du-Rhône, Vaucluse, Var, and Basses-Alpes departments, we find another *Chouannerie,* that of Provence, a *Chouannerie* whose history has still to be written. Along the entire lower and middle valley of the Rhône River, there were scattered acts of vengeance—Nemesis unchained hovered over this whole murderous region. The Pyrenees region remained in continuous ferment. Along the Cévennes mountains there were remnants of the royalist bands which had made religious war on the Convention and Directory. In most of the other departments brigandage occurred sporadically, appearing as scattered crimes. Even in the vicinity of the capital no road was entirely safe—more than a year after the establishment of the Consulate, a stagecoach was held up at Charenton [a suburb southeast of Paris].[18] Any place that was suitable for ambushes experienced a marked increase in insecurity; it seemed as though the Revolution had spread the Forest of Bondy [a legendary haunt of robbers] everywhere.

Aside from the West, the Midi, and some regions in central France, brigandage almost lost its aspect of counter-revolutionary guerilla warfare to become simple forays by deserters, vagrants, or *chauffeurs* [robbers who would burn their victims' feet until they revealed where their money was hidden]. Nevertheless, these ruffians tried to give themselves a political coloration by destroying republican symbols and by preferring to attack government officials and buyers of land confiscated from the Church or *émigrés.* Even in Paris and its suburbs, some royalist commandos, precursors of Cadoudal and his companions, dreamed of abduct-

---

[18] MS Papers of General Mortier, Commander of the Seventeenth Division. Archives of Trévise. The Duc de Trévise kindly allowed us to consult these papers.

ing or assassinating the Directors.[19] No beneficiary of the Revolution felt completely secure from attack by these armed and vagrant bands.

Against this persistent disorder, from wherever it came, the public authorities were able to do little or nothing. Although innumerable communes were in a state of siege, their means of defense were often lacking, for the continuation of the war kept the largest part of the army out of the country. The rural constabulary was poorly organized and infected by the presence in its ranks of formerly active Jacobins. The units of the National Guard—from which were recruited the flying columns assigned to chase bands of thieves and to organize roundups—were weak and disheartened. The ever changing, unstable civil authorities nowhere constituted a meaningful protective force. . . .

Wherever government action played a part, the harshest and most thoroughgoing tyranny was added to revolutionary disorder. Whoever was not in armed revolt against the law or did not evade it by subterfuge had to endure its cruelty. The revolutionaries in power, although they spurned the Jacobin label and had not reopened that famous club, still remained infected by the Jacobin spirit—the urge to persecute. Liberty existed for the Jacobins alone; they refused it to others, while ordering everyone to worship it on his knees. They had made the word divine but forbade the real thing. This is why the French welcomed Bonaparte as a liberator and so easily exchanged the oppression of wretched despots for a lofty and impartial tyranny.

Among the accepted legends about 18 Brumaire, none is more erroneous than the supposition that it brought the death of liberty. For a long time it was a historical commonplace to present Bonaparte in the Council Hall of the Five Hundred at Saint-Cloud [20] destroying a genuine legality with one stroke of his sword and smothering, while his drums rolled, the last gasps of French liberty. Such solemn nonsense can no longer be repeated in the presence of some clearly recognized and understood facts. Bonaparte can be reproached for not having established liberty, he cannot be accused of having destroyed it, for the excellent reason that on his return from Egypt it was nowhere to be found in France. He could not end something that did not exist. In

[19] See the documents cited by André Lebon, *L'Angleterre et l'émigration française de 1794 à 1801* (Paris: Plon, 1882), pp. 265–269. [Cadoudal was a Vendean leader who, in 1803–1804, plotted to assassinate Napoleon.]

[20] [The château near Paris where the last act of the *coup d'état* took place.]

the early days of the Directory, amidst violent reactionary movements, tension had started to relax and a few liberties were recognized. But the death of liberty came not on 18 Brumaire but on 18 Fructidor [September 4, 1797], when the revolutionaries, to stop a resurgence of royalism, ruthlessly seized dictatorial power again. After this *coup d'état* against the nation, almost all the liberties constitutionally guaranteed to the French were forcefully snatched away or treacherously withdrawn.

The primary right of a free people is to elect representatives and through them control the management of public affairs. All persons authorized by the constitution to exercise the rights of citizenship should cooperate in this delegation of sovereignty. In the Fructidorian Directory, according to a series of special laws, a whole category of Frenchmen—relatives of *émigrés* as well as ex-nobles who had not given formal pledges of loyalty to the Revolution—were excluded from the right to vote and to hold office. In addition, the legislature, twice purged—in Fructidor [September 1797] and in Floréal [May 1798]—did not at all represent a true image of the electorate, which already had been arbitrarily reduced in number. The representation was in essence corrupt and fictitious, a mockery.

Public platforms were available only to those revolutionaries furnished with the government's stamp of approval. The press was servile. After the coup of Fructidor a decree of deportation had been issued against the owners and editors of thirty-five opposition newspapers, a radical method of destroying them. Thereafter, a law of the year V [September 5, 1797], which was renewed in the year VI, submitted all newspapers to supervision by the police, who suppressed them at their pleasure and at their discretion. Public opinion no longer had a channel of expression. Freedom of association and assembly appeared only in the text of the constitution. At any moment arrests arbitrarily carried out and arbitrarily upheld could outrage individual liberty.

Religious liberty existed only in words. After the Terror and the great sacrilegious madness of 1793, the Convention returned to fundamentals and proclaimed religious freedom. The law of 3 Ventôse, year III [February 21, 1795], declared, "The exercise of any religious cult shall not be disturbed, and the Republic will not subsidize any of them." In this way the separation of Church and State replaced the celebrated Civil Constitution of the Clergy, and the Schismatic [Constitutional] Church lost its privileged position. The law declared all cults free of control and placed them on an equal footing before the state. In actual fact this theoretical freedom was reduced by the Convention to a minimum by the way in which it was regulated. Toward the Christian cults the state called itself neutral and remained hostile.[21] . . .

Sometimes the revolutionaries had to accept strange anomalies. In this France dotted with monasteries falling into ruin and desecrated cloisters, some female religious orders were still permitted to continue—those devoted to helping the poor and caring for the sick. Nothing else could be done, for there was no one to replace them. At the famous Hospital of Beaune in Burgundy, the sisters doffed their four-century-old garb, but managed to keep the hospital a Catholic stronghold. In a rather large number of communes and even right in the middle of Paris—at the Hôtel-Dieu [the city hospital]—the sisters, dressed as nurses, furtively continued to serve humanity.[22]

Elsewhere the anti-religious mania exceeded all limits, reaching the height of absurdity and ridiculousness. The executive order of 14 Germinal, year IV [April 3, 1796], forbade the selling of fish on what formerly had been called Friday; war was declared on fasting; fish was prohibited as Catholic contraband—to the great distress of our fisheries; in Paris, the oratory was closed in the former Carmelite chapel because the feast of Epiphany had been celebrated there;[23] in Strasbourg a merchant was fined for displaying in his shop more fish than usual on a fast day; and 350 truck gardeners were prosecuted for hallowing Sunday by not bringing their vegetables to market on that day.[24] Such severe measures continued until after Brumaire with local officials acting as the clumsy instruments of the rationalist tyranny. O Reason, what stupidities are committed in thy name! . . .

The Fructidorian Directory kept itself in power by war and victory; it succumbed in a crisis brought on by defeat and aggravated by domestic scandal. After the death of General Hoche and Bonaparte's departure for Egypt, the Directory continued

---

[21] While speaking of the revolutionaries of the year III, Antonin Debidour was quite right to say: "In general they saw that the separation of Church and State, recently put into effect, was simply a means of destroying the Church." *Histoire des rapports de l'Église et de l'État en France de 1789 à 1870* (Paris: Alcan, 1898), p. 158.

[22] See especially Léon Lallemand, *La Révolution et les pauvres* (Paris: Picard, 1898), pp. 137–146.

[23] Ludovic Sciout, *Le Directoire* (Paris: Didot, 1895–1897), III, 176.

[24] The documents are cited *ibid.*, III, 390.

the policy of conquest, or rather of plunder—occupying territories for their money, holding governments for ransom, pillag-
ing the people, making France an object of execration. Rome
was invaded. Switzerland literally sacked. After General Cham-
pionnet conquered Naples, the Austrians, who had considered
the peace of Campo-Formio only a truce, reopened hostilities;
the Congress of Rastadt had its bloody epilogue;[25] all of Germany except Prussia seemed ready to fight once more; England
supplied ships and subsidies; and finally a Russian army came
down from the North. The Second Coalition was formed. Aided
everywhere by insurrections, it threatened our conquests and
soon our frontiers. Against us was this second kings' war and
the first peoples' war.

The Directory ran dreadfully short of money. It had been
unable to solve the problems arising from an unprecedented
monetary crisis and from the ruin of public finance. No one
questioned that there was a deficit, the only issue was its size.
The executive listed the figure at 67 million francs, but the
Councils tended to reduce the estimate so as to avoid voting new
taxes.[26] When the ministers and department heads were questioned, it appeared that the abyss was bottomless. All expedients,
all subterfuges, had been tried in turn. Abroad, the conquered
territories yielded no more money. At home the taxpayers refused to pay any levies; and the government felt itself unable to
force them, since it had not succeeded in establishing a regular
method of collection. It fell more and more into the hands of a
tremendous gang of exploiters, for whom it was less an ac-
complice than a victim.

A swarm of suppliers and contractors relentlessly set upon
the Republic. Summoned to provide for the needs of the various
departments and especially the War Ministry, they turned the
regime into an object of cynical speculation. Having to deal
with a government that paid irregularly and with light-fingered
public employees, they thought only of insuring for themselves
excessive guarantees and illegal profits. They billed the state for
the graft given to its employees, forced ruinous contracts on it,
drained off the little cash that remained in the Treasury's coffers,

[25] [Two of the three French delegates to the Congress, when returning to
France in 1799, were murdered by Austrian soldiers.]
[26] According to the recent and learned work of René Stourm, *Les Finances
du Consulat* (Paris: Guillaumin, 1902), pp. 270–271, the deficit was 300 million *at the very least.*

and delivered only worthless materials.[27] This was the era of gigantic plundering and vile swindles, of massive influence peddling, and of illegal commissions and rebates to lower officials. The era of all kinds of dishonor, the age of mud after the age of blood. This nearly universal plundering found its way into the mainspring of state power and submerged it in a heap of mire; but when the spring had to be used against foreigners, everything had become decayed and rotten.

Our soldiers were without provisions, without shoes, "without pots, kettles, and mess-tins," [28] without linen for the wounded, and without medicine for the sick. And they had to fight enemies much more redoubtable than those of 1792 and 1793: in Germany Archduke Charles and in Italy the strange Russian general Suvarov, a man who joined to the extravagances of an eccentric the talents of a great leader and the soul of a crusader. With us, politics often determined the assignment of generals. What is more, the excessive length of our line of operations—stretching from Texel [an island north of Amsterdam] to Naples—offered the enemy openings for attack. Together, these causes led to a series of disasters in Germinal, Floréal, and Prairial of the year VII (March to June 1799): Jourdan defeated at Stokach in southern Baden and forced back to the Rhine; Schérer and Moreau defeated in Italy; Lombardy lost; the Cisalpine Republic swept away; Piedmont entered by Suvarov; Naples evacuated; the overthrow of all the governments established by France in Italy. Within France, agitation in the West became more serious;

---

[27] A report written after Brumaire by a former minister, General de Beurnonville, gives an idea of the way things were done in the Department of War. "It is, I believe, mathematically provable that the government overpays by more than 50 per cent for all supplies that it receives. . . . Just imagine the path a supplier has to travel. Without the minister's knowledge, he pays an enormous bribe when his contract is signed. Often his contacts take, more or less, 5 or 10 per cent of the profits. In order to put the agreement into effect, the contractor hires his own minions who get rid of the former subcontractors and who, knowing full well that the job is temporary, think only of making a killing. In return for a share of the take, their supervisors become their accomplices. Step by step, all this mounting individual greed raises the costs by fake accounting until they are often double, or more, the value of the actual goods supplied. The state thus finds itself in debt for what it has not received; and it is only by such a system that the contractor is paid back for the sacrifices that he has made to get the contract, for the losses that he has suffered by the manner in which he is paid, and for the delays in the final payment settling the account." Archives of the Ministry of War, MS Correspondance générale, 1799.

[28] Le Publiciste, 6 Thermidor, year VIII [July 25, 1800].

and in the Midi a campaign of brigandage and assassination continued. In the light of these disastrous events, the inability of the Directory stood clearly revealed. The errors and shamefulness of this dictatorship by incompetents appeared in sharp relief. An outcry of disgust and criticism arose in the army. In Paris the muzzled press could say nothing, and the political agitation of the parties continued to operate on a level above the general apathy. Nevertheless, without the Directory noticing the formation of an organized, vocal, and open opposition, the regime collapsed by itself under the weight of its own misdeeds. . . .

In the minds of its civilian authors, the *coup d'état* of 1799 was to take place for precisely the same reason as had those of 18 Fructidor and 22 Floréal. It was inspired by a passionate desire for political survival. Differing from other coups carried out by men who had nothing to lose and everything to gain, this one was the act of those who had a terrible fear of losing everything. To this motive was added, among some, the honorable desire to purify and regenerate the Republic, to start it at last on a normal course. They wanted to create a true constitutional order in place of the one that Fructidor and Floréal had virtually abolished and they wanted to insure, by a final illegal step, the reign of law.

A DEFENSE*

Albert Goodwin

For biographical information on Albert Goodwin, see the section entitled "The War of 1792."

The French Executive Directory which assumed office on 11 Brumaire year IV (2 November 1795), and was destroyed by Bonaparte's *coup d'état* of 18 Brumaire year VIII (9 November 1799), has been traditionally regarded by historians as a byword for corruption, governmental incompetence and political instability.[1] Its rule is usually associated with the financial bankruptcy of 1797, defeats of French armies in the field, administrative chaos at home and the Directors' policy of self-perpetuation in office by means of a series of "purifications" of the elected Assemblies. In 1799 the Directory is supposed to have been ripe for dissolution and France ready for Bonaparte. It is the purpose of this paper to suggest that such an interpretation does not do full justice to the governmental record of the Directory between 1795 and 1799, and that it represents an over-simplification of the situation in France on the eve of 18 Brumaire.

It is not difficult to see why, in the past, the Directors have been so harshly treated. The assumption that the Directors were themselves not exempt from the vices of corruption and immorality characteristic of French society at that date was perhaps unavoidable, especially as the Directory came to be identified in

* From Albert Goodwin, "The French Executive Directory—A Revaluation," *History*, n. s., XXII (December 1937), 201–218. The entire article is reprinted by permission of the author and the editor of *History*. Quotations originally in French have been translated by the editors.

[1] The chapter on "Brumaire" by H. A. L. Fisher in the *Cambridge Modern History*, VIII (1904), 665–88, in the main, follows rather closely the opinions of Vandal, but also expresses views which do not altogether accord with them, so that the total effect does not seem altogether consistent.

the popular mind with Barras. [This impression of Barras as representative of the general standards of the Directory, although entirely erroneous, was to some extent intelligible.] Of the thirteen individuals who at various times held office as Directors, Barras alone succeeded in retaining his position throughout, and he was undoubtedly the most colourful personality of them all. The danger of generalising from the single case of Barras is, however, obvious. Another reason why injustice has been done to the Directory is that French history between 1795 and 1799 has tended to be studied by historians, very largely for the sake of convenience, as a period of *coups d'état*.[2] This approach has had two unfortunate results. On the one hand, it has gained general acceptance for the impression that the age was one of perpetual crisis, thus distracting attention from the more solid achievements of the Directory, and, on the other, it has led to the supposition that it was this series of illegal expedients alone which ensured their survival. It is true that an informed interpretation of the *coups d'état* is essential for the understanding of the period, but due attention should be paid to other factors. Lastly, the reputation of the Directors may have suffered because it has been blackened by the apologists of Robespierre and the admirers of Bonaparte. Between Mathiez,[3] who spent a lifetime in defending the Jacobin leader, and Madelin,[4] equally intent on eulogising Bonaparte, the Directors have come in for a good deal of unmerited abuse. Few French historical scholars have been able to free themselves from partisanship in their accounts of the revolution, and the way in which the work of the Directory has been consistently underrated as a means of heightening the contrasts with the immediately preceding or following period is a good illustration of the evils implicit in such zeal. In this way a popular failure to distinguish between Barras and the other Directors, an inadequate historical approach and unconcealed historical bias have combined to enhance the evil repute and minimise the

[2] Recent examples of this treatment are A. Meynier, *Les coups d'état du Directoire*, 3 vols., and C. Brinton, *A Decade of Revolution 1789–1799*, chap. IX. Brinton, however, takes a much more favourable view of the Directory than most writers. See also Sorel, *L'Europe et la Révolution française*, vol. v, p. 11.

[3] At the time of his death in February 1932 Mathiez was engaged on a detailed study of the Directory the first volume of which, covering the period down to 18 Fructidor, was published in 1934.

[4] See particularly *La France du Directoire*; *La France de l'Empire*; *Le Consulat et l'Empire* and *Napoléon*.

achievements of the Directorate. Recently, however, the researches of French scholars, by making possible a juster appre-
ciation of the record of the Directory, have demonstrated the
necessity of re-examining the unfavourable judgments which have
often been passed on its rule.

Shortly stated, the usual indictment may be said to be based
on four main charges—that the personnel of the Directory was
both corrupt and incapable; that its administration of the finances
brought the country within measurable distance of ruin; that its
foreign policy involved an indefinite postponement of the prospects of a general peace; and, finally, that the Government could
not even fulfil the first condition of effective rule by securing
public order and individual freedom at home. What modifications
must be made in these charges in the light of the fuller evidence
which is now available?

On the score of venality there is ample authority for the view
that the Directors themselves were, with perhaps a single exception, reasonably honest. The corruption of Barras was, of course,
notorious and remains indefensible.[5] The evidence against the
rest, however, is slight. Certain passages in Thibaudeau's *Memoirs* suggest that Reubell, who for some time virtually controlled
Directorial finance, deserved censure,[6] and some suspicion was
apparently directed against Merlin de Douai and La Revellière.
It is true that Reubell's reputation for financial integrity was not
unblemished, since he had suffered disgrace for peculation under
the Terror,[7] and he was well known to be avaricious. On the
other hand, there is no real evidence against him of corruption
while a Director, and it should also be remembered that the
Commissions of Inquiry specially appointed by the Councils to
investigate his guilt in August 1799 completely exonerated him
as well as Merlin and La Revellière.[8] When he retired from the
Directory by lot on 16 May 1799, Reubell felt compelled to
accept the allowance given by his colleagues as compensation,[9]
and he died poor. The rest of the Directors seem never to have

[5] Gohier, President of the Directory on 18 Brumaire, was anxious to rid the
government of Barras and thus to make its moral standing unassailable. A.
Vandal, *L'Avènement de Bonaparte*, vol. I, p. 323.

[6] Thibaudeau, *Mémoires*, vol. II, p. 37.

[7] A. Mathiez, *Le Directoire*, p. 44.

[8] Lefebvre, Guyot, Sagnac, *La Révolution française*, p. 457.

[9] Meynier, *Les coups d'état du Directoire*, vol. II, pp. 168-9.

been the objects of contemporary criticism on the ground of their dishonesty.

How far is it true to say that the Directors were individually men without ability? For the present purpose it is only necessary to consider the members of the original Directory and three others—François de Neufchâteau, Merlin de Douai and Treilhard. Sieyès may properly be excepted, as his efforts, after he became a Director, were concentrated on the destruction of the constitution of the year III. The others may be disregarded because of the shortness of their period of office—Barthélemy was in power three and a half months, Gohier less than six months, Ducos and Moulin four and a half months. The usual opinion of the original Directory—"les Pentarques"—is that they were a group of mediocrities. If only the highest standards are applied, such a judgment would not be unfair. But if the ordinary criteria of capacity are accepted, then the Directors must be credited with more than average ability. Mature they were bound to be since article 134 of the constitution insisted that they should be at least forty years of age, and although the manner of their nomination left something to be desired,[10] they were all men of wide experience, most of them with special aptitudes and qualifications for the conduct of the departments of government they controlled. The least remarkable from the point of view of sheer ability were Le Tourneur and Barras. Le Tourneur was entirely devoid of political gifts, and in all matters of policy he followed without question the lead of his school-friend Carnot. He did, however, possess a good knowledge of the technical side of naval affairs. The Directory needed a naval expert, and Le Tourneur admirably filled the gap. Similarly, it would be hard to think of any revolutionary leader, apart from Fouché, better fitted to organise the police than Barras, whose whole life had been spent in intrigue. Nor is it accurate to regard Barras as a political cipher. Especially when resolute action was needed, Barras could be counted on, as he had already shown on 9 Thermidor and 13

[10] They were the nominees of the former members of the Convention, two-thirds of whom had been re-elected to the new Councils. The procedure for their nomination was that the Council of Five Hundred submitted a list of fifty candidates from whom the Council of Ancients made the final choice. The list drawn up by the Five Hundred consisted of forty-five complete nonentities and the five persons whom they wished to be elected. This manœuvre was completely successful in forcing a group of "hand-picked" Directors on the Ancients. Mathiez, *Le Directoire*, p. 36.

Vendémiaire.[11] That he had an eye for talent as well as for beauty is proved by those whose careers he helped to make— Bonaparte and Talleyrand, Saint-Simon and Ouvrard. Luck alone cannot account for his survival till 18 Brumaire.

La Revellière was in many ways a curious mixture, half crank, half fanatic, a botanist, student of Rousseau, high priest of the new revolutionary cult of Theophilanthropy and a believer in the *juste milieu* in politics. A sincere republican, he was consumed with a hatred of priests and aristocrats, and yet he had small liking for the rural or urban proletariat. In foreign policy he was an advocate of the war of propaganda and conquest—an attitude which he had consistently maintained ever since the day he had been the prime mover of the decree of 19 November 1792 by which the Convention had promised its aid and protection to all nations who wished to recover their liberty. His special sphere in Directorial policy was education, the *fêtes nationales* [patriotic holidays] and manufactures.

Carnot has been aptly described by Mathiez as "almost entirely a man of learning and a patriot." A former member of the Committee of Public Safety, and famous as the "Organiser of Victory," he had been nominated, in place of Sieyès, who had refused to serve as Director, in order to stem the run of French reverses on the Rhine. Carnot was a paragon of executive efficiency, and had real genius in the administration of war. He proved a failure as a Director, and for obvious reasons. He had a biting tongue and alienated his colleagues by his cynicisms. He was a convinced pacifist at a time when both Reubell and La Revellière, for different reasons, were keen supporters of foreign war. He disappointed the expectations of his Jacobin friends by evolving in the direction of the Right.[12] Lastly, although he had little or no talent for politics, he was never satisfied to confine himself to his departmental duties. Still, he can hardly be described as a mediocrity.

There is general agreement that Reubell was a man of great ability.[13] An Alsatian barrister of eminence, he had a good com-

---

[11] [On both occasions, Barras had organized troops to defend the Convention against armed popular demonstrations.]

[12] He took an active part in the suppression of the conspiracy of Babeuf and the Jacobin plot of the year IV [September 1796] at the camp of Grenelle. He was evicted from the Directory along with Barthélemy on 18 Fructidor (4 September 1797), largely because of his moderate and royalist activities.

[13] R. Guyot, *Le Directoire et la Paix*, pp. 45–9.

mand of modern languages and an encyclopædic knowledge. He owed his ascendancy over his colleagues to his industry and his strength of will. Utterly devoid of scruple and severely practical, he may be described as the main driving force behind Directorial policy. At one time he maintained a close supervision over the three most important departments of government—justice, finance and foreign affairs. Subsequently, however, he was content to delegate responsibility to ministers of proved capacity, such as Merlin and Ramel, and concentrated his own attention on the conduct of diplomatic affairs. In this sphere he identified himself with the policy of conquest and expansion which he hoped would culminate in the acquisition of the natural frontiers. As Reubell was only eliminated from the Directory by lot in May 1799, his influence upon policy was exerted throughout, and gave it a much-needed continuity.

Of François de Neufchâteau, Merlin and Treilhard, it is only necessary to say that the former was a distinguished administrator whose work as Minister of the Interior conferred lasting benefits on the French state and anticipated many of the Napoleonic reforms, and that Merlin and Treilhard were the leading jurisconsults of the day. Any government which could count on their services might well have considered itself fortunate.

The subject of Directorial finance is both technical and controversial.[14] Here attention can only be directed towards one or two points which serve to modify the severe criticisms usually passed upon it. The two leading events upon which discussion has centred are the collapse of the Assignats in 1796 and the repudiation of two-thirds of the public debt in September 1797. Both these occurrences were, in some ways, regrettable, but, by themselves, do not entail an utter condemnation of the finance of the period. Their full significance does not lie on the surface, and can only be determined by a close study of the financial situation during the Terror and later under the Consulate. Each can, moreover, be interpreted in a way which considerably eases the burden of discredit to be borne by the Directory. The collapse

[14] It is fair to say that M. Marion's standard work *Histoire financière de la France depuis 1715*, vols. III–IV, takes a highly unfavourable view of Directorial finance. Other authorities, however, such as Hawtrey, *Currency and Credit*, Chap. XV, and Pariset, *Études d'histoire révolutionnaire et contemporaine*, pp. 79–134, hold contrary opinions. See also R. Stourm, *Les Finances de l'Ancien Régime et de la Révolution*, vol. I, pp. 258–446, and the recent study *Les principes financiers de la Révolution* by J. Barthélemy in *Cahiers de la Révolution française*, vol. VI, pp. 7–44 (1937).

of the Assignats prompted, it is true, an unsuccessful attempt to stabilise the paper currency by means the *mandats territoriaux* in 1796, but this was followed by a return to a metallic currency without undue deflationary effects—a policy which may be said to have paved the way for that revival of confidence which is so often attributed to the Consulate. Similarly, the bankruptcy of 1797 should not be viewed in isolation, but be regarded as part and parcel of Ramel's economy campaign. Nor should it be overlooked that the bankruptcy itself was not only partial but conditional, and that the final blame for its becoming definite must rest with the Consulate. In fact, the suggested contrast between financial maladministration and chaos under the Directory and financial retrenchment and reform under the Consulate has no real relation to the facts, and should be abandoned. The foundation of the Bank of France in 1800 may have been symptomatic of a new regime, but it was only rendered possible by the financial reforms of the preceding period.

The immediate financial problem to be faced by the Directory was how to arrest the continued fall of the Assignats. One of the last acts of the Convention had been to establish by the law of 21 June 1795 a sliding scale of depreciation for contracts and other debts, the value of whch was to be fixed according to the quantity of Assignats actually in circulation at the time of the signing of the contract. This experiment failed because it was not applied to all contracts and because the treasury had not a sufficient reserve.[15] The first important proposal made by the Directory was for a forced loan payable in specie, grain, or in Assignats taken at 1 per cent. of their face value (6 December 1795). The manufacture of Assignats was to be discontinued and the plates broken on 21 March following. As the Assignats were worth less than 1 per cent. of their nominal value, and as receipts for payments of the forced loan were to be accepted in payment of direct taxes, this plan really amounted to a timid attempt at deflation and an effort to increase the revenue from taxation.[16] The over-valuation of the Assignats and the lack of specie for their conversion, however, effectually ensured the failure of this scheme.

The next experiment—the issue on 18 March 1796 of *mandats territoriaux*—was devised by the Finance Minister, Ramel-Nogaret. These *mandats* were in effect a new form of paper

---

[15] Mathiez, *Le Directoire*, p. 91.

[16] Lefebvre, Guyot, Sagnac, *La Révolution française*, p. 319.

money which it was hoped would gradually displace the Assignats and be immune from depreciation.[17] To render them attractive to the public they were to entitle the holders to obtain *biens nationaux* at the fixed valuation of twenty-two years' purchase of the annual value of 1790.[18] Unfortunately, however, a committee of the Council of Five Hundred made the Assignats convertible into *mandats territoriaux* at one-thirtieth of their nominal value. Thus, although the new facility provided for the acquisition of unsold national property prevented the *mandats* from depreciating immediately, they were bound to collapse eventually because of the over-valuation of the Assignats in terms of the new paper currency.[19] It had been thought that the capitalists would eagerly take up the *mandats* in order to acquire the estates of the Belgian monasteries, but the more cautious of them hesitated to buy property so near to the frontier before the conclusion of a general peace, while the speculators preferred to discredit the *mandats* in order to effect purchases at a later stage at less cost. An additional difficulty was that the new currency was not immediately available, since the government only issued *promesses de mandats*.[20] For these reasons the *mandats* failed to gain general acceptance, and despite the efforts of the government to force their currency, they quickly fell to a discount. In the course of July, August and September 1796 laws were passed whereby the *mandats* were to be accepted by the government in payment for taxes and in exchange for *biens nationaux* at their market price only. The *mandats* were finally withdrawn from circulation by a law of 4 February 1797. Thus failed the Directory's main effort at stabilisation. The failure was not, however, without its redeeming features, since it at all events prevented the inflation from getting completely out of hand, and it did in fact result in the resumption of a metallic standard.

In its essentials, the "repudiation" of 1797 was a comparatively simple operation. The law of 9 Vendémiaire year VI (30 September 1797) enacted that one-third only of the public debt

---

[17] R. G. Hawtrey, *Currency and Credit*, p. 256.

[18] Although secured upon the *biens nationaux*, the Assignats had never given holders the right to any particular share of this security. Previously the national lands had been put up for auction and sold to the highest bidder.

[19] G. Pariset, *Études d'histoire révolutionnaire et contemporaine*, p. 84. The 100-livre Assignat was then worth 7 sous, so that 100 livres *mandats* equivalent to 3000 livres Assignats would have been worth only 10 francs.

[20] Hawtrey, *Currency and Credit*, p. 256; Marion, *Histoire financière*, vol. III, p. 471.

should be consolidated and entered on the Grand Livre as a sacred charge,[21] and that the capital of the other two-thirds should be redeemed by the issue to stockholders of bearer bonds (*bons des deux tiers mobilisés*). By way of compensation, the state guaranteed that interest payments should in the future be made subject to no deductions as they had been in the past,[22] and that the *bons des deux tiers* should be available for the purchase of national property.

It is clear that many of the contemporary arguments in support of the measure were either specious or merely absurd. Such, for example, was the suggestion that no injustice to fundholders would be involved, since their stock had already lost two-thirds of its value owing to the inflation.[23] Yet repudiation ignored the possibility of a recovery in the value of the public debt and made the former losses irretrievable. Another contention was that the bankruptcy would have a depressing psychological effect on France's enemies, who would be more anxious to sue for peace when they saw the financial burdens of the French state thus lightened. If this view had been correct, the question was, Why did the Directory stop short of complete repudiation? A much more probable result would have been that the consequent loss of public credit would have prevented France herself from continuing the war. Equally it must be admitted that the bankruptcy demolished the incomes of the rentier class. An example will suffice to show the extent of the injury and to elucidate the actual nature of the operation. A rentier with a capital of 3000 livres invested in the public debt which before September 1797 had given him, at 5 per cent., 150 livres interest, now received 50 livres as interest on one-third of his capital (*tiers consolidé*) and a nominal holding of 2000 livres in *bons des deux tiers mobilisés*. In the final liquidation of 30 Ventôse year IX (21 March 1801), when the two-thirds were converted into perpetual annuities at the rate of ¼ per cent. of their capital value, the 2000 livres would be exchanged for an annuity of 5 livres. The net result was that instead of receiving 150 livres interest, the fundholder received

---

[21] The Great Book or Register of the public debt had been opened by Cambon on 24 May 1793 with the object of consolidating the debt which had been issued under various denominations before the revolution. See *Cahiers de la Révolution française,* vol. VI, pp. 39–40.

[22] In March 1795 the perpetual annuities had been made liable to a stoppage of a tenth and the life annuities to a deduction of a twentieth.

[23] Marion, *Histoire financière,* vol. III, p. 64.

55 livres, which meant that 63.34 per cent. of his capital had been destroyed.[24] In this way the state repudiated in all nearly 2,000,000,000 livres of public debt.[25] The consequent shock to public credit may be imagined. The spectre of national bankruptcy which had haunted Mirabeau in the early days of the revolution had at last materialised. In M. Barthélemy's words, "The Directory misunderstood the overriding importance of maintaining the government's credit. It thought it could evade economic laws that were inflexible, but in so doing it came to grief. The repudiation of two-thirds of the debt weighed heavily on France's credit for a long time." [26]

It is, however, necessary to say in defence of the consolidation that bankruptcy in France had really been made inevitable by the misguided financial policy of the Constituent Assembly. The issue of the Assignats and the failure to levy sufficient taxation to balance the budgets had compromised the efforts of all subsequent administrations to grapple with financial shortage.[27] The repudiation of 1797 was, in fact, only part of a larger scheme to effect reforms in the French budget. By reducing governmental expenditure from 1,000,000,000 to 616,000,000 livres, Ramel was able, for the first time in the history of revolutionary finance, to establish a balanced budget. Part of this economy was achieved by drastic reductions in the military estimates, but the main saving came from the consolidation of the public debt. The financial end in view was, therefore, sound enough in the circumstances, although the means were not. Finally, the responsibility for the final liquidation of 21 March 1801 must be borne by the Consulate. The real bankruptcy only came after the Directory had fallen.

One aspect of Directorial finance, also mainly due to Ramel, which deserves more general recognition, was the recasting of the whole system of direct and indirect taxation. Concentrated in the short interval of peace between the preliminaries of Leoben and the war of the Second Coalition [April 1797 to March 1799], these reforms present several points of interest. The new legislation relating to direct taxation was to be one of the most lasting achievements of the revolution, for it survived down to 1914.

[24] R. Stourm, *Les Finances de l'Ancien Régime et de la Révolution*, vol. II, p. 342.
[25] G. Pariset, *Études d'histoire révolutionnaire*, p. 86.
[26] *Cahiers de la Révolution française*, vol. VI, p. 44.
[27] R. Stourm, *op. cit.*, vol. II, p. 341.

Some of it was fairly obviously a direct imitation of the younger Pitt's war finance, while the altered arrangements for the assessment and collection of revenue afford one more instance of a reorganisation, the credit for which has been wrongly attributed to the Consulate. Finally, the fresh recourse to indirect taxation, itself a result of inflation, marked a significant reversal of the taxation policy of the early years of the revolution.

The first direct tax to be reorganised was the tax on trade licences (*contribution des patentes*). This had been re-established in 1795, not for fiscal purposes, but as a means of preventing unjustifiable trade practices. Some changes were introduced in the method of its assessment in 1796, and the final adjustments were made by the law of 22 October 1798. The land tax (*contribution foncière*) assumed definitive shape in the law of 23 November 1798, the new tax on doors and windows in that of 24 November. The latter duty, payable in the first case by the owner, but ultimately by the tenant, encountered considerable opposition, on the ground of its English origin. It may be regarded as a first approximation to an income tax, and the manner in which it was first doubled (1 March 1799) and then quadrupled (23 May 1799) as a means of meeting renewed war expenditure may be compared with Pitt's tripling of certain assessed taxes in 1797. Lastly, on 23 December 1798, the *contribution mobilière et personnelle* which was partly a poll tax and partly a tax on movable property was entirely reconstructed. These four direct taxes (subsequently known as *les quatre vieilles*) formed the essential structure of the French taxation system down to the outbreak of the [First] World War.[28] Equally important was the change instituted on 13 November 1798, whereby the assessment and collection of the direct taxes and the adjudications on appeals were removed from the hands of local elected bodies and entrusted to committees composed entirely of officials and working in the departments under the direct control of a commissioner of the central government. This fundamental reform was not inaugurated, but only continued by the Consulate. The only modification subsequently introduced was the change in the name of the officials.[29]

Some of the features of the legislation on direct taxation reappeared in the revival of the indirect taxes. The very adoption

---

[28] Pariset, *Études d'histoire révolutionnaire*, pp. 87–8.

[29] Lefebvre, Guyot, Sagnac, p. 442.

of indirect taxation marked a reaction against the financial policy of the Constituent Assembly which had relied almost exclusively on direct taxes. Some of the new duties, such as the highway tolls, imposed on 10 September 1797, were again adopted from England. And hardly less permanent than *les quatre vieilles* were the new mortgage, registration and stamp duties (November–December 1798).[30] Other indirect taxes which proved indispensable were those on powder and saltpetre (30 August 1797), on gold and silver ornaments (9 November 1797), playing-cards (30 September 1798) and tobacco (22 November 1798).

A tendency to exaggerate the financial straits of the government may have inclined historians to accept with greater willingness Sorel's thesis that continued European war became a necessity to the Directors.[31] The theory is at least plausible. On Sorel's view, war would ensure that the French armies would be occupied and prevented from interfering in politics at Paris, that the cost of clothing and feeding the troops would be borne by the foreigner, and that the empty coffers of the republic would be replenished by the confiscations and forced contributions levied on the conquered countries. Several unjustifiable assumptions have, however, to be made if this position is to be upheld. Sorel's assertion that France was "without industry, credit, or public confidence" is demonstrably false.[32] French industry might very well have absorbed the returned French armies—they need not necessarily have been put on half-pay. Nor should generalisations about the financial resources which the government drew from the activities of its armies abroad be accepted without caution. It requires to be proved that the war provided on balance a net income for the Directory. What figures we have point in the opposite direction.[33] Moreover, if the main danger to the executive government was felt to be the existence of a class of ambitious generals, the real solution would have been not to prolong but to curtail the war, and thus to put an end to the extravagant pretensions and illicit gains of the commanders.[34]

[30] Pariset, *ut sup.*, p. 90.

[31] *L'Europe et la Révolution française,* vol. v, p. 12.

[32] *Ibid.*

[33] In 1795 Cambon estimated the average cost of the war at 2,000,000,000 livres. The highest figure given for the total extraordinary revenues drawn from abroad is that of Sciout, who places it at between 1,000,000,000 and 1,500,-000,000. Pariset, p. 91.

[34] Meynier, *Les coups d'état du Directoire,* vol. ii, p. 185.

There could be little doubt that the country as a whole wanted peace, and the Directors knew it. On *a priori* grounds, therefore, it is conceivable that the problems of peace confronting the Directory would not have been so insuperable as they have been made out.

Nor does the actual diplomacy of the period disprove the contention that the Directors were not averse from the conclusion of a satisfactory peace. The failure of the conference at Lille in July 1797, when [the British representative] Malmesbury had Pitt's instructions to spare no efforts for peace, was not entirely the result of the purge of the moderate party in the *coup d'état* of Fructidor [35] or of the overbearing attitude of the Triumvirate [Barras, Reubell, La Revellière]. The breakdown must be placed at the door of Barras and Talleyrand, whose secret intrigues both before and after Fructidor did so much to prevent the English and French governments from reaching a frank understanding.[36] Malmesbury at the outset agreed to the preliminary conditions put forward by the French agents. Recognition was given to the Republic, the annexation of Belgium and the French treaties of alliance with Holland and Spain. At the same time, however, he excepted secret treaties and made no promise about a "general restoration" of conquered colonies. The French negotiators, Le Tourneur, former Director, Admiral Pléville Le Pelley and Maret, accepted Malmesbury's reservations, although these were quite inconsistent with the public articles of the Spanish treaty and the secret treaty with Holland. This initial ambiguity, with regard to the surrender of Dutch and Spanish colonies, was never explained to the Directory by its representatives.[37] When, therefore, Malmesbury claimed the Cape and Ceylon, the Directory refused to consider his demands. Nevertheless, such was England's desire for peace that the government was even prepared to surrender the colonial conquests without compensation. Meanwhile, as the result of a ministerial reshuffle of 16 July, Talleyrand had become Foreign Minister. His English connections, his hopes of profitable speculative dealings on the London exchange and his sincere desire for peace all inclined Talleyrand to smooth away difficulties. He and Barras accordingly encouraged Pitt to believe that the French government, in return

[35] This is the impression given by Dr. Holland Rose in his *Short Life of Pitt,* p. 143.
[36] R. Guyot, *Le Directoire et la Paix,* pp. 431–56.
[37] *Ibid.,* pp. 413–15.

for hard cash, would not insist on the surrender of the Cape and Ceylon.[38] Pitt consequently did not press the need for immediate concessions on his colleagues, and still reposed considerable faith in the prospects of the triumph of the moderates in Paris.

The precise effect of the *coup d'état* of 18 Fructidor upon the Lille conferences was that Le Tourneur, Maret and Colchen were replaced by Treilhard and Bonnier, who were instructed to present Malmesbury with a virtual ultimatum. It was to the effect that if he had not powers to cede all the English colonial conquests, he was to leave France, and not to return until he had. This new move, so far from being "a raising of the French terms," [39] marked a reversion to the original demands. The Directory had not been informed that these conditions would be unacceptable from the British point of view, and it is clear that the Directors thought that Fructidor would enable them to impose this settlement. The ultimatum was conceived not as a means to end the peace negotiations, but as a way of exacting the full price from an enemy known to be in great difficulty. Malmesbury, having no authority to make the concessions, left Lille on 17 September with little or no hope of return. The resumption of negotiations was finally prevented by the battle of Camperdown. The Directory has always been strongly criticised by English historians for its failure to close with Pitt's offers, but the responsibility must not be borne entirely by the Directors. It was the secret intrigues of French agents at Lille which stiffened the English resistance before Fructidor, and which, after the *coup d'état,* were the cause of French intransigence.

On the other hand, the approval which, under strong provocation from Bonaparte, the Directors gave to the preliminaries of Leoben and the final treaty of Campo Formio, cannot be regarded as indicative of the pacific views of the Directors. It is fairly certain that those treaties would have been rejected by the Directory if its hands had not been tied, and indeed the best interests of France demanded that Bonaparte's policy should have been set aside. The Directors had, in each case, ample room for dissatisfaction. At Leoben, Bonaparte, anxious to monopolise the credit of having concluded peace, speeded up negotiations in order to prevent the official French negotiator, General Clarke, from arriving in time to share the discussions. In the public articles of the preliminaries of peace Bonaparte renounced the

[38] Lefebvre, Guyot, Sagnac, p. 363.

[39] H. Rose, *Short Life of Pitt,* p. 143.

left bank of the Rhine, towards the acquisition of which Reubell's foreign policy had been mainly directed, and in the secret articles, by retaining the Duchy of Milan[40] and suggesting the partition of Venice, he definitely disobeyed his instructions for the first time since the inception of the Italian campaign.[41] In addition, it is clear that Bonaparte virtually conceded all that Thugut, the Austrian minister, wished to obtain. The principle of the integrity of the Empire was upheld, access to the Adriatic won, and the surrender by Austria of Belgium and Milan amply compensated for by her acquisition of part of Venice. When the articles of Leoben were read to them three of the Directors— Reubell, Barras and La Revellière—declared they were inacceptable, and the Minister for Foreign Affairs—Delacroix—also reported unfavourably on them. Yet on 30 April 1797 Reubell alone refused to sign the ratification of the preliminaries. The explanation must be sought in two ways—the Directors were compelled to accept Leoben because the French public, acquainted only with the public articles, had received the news with an enthusiasm which it would have been dangerous for the government to have damped, and, moreover, the rejection of the terms would have entailed an admission that Bonaparte's advance into Austria had in actual fact placed him in a very serious military position.[42]

These incidents were paralleled by the negotiations at Campo Formio. Bonaparte withdrew from Austrian territory without waiting for the ratification of the Leoben preliminaries by his home government, and again ignored his instructions. He had been ordered by the Directors to renew the war rather than surrender Venice, and also to insist on the compensation of Austria in Germany. The actual terms of peace, however, conceded most of the advantages to Austria. As a result of the exchange of territory, her position was strengthened both in Italy and Germany,[43] a check was placed on the ambitions of her rival Prussia, and she had the prospect of still further compensations if France

---

[40] The Directors wished for the cession of Milan to Austria and the acquisition of the left bank of the Rhine by inducing the Emperor and the German princes to accept compensation on the right bank.

[41] See the important new work by G. Ferrero, *Aventure: Bonaparte en Italie, 1796–1797*, passim.

[42] *Ibid.*, pp. 195–6. Owing to shortage of supplies and lack of co-operation from Germany, Bonaparte had been compelled either to treat with the Austrians or to retreat. He could not have continued the march on Vienna.

[43] Pariset, *La Révolution (1792–1799)*, pp. 369–70.

succeeded in wresting the left bank of the Rhine from the representatives of the Empire in the projected congress at Rastadt. On the other hand, France deserted her ally Prussia, assumed a share of responsibility for the extinction of Venice, and erected in the Cisalpine Republic an uneasy neighbour whom it would be essential in the future to protect. Once more the Directors submitted, but most unwillingly. They could not afford to forfeit the position they had just won after Fructidor, nor did they wish to see a revival of the European coalition against France, as seemed not unlikely after the failure of the Lille conferences.[44]

The net result of this double surrender on the part of the Directors was to deprive them of the initiative in French foreign policy and to substitute the Italian policy of Bonaparte for that of the natural frontiers as canvassed by Reubell. Moreover, in the years which followed Campo Formio the Directors did much successful work by assimilating the conquered territories in Belgium and on the left bank of the Rhine,[45] by protecting the Italian republics and by exerting further pressure on Great Britain. In fact, for a whole year after Fructidor, French influence on the Continent was virtually unchallenged, and the real reverses suffered by French arms and diplomacy and the revival of the second Coalition must be ascribed not to Directorial incompetence, but to the initiation of the Egyptian expedition— a venture devised by Bonaparte and Talleyrand.[46]

It is less easy to defend the inability of the Directors to secure internal peace and security. Here at least the record of the Directors was one of almost complete failure. This failure, however, only repeated the lapses of monarchical and previous revolutionary governments. Nor should it be overlooked that the task of maintaining public order in the provinces had become immeasurably more difficult under the Directory in consequence of the revival of royalism, the appearance of *chauffage* [bands of roving thieves], and the adoption of conscription (5 September 1798).[47] Conscription was applied at an unfortunate moment— just at the time when the French armies had sustained a series of severe defeats and when the prospect of starvation was greater among the fighting forces than at home. Evasion of the law and desertion both helped to swell the number of brigands, who

[44] Guyot, *Le Directoire et la Paix*, p. 508.
[45] P. Sagnac, *Le Rhin français pendant la Révolution et l'Empire*, Chap. IV.
[46] See especially E. Dard, *Napoléon et Talleyrand*, pp. 26–30.
[47] A. Vandal, *L'avènement de Bonaparte*, vol. I, p. 18.

were able to organise "reigns of terror" in various parts of the country. It is customary to blame the government for having done nothing to face up to these difficulties. A long series of measures designed especially to grapple with brigandage, however, affords little support to this criticism. One of the first acts of the Directory after its acceptance of office was to add a seventh ministry—that of general police—to the six ministries provided for in the constitution, and to institute exhaustive inquiries into the state of the *garde nationale* and the gendarmerie.[48] This investigation revealed defects which were, to some extent, remedied by a law of 17 April 1798 reforming the gendarmerie. Other administrative gaps were filled by the laws prescribing capital punishment for robbery with violence on the high roads and in private houses (15 May 1797), the law enforcing increased penalties against gaolers who connived at the escape of their prisoners (25 September 1797), and the law reforming the personnel of the criminal courts (10 January 1798).[49] It must be admitted that these changes did not affect substantial improvement, but it is evident at least that the problem had been taken in hand. Above all, it should not be forgotten that in the Vendée, where political unrest had been so continuously dangerous to previous revolutionary governments, the problem may be said to have been solved by the Directory.

It only remains to summarise the reasons for thinking that the instability of the Directory has perhaps been exaggerated. This political insecurity has been ascribed partly to the Constitution of the year III, and partly to public hostility to the Directors and the general desire for a strong executive government on the eve of Brumaire. Further investigation, however, seems to be required before this line of argument can be regarded as satisfactory.

For, in the first case, there is something to be said for the view that the main constitutional difficulties of the Directors were in the course of time solved.[50] The necessity of having a majority of at least three to two for the transaction of business may have opened the way to differences of opinion among the Directors,[51] but after Fructidor (4 September 1797) the Trium-

---

[48] M. Marion, *Le brigandage pendant la Révolution*, p. 68.
[49] M. Marion, *Le brigandage pendant la Révolution*, pp. 106, 105, 113.
[50] M. Deslandres, *Histoire constitutionnelle de la France de 1789 à 1870*, vol. I, pp. 305 *seq.*
[51] Meynier, vol. III, p. 125.

virate of Barras, Reubell and La Revellière removed this source
of weakness. It was not until Reubell retired on 16 May 1799
and was replaced by Sieyès that this solidarity of the Directors
was shaken.[52] Similarly, the lack of any power to dissolve the
Councils did not seriously hamper the Directors, since resort
could always be had to systematic corruption at the annual election of one-third of the Councils or to a *coup d'état*. Although
the right of initiating legislation lay with the Council of Five
Hundred, the Directors were not deprived of the power of giving
effect to their policy, since the machinery of Directorial messages
to the Legislative Assemblies proved an adequate substitute.
Moreover, the formal absence of the power of initiation often
provided the government with ready-made excuses when public
opinion showed itself at all critical. Nor was the tenure of the
Directory as a whole or of individual members of it really insecure. The life of the Directory was fixed at five years (Article
137)—a period which exceeded that of the Councils by two years
and that of the Assemblies of 1791 and 1793 by three. As only
one Director retired annually by lot, the political complexion of
the executive could not be effectively altered by the Councils except after a wait of three years, and even then only on the unlikely assumption that the majority in the Councils remained
stable. Finally, the substitution of three Consuls for five Directors
at Brumaire left the form of the executive government very much
the same.

Nor can French public opinion immediately before Brumaire
be described as actively hostile to the Directors. The prevailing
feeling was one of apathy rather than of antipathy. The initial
reforming zeal of the revolutionaries had dwindled, people in the
provinces had lost interest in electoral devices, and once the tide
of victory against the foreigner had turned in favour of France
the cry of *"La patrie en danger"* had lost its meaning. Now, in a
situation of this kind the government in actual possession of
power is not usually in a weak position, and it is doubtful
whether in 1799 there was a general feeling in France that the
overthrow of the Directory would do much to improve conditions. Hardly less widespread than apathy was fear—but this
fear was of a peculiar kind: it was a fear of extremes, whether
royalist or Jacobin. Fortunately for the Directors, the only
formidable opposition to their rule came from precisely these
two sources. For this reason the Directors had an easy means of

prolonging themselves in office by *coups d'état* directed now against the Right, now against the Left. This *politique de bascule* [seesaw political policy] far from being an indication of the essential instability of the government can be regarded as a source of strength. Not only was it effective, it was also consonant with the best interests of the country at large. As the representatives of moderate republicanism, the Directors could in this sense lay claim to a good deal of popular support.

Whether or not Frenchmen were willing on the eve of Brumaire to exchange the republican constitution of the year III for a military dictatorship cannot be decided with certainty. The difficulties encountered with the Council of Five Hundred at St. Cloud on 19 Brumaire, the cries of *"hors la loi"* [outlaw him] which greeted Bonaparte and the well-known sympathies of the Parisian troops, at least make it clear that the constitution was still regarded as a bulwark against dictatorship.[53] Bonaparte's military prestige had been somewhat tarnished by his abandonment of the army in Egypt[54] and little was known of his political and administrative ability. As a peacemaker, he still enjoyed the reputation he had gained at Leoben and Campo Formio, but Sieyès evidently thought that he would be willing to accept subordinate political office. Perhaps Vandal got nearest to the truth when he said of Bonaparte, "He came to power by taking advantage of his universal prestige and a gigantic misunderstanding." The theory of an "inevitable" military dictatorship has had a long inning; has not the time arrived when it should be abandoned? France in the autumn of 1799 was economically prosperous, the danger of invasion had already been averted, the reforms of Ramel and Neufchâteau were beginning to bear fruit, and the fear of reviving Jacobinism, dating back to the law of the hostages, might easily have been dealt with in the usual way. In religious matters it is difficult to believe the persecution of the priests was any more effective in practice than the measures taken to ensure public order, and although the desire for a restoration of the altars may have been pressing, there was considerable anxiety lest with it there should be associated a return of the church lands.

If Bonaparte had been forty instead of thirty, would he not have remained faithful to his original idea of becoming a Director?

[53] Vandal, vol. I, pp. 279, 396.
[54] Gohier, *Mémoires,* vol. I, p. 174.

Select Bibliography

This note includes a selection of some of the more important works on the revolutionary and Napoleonic periods. Books marked with an asterisk (*) are paperback editions in English.

I. Aids for Research

An indispensable guide for anyone doing research on the French Revolution is P. Caron, *Manuel pratique pour l'étude de la Révolution française* (new ed.; Paris: Picard, 1947). The bibliography in J. Godechot, *Les Révolutions (1770–1799)* (2nd. ed.; Paris: Presses Univ. de France, 1965), also is very helpful, especially for revolutionary movements outside France. Another excellent detailed bibliography is in C. Brinton, *A Decade of Revolution, 1789–1799* (New York: Harper & Row, 1963, orig. 1934). These works will direct students to other guides and bibliographies. To keep abreast of current scholarship on the Revolution, consult the *Annales historiques de la Révolution française, The American Historical Review,* and the *Revue historique.*

II. General Narratives

Valuable surveys of the Revolution include G. Lefebvre, *The French Revolution* (2 vols.; New York: Columbia Univ. Press, 1962–1964, orig. 1951), and C. Brinton, *A Decade of Revolution* (cited in section I). These two works place the Revolution in

its European setting. More restricted to French developments is
A. Mathiez, *The French Revolution (New York: Grosset &
Dunlap, 1964, orig. 1922–1927), exceptionally well written, very
favorable to the Revolution and Robespierre. Much less partisan
are J. M. Thompson, *The French Revolution (New York: Oxford Univ. Press, 1966, orig. 1943); A. Goodwin, *The French
Revolution (New York: Harper & Row, 1962, orig. 1953); and M.
Goehring, Geschichte der grossen Revolution (2 vols.; Tuebin-
gen: Mohr, 1950–1951). A. Soboul's La Révolution française (2
vols.; Paris: Gallimard, 1964) interprets the Revolution in terms
of class conflict, a point of view deftly challenged by A. Cobban
in The Social Interpretation of the French Revolution (Cambridge: Cambridge Univ. Press, 1964). The relevant volumes in
the New Cambridge Modern History are Volume VIII, The
American and French Revolutions, 1763–1793, edited by A.
Goodwin, and Volume IX, War and Peace in an Age of Upheaval,
1793–1830, edited by C. W. Crawley (both Cambridge: Cambridge
Univ. Press, 1965); they are useful especially for discussions of
the lesser-known countries and for nonpolitical subjects.

III. The Origins of the French Revolution

Two pamphlets give an indication of the historical controversy over the origins of the Revolution: A. Cobban, *Historians
and the Causes of the French Revolution (rev. ed.; London:
Routledge and Kegan Paul for the [British] Historical Association, 1962); and S. Idzerda, *The Background of the French
Revolution (New York: Macmillan for the American Historical
Association, 1959).

An introduction to the issue of the intellectual origins is
W. F. Church (ed.), *The Influence of the Enlightenment on the
French Revolution (Boston: Heath, 1964), with an ample and
well-chosen bibliography. On the political impact of the philo-
sophes no full length treatise in English can compare to Daniel
Mornet, Les Origines intellectuelles de la Révolution française
(Paris: Colin, 1933), or Furio Diaz, Filosophia e politica nel Set-
tecento francese (Turin: Einaudi, 1962). Joan McDonald, Rous-
seau and the French Revolution, 1762–1791 (London: The
Athlone Press, 1965), and Gordon McNeil, "The Cult of Rous-
seau and the French Revolution," Journal of the History of Ideas,
VI (1945), 197–212, describe the extent of this thinker's influence.
An excellent interpretation of European and American po-

litical developments in the late eighteenth century can be found in the first volume of R. R. Palmer, *The Age of the Democratic Revolution* (Princeton: Princeton Univ. Press, 1959). Shorter and less persuasive is J. Godechot, *France and the Atlantic Revolution of the Eighteenth Century, 1770–1799* (New York: Free Press, 1965). J. Égret, *La Pré-Révolution française (1787–1788)* (Paris: Presses Univ. de France, 1962), is a fine study of the "aristocratic revolt." See also the detailed and perceptive account by A. Goodwin, "Calonne, the Assembly of French Notables of 1787 and the Origins of the 'Révolte Nobiliaire,'" *English Historical Review*, LXI (1946), 202–234, 329–377.

Differing views on economic and social conditions in late eighteenth-century France are presented in R. W. Greenlaw (ed.), *The Economic Origins of the French Revolution* (Boston: Heath, 1958). M. Bloch's *French Rural History* (Berkeley: Univ. of California Press, 1966, orig. 1931) is a brilliant attempt to describe the leading characteristics of prerevolutionary agriculture. The massive works of C.-E. Labrousse, *Esquisse du mouvement des prix et des revenus en France au XVIIIe siècle* (Paris: Dalloz, 1933) and *La Crise de l'économie française à la fin de l'ancien régime et au début de la Révolution* (Paris: Presses Univ. de France, 1943), investigate cyclical changes in the French economy. D. Landes, "The Statistical Study of French Crises," *Journal of Economic History*, X (1950), 195–211, objects to some of Labrousse's methods.

A mine of contemporary observation is Arthur Young, *Travels in France during the Years 1787, 1788 & 1789* (Cambridge: Cambridge Univ. Press, 1950, orig. 1792).

The most noteworthy of the older treatments of French society is Alexis de Tocqueville, *The Old Regime and the French Revolution* (Garden City, N.Y.: Doubleday, 1955, orig. 1856), very freely translated by S. Gilbert. Useful recent books and articles on aspects of French society include J. McManners, *French Ecclesiastical Society under the Ancien Régime* (Manchester, Eng.: Manchester Univ. Press, 1960); F. L. Ford, *Robe and Sword: The Regrouping of the French Aristocracy after Louis XIV* (New York: Harper & Row, 1965, orig. 1953); R. Forster, "The Provincial Noble: A Reappraisal," *American Historical Review*, LXVIII (1963), 681–691; M. Reinhard, "Élite et noblesse dans la seconde moitié du XVIIIe siècle," *Revue d'histoire moderne et contemporaine*, III (1956), 5–37; A. Goodwin, "The Social Origins and Privileged Status of the French Eighteenth-

338   SELECT BIBLIOGRAPHY

Century Nobility," *Bulletin of the John Rylands Library,* XLVII
(1965), 382–403; E. Barber, **The Bourgeoisie in 18th-Century
France* (Princeton: Princeton Univ. Press, 1967, orig. 1955); and
A. Davies, "The Origins of the French Peasant Revolution of
1789," *History,* XLIX (1964), 24–41.

IV. Political History

An important synthesis of the beginnings of the Revolution
is G. Lefebvre, **The Coming of the French Revolution* (New
York: Random House, 1961, orig. 1939). Other studies include
G. Rudé, "The Outbreak of the French Revolution," *Past and
Present,* No. 8 (November 1955), 28–42; G. Lefebvre, *La Grande
Peur de 1789* (Paris: Colin, 1932); and J. Godechot, *La Prise de
la Bastille* (Paris: Gallimard, 1965), which sets this event in the
context of late-eighteenth-century political, economic, and social
developments. D. Ligou, "À Propos de la Révolution municipale,"
Revue d'histoire économique et sociale, XXXVIII (1960), 146–
177, deals with a little-studied subject and points out the many
forms the municipal revolution assumed in France.

J. Godechot, *Les Institutions de la France sous la Révolution
et l'Empire* (Paris: Presses Univ. de France, 1951), examines the
important legislation throughout the period. A. Mathiez, *Le Dix
août* (Paris: Hachette, 1931), shows how the monarchy was overthrown. Two other great events of the Revolution are traced in
S. Herbert, *The Fall of Feudalism in France* (London: Methuen,
1921); and P. Caron, *Les Massacres de septembre* (Paris: Maison
du livre français, 1935). R. R. Palmer, **Twelve Who Ruled* (New
York: Atheneum, 1965, orig. 1941), is a fascinating account of the
Reign of Terror. D. Greer has published two admirable statistical analyses, *The Incidence of the Terror during the French Revolution* and *The Incidence of the Emigration during the French
Revolution* (Cambridge, Mass.: Harvard Univ. Press, 1935 and
1951). Greer's book on the Terror is ably complemented by J. L.
Godfrey, *Revolutionary Justice: A Study of the Organization,
Personnel, and Procedure of the Paris Tribunal, 1793–1795*
(Chapel Hill: Univ. of North Carolina Press, 1951). On the fall
of Robespierre, see R. T. Bienvenu (ed.), **The Ninth of Thermidor* (New York: Oxford Univ. Press, 1968).

Political parties and factions are studied in M. J. Sydenham,
The Girondins (London: Athlone Press, 1961); C. Brinton, **The
Jacobins* (New York: Harper & Row, 1968, orig. 1930); G. Walter,

Histoire des Jacobins (Paris: Somogy, 1946); and R. B. Rose, *The Enragés* ([Carlton]: Melbourne Univ. Press, 1965).

For three significant works on the people's role in the Revolution, see G. Rudé, *The Crowd in the French Revolution* (New York: Oxford Univ. Press, 1967, orig. 1959); A. Soboul, *Les Sans-culottes parisiens en l'an II* (2 vols.; Paris: Clavreuil, 1958), of which there is an abridged translation, *The Parisian Sans-Culottes and the French Revolution, 1793–1794* (Oxford: Clarendon Press, 1964); and R. Cobb, *Les Armées révolutionnaires: Instrument de la Terreur dans les départements* (2 vols.; Paris: Mouton, 1961–1963).

Events after Thermidor are described by G. Lefebvre, *The Thermidorians,* and *The Directory* (New York: Random House, 1966 and 1967, orig. 1937 and 1946); M. Reinhard, *La France du Directoire* (Paris: Centre de documentation universitaire, 1956), lectures at the Sorbonne; and D. Thomson, *The Babeuf Plot* (London: Paul, 1947). For some of the recent research on Babeuf and his circle, consult the *Annales historiques de la Révolution française,* XXXII (Oct.–Dec. 1960); and K. Tønnesson, "The Babouvists," *Past and Present,* No. 22 (July 1962), 60–76.

Concerning the very important international aspects of the Revolution, see the second volume of R. R. Palmer, *The Age of the Democratic Revolution* (Princeton: Princeton Univ. Press, 1964); J. Godechot, *La Grande nation* (2 vols.; Paris: Aubier, 1956), which concentrates on the "sister republics" on France's eastern frontier; and R. Fugier, *La Révolution française et l'Empire napoléonien,* Volume IV of *Histoire des relations internationales,* edited by P. Renouvin (Paris: Hachette, 1954).

The counter-revolutionary movement is treated in P. Beik, *The French Revolution Seen from the Right,* published in *Transactions of the American Philosophical Society,* New Series, XLVI (1956), Part I, which describes the impact of the Revolution on the ideas of its French opponents; and J. Godechot, *La Contre-Révolution* (Paris: Presses Univ. de France, 1961), which is a survey attempting to find similarities between the counter-revolutionary movements in France and the rest of Europe. The Duc de Castries studies *Les Émigrés* (Paris: Fayard, 1962).

V. Religious History

A short introduction in English to the religious problems of the Revolution can be found in the first part of Volume I of A.

Dansette, *Religious History of Modern France* (2 vols.; New York: Herder, 1961, orig. 1948–1951). A much longer work is P. de La Gorce, *Histoire religieuse de la Révolution française* (5 vols.; Paris: Plon, Nourrit, 1909–1923), very favorable to the Church. The opposite point of view is expressed in A. Mathiez, *Rome et le clergé français sous la Constituante* (Paris: Colin, 1911). More recent and more moderate surveys include A. Latreille, *L'Église catholique et la Révolution française* (2 vols.; Paris: Hachette, 1946–1950), and J. Leflon, *La Crise révolutionnaire* (Paris: Bloud et Gay, 1949). These discussions of Catholicism are supplemented by B. C. Poland, *French Protestantism and the French Revolution, 1685–1815* (Princeton: Princeton Univ. Press, 1957).

VI. Social and Economic History

J. Kaplow (ed.), **New Perspectives on the French Revolution: Readings in Historical Sociology* (New York: Wiley, 1965), is a collection of articles for advanced students. N. Hampson, **A Social History of the French Revolution* (Toronto: Univ. of Toronto Press, 1967, orig. 1963), includes much political history as well. J. Robiquet, *Daily Life in the French Revolution* (London: Weidenfeld and Nicholson, 1964, orig. 1938), is more serious than its title suggests. R. Cobb shows the impact of the Revolution on ordinary people in the following: *Terreur et subsistances* (Paris: Clavreuil, 1965); "The Revolutionary Mentality in France, 1793–94," *History*, XLII (1957), 181–196; and "The People in the French Revolution," *Past and Present*, No. 15 (April 1959), 60–72. G. Lefebvre, *Les Paysans du Nord pendant la Révolution française* (Bari: Laterza, 1959, orig. 1924), is a classic analysis in depth; his *Études sur la Révolution française* (2nd ed.; Paris: Presses Univ. de France, 1963), allows one to sample his shorter writings on social and economic problems. A. Soboul has published some of his articles on social history in *Paysans, Sans-culottes et Jacobins* (Paris: Clavreuil, 1966). A useful monograph is S. Harris, *The Assignats* (Cambridge, Mass.: Harvard Univ. Press, 1930).

VII. Military History

A general introduction can be found in two brief works by S. Wilkinson, *The French Army before Napoleon* and *The Rise of General Bonaparte* (Oxford: Clarendon Press, 1915 and 1930). More detailed studies are A. Chuquet, *Les Guerres de la Révolution* (11 vols.; Paris: Cerf and Chailley, 1886–1896), which stops after the battle of Hondschoote (September 1793); and R. W. Phipps, *The Armies of the First French Republic* (5 vols.; London: H. Milford for Oxford Univ. Press, 1926–1939), which carries the story to Brumaire but is often unsatisfactory. R. S. Quimby, *The Background of Napoleonic Warfare* (New York: Columbia Univ. Press, 1957); and M. Lauerma, *L'Artillerie de campagne française pendant les guerres de la Révolution* (Helsinki: Suomalainen Tiedeakatemia, 1956), are excellent, the first dealing with the theory of revolutionary warfare, the second with its practices. A. Soboul, *Les Soldats de l'an II* (Paris: Club français du livre, 1959), is an account of the administration and the equipping of the French armies. Reinhard's biography of Carnot (cited in section VIII) is also recommended.

The best study of the revolutionary navy is L. Lévy-Schneider, *Le Conventionnel Jeanbon Saint-André* (2 vols.; Paris: Alcan, 1901), a biography of the Committee of Public Safety's maritime expert. A short, well-researched monograph is N. Hampson, *La Marine de l'an II* (Paris: Rivière, 1959). Mahan's important work on seapower from 1793 to 1812 is cited in section IX.

VIII. Biographies

Brief studies of some of the outstanding figures can be found in J. M. Thompson, *Leaders of the French Revolution* (New York: Harper & Row, 1967, orig. 1929); and R. R. Palmer, *Twelve Who Ruled* (cited in section IV). Longer accounts of the early leaders include L. Gottschalk, *Lafayette* (4 vols.; Chicago: Univ. of Chicago Press, 1935–1950), which covers his career before the French Revolution and does so with verve and sympathy; O. Welch, *Mirabeau* (London: Cape, 1951); and J. Clapham, *The Abbé Sieyès* (London: King, 1912).

The lives of later revolutionary figures are described in E. Ellery, *Brissot de Warville* (Boston: Houghton Mifflin, 1915); H. Wendel, *Danton* (New Haven: Yale Univ. Press, 1935, orig. 1931); J. Massin, *Marat* (Paris: Club français du livre, 1960); L. Gottschalk, *Jean-Paul Marat* (Chicago: Univ. of Chicago Press, 1967, orig. 1927); L. Jacob, *Hébert* (Paris: Gallimard, 1960); J. M. Thompson, *Robespierre* (2 vols.; Oxford: Blackwell, 1935); G. Rudé (ed.), *Robespierre* (Englewood Cliffs, N.J.: Prentice-Hall,

1967); L. Gershoy, *Bertrand Barère* (Princeton: Princeton Univ. Press, 1962); E. Curtis, *Saint-Just* (New York: Columbia Univ. Press, 1935); M. Reinhard, *Le Grand Carnot* (2 vols.; Paris: Hachette, 1950–1952); G. Robison, *Revellière-Lépeaux* (New York: Columbia Univ. Press, 1938); and G. D. Homan, "Jean-François Reubell, Director," *French Historical Studies*, I (Fall 1960), 416–435.

IX. The Aftermath: Napoleon

The standard survey of the period is G. Lefebvre, *Napoléon* (5th ed.; Paris: Presses Univ. de France, 1966); an English translation is in preparation. Shorter and less sympathetic to Napoleon is G. Bruun, *Europe and the French Imperium, 1799–1814* (New York: Harper & Row, 1963, orig. 1938), with an up-to-date bibliography, while J. Godechot, *L'Europe et l'Amérique à l'époque napoléonienne* (Paris: Presses Univ. de France, 1967), briefly treats the Atlantic world and includes a large bibliography.

The best recent biography is F. Markham, *Napoleon* (New York: New American Library, 1964); such older works as J. H. Rose, *Life of Napoleon I* (2 vols.; New York: Macmillan, 1901–1902); and A. Fournier, *Napoleon I* (2 vols.; New York: Holt, 1911, orig. 1886–1889), are still valuable. F. Kircheisen and L. Madelin devoted their lives to investigating this period. As summaries of their views, see Kircheisen's *Napoleon* (New York: Harcourt, Brace, 1932), and Madelin's *The Consulate and the Empire* (2 vols.; New York: Putnam's, 1934–1936); both find much to admire in the Corsican. J. M. Thompson, *Napoleon Bonaparte* (Oxford: Blackwell, 1951), is inferior to the same author's books on the Revolution. P. Geyl, *Napoleon: For and Against* (New Haven: Yale Univ. Press, 1963, orig. 1946), admirably traces the varying interpretations by French historians.

Few of the many memoirs are of lasting value; among those that are, see especially *The Adventures of General Marbot* (New York: Scribner's, 1935, orig. 1891) and *Les Cahiers du Capitaine Coignet* (Paris: Hachette, 1883) for military life; *Memoirs of Queen Hortense* (2 vols.; New York: Cosmopolitan, 1927), by Napoleon's stepdaughter; A. de Caulaincourt, *With Napoleon in Russia* (New York: Grosset & Dunlap, 1959, orig. 1933) and his *No Peace with Napoleon* (New York: Morrow, 1936, orig. 1933); and H.-G. Bertrand, *Cahiers de Sainte-Hélène* (3 vols.; Paris: Sulliver, 1949–1959).

Napoleon's own writings can be sampled in J. M. Thompson (ed.), *Napoleon's Letters* (Everyman ed.; New York: Dutton, 1954); and J. E. Howard (ed.), *Letters and Documents of Napoleon* (London: Cresset, 1961—). J. C. Herold, *The Mind of Napoleon* (New York: Columbia Univ. Press, 1961, orig. 1955), is a skillfully prepared collection of his opinions on various themes, taken primarily from his conversations and correspondence.

Napoleon's rise to power has called forth several dramatic accounts. G. Ferrero, *The Gamble: Bonaparte in Italy, 1796–1797* (New York: Walker, 1961, orig. 1936), discusses this episode in tendentious fashion and is not so reliable as the fascinating and critical J. C. Herold, *Bonaparte in Egypt* (New York: Harper & Row, 1962). See also A. Vandal, *L'Avènement de Bonaparte* (2 vols.; Paris: Plon, Nourrit, 1902–1907).

The First Consul's reorganization of French institutions is described in F. Ponteil, *Napoléon Ier et l'organisation autoritaire de la France* (Paris: Colin, 1956); J. Godechot, *Les Institutions de la France sous la Révolution et l'Empire* (cited in section IV); and H. H. Walsh, *The Concordat of 1801* (New York: Columbia Univ. Press, 1933). In English, the best survey is R. B. Holtman, *The Napoleonic Revolution* (Philadelphia: Lippincott, 1967).

For Napoleonic France's diplomatic history, consult the following: R. Fugier, *La Révolution française et l'Empire napoléonien* (cited in section IV); H. C. Deutsch, *The Genesis of Napoleonic Imperialism* (Cambridge, Mass.: Harvard Univ. Press, 1938); O. Connelly, *Napoleon's Satellite Kingdoms* (New York: Free Press, 1965); J. S. Watson, *The Reign of George III* (Oxford: Clarendon Press, 1960); the excellent work by F. Crouzet, *L'Économie britannique et le blocus continental (1806–1813)* (2 vols.; Paris: Presses Univ. de France, 1958); G. Lovett, *Napoleon and the Birth of Modern Spain* (2 vols.; New York: New York Univ. Press, 1966); and L. Strakhovsky, *Alexander I of Russia* (New York: Norton, 1947). J. Leflon, *Pie VII* (Paris: Plon, 1958), is the first volume of a major biography.

Important works on military affairs include D. Chandler, *The Campaigns of Napoleon* (New York: Macmillan, 1966); V. Esposito and J. Elting, *A Military History and Atlas of the Napoleonic Wars* (New York: Praeger, 1964); and A. T. Mahan, *The Influence of Seapower upon the French Revolution and Empire (1793–1812)* (2 vols.; Boston: Little, Brown, 1892). More specialized accounts are P. Mackesy, *The War in the Mediterranean,*

1803–1810 (London: Longmans, Green, 1957); D. J. Goodspeed, *The British Campaigns in the Peninsula, 1808–1814* (Ottawa: Army Headquarters, 1958); P. de Ségur, *Napoleon's Russian Campaign* (Boston: Houghton Mifflin, 1958, orig. 1825); E. Tarlé, *Napoleon's Invasion of Russia, 1812* (New York: Oxford Univ. Press, 1942), by a Soviet historian; Henry Houssaye, *1814* (Paris: Perrin, 1888); Carola Oman, *Nelson* (Garden City, N.Y.: Doubleday, 1946); and R. Margerit, *Waterloo* (Paris: Gallimard, 1964).

Some noteworthy biographies of leading figures of the Napoleonic period are E. Knapton, *Empress Josephine* (Cambridge, Mass.: Harvard Univ. Press, 1963); W. Geer, *Napoleon and His Family: The Story of a Corsican Clan* (3 vols.; New York: Brentano's, 1927–1929); G. Six, *Les Généraux de la Révolution et de l'Empire* (Paris: Bordas, 1948); R. F. Delderfield, *Napoleon's Marshals* (Philadelphia: Chilton, 1966), a popular account; J. C. Herold, **Mistress to an Age: A Life of Madame de Staël* (Indianapolis: Bobbs-Merrill, 1962, orig. 1958); C. Brinton, **The Lives of Talleyrand* (New York: Norton, 1963, orig. 1936); G. Lacour-Gayet, *Talleyrand* (4 vols.; Paris: Payot, 1928–1934); and L. Madelin, *Fouché* (2 vols.; Paris: Plon, Nourrit, 1900).